THE MEMBER OF PARLIAMENT
AND HIS INFORMATION

THE MEMBER OF PARLIAMENT
AND HIS INFORMATION

by
ANTHONY BARKER
Lecturer in Government, University of Essex

and
MICHAEL RUSH
Lecturer in Politics, University of Exeter

for
POLITICAL AND ECONOMIC
PLANNING
and
THE STUDY OF PARLIAMENT
GROUP

London
GEORGE ALLEN & UNWIN LTD
RUSKIN HOUSE   MUSEUM STREET

PRINTED IN GREAT BRITAIN
in 11 on 12pt Times type
BY ABERDEEN UNIVERSITY PRESS

ACKNOWLEDGEMENTS

This book results from a project initiated by PEP together with the Study of Parliament Group. PEP, where the study was undertaken, was responsible for its management; responsibility for guiding the research was shared by PEP and the Study of Parliament Group's sub-committee on parliamentary research and information, under its Chairman, Professor Peter G. Richards. It should however be made clear that while the Study of Parliament Group occasionally publishes formal statements of its considered view on aspects of parliamentary affairs this book is not one of these. While the Group was associated with PEP in initiating and guiding the research project, it bears no responsibility for the way in which the results are presented nor for any opinions expressed.

The study was carried out by Anthony Barker, of the Department of Government, the University of Essex, and Michael Rush, of the Department of Politics, the University of Exeter. Patricia Thomas, as research assistant, undertook (among other tasks) the parliamentary postbag analysis; William Plowden, Department of Government, London School of Economics wrote the section on six 'Roads' organisations; Elizabeth Green together with other members of the PEP staff, provided the secretarial help; and Douglas Pitt, of the University of Exeter, assisted in the final preparation of the manuscript.

The study could not have been completed without the support and co-operation of many people, particularly the 111 Members of Parliament whose responses to the questions in the sample survey interviews make up the core of the book and on which rest the greater part of any claim that it may have to being a contribution to parliamentary studies in Britain. Other Members, including some Ministers, who were not included in the formal sample also gave their time to help the authors; and a special debt of gratitude is due to those Members and their secretaries who agreed to the rigours of month-long analyses of their parliamentary postbags. A wide variety of people, other than MPs, were also questioned during the course of the project. These provided background material and advice or were themselves engaged in trying, in various ways, to offer Members information and arguments on many aspects of public affairs.

ACKNOWLEDGEMENTS

Some appear by name in the text, while others, including members of the staff of Parliament, must remain anonymous. Those concerned with this project wish to express their warm appreciation and thanks to all, in Parliament and elsewhere, who contributed in their several ways to the conclusion of the study, and in particular to those who read and commented on the text at draft stage.

The study was financed by a grant from the Social Science Research Council, with additional assistance from the Universities of Exeter and Western Ontario.

CONTENTS

9

CONTENTS

FIGURES

11

CHAPTER I

INTRODUCTION

1. THE SCOPE AND NATURE OF THE MP'S 'INFORMATION'

This is a book about British Members of Parliament and their work. It is the first such book to be based on a survey of a sample of Members which asks them many questions about their duties and their opinions of their work and of their place in the British political system. Our interest has been the sources of political information enjoyed by MPs, the use they make of this information and what they think of the way they are kept informed on the flow of the country's affairs. Politicians have a rather unusual attitude to political knowledge; when most of us hear some statement which claims to describe the way the world is, or ought to be, we will usually ask only the double-barrelled question: 'Is it true, and if so, is it significant?' But when a political leader or activist hears it, he will ask further questions: 'Whether or not it is a true statement, do people believe it to be true? And, if they do, who are these people and how strongly do they feel about it?' The importance of the fact that certain people believe in something, however dubious its claim to truth, is one of the elementary canons of the study of politics which gives the field a distinctive, if not always a very intellectually attractive, flavour. In political life, therefore, there are two kinds of facts: facts about situations and facts about people's opinions of those situations. The political leader, whether in an English parish council meeting or in the Central Committee of the Communist Party of the Soviet Union, needs some knowledge about both kinds of facts before he can calculate his reaction to them.

As a result there is in the political world an enormous overlap between the meanings of words such as 'information', 'opinion', 'influence' and 'pressure'. The common phrases that someone is 'very well-informed' or that the diplomatic correspondent's contact is a 'usually well-informed source' are certainly not intended to convey merely that a person has technical knowledge of the subject: such phrases are not synonyms of 'expert' or 'specialist' in the field which is currently the subject of a political issue. They mean rather that a person can identify the people whose opinions will count in the issue and also knows what their opinions are. The really authoritative person will also know a good deal about the issue itself and thus combine technical and political knowledge of the affair. Newspapers and broadcasters divide these aspects of political affairs between the specialist in the field concerned (such as the aviation correspondent) and the political correspondent (who will probably be in the privileged group of parliamentary 'Lobby' journalists). Journalists specialise in this way because of the complexity of information: the 'field' specialist concentrates on the technical information with which Government officials and ministers are primarily concerned and the political or Lobby man tries to follow the trends of political opinion among the MPs of all parties, their whips and frontbench leaders. On major issues information is thus very complex and very likely to be of a political or tactical nature as well as technical. On such issues party management and policy-making are closely connected and, on the most contentious issues, may become virtually indistinguishable.

The 'package' of post-devaluation cuts and postponements in public expenditure programmes of early 1968 was a major example of these twin characteristics of 'information' on political issues. The example was so clear because of the highly publicised marathon Cabinet meetings and the unprecedented range of the expenditure review, based on the Prime Minister's promise that all fields would be examined and no 'sacred cows' excused scrutiny.

The major decision to advance the date of withdrawal from 'East of Suez' from about 1975 to 1971 and the cancellation of the order for American F111 aircraft may be taken as examples from among the 'package' cuts of the great complexity of political 'information'. Like the Government's earlier decision for withdrawal by 1975, the 1968 East of Suez decision must have been based on an amalgam of financial, technical and political information drawn from such factors as estimates of likely future costs, especially in foreign exchange, estimates of the practical capability of the forces which were due to continue to serve in the area, estimates of British military and diplomatic advice on the political background of any conceivable future operations by these forces, and estimates of what 'public opinion' in general, and Press, Opposition and Parliamentary Labour Party opinion in particular, would be on the subject. A similar mixture of technical information or speculation about the aircraft's performance and its possible weight problems would have been combined together with such political considerations as RAF morale and 'public opinion' to make the cancellation of F111 a complicated formula for decision.

These two major defence and overseas policy matters would then have been placed alongside other, mainly civilian, expenditure options when the 'package' was assembled by the Prime Minister and his Cabinet colleagues. At this stage, the mainly factual or 'objective' information about the many different items involved, which had been assembled by the Departments and the Treasury, would have been confronted with the 'subjective' political intelligence gathered by the Government Chief Whip (who attends Cabinet meetings) and shaped by the political judgements of Cabinet members to make up what the Government would hope to be a politically fair and balanced 'package'. Thus, for the final decisions, the 'objective' and the political aspects of the whole affair would need to be reviewed together. Technical facts, expert assessments, parliamentary opinions, threats of revolt and abstention in the lobbies and even resignation in the Cabinet room itself—all are 'information' for the political leaders.

At the admittedly less complicated level of the backbench MP we see this very wide range of 'information' as the optimum ambit for our study. It is incomplete since details of the more purely political and tactical aspects of these matters are not vouchsafed to outside enquirers, even in confidential interviews of the kind we have conducted. If one Member, Mr A, learns in the bar that his co-partisan Mr B, intends to take a certain line on an issue, and if this piece of information helps Mr A to decide to take the same, or a deliberately different, line we did not think it likely that Mr A would tell us since he, in common with the rest of us, likes to appear to form opinions on the merits of cases rather than on personal or tactical grounds. The more easily discernible and discussable aspects of 'information for MPs' therefore received the priority within our limited interview time. 'Information' is, in sum, a very broad word.

A second basic point also needs to be made at the outset. Politicians are advocates of public issues and use 'information' of various kinds to support their opinions. This means that they are selective in their information up to and beyond the point where they will ignore or suppress information which may undermine the force of their case or the information on which they feel it is based. We all do this, of course, in our attitudes to affairs. This basic device of choosing information on an issue to suit an already firmly settled opinion appeared in our survey interviews in various forms. It was naturally most obvious in those sections which asked MPs about the constant stream of unsolicited printed material which comes to them from 'pressure groups' and from the embassies and agents of overseas governments. Many Members replied that they pick out the 5 or 10 per cent of this material which 'interests' them, often meaning either that which supports their established view with fresh ammunition and knowledge or which comes from sources whom they actively oppose: they study these latter items as one studies any enemy propaganda, to 'read between the lines and spot trends' (as one Labour Member described his own close interest in material received from the Smith regime in Rhodesia).

The defence issue since 1964 again provides a perfect example of how 'information' is the handmaiden of policy and action in the parliamentarian's view. The feeling among Labour MPs since 1964 that their new Government must make a serious attack on the level of military spending seems to have grown steadily, partly with the infusion of forty-six extra Members in 1966 and partly with the growing difficulty of maintaining social services expenditure. As a result, defence spending was under almost continuous official review between 1964 and early 1968 when the strategic decisions on 'East of Suez' and the F111 were taken and began to be digested by the armed services.

When MPs have a political view on a major issue which they are prepared to press upon their leaders at party meetings, in the 'early day motions' which Members can sign, in speeches in the country or in the Chamber, or even in the form of abstaining in a relevant division, it does not follow that they have a correspondingly strong desire for factual information on the matter. The two or three Members whom we interviewed who make defence a special interest pointed out that, despite the great expenditure, defence is not widely studied among their colleagues. One Labour respondent interested in defence, Ivor Richard (Member for Baron's Court since 1964) believes this is not merely because of its technical difficulty: all public policy fields are technical and challenging if one is seriously concerned to understand them. As he sees it, the older school of Conservatives interested in defence are really amateur lobbyists for the three services, especially, perhaps, the one they served in professionally or in wartime. It is not difficult to make out a case for a particular item, such as an aircraft carrier or a Scottish regiment, outside the overall context of defence costing. Richard believes that on his own side of the House it is not defence but total defence expenditure which causes the interest. This financial approach is quite different, however, from the long-term interest in defence estimates maintained, for example, by Col. (now Lord) Wigg throughout his period in the House from 1945 which led him some years ago to propose (and Richard Crossman to support) a permanent select committee of the House specialising in the defence estimates.

In 1967, a fairly senior Minister went to a meeting of the Defence group of the PLP soon after seventy-five Labour Members has signed a motion calling for reductions in defence spending to describe the methods and problems of the costing aspects of the Government's current 'Defence Review'. Four Members attended. By contrast, when broad policy was due to be debated, this subject group has, like the Foreign Affairs group, been so well attended since 1964 as to be in effect a party meeting under a different chairman. We gained some idea, during other interviews, of why this apparent discrepancy exists. The Labour supporters of that and other similar motions are often anxious to see defence cuts because of their concern for social and economic investment. If housing or education are their particular interests they will concentrate on these, and ask of Labour Ministers in charge of defence not that they should produce information but that they should achieve results. The nuts and bolts of the policy do not interest them—only the dismantling of policy structures such as the Singapore base or the BAOR support costs situation. If major defence cuts are made and extra public money becomes available for housing or education these Members will certainly be interested in details in these fields and would expect their colleagues who follow defence problems to have the time to offer only the same general political support to Ministers on the building of new comprehensive schools or technical colleges as they themselves are able to offer their Government on the achievement of defence cuts.

Because our survey necessarily concentrates on less contentious and confidential sources of information than the complicated lattice-work of facts, rumours, opinions and pressures which lie behind such major parliamentary issues, we wish to emphasise these two points at the outset: for a politician, 'information on public affairs' is a very broad concept indeed, of which we have surveyed only the more amenable and available fields; and he needs 'information' only partly for its own intrinsic sake and, beyond that, judges it in the practical, political terms of what good it does him and his political position to take the trouble to absorb it. Thus, a study of MPs 'sources of information' takes one very wide, for the reasons we have advanced. Throughout this book other political and parliamentary matters are touched on which it was beyond our brief, and our resources, to examine fully although in almost all cases no other study has yet been made. Examples include the local public status of the individual MP in his constituency, the status within the political system of Members as a whole, several aspects of parliamentary procedure and possible reform, the accommodation problems within that part of the Palace of Westminster currently controlled by the Commons, the relationship between Parliament and television (one aspect of which we have surveyed) and whether Parliament is losing the battle for power and influence with the Executive branch of Government comprising Ministers and their officials. Some of these matters are already widely discussed although fewer are empirically studied; we can only indicate in our text where we think an interesting further line of enquiry may exist.

2. THE BACKGROUND TO OUR SURVEY

Why was it thought necessary to conduct a survey on the subject of the flow of information about public affairs to MPs? One answer is that MPs fulfil an important role in the political system. Certainly MPs are regarded by some people as important individuals who are able or may be able to influence the course of affairs, whether national or local, public or private, as is suggested by the number of letters which MPs receive from the public or the extent to which various outside interests seek to present their views to MPs. What is rather more difficult is to define the role of the MP. The problem is complicated by the fact that there is a degree of conflict between theory and practice in that the work of Parliament in general and the House of Commons in particular is carried on in an atmosphere of lip-service to a number of constitutional norms, such as the supremacy of Parliament, individual and collective ministerial responsibility, the official absence of parties and so on, all of which are in practice subordinated to the political realities of Cabinet government whereby the government of the day normally controls the House of Commons rather than the House of Commons controlling the government. Thus the role of the Member is not easy to define, whilst Members themselves are by no means agreed as to what their role is, still less what it ought to be. Nevertheless, unless MPs are nothing more than political eunuchs, they need information whatever their role. If, for example, their role is to sustain or oppose the government of the day, they need information to do this effectively; or, if their role is to scrutinise the activities of the government, they need information; or, if their role is to represent their constituents and to defend their interests, once again they need information. Their role may, of course, be multiple in nature: indeed, it is not difficult to show that MPs do variously sustain or oppose the government of the day, that they do seek to scrutinise the activities of the government, and that they do seek to represent their constituents, although these do not necessarily represent the sum total of their activities; and on all these matters they need information on which they can base their actions.

Information is therefore crucial to the MP, but, as we have suggested in the first section of this chapter, not only does information have a special meaning for the MP but it is also extremely complex. Furthermore, this complexity is increasing rather than decreasing. The abandonment of *laissez-faire*, the development of the welfare state and modern scientific and technological advances have all contributed to the growing complexity of public affairs and, therefore, of information. Not only is information more complex but ever increasing and there are a number of basic questions which are vital to the relationship between MPs and information.

First, how much information on public affairs reaches MPs? Whilst it is doubtful whether an accurate, quantifiable answer to this question is possible under present circumstances, it is possible to examine whether the amount is very large and, much more importantly, whether MPs are denied any significant amount of information. It may also be possible to examine whether any information that is denied MPs is necessarily important information.

Second, whatever amount of information MPs do receive, is it sufficient for them to fulfil their role in the political system? As we have already pointed out perceptions of the latter vary, but the question remains crucial and can, in any case, be related to various roles.

Third, again whatever amount of information they receive, are MPs able to cope with it? Clearly this may vary from Member to Member and, although we have not been able to examine the adequacy of all the facilities and resources that Members have at their disposal, we have sought to examine some of the more important from the point of view of dealing with information.

Fourth, if improvements, either in the amount of information or the means of dealing with it, are desirable or necessary, what are these improvements? Inevitably and deliberately we are entering the subjective area of our topic. It is, however, a vital area and a major part of our survey is devoted to the views of MPs on these matters, apart from any observations of our own which we make from time to time.

Finally, and even more subjectively, what are the chances of any improvements that are suggested being realised?

We have not sought to delineate the role of the Member of Parliament, partly because it is beyond our brief but more particularly because the subjects of our study—the MPs—do not have a single perception of their role. We have, nevertheless, assumed that at its minimal level the role of the MP does embrace the three functions mentioned above: to sustain or oppose the government of the day, to scrutinise the activities of the government, and to represent their constituents; and we have done this because it was clear to us from our interviews that the majority of our respondents accepted these functions.

Just as these three functions formed a vital part of the background to our study, so also did another factor—the attitude of Members towards the reform of Parliament. Once again we did not attempt to examine this question systematically, but reform of the House of Commons in particular was frequently mentioned by our respondents. Although we feel that some of our survey results are quite striking and of considerable interest to parliamentary reformers, our work has not been a 'reformist' exercise in this sense: we hope its finding will impartially assist all who follow the House's affairs, whatever views each observer may hold.

We could not, however, ignore that fact when our project began in late 1966 there was a well-established climate of reformist discussion and controversy, of which we became increasingly aware as we conducted our interviews and other aspects of our research. This climate of public discussion about the 'decline' and 'reform' of Parliament developed in the latter half of the 1959–64 Parliament, when many national institutions and alleged national habits of mind were coming under increasing attack from political and cultural observers. Although here had been a Commons' Select Committee on Procedure in 1958–9, it had left almost undisturbed a set of standing orders and practices which had changed very little since the reforms of 1946–7—and these changes had been designed mainly to strengthen the Government rather than private Members. Demand for a new select committee therefore built up towards the end of the 1959–64 Parliament and both Labour and Conservative leaders promised to meet this demand if they won the election, resulting in the setting up of a Select Committee on Procedure in November 1964. When the 1966 election was held this committee had by no means finished its work and it continued into the 1966 Parliament with a minimum of interruption.[1]

Since the election of October 1964 produced a change of majority party it naturally involved a turnover in the personnel of the House of Commons over and above that produced by the replacement of retiring Members, and this was followed by more extensive changes in the election of March 1966. This

---

[1] For an account of reformist activity within the House 1964–6, see A. Barker, 'Parliament and Patience', *Political Studies*, XV, February 1, 1967; reprinted in B. Crick, *The Reform of Parliament*, Weidenfeld & Nicolson, 2nd (rev.) ed., 1968.

turnover of personnel was important to our research for two reasons: first, because any of the Labour newcomers were labelled as 'reformers',[1] thus contributing to the reformist atmosphere described above; and second, because there were important changes in the composition of the House of Commons. Taking the House as a whole, in 1966, over one-third of its Members not serving in the Government had entered the Commons at or since the General Election of 1964; and this proportion rose to just over one-half when Labour backbenchers were viewed by themselves. It was clear that the quite rapidly changing membership of the House, viewed in the personal terms of age, education and general experience, would be a significant focus for analysis—at least as important as the recent party swing from Conservative to Labour and possibly more significant in the long run. We return to the subject of parliamentary recruitment in Chapter VII.

At the same time as the development of the reformist atmosphere the literature on parliamentary reform became quite extensive. Bernard Crick's 'Fabian Tract' of 1959 grew into his widely influential *The Reform of Parliament*, while the pseudonymous *What's wrong with Parliament?*[2] by Hill and Whichelow is an essential companion work, to name but two of the most important contributions. A newspaper's survey of 'what MPs think of their jobs' (which had unfortunately received only a 25 per cent response from all MPs and only about a 33 per cent response from backbenchers) was conducted in 1963 and reprinted in Professor Crick's book; there was otherwise a dearth of survey evidence of what Members of the House, whose alleged weaknesses and failures were rapidly becoming a favourite topic for the Press and broadcasters, themselves thought about such things. This unfortunately robs a more recent survey such as ours of a basis for comparison.

This lack of basic information about the working of Parliament was a major factor in the formation of the Study of Parliament Group in 1963. This is a private group composed, in roughly equal proportions, of university scholars in this field

---

[1] See, for example, an editorial in *The Guardian*, April 18, 1966; comments in the *New Statesman*, April 8 and 29, 1966; and the article 'New MPs have kept their zeal for reform' in *The Times*, June 6, 1966.

[2] op. cit., 1st ed., 1964; 2nd (rev.) ed., 1968 and Penguin, 1964 respectively. For a more extensive bibliography see A. Barker, 'Parliamentary Studies, 1961–65: a Bibliography and Comment', in *Political Quarterly*, July–September 1965.

and officers of the two Houses. The Group's first main enterprise was to present comprehensive evidence to the Select Committee on Procedure set up in November 1964: this initiative was welcomed by both the committee itself and the Press. The Group then co-operated with Political and Economic Planning in proposing to the newly-established official Social Science Research on Parliament a research project.

The aspect of Parliament's work which was chosen for this first project was the 'research and information' needs of Members of the Commons. It has long been said by political commentators that modern governments do not inform the public properly of the background to their decision; and as representatives of the public, it is claimed, MPs could and should press for more information on things for which Ministers are supposed to be responsible to them and for which Members themselves are ultimately responsible to their constituents. Whatever the merits of these claims information is clearly of crucial importance to Members of Parliament and a study of their 'research and information' needs thus seemed to deserve the first priority for academic study; and this book is the main result, with the survey results from our interviews forming the framework. A certain amount of research and enquiry has been pursued apart from the interviews, notably William Plowden's account of the 'Roads lobby', and the report of the interview results is also set in a certain amount of discussion intended to put the data into context.

3. A NOTE ON OUR SURVEY METHODS

In choosing which aspects of 'information for Parliament' to include in the limited time available for each interview with Members we concentrated, as we have already explained, on the more straightforward and accessible topics. We were concious of the danger of imposing on Members a framework for the concept of 'political information' which would impede the discovery of how they themselves see their situation: informal discussions with some Members who knew of our project helped with this problem and carried us towards a draft interview guide. This draft document was then improved following its use in test interviews with several Members who had not fallen into our formal sample.

Our final interview guide (together with some extra questions which most Members answered after our interview and returned by post) appears in the Appendix. Its outline structure is, very broadly, repeated in the structure of the book. It proceeded from the Member's contacts with his electorate, his own local party and local authority, to national matters such as the material he receives from organised interest groups; the help he gets from his party's national headquarters; the value to him of parliamentary proceedings as sources of information; and his use of the House of Commons Library.

We then often turned the matter round and asked the Member to name a special interest and describe how he kept informed on it; the purpose of this exercise was to catch any unusual or specialised channel of information which we otherwise would not hear about. Finally, we related these channels of information to the Member's political conception of his parliamentary role and the place of the House of Commons by asking some questions on the limits of the House's knowledge in a system of ministerial responsibility and Cabinet decision-making. The 'specialised select committee' idea appeared at this stage in the context of how far the Member felt any government would permit the House to become better informed on national affairs. This interview guide, like many others, tried to tread the narrow path between obtaining plain facts about its subject, which were suitable for tabular analysis, while at the same time obtaining richer, if less precise, material about what MPs think of their political role. The interviews were conducted at the House, usually in private rooms, or in Members' business offices or homes; their length, intended to be about forty minutes, ranged from a very few severely abbreviated cases of fifteen minutes to long and somewhat rambling sessions of five to six hours during all-night sittings when the conversation occasionally veered back in the direction of the interview guide. Except when there was severe pressure of time we always tended in the direction of encouraging the Member to answer questions in his own way since we felt that this would not only produce a more sincere and useful answer but also uncover interesting examples and anecdotes which may have thrown light on other aspects of our study; this latter assumption proved correct especially in those fields such as attitudes to the 'specialised committee' and the House's Library which are not easily quantifiable in terms of coded responses to a formal question. Since nearly all Members are extremely kind and patient with outside inquiries asking about Parliament's affairs at whatever level of sophistication, they will agree to answer plain, formal questions, suitable for computer analysis, although, like many of the other sampled specimens of social science, they dislike the 'forced choice' nature of this approach. Some Members would rather expand generally on a topic and the interviewer must try to prevent too much embroidery on too little cloth; we therefore aimed at conducting a guided discussion with each Member which was flexible enough to allow him to put his thoughts in his own way while serving the ends of our study. Members of Parliament are, of course, extremely sophisticated interviewees since even the least nationally-known Member who plays the least vocal role in the affairs of the House is quite used (unless he is very new to politics) either to the formal interview of a reporter from his local Press or the constant requests for his considered opinion on affairs coming from his local councillors, his constituents and others who write to him, and, perhaps above all, the stalwarts in his local party. Members are therefore far more likely than almost any other group in the community (saving academics) to complain of an ambiguity or half-hidden implication in a question, or to protest (usually in the case of a postal questionnaire) that the 'forced choice' question does not permit them to give what they believe to be the politically correct answer—and they are quite right to do so, of course. We hope that those Members who gave us their time to contribute to this survey found it as interesting and worthwhile as we did from our viewpoint as students of Parliament.

The sample on which our survey was based was drawn from the membership of the House of Commons as it stood on January 1, 1967. On this date there were 627 Members of Parliament. All those receiving an official salary (i.e. the Speaker, members of the Government, the Leader of the Opposition and the Opposition Chief Whip) were, however, excluded from consideration, leaving a total population of 531, made up of backbenchers of all parties and all but two of the Conservative Opposition frontbenchers. (These official Opposition spokesmen were included partly because we wished to see whether there was any contrast between them and backbenchers, especially their own Conservative backbenchers, and partly because we were interested in examining the problems of information which face official Opposition spokesmen.) This population of 531 was then broken down into various categories according to party affiliation, age, education, occupation and parliamentary

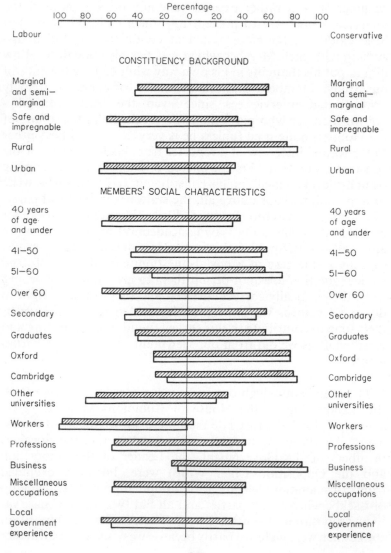

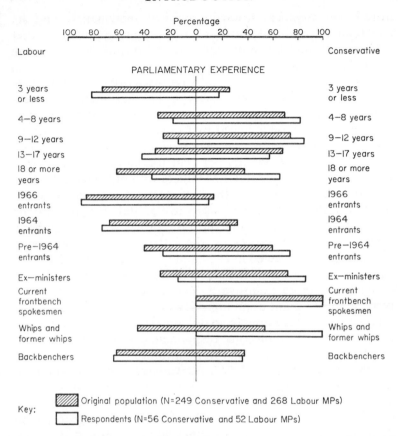

Figure 1. *Distribution of selected characteristics of our original population and respondents.*

service and experience. The Labour Members were also grouped according to whether their candidatures had been sponsored by trade unions, by the Co-operative Party or by Constituency Labour Parties.

At the time of the survey there were twenty-six women MPs, of whom seven were asked for interviews and four agreed. We did not feel, however, that any meaningful statistical analysis could be undertaken with so small a group and our women respondents were included with other Members in subsequent analyses.

The sample was structured in respect of party, age and education because we felt that these factors might affect the attitude of Members towards political information and its availability. The breakdowns of the original population and of the sample are shown in Figure 1, and further details appear in the Appendix.

The sample of 177 is statistically representative of the population of 531 in every respect except that it somewhat under-represents the trade-union sponsored Labour Members and over-represents those financed by Constituency Labour Parties.

The overall response rate was 62·7 per cent (i.e. 111 MPs), although it varied from 100 per cent for Labour Co-operative MPs to 33·3 per cent for those Members with only an elementary education. On a party basis the best response rate was from the Liberals, followed by the Conservatives, and then by Labour Members. Broadly speaking the rate varied with a Member's age and education, especially the latter. Younger Members, particularly those elected in 1964 and since, were generally more willing to see us than their older and longer-serving colleagues. Similarly the more extensive a Member's education the more likely he was to grant us an interview.

These varying responses from different sub-groups of Members meant that as a whole our respondents were somewhat less representative of the original population of 531 Members than was the original sample of 177. As we have said, our sample of 177 itself rather under-represented those Labour Members who are union-sponsored. Since these Members tend to be older and less extensively educated than other Labour Members (or than all other MPs) they became further under-represented in our findings through the relative unwillingness of these types of Member to participate in our survey. This has meant that workers, union-sponsored Members, Members over the age of fifty-five, Members elected before 1964 and Labour Members as a whole are all groups which are under-represented to some extent in our findings by this 'double bias' against working-class Members.

We may perhaps plead that our sample's bias against this type of Member was slight compared with the unfortunate effects of under-response by those who were sampled and approached: for example, the 'Elementary education only' group constituted 11·3 per cent of the population of 531 Members and 10·2 per cent of our sample of 177 but they constituted only 5·4 per cent of the respondents. 17·7 per cent of the population were 'Workers' and 15·2 per cent appeared in our sample, yet only 9 per cent of the respondents fell into this category. The figures for 'Over-sixties' were 18·4 per cent in the population, 18·1 per cent in the sample and 13·5 per cent in the group who responded. The effect of this under-response on our knowledge of the viewpoint of union-sponsored Labour Members is seen by a glance at the eleven who did agree to see us: eight had been elected in 1964 or since, one had been elected in 1960 and only two before then. In analysing the material gathered from our interviews, therefore, not only is it necessary to bear in mind that those trade union Members who did respond to our request are not typical of the older type of union MP, but that other groups are consequently somewhat over-represented and we have endeavoured to take these factors into account. In spite of these points we regard our group of respondents as sufficiently representative of backbench and Opposition frontbench Members of the House of Commons to provide a reliable basis for studying our subject: the sources of political information available to and used by non-ministerial Members of the House of Commons in 1967.

CHAPTER II

THE MEMBER'S VIEW OF THE INFORMATION NETWORK

FOREWORD

This chapter attempts to discuss, in general terms but with several specific examples or cases, the large and very varied flow of information on all public affairs available to Members of Parliament except that which is specifically covered in the other chapters concerning the Member's constituency, his party and his activity within the Palace of Westminster. This discussion will thus mainly be concerned with different examples of nationally organised interests and opinions as opposed to the local matters appearing in Chapter IV on the Member's constituency.

We call this complex, residual field of study an 'information network' and will try to describe it with the Member's point of view in mind. It is, of course, usual to refer to diagrams and models of communication as 'networks' or 'trees': a message can travel out from its source and be received in several different parts of the network, sometimes after following one of several alternative possible paths. Every political system, however simple, has some normal framework by which messages flow and in Britain's case this framework is, of course, extremely complex.

The British arrangements for consultation within the political elite, and between that elite and other powerful or authoritative groups in society, have traditionally been characterised as being both subtle and intimate: Lord Northcliffe wished that he could control the 'magic square mile' of London S.W.1, centred on the Palace of Westminster and Whitehall, which has more recently acquired a narrower cliché identification from C. P. Snow's *The Corridors of Power*. Essentially, the flow of information of all kinds in a political system is called a 'network' because its lines or paths cross: there is, therefore, often more than one way in which a particular message or fact can travel from its source to a particular recipient. Its recipient (specifically in our present context, the Member of Parliament) may receive this message in several ways—and perhaps in several versions—because he is exposed to so many lines of the network.

The Member observes the constant activity of the Westminster lobbies, the Press and broadcasters and national organisations of every kind as a daily routine of thousands of messages, often repeating, confirming or contradicting each other from which he picks out a selection as he goes about his parliamentary day.

Some other people, who also follow politics particularly closely, will have a similar, although not identical, experience: they will read the same newspapers as the Member, see the same television programmes and even, possibly look at the daily *Hansard* report of Commons debates. They will read the parliamentary sketch-writer's account of the atmosphere in the House the day before and generally keep up with the flow of events, great and small. In particular, they will share the experience of constantly cross-checking the intelligence they receive by reading it (or some commentary on it) in several papers and magazines, seeing well-known political figures discuss it on television and discussing it themselves with friends and colleagues who may add new information, either on the facts themselves or on what others have said about them. These very politically aware people are, of course, themselves involved in a complex network and play their part in sustaining it, just as MPs do.

These people's situation is different, however, from that of the actively interested Member of Parliament in three significant respects: they lack the personal contacts with other Members and the lobby journalists which make up the Member's own participation in the specifically parliamentary network of information; they are not at the receiving end of a wide variety of opinion sent to Members by organised interest groups; and they do not share the attitude to the mass media of the politician who knows that something could happen at any time to bring publicity on to him and turn him, briefly, from a mere consumer of the mass media into a contributor to its flow of information. The politically interested citizen is, in short, a private person whereas even the least well-known

2   33

Member must be counted as at least a potential public figure, standing closer to the springs of political information and action.

Unlike a private citizen, the Member is not free merely to absorb all the information on public affairs he wishes while contributing nothing himself in the form of a public decision on where he stands on certain issues. British MPs do not have to take many personal legislative decisions, although those which have concerned them on free votes in the House in recent years on such subjects as hanging or abortion were probably quite taxing for some concerned, yet doubtful, Members. Apart from the 'conscience issues' linked, by convention, to the free votes in the Commons, in which most Members feel they should participate, there is also a constant flow of issues on which Members can take a public stand if they want to: the organised interest groups know this and supply Members with a stream of printed material designed to engage their general interest and sympathy or to call for positive political support. Being public persons, MPs know they are always liable to be called upon publicly to support or assist any number of political or social developments and so build up a certain political record and reputation.

The private citizen is, of course, free to be as active in as many causes as he likes but he is not a public actor in these things as is any MP: the two individuals may well, as a result, develop different attitudes to the 'information network' and we set out to sketch some features of the MPs' attitudes. Our resources did not permit the systematic comparison of a sample of Members with other groups such as journalists, academics, or voters as a whole. We chose instead to attempt to interview a large sample (one third) of all private Members because we expected a great variety of experience and opinion among them on this general phenomenon, the 'information network'. The relative views of this network held by Members who either have or do not have regular 'outside' jobs in addition to their parliamentary duties forms an important element in this variety of experience. We return to this matter in Section 2 of Chapter VII: in the present context it is sufficient to note that a Member's regular employment in some field is obviously an important factor in his perceptions of that field and that this may influence his views on any relevant political questions.

In this Chapter we present both findings from our interviews with Members and other research results: they do not form a systematic pattern of topics but were chosen for study for their intrinsic interest. They are: survey findings and other material on MPs' use of television, magazines, etc., and their receipt of printed circulars and letters on national issues; two accounts of some particular British interest groups' links with Members; and two aspects of information for Members in the international affairs field.[1]

1. MPS' USE OF THE MASS MEDIA

As we know, from general knowledge of the House, that members receive a great deal of material from organised interest groups which is either specifically prepared for them

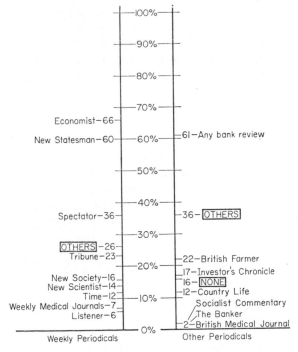

Figure 2. *Respondents' choice of periodicals*. (See Appendix, table 1).
(N—105: 52 Conservative, 50 Labour and 3 Liberal MPs)

[1] See contents for details of the sections of this Chapter.

or which is of a very narrow and specialist nature, we tried to obtain some idea of how much attention they paid to the popular published sources which anyone can see, or buy and read. Similarly, as we knew MPs hear a lot of political talk around the House, we wanted to ask them how often they shared, with that portion of the public which watches them, the discussions and other items on politics and social affairs available to all on television. Our questions concern weekly and other periodicals, books and seeing public affairs programmes on television. We also asked whether Members found more time for periodicals, books and these programmes during recesses than the parts of the year when the House is in session.

The two weekly periodicals which are most widely read by our respondents are the *Economist* and the *New Statesman*, with 66 per cent and 60 per cent respectively. A considerable way behind comes the *Spectator*, with just over one-third citing it, followed by *Tribune* and *New Society*. Party differences are about what one would expect, although the surprise may be that, for example, two Conservatives among our respondents read *Tribune* rather than that the fifty others do not. The overall favourite, the *Economist*, receives 73 per cent of the Conservatives' main attention against only 56 per cent from Labour: perhaps an example of 'image-lag' from the days when it was still a plainly anti-Labour paper before its modern phase of being impartially scathing about one or all parties. One-third of Conservatives read the *New Statesman* and one-fifth of Labour Members the *Spectator*, without which 'opposition' patronage both would slip down the all-party scale of Figure 2. The *Statesman* is much more popular among Labour Members than is the *Spectator* among Conservatives, with 90 per cent of our Labour respondents reading the *Statesman*, but only 50 per cent of our Conservative respondents reading the *Spectator*.

It is interesting to see the popularity of the 'political weeklies' as a group: these general, but highly politically oriented, papers are much more popular than specialist journals. These terms are slippery, however, since the *Economist* contains some very specialised City and trade material while the apparently narrower *New Society* is, in fact, very broad in its conception of the social sciences; *Tribune* again could be seen as a specialist publication although, of course, it does comment vigorously on the passing political scene. Most of the publications in the

'Other' group, which amounted to 26 per cent, are specialist items. The greater popularity among Labour MPs of medical journals and of *New Society* is natural, as more trained people from these fields are on the Labour benches. Observers of Labour's public devotions since 1964 to the technological revolution and the harnessing of science to socialism may note that 7 per cent more Conservatives than Labour Members cited *New Scientist*.

Among the other periodicals the bank reviews, taken together, score very high at 61 per cent, with both parties equally enthusiastic. We noted when asking Members about the unsolicited printed material they received how highly they rate the banks' information, Barclay's review being mentioned particularly. The equal patronage of these reviews by Labour and Conservative Members may be a small sidelight on the way the PLP is changing. A more traditional pattern remains on rural and stock exchange affairs: there are much greater appetites among Conservatives for *The British Farmer* (which is produced by the National Farmers' Union and would therefore be received automatically by the greater number of Union members on the Conservative side) and for *Country Life* and the *Investors Chronicle*. 36 per cent of the Members suggested other publications than those listed in the figure—a sign of the more specialist nature of Members' attention to monthly and less frequent publications. Labour Members mentioned these other titles rather more than did Conservatives which may suggest a rather broader range of interests on their side. *The Banker* and *Socialist Commentary* were in this residual class and the lack of support they seem to enjoy from Conservative and Labour Members respectively is of some interest.

Members (particularly newer ones) often openly regret that their parliamentary and other activities seem to prevent them continuing to extend their knowledge. Their life as Members seems to be an infinite series of short-run goals and routine tasks which do not always subside to a manageable level after a Member has 'learned the ropes' of Westminster and gained experience of doing most of a Member's possible tasks (including, even, promoting a private Member's bill) at least once. 'Living off intellectual capital' is the common phrase for this situation: the Member feels so dominated by the techniques of his duties and the flow of events and activities that he has no time to gain new knowledge. Because there is a good deal of information on the background to politics which appears in and remains confined to books, we asked Members: 'When the House is sitting are you usually in the course of reading all or most of a book which is about political, international or social affairs?'

The response may surprise those who have noticed how often one sees a Member about the House carrying a book of any kind[1]: three-quarters of our respondents replied 'yes' (80 per cent of Labour Members, 69 per cent of Conservatives and all three Liberals).

The party difference between Labour and Conservative respondents replying positively is noticeable rather than great. But this party difference is the basic dichotomy in these responses, running through other bases of comparison. Thus years of parliamentary service is not a factor although the notably more highly educated 1966 intake into all parties (especially, perhaps, Labour's famous group of university lecturers, three of whom appeared among our respondents) did record the highest positive response. This is certainly a mere reflection of the educational distinction in these figures which is naturally sharp, with 80 per cent of graduates, compared with just over a third of non-graduates replying that they usually were reading such a book. In spite of this strong cross-party factor, the party difference prevailed: Labour graduates were more likely to reply 'yes' than Conservative graduates and Labour non-graduates were similarly placed to Conservative non-graduates. Another slight difference which emerged was between Conservative Opposition frontbench spokesmen and the rest of our respondents who were, of course, all backbenchers.[2] Most of these spokesmen replied 'no' and were not prominent in claiming to read more of these books during recesses when their particularly taxing parliamentary duties are suspended. But our group of Opposition spokesmen was too

[1] Charles Clapp's similar question about reading books in *The Congressman: his work as he sees it* (Brookings, 1963) also produced high figures (apparently based on Congressmen reading while on planes to and from Washington). Richard Rose, who has experience of Congress, expressed surprise at Clapp's figures: see his review of Clapp, *Parliamentary Affairs*, XVIII (Spring 1965), p. 217.

[2] See Chapter V, Section 1 on the Liberals' position as specialised party spokesmen.

small for any firm judgements to be made about all of the Opposition frontbench.

For obvious reasons we felt the need to check whether Members managed more reading of political books during the recesses. Nearly three-quarters of all Members replied that they did, with a higher proportion of Conservatives making this claim than Labour Members, thus offsetting their replies about such reading during the session. Again, the graduates replied that they did extra reading more often than non-graduates, thus widening the gap between these groups. But while Conservative graduates and non-graduates were equally likely to say that they read more during recesses, there was a difference between Labour graduates and their non-graduate colleagues of whom only little more than half said they read more books and periodicals on public affairs in the recesses than they did during the sessions. Some Members catch up on their outside jobs during recesses (notably doctors, solicitors, accountants and others in partnerships) and thus may read less about politics. Others lack the hours of travelling to Westminster and back each week which, some Members told us, give them their only real chance to read solidly. One Yorkshire Member who reads less in recesses gave a simple explanation: 'No trains.'

In general, the evidence on this topic is that Members' claims are remarkably high in view of the taxing and distractive nature of parliamentary life and that formal educational background is very influential in shaping behaviour, probably by establishing (or not) reading tastes and habits before the Member enters Parliament. But the survival of the Labour 'lead' on this topic across the educational trend is interesting: it is probably one element of that elusive concept—the difference in the established psychology, esprit or 'style' of the two parliamentary parties which lies behind the attitudes to 'information and research' which concern us in this study.

We had several reasons for wanting to ask Members about their watching television programmes on public affairs. More than nine in every ten households in the country now have television sets receiving at least one of the three national services yet there are no figures for MPs' viewing, either as a group or in comparison with the national habits. Perceptions can be developed among the electorate by things seen on television, not because everyone necessarily watches a particular programme or series, but because, over time and with people talking about programmes to each other, certain points are made and images created.

As MPs are a very small group holding a unique position in relation to television's coverage of political and social questions it is very difficult to compare their replies to survey questions with anyone else's, but we hoped to gain at least an impression of their own use of television for political information by asking our respondents: 'When the House is sitting do you see the current affairs programmes on TV—either individual features, or regular magazines like "Panorama", "24 Hours" or "This Week"?' Members gave their responses on a sheet of supplementary questions, not covered in our oral interviews, and could also make any additional written reply or comment.

Taking all respondents on this question together, they fall into three equal parts, if the handful of non-viewers (5 per cent) of these programmes is ignored. Approximately one-third replied that they see at least one current affairs programme every week during the session; a further third said they see such programmes about once a month, and the remainder said they see them more rarely. But this even spread conceals sharp party differences with 42 per cent of Labour Members watching at least one programme a week compared with only a quarter of Conservatives.[1] There are, again, educational differences which cross partly lines. Graduates are less likely to watch such programmes than non-graduates, although party remains a significant distinction: Labour graduates are more likely to watch them than Conservative graduates and Labour non-graduates view these programmes more frequently than Conservative non-graduates.

Looking at Members' occupational divisions, workers are the most avid viewers followed by the group with miscellaneous occupations. Professionals and businessmen are considerably less likely to see current affairs programmes as often as once a week, perhaps because of their heavier involvement in outside

[1] Some Members replied that they regularly watch several of these programmes and it is worth noting that the maximum possible was about eight: (seven regular editions of 'magazine' programmes plus any individual 'documentaries' which perhaps appear about once a week).

jobs during the day which requires them to do parliamentary tasks, such as dealing with certain postbag items or conducting business with colleagues, during the evening when these programmes are broadcast.

Except for a higher viewing rate among the 1966 intake there is little difference in respect of years of parliamentary service. Backbenchers of all parties watch more of these programmes than Opposition frontbench spokesmen, although our group of these spokesmen was too small for any clear result.

We then asked whether the Members watch more of these programmes during parliamentary recesses: 70 per cent replied that they did, and a quarter said they watched no more or fewer of them; 4 per cent of them watched none at all during recesses. There was little party difference or any novel feature within these figures compared with the main question on viewing during the parliamentary sessions. The situation during recesses therefore reinforces the differences among our respondents seen during the session, except that Conservatives catch up a little with Labour's overall viewing in recesses, as Appendix, Table 2b shows.

Watching these programmes on any given evening is an experience which the Member is sharing with part of his electorate. It would be interesting to know whether backbench MPs watch these programmes more or less than the rest of the population because that data would provide one indicator of how completely television has penetrated the political system at its professional levels. If, for example, nearly everyone in the country has access to television and a certain proportion see current affairs programmes, while only a much smaller proportion of MPs are watching, it is likely that the electors will grow away from the Members in some of the images and conceptions which they develop partly as a result of watching TV. The MPs could gradually get out of touch, either on issues themselves or on the many background assumptions or 'style' of politics. There are certainly anomalies in the relationship of some aspects of party politics to television.[1] And it would be valuable to know where backbench MPs stand on their consumption and opinions of this medium compared with everyone else.

[1] For example, there is virtually no attempt by the parties to time and relate their doorstep activity to the messages entering the home from the parties' leaders through the TV set standing, probably, only a few feet from the doorstep inside the front sitting room.

41

As far as we could discover, no previous figures exist on the viewing habits of MPs. A study by Ian Budge of Essex University of British political homogeneity, based on a survey in 1962, offers some background information on the question.[1] Dr Budge sampled (using random-number selection) 59 MPs and candidates from about 180 in the London area and compared *inter alia* their sources of political information with those of 147 adults sampled from the electorate of Brentford and Chiswick, a marginal constituency in West London. He found that the MPs and candidates (the 'political leaders') relied more on their reading of newspapers and journals for information about politics than did the electors: 75 per cent of them cited newspapers, magazines and journals as one of their main sources against 51 per cent of electors making this response. Only 22 per cent of electors said TV was their main source but not one of the leaders said so. The 'leaders' exposure to politics through newspapers was, predictably, higher than the electors (as measured by the Trenaman-McQuail scale).[2] The difference between the two groups on newspaper exposure was far greater than on the similar rating for the exposure to politics through TV. On TV exposure the figures were:

Exposure Scale	'Political leaders'	Electors
	per cent	per cent
High: Score 6+	4	7
Medium: Score 3, 4, 5	55	47
Low: Score 2—	41	46
Total	100	100
Respondents not ascertained	12	16

Figure 3. *Exposure to politics through TV of 'leaders' and electors: 1962 London survey.*

Thus the 'leaders' had about the same amount of exposure to politics from TV as the electorate but also read much more in the Press and magazines to give them a generally higher level

[1] Details of this work appears in Ian Budge, *Agreement and the Stability of Democracy*, Markham (Chicago), 1970.
[2] J. Trenaman and D. McQuail, *Television and The Political Image*, Methuen, 1961.

of political knowledge. Some of these 'leaders' were MPs and the rest adopted candidates. Dr Budge checked for any differences between the MPs and the adopted candidates on all aspects of his survey and found few of any significance, with none in regard to political information or exposure to the media. Although the numbers of individuals involved were not large, any substantial differences between the behaviour of the MPs and the candidates would have registered in these checks.

A second oblique approach to obtaining some background knowledge for our own sample survey is afforded by the Marplan Ltd's survey, 'Television and the Managerial and Professional Classes' undertaken in 1965 for the ITA.[1] This survey compared the TV viewing habits of these people (the 'AB' socio-economic group) with those of the rest of the population regarding all kinds of programme divided into six types, of which two were 'news and current affairs' and 'political' (i.e. party political) programmes. The results showed that the ABs watched a very small, possibly insignificant amount more news and current affairs programmes than did the other respondents. Approximately three-quarters of all respondents had seen at least one newscast during the previous week and about one-fifth had seen at least one edition of the daily news magazines, 'Dateline' or 'Tonight'. The ABs were 3 per cent up on the others in both cases but registered only 24 per cent as having seen even one of the possible total of ten transmissions. The gap between ABs and the others widened a little when the survey asked whether respondents had seen one of the four weekly comment and reporting programmes: 'This Week', 'Gallery', 'World In Action' or 'Panorama'. 23 per cent of ABs claimed to have seen at least one of these four offerings against 16 per cent of the other respondents.

The data from Dr Budge, Marplan and our questions to MPs are not, of course, directly comparable. The respective responses of the 'leaders', the ABs and the Members do suggest, however, that Members are probably rather more in touch with public affairs television than is the AB class in which most (but

[1] We are indebted to Dr I. R. Haldane of ITA for a sight of this survey, for permission to quote from it and for advice on sources in this field. We also acknowledge assistance from TAM Ltd, BBC Audience Research Department and Dr Jay Blumler, Director of the Centre for Television Studies, University of Leeds.

not all) Members would be counted if they were not in Parliament (and thus in an unusual social class position). The gap between MPs and the rest of the electorate is thus even wider although the Labour-Conservative difference on Members' viewing should be remembered here, with Conservatives watching less and thus conforming more closely to the apparent level of the general public.

These points are now informally set out together while bearing in mind that different groups of respondents were being asked rather different questions about this kind of TV programme:

(Survey: 1962 Dr Ian Budge)	'Leaders'	Electors
Percentage scoring medium or high on TV exposure scale	59	54

(Survey: 1965 Marplan/ITA)	ABS	Others
Percentage claiming to have seen at least one edition (out of 10 possible) of either 'Dateline' or 'Tonight' during previous week.	24	21

(Survey: 1965 Marplan/ITA)	ABS	Others
Percentage claiming to have seen at least one of 'Panorama', 'World in Action', 'Gallery' or 'This Week' (out of 4 possible) during previous week.	23	16

(Survey: the present study)	MPS
Percentage of MPs claiming to see at least once a week either regular editions of 'Panorama', '24 hours', 'This Week', etc., or *ad hoc* individual programmes (estimate 8 possible).	32

Figure 4. *Some TV viewing data.*

On the basis of this very tentative discussion we feel there are grounds for believing that backbench MPs as a whole more than match the electors' appetite for public affairs television (although this may not be so true of Conservative Members or of all Members who are graduates) bearing in mind that this public appetite is notably modest.

Like anyone else, a Member's decision to watch a programme

44

(whether in the viewing rooms high up in the Palace of West-minster or at home) may be conditioned by his attitudes to the television organisations (the BBC and the programme companies of the commercial channel) and to the general contribution of television to the national life. We noted in the introduction to this chapter that one factor which distinguishes a Member's consumption of all mass media from that of a private citizen is the constant prospect that he could be one of their items of news and comment, either by being talked or written about by others or by being invited to make contributions of his own. He may therefore have views on the frequency of his own contributions, in the form of giving interviews to reporters or appearing on the screen or radio, or on the choice of other Members which editors, reporters and producers make. Apart from this potential personal relationship with the media a Member may well have views on the recent 'rise' of some kinds of political programme: even the youngest MP can probably recall the period before the 1959 election when television played a very restricted role, particularly during by-election and general election campaigns. It is also likely that the growth of opinion in the House favouring some system of televising debates (which presumably was greatly accelerated by the more favourable views of the 1964 and 1966 intakes compared with the Members who left the House in those years) reflects a developing attitude to all aspects of TV as a vehicle for politics, which will probably ensure that Members continue their own viewing to keep pace with, or even to run ahead of, general public demand for such programmes: indeed, we believe that MPs have probably reached the latter stage already.

MPs talk about Current Affairs Progammes on TV

'I watch as often as possible, it's most valuable.' (Conservative, high claim)

'I'm usually dealing with other matters such as constituency work.' (Labour, low claim)

'I don't watch or have TV.' (Conservative ex-Minister, low claim)

'I have no TV at home but I try to see these programmes as I like them and recognise their importance.' (Labour, low claim)

'Definitely no: I have never been in the television room at the House.' (Labour, low claim)

'The political clock makes TV viewing more difficult than we would wish.' (Conservative, medium claim)

'I do wish I could see more.' (Labour, low claim)

'My outside speaking engagements prevent this.' (Conservative, low claim)

'I haven't got a TV set.' (Conservative, low claim)

'I don't see a current affairs programme on TV as often as once a month nor more frequently in the parliamentary recess if I can help it.' (Conservative, low claim)

'I never see these programmes.' (Conservative, low claim)

'I see at least one of these programmes every week during the session and more if possible.' (Conservative, high claim)

'The public ask us questions about things they have seen on TV, so it's almost as essential as the Press for information.' (Labour, high claim)

'TV should be used more widely and more deeply as a medium in our field.' (Labour, high claim)

'I don't see these programmes as often as once a month and then only when I happen to notice something of interest to me which is *not* very often.' (Conservative, low claim)

There may be room for doubt whether a public opinion poll is itself a 'mass medium' of information or a piece of information in its own right. Skirting that nice point, we believe its place in our Chapter on the MP's view on the 'information network' is here with the mass media of books, magazine journalism and broadcasting. There is no doubt that the opinion poll has increased its importance as a source of information on public affairs. The trend in political polling is to diversify from the basic, traditional exercise which asks a sample of people how they intend to vote and then attempts to predict the result of an election. It is now possible to study as many as two or three polls each week, appearing in about half a dozen newspapers, on different public issues of varying breadth and specialist importance. Public opinion polls go together with the evidence of many surveys (such as that offered about non-ministerial MPs in this present study) to swell the growing stream of empirical knowledge about the community which is already altering the attitudes and styles of younger politicians and mass media people and will doubtless continue to do so until the tone of political affairs is generally rather different.

How far political strife will be altered in its basic drives by the presence of 'facts' on how the country behaves, what it thinks or what it wants on some topic is a very broad question, although it may, at once, be doubted whether change will be either rapid or radical. The status of such 'facts' is always open to question, if nothing more damaging. Any poll or survey can be incompetent, deliberately rigged or both and a glance at American politics during the 1968 presidential campaign with secret polls, partly-leaked secret polls, competent and authoritative published polls and hundreds of the most inept exercises by local newspapers, radio stations and high school children all being publicised or leaked on an almost equal footing, showed clearly that the good may easily be driven out by the bad.[1]

Even if all published poll and survey findings could carry a guarantee of their authors' competence and honesty there would, in the British Parliament at least, be formidable hostility to substituting them for the Members' (and also, presumably, the peers') right to exercise what Walter Bagehot described and venerated as 'the expressive function', that is 'to express the mind of the English people on all matters which come before it'.

That this function is also the prerogative of Welsh Members in respect of the Welsh people was vigorously asserted by Idwal Jones (Labour, Wrexham) when he was confronted with a Gallup poll, published in national and Welsh papers showing that many more Welsh people favoured abolishing present legal restrictions on activities on Sunday afternoons than may once have been the case or than Mr Jones currently approved of. The occasion was the standing committee of the House considering the details of the Sunday Entertainments Bill, 1967, a

[1] There were reports that, for the first time in about thirty years' work, the American polls were being significantly hampered by voters' refusals to be interviewed. This may prove to have been a temporary phenomenon associated with a mediocre campaign atmosphere.

private Member's measure sponsored by William Hamling (Labour, Woolwich West). Mr Jones asserted that the restricted Welsh Sunday was a cultural heritage which Welsh people did not (or should not) wish to see changed. He quoted the leaders of the Welsh Nationalist Party as being in favour of the *status quo* and merely re-asserted that fact when it was pointed out that the poll showed how voters who gave that party as their current voting choice did not particularly agree with those leaders. Although they were no political friends of his, Mr Jones continued to grant authority to them despite evidence of their unrepresentativeness on that point.[1]

Mr Jones's argument was, of course, that Members have a duty to decide what they think best irrespective of information to the contrary coming from their electors. Burke's famous lesson to the electors of Bristol is always to hand even in the wider context of a national opinion poll. David Ennals, the Home Office junior minister on the standing committee said: 'We have had great difficulty in trying to assess the general views of the people. There have been Gallup polls which would suggest that the general view of the people was that they wanted complete freedom after two p.m. on Sundays as the bill suggests . . . That may be right or not; it is difficult to tell. I do not think that we, as a committee, can simply legislate on the basis of generalisations about the general will of the country. We have to try to apply our own attentions to the matter.'[2]

An ally of Mr Jones against the Sunday bill was Sir Cyril Black (Conservative, Wimbledon) who challenged the bill's supporters on the known fact that hanging for murder had been abolished by the House on a free vote for five years, although every poll had shown this to be against majority public opinion. He accused his opponents of supporting poll findings only when it suited their own established policies. The undoubted truth of this charge (provided that it is universally laid to all MPs and all others with strong opinions on affairs) recalls our Introduction's point that politicians judge 'information' by its usefulness and suitability to their purposes. Mr Ennals, as Minister, took an official middle course on Sunday Entertainments and called the Gallup poll 'generalisations', which

---

[1] H.C. Official Report, Standing Committee 'C' (Sunday Entertainments Bill), Third Sitting (February 14, 1968), cc. 110–12.
[2] ibid. Fourth Sitting (February 21, 1968), c. 179.

(except in the purely arithmetical sense) is precisely what a competent poll is not. But as Minister with responsibility for race relations affairs he was, at this time, leaning very heavily in his public speeches on the social facts revealed in the PEP report *Racial Discrimination In Britain* because he wished to bring home to people a situation which, he obviously was convinced, had been accurately described by the same sample survey methods.

As D. N. Chester has written, the public opinion poll is now 'an alternative measure'[1] of what Bagehot called the mind of the English (and of the Welsh). Like universal literacy, mass suffrage and mass television before it, the opinion poll will undoubtedly alter political operations and is potentially a major new source of information to Parliament. But it will inevitably seem to elected representatives who dislike what a particular poll claims to reveal as 'true public opinion' to be a threat rather than a tool. It will always be a weapon rather than a tool for their opponents on that particular issue who do like what that particular poll says. Maximum play will be made with technical problems (such as the proper comparability of different polls on a topic) and the competence and motives, respectively, of those who conduct polls and those who pay for them. Politicians will, no doubt, continue to use poll findings as its suits them politically while preserving the same basic attitude towards such a mechanistic affair as the established portrait painters of the day maintained towards the early photographers.

2. MEMBERS' POSTBAGS ON NATIONAL ISSUES

There are national 'public opinions' on British relations with Nepal, Manchester taking water from Ullswater, the farm-gate price of milk and the supply of engineering apprentices. MPs receive some letters and much printed material offering opinion and information on hundreds of issues which count as national, however small or sectionally-based that issue may seem to be. They are national issues—albeit of a minor kind—because the people who care about them may live anywhere in Britain and because the promotion of their particular cause lies with the

---

[1] D. N. Chester, 'The British Parliament 1939–66', in *Parliamentary Affairs*, XIX. 4 (Autumn 1966), p. 425.

Government, in part at least: that is why they give their views to MPs.

Concentrating first on individual letters which appear, at least, to be directed specifically to an individual MP, we asked our respondents to say, if they could, how many such letters they received from outside their own constituencies.[1]

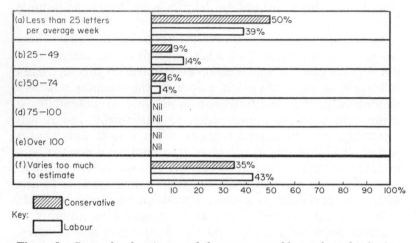

Key:
Conservative
Labour

Figure 5. *Respondents' estimates of the average weekly number of individual letters received from outside their constituencies.* (See Appendix, Table 3.)
(N—90 (excluding 14 'Don't know's): 46 Conservative and 44 Labour MPs).

Two-fifths of the Members answering this question could not offer any average estimate because variation is too great. The other Members estimated along the lines shown in the Figure: about two-fifths said they received fewer than twenty each week and nearly one third received fewer than ten.

There is some evidence here that Labour MPs receive more individual letters from outside their constituencies than do Conservatives, which may indicate the tendency for some people and organisations to write to Government supporters in the hope of their more readily influencing Ministers. Another speculation, based on our general study of Members' postbags,[2]

[1] This distinction between printed items and personal letters is often forgotten, sometimes by Members themselves when referring publicly to their postbags. Outside observers can also be careless in considering overall figures of parliamentary post: see D. G. Crockett, 'The MP and his Constituents', in *Parliamentary Affairs*, XX, 3 (Summer 1967), p. 282.

[2] This detailed analysis of some twenty-four Members' parliamentary postbags for four weeks each was undertaken by our research assistant Patricia

50

is that Labour Members receive more 'ideological' letters, possible from party supporters who wish to discuss national issues or express enthusiasm or disappointment at what they see as the Labour Government's policies. Further analysis shows a trend for these letters to increase with a Member's years of service. We shall see that a similar trend appears when Members' estimates of the number of printed circulars which they receive are examined. There is certainly no apparent reason for believing that longer-serving Members are likely to be better-known to the public, as some of the least prominent MPs have served for long periods in the House. Nonetheless, it is possible that the longer an MP serves the greater chance he has of being identified by the public with particular issues, or types of issues, based on his record of activity in previous years.

Letters on national affairs are clearly not a major item for most Members. Very many Members said of their own accord that this flow is small unless a Member becomes involved in some issue which attracts publicity or unless there is a national campaign on, such as the battle over the Medical Termination of Pregnancy Bill (which became the Abortion Act, 1967). Two Members (one in each main party) told us they received very few of these letters because they were silent in the House. The inference of this statement is that publicity, and thus letters, would flow to them if they simply spoke more often in the House, but that would, in fact, depend upon whether the mass media chose to report their remarks. One Opposition frontbench spokesman said that although his appearances on radio and TV generated letters, this was not true of his speeches in the House. A backbench Labour Member, on the other hand, recounted how she had received so much national correspondence after raising a very 'popular', although controversial, matter in the House that she had been deterred from doing so again, preferring instead to try to press her case with Ministers in personal conversations. The difference in the apparent role

---

Thomas in 1967 (mostly with MPs who had not fallen into our interviewing sample). Although the exercise did not achieve the quantitative reliability originally intended (owing to various practical problems such as post arriving at several London and constituency addresses) it did show us the character and variety of Member's postbags and illuminated our work on this chapter and Chapter IV (on the Member's view of his constituency). As well as counting and classifying all relevant items in these postbags, Miss Thomas gathered data from Members on which of the printed items they looked at.

of speeches or Questions in the House is plain: this frontbench spokesman happens to speak for the Conservatives on a subject which is even further away from everyday life than is political debate on matters such as housing and health, while the lady Member had raised an issue on which probably every person feels qualified to pass an opinion. The popular and general news media ignore the one topic and splash the other. The House is a news source and not (except, perhaps, for *Hansard* whose readership is not what it was) a mass medium for news; Members are totally dependent on the editorial decisions of the media on which of their activities will interest the public, and only a continuous (or nearly so) radio or television broadcast of parliamentary proceedings direct to the country would allow the House to escape these editorial judgements.[1]

Members therefore attract letters from the country as a whole by being active on an issue which the media think worth covering. The effect of such activity can last a long time once the association is made in the mind of people who make up the public opinion on that issue. Any MP whose private Member's bill gets at least a second reading may expect to receive some letters from people affected by that branch of the law for years afterwards—often people whose own personal concern for the topic may post-date the bill but who have been studying the subject's history and background because they now find them-selves involved. For the most part, however, the reaction to a Member taking a position on an issue and gaining publicity by so doing is fairly quick and short-lived after the Member ceases his activities, or ceases to get publicity for them. The out-standing example of modern politics is, of course, the 65,000 letters received by Enoch Powell following his speech to the Birmingham Conservative Political Centre in the spring of 1968.[2]

Another example of the major generation of letters by public activity is Duncan Sandy's national campaign to restore hanging in certain cases of murder. During the winter of

[1] This obvious enough point is overlooked by those who treat the proposal for an edited daily TV presentation of the House's proceedings as some major precedent. Parliament has already made one small inroad into the media's freedom by requiring the BBC to broadcast a daily account of proceedings (which—in 'Today in Parliament'—occupies fifteen minutes for both Houses together).

[2] See *Daily Telegraph*, May 3, 1968. A figure of over 100,000 is cited in Keesing's *Contemporary Archives*, 1968, p. 22783.

1967–8, Mr Sandys sent a long standard letter together with a memorandum to every weekly newspaper in England, Scotland and Wales and saw it published widely. It described his petition to Parliament for the restoration of capital punishment and offered general and statistical arguments in its support. He wrote that he had received 'a vast number of letters expressing agreement, many of them enclosing cheques or postal orders', and concluded, 'Those who wish to help should write to me at the House of Commons.'[1] Mr Sandys's exercise was, of course, purely political, in aid of his legislative aim: the only 'information' he could draw from it was the simple number and opinions of his correspondents on the subject as people could hardly tell him of murders they had known about which official statistics did not cover. In Mr Powell's famous speech, however, he did employ information about coloured immigrants' alleged behaviour which he claimed had reached him in a letter from a member of the public.

The Member involved in public exchanges on an issue stimulates letters in the hope that they will reveal not only the existence of citizens who agree with him but also new facts and examples which he will use as ammunition. There are frequent examples in *Hansard* of Members claiming that their post-bag reveals public concern on an issue along lines similar to the Member's own concern. During a short debate on sonic booms following 'tests' on technical effects and of public reaction conducted by the Ministry of Technology in July 1967, Ivor Richard said that the Government had not justified a second round of supersonic flights and boom tests. Such flights should not take place at all over land. On this subject he had, 'received more letters than on any other except factory farming and capital punishment, and the number of people who were in favour of the sonic boom tests was infinitesimal'. Robert Cooke (Conservative Member for Bristol West since 1957) spoke against sonic booms and their testing on several grounds and said that in all his experience as an MP he had never had a more formidable and responsible batch of correspondence on any subject.[2]

Although a very large number of Members mentioned to us that their appearance on TV or a story about them in a national daily newspaper or (for a different or narrower milieu

---

[1] See, for example, the Ipswich *Evening Star*, November 20, 1967.

[2] Reported in *Daily Telegraph*, July 26, 1967.

of potential correspondents) a letter by them in *The Times* would always produce a certain number of letters from different parts of the country, the main factor in the fluctuation which characterises this kind of post is the rise and fall of national campaigns on certain issues. We were very fortunate to survey backbenchers during the climax of the 1966–7 campaigns on abortion and can include in this Chapter some Members' experiences on that issue as it was reflected in their postbags. As David Wood of *The Times* described it:

'The voice of the people has been coming through to Westminster very stridently for six months, with all the signs of energetic organisation by Roman Catholic guilds and groups and by the Society for the Protection of Unborn Children on one side, and by the Abortion Law Reform Association in the forefront on the other.'[1]

Some of our respondents' comments which we reproduce here show that the 'quality' of abortion letters varied from the very closely argued to the very stereotyped, some of which bore signs of being copied out under the guidance of an opinion leader. These stereotyped letters are one degree of individuality above the 'printed postcard' campaign (where people merely add their name and address to a printed and paid message card and send it to Members) which, in turn, is itself only a little different form of the traditional, but still quite popular, parliamentary petition.

The comments we print here also show that the Roman Catholic forces were not unanimous in their hostility to the bill and some Members suggested that their constituency's Catholic bishop was not encouraging a campaign against the bill or, more commonly, was being neutral and allowing the local priests to organise their people against the bill or not, according to their own views or perceptions of their congregations' views. It has been suggested that Roman Catholics are the only 'true' pressure group in British politics as no other body is continuously poised to raise a campaign on a variety of issues by ordering their local professional leaders, the priests and bishops, to obtain the desired mass response from their followers. On the basis of our limited information from the 1966–7

[1] 'Postbag pressures on MPs', *The Times*, January 27, 1967.

session we would speculate that the Roman Catholics were, on this issue at least, less monolithic in their reaction than this comment allows and that local priests are moving towards Anglican priests in their individual freedom either to preach and organise against legislation which official Catholic teaching opposes, or to keep quiet.

It may also be significant that the National Health Service (Family Planning) Bill, which provided for the considerable extension of contraceptive advice and dispensing facilities to all persons, without mentioning permitted ages or marital status, went through Parliament during the same session as a virtually unopposed bill and with absolutely minimal public hostility, as shown in Members' postbags. The sponsor of this bill, Edwin Brooks (Labour Member for Bebington) was congratulated by a Labour colleague and envied for his great courage in introducing such a bill when he held a marginal seat near Merseyside—the centre of the Catholic vote in England. Mr Brooks was able to tell his colleague that he had received no hostile letters from Bebington, only half a dozen from the whole of Merseyside, and none from anywhere else.

MPs talk about their 1966-7 postbags on Abortion

'I got letters for and against: my position was known locally.' (Labour, Northern England—a key Roman Catholic opponent of the bill)

'Some R.C. stuff from elsewhere but none of the *real* pressure that others have had. No doubt my strong position supporting the bill is known in my constituency and dissuaded the local clergy, etc. from lobbying against the bill.' (Labour, Midlands)

'I have an actively anti-bill Roman Catholic priest which leads to letters arriving from his flock.' (Conservative, Northern England)

'On abortion? Only two letters from my constituency, one on each side. My local Catholic priest is very liberal: I'm pro-bill.' (Labour, Wales)

'I got the usual R.C. abortion letters: I replied that I agreed with them.' (Labour, Midlands)

'I got a wave of stereotyped letters against the bill plus a 1500 strong petition: then about 30 pro-bill letters. Apart from cranks and major issues like this, my constituency does not produce letters on issues.' (Labour Northern England)

'I got about 60–70 letters against the bill and about 20 for it. I answered fully and personally all non-stereotyped letters as I do on all other issues.' (Labour, Midlands)

'A steady flow of three to four stereotyped letters against the bill each day over a period plus one major petition with perhaps ten thousand names altogether, several thousand from my constituency, which I declined to present to Parliament. I got a few better-quality letters favouring the bill.' (Labour, London)

'My public support for the Society for the Protection of Unborn Children led to a lot of support from the public. I got 150 letters from the constituency and 250 from outside, mostly anti-bill.' (Labour, Northern England)

'I've had only three individual letters from my constituency against the bill and none at all for it.' (Conservative, London)

'I'm pro-bill. Quality letters were pro-bill: more of the stereotype ones against.' (Conservative, London)

'A lot on abortion: the first R.C. wave was stereotyped. The local priest was active against the bill: later the pro-bill stuff came in and was of higher quality. I am pro-bill.' (Labour, London)

'I am associated with this bill and have links with ALRA: their letters are sophisticated and individually written.' (Conservative, Southern England)

'Although constituency letters on issues vary with the weather I've had a lot on abortion: nearly 100. All of them against the bill.' (Conservative, Northern England)

'I've had six or seven constituency letters pro-bill, and one petition from 150 R.C.s and five to six letters against the bill. The printed circulars on abortion were badly timed, e.g. the anti-abortion pressure all came after the second reading decision. The social clause led to a flood of stuff after the gynaecologists' report. The gynaecologists were so slow to react to the contents of the bill.' (Liberal)

'I received a small petition against the bill, signed by about twenty members of the Mothers' Union branch at a local church, with a covering letter from the vicar saying that they had signed it following his lecture to them outlining the provisions of the bill.'   (Labour, London)

During the same session Eric Heffer (Labour Member for Liverpool, Walton) was trying to pass a private Member's bill to make illegal the coursing of live hares. This roused the 'lobby' which several Members assured us is the main centre of letter-writing campaigns to MPs—the 'animal lobby'. This same general body of opinion (which covers several special approaches to animal welfare such as anti-vivisection, moorland ponies and sheep and anti-blood sports as well as the general 'RSPCA approach') was active simultaneously on the latest chapter in the business of exporting live animals.

Another campaign of that session concerned legalising off-shore radio stations. The Free Radio Association was formed in early 1967 to organise listener support for the pirate stations, several of which broadcast repeated appeals to their listeners to join it and work for its aims. It was a classic case of the novel 'promotional' interest group as opposed to its major foe, the Copyright Council, which is an equally typical 'protective' group. The Council apparently enjoyed such good access to the Government that, apart from a few letters in *The Times* and *Daily Telegraph* and an article in *Punch* by its president, Sir Alan Herbert, it hardly lifted a finger by way of a public campaign for its views. The Free Radio Association, however, had to build itself up as an organisation while rallying support for its aims: direct political pressure therefore came near the bottom of the list in this much-broadcast statement over the pirate wavelengths: 'the FRA will be holding meetings, issuing badges and car stickers, organising petitions, publishing leaflets, lobbying MPs and lots more besides.'[1] Despite the enormous handicap of organising a 'fire brigade' interest group at very short notice among mainly non-political and non-voting young

---

[1] We are indebted to Christine Rose's B.A. dissertation, 'Pirate Radio and the Government, 1964-8' (University of Essex, 1968), for this information about FRA and the Copyright Council.

people, the FRA did very well to get the number of letters in to MPs that they achieved. The Press wondered at the time whether enough Labour MPs would be frightened by the volume of this pressure into suggesting to the Government that a compromise with the pirates would be a prudent policy, and we met quite a few Members whose postbags on the issue had surprised them by their volume, if not impressed them by their 'quality'.

Members are, we believe, very much influenced in their view of a campaign by the size of its 'quality' element (if any) as was Mr Cooke, for example, on sonic booms. Reported comments on abortion show how often Members distinguish between the original, or, at least, reasoned, letter and the simple, rather stereotyped assertion of opinion. There are dangers in dismissing uneducated letter-writers or balancing them off in a ratio of five or ten to one against a closely reasoned and reasonable letter on the other side of the issue. We formed the impression during our interviews that many Members were doing this when assessing their post on the abortion issue. To some degree it is a natural and reasonable reaction, but a Member's attitude may be based simply on his boredom with repetitive and unoriginal messages. It is as well to remember that an ill-educated constituent is just as capable as an articulate one of withholding his vote at the next general election. This comparison between the two individuals is not affected by the general reality that few British voters do seem, in fact, to apply such personal sanctions, preferring usually to vote for the Government they want rather than reviewing their MP's record on non-partisan issues. The ladies of the Mother's Union who signed the small petition described in our Members' quoted comments on abortion postbags may have signed very much under the eye of their vicar and they may not have felt at all strongly on the issue, but this is not certain. Because the petition, group letter or printed postcard is the rather public or collective approach usually adopted by most people, it does not follow that they feel less strongly than the person who sits down at home to write a reasoned, individual letter.

One further campaign of 1967–8 is worth mentioning because it was different in design from abortion, animal welfare and free radio. The National Union of Students campaigned against the raising of overseas students' fees. It asked the officers of affiliated student unions to lobby the MPs for their university's city while, at the same time, getting individual students in their unions to write to their home town's Member. Thus many Members got some 'constituency' letters from individual students while Members with universities and colleges in or near their constituencies were supposed to receive extra pressure from personal meetings with elected student officers. One Labour Member was drawn into this issue to the extent of abstaining from supporting the Government partly by the strong opinions against the policy held by colleagues in the House but, as he freely concedes, partly by the students' case which had reached him by both these methods.[1]

One kind of letter-writing campaign on national issues is in a class by itself. Occasionally, all or some MPs receive handwritten letters from a single person; they are, understandably, fairly uncommon but during our analysis of Members' postbags we saw a handwritten card and a similarly-produced letter appearing in the postbags of several Members simultaneously. The potscard called for 'England for the English' and denounced Celtic hegemony, as finally revealed by the moving of the Mint to South Wales, while the letter offered a message from God warning that the Yellow Peril would overwhelm Britain if she failed to mend her ways.

The letter-writing campaign to Members merges gradually with the more impersonal material they receive. The pure stereotyped letter, following an identical form, or an obviously organised variation of wording, is next in a scale of 'quality' to the printed postcards we have mentioned. One Member told us he had entirely discounted the signing and posting of printed and paid postcards protesting against the breathalyser tests by customers in some of his constituency's pubs who had picked them up from the counter, on the grounds that 'they came from the licensed victuallers, not from my constituents'—a course which may, as we have noted, have its dangers.

Beyond the printed postcard campaigns lie the many kinds of obviously impersonal material on many aspects of national affairs. We asked Members to estimate their total postbag except the letters etc. coming from their constituency. Figure 6

---

[1] This work on MPS was not, of course, the full extent of the lobby activity although it is our context in this study. As with the Free Radio Association's promise of public meetings, the students provided other demonstrations of opinion, e.g. a very large march through the centre of Bristol.

is, therefore, their estimate of the letters we have just discussed plus all printed circulars, periodicals, 'public relations' brochures, etc.

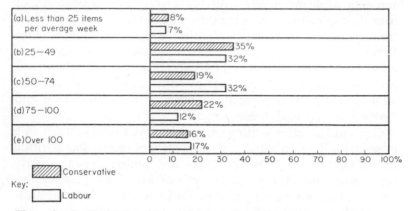

Key:

Figure 6. *Respondents' estimates of the average weekly number of postbag items received from outside their constituencies.* (See Appendix, Table 4.)

(N—78 (excluding 26 'Don't know's): 37 Conservative and 41 Labour MPs)

Two-thirds of our respondents said they received fewer than seventy-five circulars and letters from outside their constituencies in an average week; two-fifths received fewer than fifty items per week and only about one sixth (16 per cent) claimed totals of more than one hundred in an average week. Taking circulars alone, there seems to be evidence that Labour Members receive more of them than Conservatives but we judge this to be a simple consequence of their seeing this material for themselves while sorting out their post. Our reasons for this are that although some Members with secretaries (e.g. Renee Short, Labour, Wolverhampton NE) deliberately open and sort all their post themselves, it was clear to us that many Members with secretaries regard protection from the routine printed stuff as part of the secretary's purpose and value. Conservatives more commonly have this service and they were more likely not to know the volume of their total mail ('Don't know': 'Vast amount'): they often specified that discarding or filing circulars was their secretary's job. Of course, Labour Members may actually receive more of this material, perhaps because some organisations think that Government supporters are better able to influence Ministers. There is also some evidence from our

60

respondents' estimates that longer-serving Members receive more printed circulars and suchlike, as they appeared to in the case of personally directed letters. As we have suggested, a Member's long-term record probably leads to a gradual increase in the volume of his postbag. Thus we found that, in estimating the *total* number of items they received, 56 per cent of these claiming less than fifty items per week had served three years or less in the House, whereas of those claiming fifty or more items per week 62 per cent had served four or more years and 47 per cent nine or more years.

We asked Members their 'general opinion of the printed and published material you get sent from organisations, firms, embassies, etc.' Members gave the hostile answers we expected, but with an undercurrent of acceptance or even welcome for those items which any particular Member finds interesting. We coded the responses into eight statements (Figure 7).

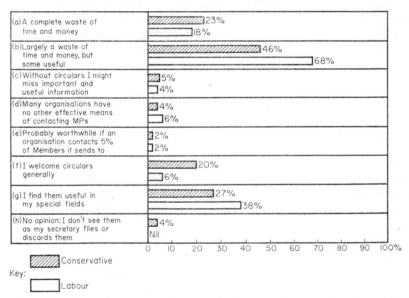

Key:
▨ Conservative
☐ Labour

Figure 7. *Respondents' general opinion of printed circulars, etc.* (See Appendix, Table 5.)

(N—106: 56 Conservatives and 50 Labour MPs)

Three-quarters of our 107 respondents thought the sending of these cirulars and printed items to them was largely or completely a waste of both the organisation's money and the

Member's time. But one-third of the Members agreed that they found some of these items useful sources of knowledge in their own special fields of interest. About one-fifth of the Members were solidly against the whole business and little more than one-eighth were in favour of it, offering a general welcome to circulars on any subject.

Party differences on this matter while not sharp, are interesting: a few more Conservatives than Labour Members are really hostile to this flow of material but more Labour Members gave a critical tone to their overall attitude by declaring that circulars are largely, but not wholly, a waste of time and by being less likely than Conservatives to say they welcome them generally. It is important to note that in spite of Labour Members objecting to circulars as largely a waste of time, notably more of them said they found them useful in their special fields: a possible confirmation of Labour MPs being more 'specialist-minded'. Only a couple of Conservatives said flatly that they had no view because their secretaries dealt with all routine post but their position was in effect shared by a limited group of Members (mainly, but certainly not entirely, Conservatives) who clearly did not now bother with this post but who perhaps remembered the days when, lacking a secretary, they had been obliged to do so and thus offered us an opinion on it. It may well be that the rather more favourable attitude to circulars among Conservatives is due to their seeing only those in their special fields which they have told their secretaries to retain, without having to bother with the rest. On the other hand, many Members told us in passing that it is little trouble to throw away the 95 per cent they do not want since they recognise the wrappers of the unwanted regular items and discard them unopened.

Apart from the differences between parties, we also found some differences in respect of parliamentary service. Longer-serving Members generally were more likely to say that circulars are a complete waste of time and money, this being the view of more than a quarter of our respondents with nine or more years of service in the House. Looking at education, the diversity of views among graduate MPs is aptly illustrated by their great hostility compared with non-graduates to the indiscriminate nature of much of the material which MPs receive: they are more likely, as a group, to feel that the organisations concerned should become more selective among Members. Yet more graduates than non-graduates said that they welcomed circulars generally.

Two-fifths of our respondents thought that the circulars which fell within their special interests were excellent or well-presented and a similar proportion felt that the quality varied considerably. Less than an eighth regarded such material as being generally poorly presented, leaving the two Conservatives who said that they never saw any circulars as their secretaries dealt with them.

There was no significant difference between the major parties, although some differences were found among MPs of different educational background, the most critical being graduates and the least critical those with an only elementary education or non-graduate further education. Again, we found that Members who were graduates had more diversified views than other Members. The longer-serving Members were, as we have seen, more likely to be unreservedly opposed to this flow of material even if a small proportion of it did fall within any special field of their own interest. Conversely, Members elected in 1959 or since were more likely to reply that, although this practice is largely a waste of time and money, they found value in some of the stuff they received. They were also more likely to reply that they found such information useful when it concerned their special fields. These views were even more pronounced among those who entered the Commons in 1964 and 1966.

The point of view of MPs on this aspect of their parliamentary work can be summed up by saying that they are really rather hostile to the aggregate flow of printed and duplicated material which a large number of organisations of many different kinds believe it worthwhile to post to them. This general irritation is, however, significantly neutralised by Members' welcome for a mere handful of the stuff they get which they do find useful. Members who take this majority position often spoke of the need for selectivity: why should they receive twenty unwanted items, which they discard, for every item which lies in their special fields and which therefore has a chance of being looked at? The newer Members were particularly likely to regret the waste and the inefficiency which they believed was involved: 'I can't yet bring myself to throw away extremely expensive and attractive glossy colour brochures as it would be a shocking waste—so I take them home for my wife to look at and then she throws them away', said a younger Conservative. We were often told that a Member was not at all averse to being lobbied, even by a group whose aims are far removed from his own special interests. The argument ran that a half-hour talk with an organisation's representative, allowing the Member to question and comment, would tell the Member more about the problem than a good deal of printed material which he may read—and an infinite amount which he discards unread.

Some Members, however, are less hostile to all this unsolicited impersonal material and sympathise with the problem faced by the small organisation in selecting the 'correct' MPs to receive a circular. This important problem of selectivity and personal contacts with Members is mentioned again in the following sections of this chapter by William Plowden, discussing six major organisations in the 'Roads lobby', and by us in the context of the much less well-endowed National Council for Civil Liberties. Lacking a truly selective and personal approach (which is, of course, an expensive way for an organisation to conduct parliamentary relations) some printed material sent to MPs has a bogus individuality instead. One of our respondents found brochures from a company arriving at his home address marked 'private and confidential'. He sent some of them to the private address of the company's chairman, similarly marked and with a covering note. As he had expected, the chairman was unaware of the methods of his company's PR agent and had them altered.

Although 'lack of selectivity' and of 'a personal touch' was probably the most common complaint among our respondents, there was also a general feeling that these printed circulars and brochures did not offer what we in our Introduction, have called 'facts about situations' so much as information about the organisation's opinion of that situation. As we have said, there is very little 'pure' information to be had in politics and it is not surprising that the messages sent to MPs by organised interests, at some trouble and expense, should contain those interests' views as well as basic facts about the situation in question. It is, of course, the essential doctrine of good public relations that arguments should not be thrust at the person to be influenced nor blatantly selected facts disguised as the objective truth. As the senior practitioner of parliamentary PR, Lt.

Cdr. C. C. Powell of Watney and Powell, has emphasised, 'a sense of proportion and due regard for *other* aspects of the matter which Parliament may have to consider', is needed when interest groups draft their material to be sent to all or some MPS:

'It is essential to avoid bias, hysteria or exaggeration especially if Parliament is to have respect for the views of any organisation over any length of time, and it is important to remember that Members, very properly, resent being confused, or invited to study documents which waste their time . . .'[1]

Cdr. Powell also advised his colleagues not to send MPS long documents unless the case really required it (and then to attach a summary) and to remember that timeliness is essential: a good brief is useless if it arrives too late. These two points were the subject of the other major complaints of our respondents. Cdr. Powell gave this advice, which every MP to whom we spoke would applaud, in 1955 but the complaints we collected from Members were voiced in 1967. Moreover, none of our longer-serving Members mentioned that parliamentary public relations of this kind had improved along these lines (although, to be fair, we did not specifically ask them). We therefore asked Cdr. Powell whether, as a continuous practitioner in this field over the years, he had noticed any better observance of his precepts: his reply was not encouraging, observing an increase, 'rather more in quantity than in quality and to some extent this may be due to the proliferation of PR organisations, who do not pay sufficient attention to what are the particular requirements of MPS'.[2]

MPs talk about printed circulars and brochures

'I ignore some, such as South African material, but find others, such as from tenants' associations, valuable.' (Labour)

'It's not really worth their sending it because they're not read: they should be selective among Members and send a precis on the front.' (Liberal)

[1] C. C. Powell: address to London meeting of the Institute of Public Relations, September 27, 1955.
[2] Letter to the authors.

'The things I'm interested in, such as Vietnam are very valuable, but printed material rarely alters an experienced man's mind when he's held a general view on an issue for years. MPs therefore tend to pick out the things they can use to support their views.' (Labour)

'Most is blatant propaganda and is thrown out, e.g. Chinese and Spanish diplomatic stuff.' (Conservative)

'I'm a strong believer in anybody's right to express themselves to MPs. Nearly all this bumph is open, plain and honest. MPs can tell disguised or dishonest stuff easily.' (Conservative)

'I rate the diplomatic flow of stuff very low although foreign affairs is an interest of mine.' (Conservative)

'The French embassy material is very useful to a foreign affairs specialist like myself.' (Conservative)

'I have a low opinion in particular of the very extravagent stuff. Too much money is spent, for example, on glossy PR for BBC and ITV programmes which an MP is most unlikely to be able to see.' (Conservative)

'We're lumbered with stuff: it's terrible, the waste.' (Labour)

'There's no other way for them to do it. If 5 per cent of MPs are interested in something, it's probably worthwhile to send it.' (Labour)

'Even from the most prominent bodies, such as CBI and the Iron & Steel Federation, the quality can be low and its arrival too late. The Federation should have had a man with us in the standing committee on steel re-nationalisation for instant briefing.' (Conservative)

'It is good that we read what outsiders are saying: it wouldn't do if all or much of MPs reading was specially designed for us.' (Conservative)

'All commercial sources are untrustworthy except the bank reviews, especially Barclays.' (Labour)

'If they could all agree on some standard format, like a Minister's papers, they would get more attention.' (Conservative)

'I always skim the stuff to keep informed: that way I don't have to read books.' (Conservative)

'Receiving this flood of stuff certainly has a psychological impact on MPs and makes them feel important.' (Conservative)

'It's fabulous; stupendous' (Member describing the flow of this material. Pressed for an estimate, he reckoned four to six items per day)

'The large waste paper baskets they give us here are the most important tool of our trade.' (Labour)

There is clearly a need felt by Members for some of the material sent them by organised interest groups. Most of this flow is wasted but a little of it is read and perhaps kept at least for a time. If it comes at the right time it can be turned to by some Members with particular gratitude to help them form a judgement. The major private Members' bills often present MPs with decisions which they feel they should take but which they have not thought much about in the past. One such matter current during our interviews was the so-called 'social clause' of the abortion bill which the House had to consider and decide upon on the bill's report stage, after its long period in the standing committee. The clause provided that a woman could legally claim an abortion if two doctors certified that the extra child's presence in the family would prejudice her ability to cope with her existing children and generally damage their family environment: no specific medical or mental risk to the safe delivery of the unborn child was necessary to this decision. Several Members we spoke to wanted information on the social background to this proposal unadorned with the general philosophical or religious arguments on abortion with which they were, by this stage of the bill, thoroughly familiar. They seemed to be unsatisfied with the material they received from the main abortion protagonists and the main latecomers on the scene, the organised gynaecologists. These Members' difficulty points towards the House of Commons Library as a potentially better source of impartial advice on how a fair judgement of the 'social clause' of that bill may have been made—assuming, of course, that the 'relevant social facts' of such a morally taxing question are available which, on this matter, was hardly the case. Where facts are limited the exchange of opposing opinions tends to increase to take their place.

Although the 'rationality' and 'efficiency' of the modern

processes of trying to influence the thinking and perceptions of Members of Parliament leaves a great deal to be desired, there is, of course, no question of people and organised groups being free to send their material as often and in whatever form they like. Members, for their part, are free to ignore it but they may, conceivably, run into political trouble if they do. Judging from our interviews, we would expect all Members to accept that they should be open to information and influence from anybody— provided they do not have to reply in a way which would reveal whether or not they have studied what they were sent. The contrast with the letter allegedly sent by Anthony Henley[1] in 1727 is almost complete:

> 'Gentlemen:
> I received yours and am surprised by your insolence in troubling me about the Excise.
> You know what I very well know, that I Bought you. And I know, what perhaps you think I don't know, you are now selling yourselves to somebody Else. And I know what you don't know, that I am buying another Borough.
> May God's curse light on you all. May your houses be as open and common to all Excise Officers as your Wifes and Daughters were to me when I stood for your Scoundrell Corporation.
>
> Yours,
> Anthony Henley.'

> House of Commons
> London
> S.W.1.

Thank you so much for your kind letter. It was nice of you to write.

I am very glad to know that you agree with the line I have been taking. I have been much encouraged by the many letters of support, which I have received from all over Britain and from overseas.

Please forgive me for not answering sooner. But I have been extremely busy just lately, and have had to make one or two journeys abroad.

> With best wishes,
> Yours sincerely,

[1] We are grateful to Lord Henley for providing us with the text of this letter.

(Text of a stock, all-purpose reply letter sent by one current MP to people who write giving their support to his political views on any of a number of issues.)

Clearly, the extension of the franchise and the elimination of corrupt electoral practices since 1727 have improved politicians' civility rather than their prose style.

So far we have considered the information network of mass media and interest groups through the eyes of a Member of Parliament and this, indeed, is the perspective of our whole study. The next three sections of this Chapter, however, try to see parts of the information network from the viewpoint of a few of the organised interest groups and other bodies which seek to inform the country, including MPs, of their policies and views.

3. MPS AND THE 'ROADS LOBBY'

by William Plowden

In any field, the non-specialist and perhaps uncommitted MP needs to be able to evaluate the information reaching him from various sources, and to have some idea of which sources are the most reliable. For the outside organisation, the problems concern the sort of information to supply. Arguments or simply facts? To which MPs: all, or a few? If only a few, how to select them? and how to communicate—personally and informally, or in a printed memorandum sent through the post?

Everybody uses a road at one time or another, even if only in a hearse, and MPs are no exception. They are in fact exceptional in the considerable amount they drive on the roads, and the distances which many of them cover. Of the 63 per cent of all MPs who replied to a 1967 questionnaire from the British Heart Foundation, only 3 per cent admitted to never driving a car; 47 per cent drove 10,000 miles a year, and 14 per cent did over 20,000. Whatever the policies of their parties, MPs might thus be expected to have views on roads. This section considers the efforts of some of the organisations making up what Professor Finer conveniently labelled the 'Roads lobby'[1] to mobilise or modify those views and bring them to bear on the wider questions of roads policy in general.

[1] *Political Quarterly*, 1958, I, pp. 47–58.

The organisations studied include two 'pressure groups' specifically concerned with propaganda for the road-building programme, the Roads Campaign Council and the British Road Federation; the two main 'motoring organisations' proper, the Royal Automobile Club and the Automobile Association; and two major trade associations, the Road Haulage Association and the Society of Motor Manufacturers and Traders. Even this select list of six bodies shows that the 'Roads lobby' is a very heterogeneous group. There are real differences in its constituent members' objectives, which may at times conflict— although the post-war years have seen nothing to match the furious rows of the 1920s between the various road-users over the incidence and distribution of road taxation. These differences, and also differences in constitutions, in views about the role of Parliament in the making of policy, in relationships with other political institutions—such as the electorate, or Government Departments—affect the use which these organisations try to make of Parliament and the way they communicate with MPs.

The histories, objectives and activities of these six organisations vary widely. Both the Roads Campaign Council and the British Road Federation differ from the others in that their major task is to influence opinion. Both bodies are the creation of other autonomous groups who 'subscribe' (rather than belong) to them, for the purpose of presenting to public and official opinion an agreed case for road transport and road-building.

The RCC was started in 1955, largely on the initiative of the chairman of the RAC, Wilfrid Andrews. It described itself as being backed by about a dozen of 'the principal organisations concerned with the manufacture, maintenance and use of roads', including all the other five discussed here; its original executive committee of five included the chairman of the AA and the RAC and senior representatives of the Society of Motor Manufacturers and Traders, BRF and the Motor Agents' Association. The RCC's original purpose was to organise a short, sharp publicity campaign demanding increased expenditure on roads, but it has stayed in being ever since.

The British Road Federation dates from 1932. It grew out of a conference of various road interests formed to prepare a reply to the report of the 'Salter Conference' on competition between road and rail transport. It described itself at the time as 'the one representative body which is making efforts to combat the sinister and distorted propaganda of the railways in their efforts to enslave British industry'. Its original objects included:

'To promote, support or oppose bills in or Acts of Parliament . . .' 'To confer with and make proposals and representations on the objects of the Federation to British and foreign governments and Government Departments . . . and as far as possible to secure the adoption of such proposals and representations and to obtain representation in Parliament and on Government committees . . .' 'To render assistance to candidates in any parliamentary municipal or other election.'

Today its general purpose is 'the promotion of road development and road transport in the interests of all road users'. It is concerned both with roads and road investment, and with general transport policy and its legislative framework. Its hundred-odd subscribing associations and major companies comprise over 35,000 firms, with interests in either the building or the use of roads. They thus include public hauliers, and those who distribute their own goods on their own account (bakers, timber merchants, launderers, funeral directors); suppliers of construction equipment and materials; and those with a general interest in the roads programme (the AA and motor manufacturers). The RAC does not belong, on the grounds that it puts its main weight behind the Roads Campaign Council.

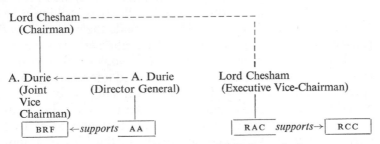

Figure 8.   *Links between four 'Roads lobby' organisations.*
(*Note:* The dotted lines indicate that the links concerned are in a personal capacity.)

But the RAC's Executive Vice-Chairman, Lord Chesham,[1] is—in a personal capacity—the Chairman of the BRF; its two

[1] Joint Parliamentary Secretary (Lords), Ministry of Transport, 1959–64.

Vice-Chairmen are the Director General of the AA, A. C. Durie, and A. P. de Boer (a director of William Cory & Sons Ltd, a firm of coal and oil contractors, exporters, ship owners, lighter-men, etc.) In 1966 the BRF's income was £41,600; some members also contributed in kind (e.g. by printing some BRF publications without charge).

Of the six organisations discussed here, it is probably the RCC for whom parliamentary contacts have been most impor-tant. Established to put across a message on behalf of corporate subscribers which already had their own channels of com-munication with the Government, the RCC from the beginning concentrated on direct attempts to influence parliamentary and public opinion. Its contacts with MPs are institutionalised in the shape of the all-party Roads Study Group. This grew out of an original RCC proposal to create a group of MPs to press for its objectives within Parliament. But Geoffrey Wilson (Con-servative Member for Truro) who was then chairman of the Conservative party group on transport, recalls that he pointed out that both parties already had their own transport groups. He suggested that, to avoid overlapping, members of these two groups should meet together to discuss the facts, as far as was possible, on a non-party basis. The resultant Roads Study Group, set up in 1957, has joint Conservative and Labour chairmen. Mr Wilson has been the Conservative chairman since the beginning; the present Labour chairman, Archie Manuel (Labour Member for Central Ayrshire) was preceded by Ernest Davies and Ernest Popplewell. (It is striking that of these four MPs all, except Mr Davies, made their careers on the railways.) The Group has no fixed membership. It is serviced by the RCC, which has always been responsible for arranging the Group's programme; this has included addresses by outside speakers, and visits to study both British and—perhaps a more effective way of encouraging any latent interest in roads—Continental highway developments. (In the summer of 1965 a party of twelve MPs visited Birmingham, the Port of London, Rotterdam and Düsseldorf.)

The RCC does not, however, confine its activities to the Roads Study Group. It has published several studies of road problems, including one commissioned from Professor Victor Morgan and published in October 1965 under the title *Econ-omic and Financial Aspects of Road Improvement*; the RCC sent a copy to every MP—and a synopsis, with comments, to every candidate in the 1966 General Election.

Geoffrey Wilson's view is that, although transport policy is potentially a highly controversial topic, the Roads Study Group has worked extremely well and has done much to ease the bitterness of the controversy. Although, with the Conservatives in Opposition, the shadow Minister of Transport has now replaced Mr Wilson as chairman of the Conservative party group on transport, Mr Wilson retains his position on the Roads Study Group to preserve its all-party nature.

But the RCC—despite Professor Finer's 1966 comment that it enjoyed 'high repute'[1] with Press and MPs—is not what it was. Possibly as a function of declining support, its activities have dwindled from the peak they reached in the late 1950s. The BRF acted for several years as the RCC's research and information unit, and gave much space to RCC activities in its own annual report; but after 1963 this agreement was not renewed, and the BRF withdrew its representatives from RCC committees. The same year the AA reported that despite its founder membership of the RCC, it felt that the roads programme still failed to reflect the urgency of the situation, and accordingly was joining forces with the BRF; today it has little contact with the RCC. The RCC still periodically arranges speakers for Roads Study Group meetings—in July 1967 the chairman of the Humber Development Committee spoke to them on the need for the Humber bridge—but its most recent foreign visit was the Düsseldorf trip in 1965; and the Morgan report is its latest major publication. Its continued existence seems to depend largely on support from the Motor Agents' Association and from the RAC, in whose building its office is located and from whose staff its own Information Secretary is formally seconded. The declining role of the RCC is in striking contrast to the growth of expenditure on trunk roads; this almost quadrupled between 1956 and 1962 and then almost doubled again by 1965, at constant prices.

The position of the BRF is very different. Compared with the rather shrill tone of much RCC propaganda and the polemical sectionalism of its own early days, the BRF's public style is notably restrained.

This is appropriate, for the BRF has grown into perhaps the

[1] *Anonymous Empire*, 2nd (rev.) ed., Pall Mall, 1966, p. 92.

most respectable and influential organisation in its field. Its status is simply illustrated: in 1966, for example, the Duke of Edinburgh patronised and the Minister of Transport, Mrs Castle, opened the fifth World Meeting in London of the International Roads Federation, organised by the BRF; the same year, BRF organised a symposium on road administration and finance at which the speakers included not only academics, but the chairman of the British Railways Board and senior officials from the Ministry of Transport.

The provision of information, in the widest sense, is the BRF's business—whether acting as middleman, as above, or making its own compilations, or sponsoring research projects such as the three-year survey being carried out at Newcastle into the value of motorways to industry. For MPs, the BRF's information activities fall into three main categories. All MPs are sent copies of the BRF factual surveys and compilations, such as the annual *Basic Road Statistics*, twice-yearly progress reports on motorway construction, the BRF's own annual report and monthly bulletin, and periodic reports on subjects such as road communications with docks and airports. The BRF justifies this wide coverage with the argument that since the state of British roads affects in some degree most other economic activities, the subject should concern all MPs; hence some of its publications are specifically aimed at emphasising the relationship between roads and other sectors. On the same principle, the BRF sent all candidates in the 1964 and 1966 elections leaflets outlining its view of Britain's road needs. (Before the 1966 election candidates also got a letter inviting their support for a national roads board: of the 35 per cent who replied 36 per cent approved and 22 per cent agreed that the idea deserved further study.)

The BRF also briefs MPs for specific parliamentary occasions. Like most of the other organisations discussed here, it generally assumes that, beyond its own and its members' first-hand contacts with MPs, the limits of active parliamentary interest in roads (peers apart) are probably largely set by the membership of the party transport groups and the Roads Study Group. (Although technically these three groups have no formal membership, they have their own officers, and there is no difficulty in finding out the names of those MPs who attend regularly and show an interest in roads affairs.)

In practice the BRF prefers to leave the choice of MPs to receive briefing material to the adviser whom it has retained since the war, Lt. Cdr. Christopher Powell. In fact this produces a fairly wide circulation, though this is adapted according to the occasion. Cdr. Powell's own view is that it is sometimes both invidious and uneconomic to be too selective; it costs more in time and effort to try—not always successfully—to identify the 'really' interested MP than is saved by sending out 100 rather than 600 copies of the brief. However, if an MP is known to be especially interested, he may get a special note, or at least a personal covering letter.

The BRF's third type of contact with MPs is outside the context of the national roads programme altogether. One of its main activities is at the regional level, where it tries to act as a middleman in helping local authorities to devise and to promote highway schemes which cross the boundaries of individual highway authorities. Thus in 1966 the BRF co-operated with the Lancashire County Council in bringing together local highway authorities to agree on pressing for the inclusion of four major new Lancashire road developments in the national programme. This scheme was publicly endorsed by the county council at a conference sponsored by the BRF, and was given further publicity in a typically elegant BRF publication under the title *Lancashire Needs*.

In this exercise the BRF's contact with MPs were extremely selective. In the first place, only a limited number of MPs mainly local, were concerned. Second, contact with MPs was made, and publicity to draw the Government's attention to the proposals encouraged, only relatively late—when the scheme had been approved by all the local authorities concerned. Third, even then it was left to the local authorities to make this contact with local MPs, in an attempt to gain their support for the schemes. All this reflected accurately the BRF's view that the role of the MP in these cases is distinctive, but limited. There is no point in raising dust at Westminster until agreement has been reached locally—with planning officers, surveyors, industrialists, councillors. When local lines are cleared, the time has come for pressure at the centre—and then preferably in response to a local stimulus. In the BRF's view, it is in this kind of operation that the MP can be most effective—not in battles about the shape of the roads programme as a whole. Local schemes are comprehensible, the facts on them are easily available from the constituency sources, and even Government party Members can join in pressing for action in a way which might be inhibited in discussion of national policy. (The findings of a survey of Yorkshire and Humberside, similar to, though rather more elaborate than the Lancashire one, were published in the summer of 1968.)

The *raison d'être* of the BRF (and of the RCC) is to perform fairly specific functions, which are—in the broadest sense— largely political, on behalf of members who support them for those ends and who are themselves organisations specialising in some aspect of the roads and vehicle industries. In contrast, the RAC and AA have a mass membership of private individuals, most of whom may reasonably be judged as more interested in the services they receive (breakdown, garages, touring informa- tion, etc.) than in the two bodies' published views on matters of political policy. How far this mass membership sees itself as a separate 'motoring class' is uncertain, yet it is clear that, as ordinary citizens, these members have no special means of communication with the Government about roads and motor- ing. So the RAC and AA have the double task of acting as a channel of communication on motoring matters between the citizen and the Government and of trying to give political weight and shape to their own views by enlisting approval for their political activities among their mass membership. They want, in short, to appear to be speaking for an 'interest' in the community—'the motorist'—which is as distinct and united in its operation as it is plainly large in sheer size. In its annual report for 1963, the AA thought it worth reminding its members that—

'Because of its large membership, the AA is able to speak with authority on behalf of motorists as a whole and is regarded both by central and local government as a powerful and responsible influence in motoring affairs.'

Both the RAC and the AA have made this claim from the earliest days of the motor vehicle, when 'motoring' was an expensive, skilled and often anti-social leisure occupation of the upper and middle classes. The old Automobile Club, founded in 1897, was a club, and the RAC has always seen itself as rather more stylish than its pushing rival, founded nearly a decade later as a motorists' defence organisation against the police.

In Edwardian days, both of them lobbied—publicly and privately—Ministers, civil servants, MPs, other road users, and local authorities: about levels and methods of taxation; building, maintenance and financing of roads; speed limits and other restrictions on the use of private cars. They still do. But by 1967 the membership of the RAC had grown to 1·5 million, the AA's to 3·7 million; the subscription income of the RAC (which does not publish its accounts) must be at least £3 million a year, and in 1967 the AA's income from all sources was over £13 million. With this growth came some doubt as to what their proper functions were; critics have had their own ideas, and the organisations have been chided by politicians, by the Consumer Council, by the Prices and Income Board, by motoring correspondents and by their own individual members, for failing to do 'their job' properly.

This doubt is one of the factors which has weakened the RAC and AA claims to negotiate with Governments. Their claims rest on, among other things, the residual status of the organisations as experts on motoring; on the value of the services, such as sign-posting and traffic control, which they provide free of charge; and on their still virtually exclusive status as motorists' organisations. But these claims are qualified not not only by public criticism of the organisations' activities, but also by the challenge to their expert status from all the individuals and organisations (including millions of non-member car drivers) which did not exist in the early 1900s and which now know at least as much as the organisations about driving motor vehicles; and by the facts that their managements neither 'represent' the mass of their members in any modern sense (since they are not elected by them), nor can pretend to 'deliver' their votes to any particular political party (given the realities of British voting behaviour).

Thus Governments have long found advantages in maintaining regular contacts with the motoring organisations, which are represented on official committees and working parties, and which are also consulted, or listened to, on many individual topics. But Governments also find it possible totally to disregard their views if necessary. This makes for an ambivalent relationship, in which continued private co-operation is overlaid by public bickering. Mrs Barabara Castle's regime at the Ministry of Transport was the subject of vigorous and sometimes extravagant attacks by the RAC and the AA, reaching a state of what one moderate motoring correspondent described in early 1967 as 'almost open war'. Mrs Castle herself, in a press interview in summer 1967, brushed aside the organisations' criticisms with the comments that their managements were not democratically elected and that their reactions were so stereotyped that they had no effect on the general public.

It is against this background that the relationships of the RAC and AA with MPs must be seen. Attempts to organise large-scale parliamentary protest have always been a regular part of their activities since the war. In recent years they have taken an interest in parliamentary activities involving road safety, parking meter charges, animals on the highway, the 'totting-up' procedure for motoring offences, illuminated warning signs for motorways, hire purchase of motor vehicles, the Highway Code, driving licences and certificates of insurance, London government, the Royal Commission on the Police, the grading of petrol, anchorage points for safety belts, speed limits, court procedures, companies legislation, drink and driving, and the selection and training of traffic wardens. Over much of this field they have co-ordinated their activities as far as possible, as is described below. But their individual styles are still very different.

The RAC in the 1960s is still recognisably the same body that negotiated with Asquith and Lloyd George over motor taxation in 1908–9. Its sometimes sturdily individualistic comments occasionally imply a wishful belief that things have not changed very much since then. It has a central committee of about forty members, including its chairman, Wilfrid Andrews, who has held office since 1945, and three MPs (Thomas Galbraith[1], Arthur Palmer (Labour Member for Bristol Central) and Sir Clive Bossom (Conservative, Leominster)). It also has an executive committee of twelve, which includes no MPs.

The RAC's 'public policy activities' are described in a published annual report, which tells—to quote the two most recent reports—how

[1] Joint parliamentary Secretary, Ministry of Transport, 1963–4; Conservative Member for Glasgow, Hillhead.

'detailed information was provided to MPs and the Press to ensure that the Club's views were made known on a variety of matters which were the subject of debate and Questions in both Houses of Parliament'.

These activities are subject to the formal scrutiny of the Club's Public Policy Committee. This has about twenty members, including (in 1966–7) Sir Clive Bossom, Lord Nugent[1] and the RAC's Executive Vice-Chairman, Lord Chesham. This Committee, which meets about five times a year, is serviced by a full-time executive staff of two, who are responsible for scrutinising *Hansard* to note which MPs take an interest in motoring matters, for communications with these and other MPs, and for attending Commons debates and standing committees, and meetings of the Roads Study Group.

Like other organisations, the RAC takes as the nucleus of its contacts among MPs the active 'roads' members of the party transport groups. It does not rely unduly heavily on the parliamentary services of the four MPs who sit on its committees; their main liaison role is seen as being to explain to other committee members the significance and prospects of current parliamentary developments. The RAC public policy staff do not have a great deal of regular contact with the research departments of the three political parties; contacts with the Opposition tend to be made directly through frontbench transport spokesmen. In general, RAC policy is to communicate with MPs for specific purposes—i.e. to brief them for public argument about issues on which the RAC have failed to get satisfaction in private discussion, whether from the Government, from MPs introducing private Members' bills or from the sponsors of private bills. Thus the RAC does not aim in the same way as, for instance, the BRF, simply to keep MPs informed of developments of interest to it. It hopes that MPs who are themselves RAC members— club officials do not know exactly how many of these there are— will keep up to date by reading the Club's regular publications (although during the Club's running battle with the Ministry of Transport in 1965 over the 70 m.p.h. speed limit, it did take trouble to keep MPs abreast of events by sending them periodic memoranda). The number of MPs receiving copies of RAC briefs

[1] Member for Guildford, 1950–66; Joint Parliamentary Secretary, Ministry of Transport, 1957–9.

varies between 50 and 100; in preparation for the second reading of the Transport Bill in December 1967, about 100 MPs received a RAC memorandum objecting to the powers given by the bill to local authorities to use the revenue from parking meters to finance off-street parking and other highway improvements (which the RAC felt should be financed from central funds). The RAC estimates that it has about 100 regular contacts (in this sense) among MPs at any one time.

The activities of the AA are similar in kind to those of the RAC, but rather more elaborate. It too still retains traces of the grand style; its annual general meeting is at the Savoy Hotel, presided over by its President, the Duke of Norfolk (whose predecessor was the Duke of Edinburgh). But in recent years the AA has been undergoing some radical administrative changes. In 1964 it modernised its whole management structure, replacing two joint secretaries with a Director-General (Mr Durie, formerly a managing director of Shell-Mex and BP). Some observers consider that the AA, its attacks on Mrs Castle notwithstanding, is now making a determined effort to shake off any image of itself as the uninhibited spokesman for the irresponsible private motorist.

Parliamentary liaison is the task of the AA's public relations division, which shared in the recent re-organisation. It is the particular responsibility of the head of this division, Basil Rogers. Mr Rogers was from 1955 to 1963 the Secretary of the Roads Campaign Council, and has been able to draw on the parliamentary experience he gained there in pursuing the AA's current policy of establishing closer relations with MPs. Characteristic of this attention to Parliament is an AA leaflet, first produced in 1965, *The AA and Parliament*. This, which was sent to every MP, told them:

'There are no doubt many occasions when a Member of Parlia-advice. The AA is ready to provide any information or assistance ment, faced with a motoring or transport problem, needs expert required, and places its full resources at the disposal of Members of Parliament.'

Although the AA thus proffers its services to all MPs it—like the RAC—does not aim to keep MPs informed of the AA point of view unless parliamentary developments require it. This is consistent with their view that indiscriminate propaganda is not merely a waste of time and effort, but can be actually counter-productive. One weakness of motoring affairs as a subject of parliamentary discussion is that everybody, as a road user, considers himself an expert and has something to say; debates become diffuse, and ill-informed criticism can easily be dismissed by Government spokesmen. As the AA see it, concentrating information on relatively few MPs is, firstly, realistic: not more than a dozen backbenchers can take part in a normal day's debate. Secondly, MPs will tend to take a closer and thus more effective interest in a subject if they feel that it calls for some real expertise—and that they are recognised as having this.

In practice the AA, again like the RAC, estimates that in a single session it will communicate with about 100 MPs, the Labour and Conservative party transport groups being the hard core. For major debates, about seventy-five MPs will normally get an AA brief. About this number were briefed for the debate on the White Paper on transport policy (Cmnd. 3057) in February 1967; the AA told them that the Ministry of Transport seemed wedded to 'a gospel of defeatism and despair with the problems of living with the car in a modern society'. As with the RAC, there are exceptions to selectivity: in 1965, for the discussion on the Finance Bill, every MP was sent an AA protest against increases in road tax and goods vehicle licence fees.

The AA sees its contacts with Parliament as political but strictly non-partisan, and it has been equally critical of Governments of both parties. Although on most major issues it clearly makes sense to concentrate efforts on the Opposition of the day, the AA does not try to conceal its lines of argument either from MPs on the Government side or from Government Departments—and indeed sometimes sends copies of its critical memoranda to both (as it did before the debate on Cmnd. 3057). At the same time, the AA feels that briefing is not best conducted through the postbag. Apart from informal contacts with individual MPs—which are possibly the most fruitful form of communication—the AA organises periodic parliamentary lunches, to which MPs from all parties are invited. The same philosophy is behind the separate working dinners which are usually given each year—sometimes as a preliminary to the Finance Bill debates—for the members of the transport, finance and economic groups of each party. The AA has one MP on its governing committee—Esmond Wright (Conservative, Glasgow Pollock) who was a committee member before he became an MP. There is no set AA policy about the appointing of MPs, although in fact in recent years only two other MPs have sat on the committee: the AA's present Chairman, Lord Brentford (who as Conservative MP for Chichester from 1942 to 1958 was a committee member until he resigned on becoming a junior Minister in 1951) and Sir David Renton (Conservative, Huntingdon, who also later resigned from the committee for the same reason).

But this is not the whole of the two motoring organisations' parliamentary activity. Where possible, their efforts are co-ordinated by another body, their Standing Joint Committee. Its formal terms of reference are

'to co-ordinate the views of the motoring organisations including the Royal Scottish Automobile Club and to ensure that a united front is presented in comment and discussion on matters of policy affecting the motoring public'.

The SJC came into being in 1944. It replaces the old Motor Legislation Committee, which acted as the political branch of a mixed group of motor and road interests—including the AA, and latterly the RAC—from 1918 to 1943. It meets four times a year; it has four members from each of the three organisations and three joint secretaries (including the deputy head of the AA's public relations department and his opposite number from the RAC).

It is not always easy to distinguish the activities of the SJC from those of its constituent bodes; the ground covered in its annual report is often identical with much of that in the report of the RAC's public policy committee (and with the rather briefer account in the AA's annual report). One or two specific functions are normally reserved for it, such as petitioning against private bills. In this it acts through its own parliamentary agent, Colin McCulloch of Martin & Co. Typical of the kind of provision in private legislation that concerns the motoring organisations was a clause in the Portsmouth Corporation Bill, introduced in the 1966–7 session, which would have empowered the Portsmouth Corporation to close off part of the esplanade, to charge motor vehicles for parking on it and to use the revenue for general amenity purposes. The motoring organisations objected on principle both to charging for parking on the highway and to the diversion of the revenue to non-highway purposes. A petition was instituted, and the clause was deleted.

Apart from dealing with private bills, the SJC aims to deal with major policy matters on which there is time—and scope— to agree a common line. Thus, although by mid-1967 the RAC and AA positions on the carrying-out of breath tests under the Road Safety Act had grown slightly apart—with Mr Durie of the AA writing to the *Times* to commend an editorial which had criticised the attitude of the RAC—the initial discussions with the Ministry of Transport and Home Office about random breath tests in 1965–6 were conducted by the SJC. It was an SJC brief (consisting of a covering note plus separate legal and medical arguments against random tests) which was sent to about sixty MPs in early 1966; and draft amendments were prepared for the committee stage of the bill under the auspices of the SJC. Again, the SJC has sent a statement to all candidates at recent General Elections (plus, in 1964 and 1966, questionnaires asking for their views on roads, taxes, and parking). The RAC and AA supported this initiative with separate letters to the candidates drawing attention to the SJC material; both bodies are, of course, interested in the replies to the questionnaire—particularly as indicating potentially useful contacts among new MPs.

The SJC's parliamentary agent is an important link in the motoring organisations' contacts with Parliament. He acts for them on private legislation and is also responsible for drafting agreed amendments incorporating their views to public legislation. He also plays some part in selecting suitable MPs to move these amendments at the bill's standing committee stage and—if he thinks it appropriate—in circulating briefs supporting the amendments to other members of the standing committee. Occasionally he helps the SJC in choosing MPs at large, to receive copies of general briefing material. He keeps in touch with the organisation by attending the SJC's quarterly meetings; he will draw their attention to parliamentary developments likely to be of interest to them, but waits for instructions before taking any action.

Jointly and severally, the motoring organisations pay a lot of attention to Parliament—and give this attention some prominence in their annual reports. By contrast, in the recent annual reports of the Society of Motor Manufacturers and Traders, and the Road Haulage Association, the word 'Parliament' occurs but rarely. As trade associations, both these organisations concentrate mainly on non-political activities. But both are inevitably engaged in politics; they represent major economic interests whose relationships with the Government have grown increasingly close in recent years for the familiar reasons that, first, they possess detailed knowledge of their own specialised activities which interventionist Governments need to share—and, secondly, Governments are anxious, other things being equal, to disrupt their activities as little as possible. Both the SMMT and the RHA have their own links with Parliament; for instance, Roger Gresham Cooke (Conservative Member for Twickenham) is a former Director of the SMMT, as well as having been chairman of the BRF's Highways Committee and the joint secretary of the Conservative Party Transport group. But for neither of them is day-to-day parliamentary liaison normally of prime importance.

For the Road Haulage Association in particular, however, things are not always normal. Alone of the organisations discussed here, the RHA represents an interest which has been and still is a major topic of party politics. It grew originally out of the Long Distance Road Haulage Committee, a body formed to put the views of the big hauliers to the Royal Commission on Transport of 1930; it was reorganised in 1944, and by the second half of 1945 was actively engaged in the campaign to defend the interests of commercial haulage operators against nationalisation. It has been engaged in the periodic battle over the shape of the road haulage industry ever since. Today it sees itself as standing for

'the complete freedom of choice in transport services by trade and industry and for full and natural development of each form of transport . . . without fiscal and political distortion'.

The RHA has nearly 18,000 members, operating 173,000 of the vehicles licensed for public haulage (nearly three-quarters of the total). In 1945 its subscription income was £74,000 and its total assets were worth £61,000; in 1966 subscriptions came to

£229,000, and the total balance carried forward at the end of the year was £338,000.

The history of the RHA's relationships with Parliament shows a remarkable contrast between periods of intense activity while road haulage has been under political discussion, and fairly intermittent contact at other times. The first annual report of the reorganised RHA recorded that in 1945 its 'Parliamentary Committee, in conjunction with the parliamentary agents and Political Adviser, is actively engaged in building up parliamentary contacts'. In fact, the nature of the arguments over road haulage from 1945 inevitably drive the RHA mainly into contact with the Conservatives; between 1945 and 1956 it was in fairly continuous contact with Conservative MPs, in Opposition and in Government, in attempts successively to resist and then to reverse nationalisation. The RHA recalls that in 1956 about sixty Conservative MPs attended a meeting called by the RHA to express its views on the Government's decision to halt the process of denationalisation.

The significance of this meeting was that it was to be the last of its kind; although the outcome of the campaign may have encouraged some RHA members to an exaggerated belief in the efficacy of parliamentary intervention, during the next ten years the RHA's contacts with Parliament became increasingly sporadic. The only mention of parliamentary activities in the RHA's reports between 1957 and 1959 refers to private bills (on which it was noted that 'action taken by the Association has been such that points on bills have been adjusted by negotiation', and that there had thus been no need for petitions)—which implies, even had there been anything to report, a fairly limited view of the scope of relevant parliamentary action. During this period there were occasional contacts with MPs on individual subjects: 500 MPs were sent a memorandum on the Channel Tunnel, a handful were in touch in connection with the Road Safety Bill, statements of RHA policy were circulated to MPs in 1958 and again in 1963. But the RHA's only regular communication with MPs has been to send copies of its annual reports to about 200 of them; these—estimated by the RHA to be the absolute maximum with even a marginal interest in road haulage—are selected on the basis of their active membership of the two main parties' transport groups and of any signs of interest to be found in *Hansard*.

There seems to have been several reasons for this relative lack of attention to Parliament. First, the RHA subscribes to the British Road Federation and—unlike some other subscribers— deliberately leaves political activity on the subject of the roads programme to that body. Secondly, scope for effective parliamentary liaison is limited by the fact that the RHA has not found it possible, even during periods of political calm, to establish road haulage as a non-partisan topic on which an MP of any party is a potential spokesman. It has never achieved close links with Labour MPs interested in road transport; an attempt in 1964 to strike up a relationship with the Labour Transport group during the hearings of the Geddes committee on licensing had no lasting effects. When in 1961 the RHA was deeply involved in an appeal against a decision by the Transport Tribunal, it was the Conservative Transport group with which it kept in touch. Today the RHA regretfully considers its only regular contact with the Labour group as being the invitation sent to its chairman for the RHA's annual dinner.

The other major reason is the relative inadequacy of parliamentary discussion as a means of getting things done. Detailed negotiations with Government departments are quicker and more effective in settling technical questions than are broad debates in the House of Commons where the few MPs who know something about road haulage do not often succeed in fully deploying their expertise. The RHA relies heavily on its contacts with Departments and Ministers; its protests in 1965 against the Government's investment incentive proposals were addressed not to MPs but to the Prime Minister, the Chancellor, the Department of Economic Affairs and the Board of Trade. In 1966 it reorganised its structure to cope with 'rapid consultations with the Government and rapid decisions on behalf of members . . .'.[1] At the same time, the RHA pays great attention to public opinion at large; in recent years considerable efforts have gone into analysing and improving the public image of road transport, and in 1966 the RHA commissioned a survey of opinion about itself and about the haulage industry in general.

But all this applies to normal times. In 1967–8 road haulage was once more at the centre of political argument. The RHA saw the Transport Bill, published in December 1967, as presenting a 'very grave threat to users of road transport throughout

[1] RHA Annual Report for 1966.

the country'. To meet this threat the RHA, after a decade's lull, embarked on a massive programme of parliamentary action with active help of Aims of Industry, a promotional organisation for private enterprise. Before the second reading of the Bill, it wrote to all MPs: it explained its objections to some of the Bill's provisions, but also made the point that the RHA was fighting only these—not the Government, nor the Ministry of Transport (nor the Minister), nor even the Bill as such. As well as making this general appeal, the RHA provided a brief for the Conservative Research Department[1] to circulate to Opposition MPs of the Department's own choice. On the day of the second reading, a large number of representatives of RHA's member firms lobbied their MPs at Westminster.

For the standing committee stage of the Bill, the RHA accepted that its allies on major points were more likely to be found on the Conservative side, and kept in close touch with the Opposition transport spokesmen led by Peter Walker. At the same time, it hoped to persuade Labour Members to put the road haulage case on some aspects of the Bill, not all of which were expected to be opposed by the Conservatives. It also did everything possible to involve MPs of all parties at constituency level: local MPs were invited to a series of public rallies held in major cities and branches of the RHA were encouraged to make contact with their own MPs. Finally, as part of an intensive publicity campaign, co-ordinated by a specially engaged public relations expert (financed by an increase in the RHA's 'publicity levy' on its members from two shillings per vehicle to four shillings) leaflets were sent to road hauliers and their employees, and to management in other sectors of industry, encouraging them to

'Write to your MP. This is NOT a waste of time. You have a vote. Your mates/employees have votes. Your friends and colleagues have votes. MPs ARE influenced by voters' letters.'

In present circumstances, it is hard to imagine the Society of Motor Manufacturers and Traders engaging in a parliamentary campaign of this sort. By comparison with the RHA,

[1] See Chapter V, Section 1 on the Conservative Research Department's relationship with the steel industry's trade association when re-nationalisation was proceeding.

it represents an economic interest which has in general been spared direct interference by Governments of either party—although it has been peculiarly vulnerable to the effects of their economic and fiscal policies. The SMMT is the central trade association of the motor industry. It was founded in 1902; for long its political role consisted mainly of following the vociferous lead of the AA in the Motor Legislation Committee. Today it has 16,000 member firms, engaged in making and dealing with motor vehicles and their component parts (including caravans, farm machinery and so on).

The SMMT's working relationships with Parliament seem to be even more diffuse than those of the RHA. Like the British Road Federation, the SMMT leaves much of the work to a professional parliamentary consultant—and again like the BRF, it retains Lt. Cdr. Powell for this purpose. He keeps in touch with the SMMT by attending meetings of its Public Affairs Committee (whose main attention is devoted to press publicity). The SMMT has one regular means of communicating with MPs: the *Motor Industry Bulletin* which was started in 1957 specifically to keep MPs (and peers) informed. It appears about three times a year, has a parliamentary section which records the main subjects of interest to the motor industry discussed in Parliament, and is sent to all MPs.

The SMMT occasionally arranges visits for MPs, for instance to the Motor Industry Research Association; and speakers connected with the industry, if not with the SMMT as such, quite often address the parties' transport groups or the all-party Parliamentary and Scientific Committee (of which Commander Powell has been the Secretary since its foundation in 1940). But apart from this, the SMMT itself—as opposed to individual members of the motor industry—has few formal contacts with MPs.

There are two basic reasons for this—and two main ways in which the parliamentary process is by-passed. In the first place, the SMMT, as a trade association attempting to represent the common interests of a diverse group of independent undertakings, is often not the appropriate channel for dealing with individual problems. These can be most simply raised by the sector of the industry concerned—often directly with Ministers by chairmen of big firms. Even much parliamentary discussion of motor industry problems is on a constituency level, with arguments deployed in relation to redundancies at Coventry or Dagenham.

Secondly, like other economic interests, the motor industry—often acting through the SMMT—is engaged in a continuous process of consultation with the Government, both formally and informally, which makes much parliamentary participation superfluous. This is not a new development; the National Advisory Council for the Motor Manufacturing Industry—with which the motor industry's official Economic Development Committee (or 'Little Neddy') now coexists in uneasy parallel—was set up as long ago as 1946, to provide for regular consultation between Government and the industry. But the number of Government bodies the industry now has to deal with was the subject of some not entirely jocular comment by the SMMT's President, Sir George Harriman, in October 1967; and a working party which the SMMT set up to consider its own role commented in July 1967 that

'Parliaments, departmental responsibilities, policies and staffs change as never before. Whereas industries used to look to Government Departments for continuity of thought, policy and action, now the reverse is often the case.'

It would certainly be logical to feel that this situation would only be exacerbated by trying to impose on it a system of working relationships with MPs. As long as private negotiations can produce results, nothing is gained from raising a subject in Parliament—especially if negotiations are still in progress. It can be agreed that parliamentary discussion of technical and economic subjects is, firstly, often superficial and inadequate; and secondly, that by being forced into a gladiatorial mould it both distorts the issues and gives a misleading—and possibly damaging—public impression of the industry's true relations with government.

The SMMT seem to do their best to avoid public argument where possible. Although they gladly supply information to MPs on request, they do not always encourage them to make public use of this. One prominent back-bencher with a wide knowledge of the motor industry mentioned an occasion when he had wished to raise in the House a technical matter about certain equipment for motor vehicles, but on consulting the

SMMT had been advised not to do so on the grounds that they were already discussing it privately with Government Departments.

The Six Bodies

The contrast between the parliamentary activities of the SMMT or the RHA on one hand and the RAC or the AA on the other shows very clearly that the concept of a 'Roads lobby' can be misleading if it is taken to imply common political styles. The reports of the AA and RAC and of their Standing Joint Committee specifically draw attention to the organisations' efforts to keep MPs informed of and active in their affairs. The SMMT tends to play down this side of its activities. The RHA, except when the whole position of the interests it serves has been at stake in circumstances where private negotiations are unlikely to produce results, seems to have regarded its affairs as too serious to be bandied about on the floor of the House of Commons; in normal times, its concern with public opinion at large has been in striking contrast to its apparent lack of concern with the views of MPs, and scepticism about the effects of parliamentary intervention on either the Government or the electorate.

Nonetheless, all these six organisations do undertake to provide certain sorts of information for MPs. What needs to be asked is whether their information activities, severally or collectively, are of value to MPs.

The subject matter of the information varies widely. It follows from the nature of each organisation that, although all share a common interest in the roads system itself, the BRF and RCC activities have been much more closely related to this single subject than have those of the RAC or AA; and equally that the RHA and SMMT are often concerned about issues, like vehicle taxation, which do not directly bear on roads as such. 'Single subject' organisations have an initial advantage in that they are easily identified with their subject; anyone receiving a communication from them knows roughly what it will be about and may have some idea of whether it is likely to be worth studying. But communications from the motoring organisations might refer to any of the range of topics listed above and cannot be expected to be equally authoritative on all of them.

The value to MPs of any information will be affected by its

accuracy, and by its objectivity. The idea of objectivity is only partly relevant. It clearly has very little application in discussing 'argumentative' information; nobody would expect the RHA to put the case for transferring goods from roads to railways, nor the SMMT for restraining home demand for motor vehicles. Bias is much more of a danger in relation to questions of fact, where there is a possibility that facts will be selected, or distorted, to suit an argument. The files of the Public Record Office contain a classic memorandum many years ago by the SMMT to the Ministry of Transport, seeking to show that motor taxation was hitting sales by comparing registrations in August one year with those in the following February. In the committee stage of the Road Traffic Bill in 1955, David Renton, who was at that time a member of the AA's executive committee, dissociated himself from the anti-meter material which had been widely circulated to MPs by the AA, and attacked it—with the support of the Opposition—as inaccurate and misleading. The AA goes boldly out to meet the doubts which incidents such as these may cause; in *The AA and Parliament* it declares 'The AA does *not* believe in "The Motorist right or wrong". It can therefore be relied upon to give factual and impartial information.'

In general, the claim seems to be a fair one. It is widely agreed, even within the Ministry of Transport, that the facts supplied by these organisations—whatever the validity of the arguments they are used to sustain—are accurate and reliable. To this extent they are of value to MPs or to anyone else. The problems of roads and their users are only one of the fields in which anyone producing information is likely to be performing a public service. A notable example is the periodic *Financial Times* feature which provides the only reliable published estimate of British motor manufacturers' production of each model. For this reason it has been possible for the BRF above all to build a reputation for responsibility and authoritativeness, based largely on the accurate comprehensive information which it provides about roads.

Given the BRF material and official publications such as the Ministry of Transport's annual *Highway Statistics* and *Roads Report*, MPs are at least not short of facts. Where problems do arise is on interpretation. One must again recognise the legitimate distinction between argumentative and factual information:

there is bound to be a difference in kind between an SJC attack on random breath tests, and BRF statistics of motorway construction. Interpretation of facts relating to roads is a problem firstly in a technical sense. The amount and variety of fact available make analysis, and still more comparison, a tricky affair: published figures for roads expenditure variously relate to England, and Great Britain; to 'Exchequer' expenditure (excluding rate-borne) and 'public' (including rate-borne); to real and to constant prices; to payments made, and commitments entered into (Ministers have had trouble on this one); and there are other complications such as the basis of *Highway Statistics* which relates to the calender year, while *Roads Report* is based on the financial year.

Interpretation is a problem also in the sense that the arguments based on the facts may vary. Despite its federal status, the BRF is far from being the only body making public pronouncements about roads; the AA, although supporting the BRF, will always seize the chance to make a point about any aspect of the roads programme, as will the RAC and the RCC.

On the question of road pricing there is a curious contrast between statements by AA spokesmen on the lines that 'from the motorists' and business point of view, road pricing would be the first death knell', and pronouncements by Mr Durie, usually wearing his BRF hat, that road pricing would be acceptable as part of the political price of an independently financed national road-building board. Some people might not be able to follow the logic of the motoring organisations' public protests against the diversion of parking revenue whether to road or non-road purposes. In the battle about the 70 m.p.h. speed limit, the statistics available at least up till late 1967 lent themselves equally convincingly to the Ministry of Transport's contention that the limit did save lives and to the motoring organisations' (and Conservative Opposition's) insistence that it was too soon to tell.

Difficulties and variations in interpretation lend force to complaints which may be heard among MPs that these 'roads' organisations—in common with others—'do not understand what MPs need'. The sense of this seems to be that interests who want to put across a point of view should take more account of what an individual MP wants; there is too much reliance on blanket briefing in stereotyped form, and a failure to appreciate the value of personal contacts and face-to-face briefing—for which meetings with backbench committees, or social occasions, whatever their other functions, are no substitute. Interests should take the trouble to identify and to concentrate on individual MPs who are prepared to work at the subject; this means discussing it thoroughly with them, to make sure both that complex points are understood, and that all the necessary material has been provided. One current Opposition transport spokesman said that of the mass of information he received from roads interests, very little that he had not specifically asked for was of much use. Another felt that, where outside interests felt themselves threatened by Government policy, the Opposition frontbencher had no difficulty in finding out what he needed to know. Nonetheless, in briefing himself for the Transport Bill, he had found it necessary to approach the interests affected, and to travel round the country talking to them.

On the other side is the problem with which both the BRF and the AA, in rather different ways, have specifically tried to deal; that precisely because—as the British Heart Foundation's findings show—so many MPs have regular personal experience of driving, questions of roads policy risk not being treated as the complex and specialist subject they are. Observation of meetings of the Parliamentary and Scientific Committee confirms that attendance when 'transport' is to be discussed is always above average; and that, at the same time, transport matters tend to be discussed very much in practical and applied, and not in more scientific and analytical terms. *Hansard* shows debates on roads, from the earliest days of the motor vehicle, studded with pointless personal reminiscences about narrow escapes and alarming motoring experiences.

Of the six organisations, only the SMMT and the RHA seem not to have had regular contacts with the Opposition of the day— the SMMT because the motor industry's main problems have been dealt with in direct negotiations between industry leaders and Governments; and the RHA because during the years of Conservative Government it never established a working relationship with the Labour Opposition. To some extent, relationships with the Opposition party's MPs have been backed up by contacts with its research department; but these contacts seem to have been usually related *ad hoc* to particular pieces of controversial legislation, and were often initiated by the party officials themselves. Often, these links were, in any case, short-circuited by the organisations' personal contacts with MPs of that party. Insofar as this was true in 1967 of the Conservative Research Department, it may have been partly because they were still re-establishing relationships which had atrophied during the years of Conservative Governments. Transport House has certainly never built up a working relationship with any of these six organisations, even when Labour was in Opposition: the section on transport in the 1964 handbook for Labour speakers was based on BRF material—which arrives through the post—and a series of articles which had appeared in *The Times*. In general, these organisations and the party research departments seem not to have developed the kind of regularised relationships which one might have expected to develop to match the Minister of Transport's staff of permanent civil servants.

Relationships between MPs and those organisations might be improved by creating a new specialised select committee of the House in this field—perhaps dealing with transport, or communications. Giving evidence to such a committee would not be a novel exercise for these organisations. From the early years of this century the RAC, AA and SMMT have readily come before royal commissions, departmental committees, standing and *ad hoc* select committees of both Houses of Parliament. The origins of the RHA lay in precisely this function; and the BRF, as its original articles make clear, has always seen one of its main tasks to be making 'proposals and representations'. In the spring of 1967, to take a recent example, the RAC, AA and SMMT all appeared before the Commons Estimates Committee, which was considering road research, and gave their views on the status and activities of the Ministry of Transport's Road Research Laboratory. They were fairly critical; thus, for the RAC, Lord Chesham said:

'Many of us . . . did not care for the presentation of the (Laboratory's) Interim Report on the 70 m.p.h. speed limit, because it seemed to us that selected facts had been included which slanted opinion towards the speed limit, and it was hardly as scientific as one would have expected from the Road Research Laboratory.'

Later, he added that the motoring organisations felt that they were not adequately consulted about the Laboratory's activities.

In fact, none of these organisations seem to have strong or distinct opinions about creating a new specialised select committee which would give them a more or less permanent channel of communication with Parliament—although in general their representatives, speaking personally to the author, were not hostile to the idea. Only one organisation seemed cool, apparently feeling that such a committee of MPs would do nothing to improve the organisation's own already satisfactory contacts with MPs and would, if anything, merely institutionalise competition for parliamentary attention from other interests.

But any prescription for 'improving' the parliamentary activities of these organisations must recognise that they are directed only in part towards Parliament. Their other, indeed sometimes their main function, is to demonstrate to their own members or supporters that at the political level their interests are being defended as vigorously as possible. The AA's annual report, which goes to all AA members, always devotes space to the AA's part in the main parliamentary events of the year; the RAC does likewise, and copies of the detailed report of its Public Policy Committee are available to members on request. The representative of one organisation agreed that negotiations with Government Departments, or private discussions with MPs, were much more likely to produce results than last minute mass briefing. But neither of these could be publicised adequately afterwards; a member demanding to know what the organisation was doing about an issue could be more easily satisfied with a reference to a well-publicised mass briefing of MPs than with an assurance that confidential negotiations with a Government Department were proceeding satisfactorily (and there will always be the suspicion that too much private discussion may end in a 'sell-out'). Another of these six organisations felt that being able to inform the membership about it was the only real advantage to be gained from its parliamentary activity. A 'roads' MP suggested that it was precisely because organisations were so preoccupied with the impact of their parliamentary activity on their own members that its impact on MPs was so uncertain. Nothing destroys any organisation's credibility with MPs quicker and more completely than the impression that in sending them its material it is really addressing its supporters rather than Members. Most of the organisations discussed here are aware of this danger. For them the problem is to strike the right balance between the most effective briefing of MPs and the need to be seen by their members and the public to be 'going through the motions'.

4. THE PARLIAMENTARY LINKS OF THE NATIONAL COUNCIL FOR CIVIL LIBERTIES

The six 'roads' organisations analysed by William Plowden are all wealthy. They either enjoy the subscription support of the various sections of the industries connected with the supply and use of vehicles or they are mass organisations of private car owners. The British Road Federation's 1966 income was £41,600 plus services in kind; the Road Haulage Association collected £229,000 in 1966 subscriptions and the RAC at least £3m in 1967. The giant of these six groups, the AA, received total income of over £13m in 1967. Of these bodies the two mass 'motoring organisations' try to cut the widest swathe in the field of roads-vehicles-driving and membership services. As William Plowden has shown, the AA's and RAC's ranges of public interest are very wide.

Most organised interest groups which try (or would like to try) to influence MPs and the Government by supplying information and opinions to them have far less money than these 'roads' groups. This is particularly true of promotional groups which exist to see some proposal or set of values adopted into law or into social behaviour; representational or other protective groups such as at least five of these six 'roads' bodies (the Roads Campaign Council is a border-line case) usually have more money, as well as better access to the Government because the members whose interests they protect are glad to pay for this service through their subscriptions.

Among promotional groups, the entirely non-economic ones, which can claim no one's subscription to be a necessary levy on their economic well-being, are perhaps the least well-funded. These groups are, in the eyes of their members and supporters at least, the 'good causes' which one ought to support from conviction or on principle. They are not, of course, a close-knit group of like-minded organisations and sometimes do battle with each other. We saw in the section of this chapter dealing with letters and other activity concerning abortion that two organised interests in the field of social policy, the established ALRA and the newly-founded Society for the Protection of Unborn Children, were direct rivals. The British Field Sports Society is a rival of the League Against Cruel Sports and the Hunt Saboteurs, their members sometimes dramatising the organised interest group system by hunting each other in country lanes and woods, the fox or stag serving as a political catalyst.

The National Council for Civil Liberties (NCCL) is a 'good cause' group of this kind. It exists to promote the civil liberties and freedom from restriction or harrassment of every person or group in the country especially when this is alleged to exist on the traditional grounds of religious, ethnic, sex or class discrimination. It is like many other liberal causes in being small and poor while enjoying a reputation which outruns its resources. Having this reputation and being widely known constantly brings more work and even broader boundaries for concern to the Council.

It could be said that the NCCL combines the features of both main types of organised interest groups as they have been classified by political scientists: it is 'promotional' in that it stresses the need to encourage the civil liberties of all citizens, especially discriminated groups such as gypsies or Commonwealth immigrants, while being 'protective' of these liberties on matters where the Council feels liberty is being threatened. Because the promotional side has to be seen as longer-term policies while the protective side involves immediate 'cases', the Council often seems to be reacting to what it considers to be erosions of existing standards rather than working in detail to raise standards. If the AA's list of relevant topics is long, the Council's is formidable. Even half a dozen editions of its monthly newsletter, *Civil Liberty*, provide examples of an almost motley collection of topics: identification of police from numbers or names on uniforms; the behaviour of a certain judge; the right to picket during industrial disputes; allegations against the London police; rights of gypsies; drugs and police powers; conditions and events in Durham Prison; and the rights of foreigners in legal political demonstrations. Some of these matters are possibly isolated cases but, as the newsletter often says, they may show a certain state of affairs which requires study and possible reform.

We choose to describe the parliamentary links of NCCL because, although it is as modestly financed as many other groups interested in public affairs, it stands out from most of them in the great range of interests and their very high political content, which makes contact with MPs not merely desirable but essential. An organisation for protecting and advancing 'civil liberty' is dealing in an abstraction whose practical aspects are very varied. Our civil liberties may be held by some people to be threatened on many occasions which others may dismiss as being no threats at all. Is it a denial of one man's 'civil liberty' to sell his house as he chooses, for Parliament to pass a law which is designed to promote another man's 'civil liberty' to buy any house he can afford? People disagree about this while according the same high status in their statements to 'liberty'. The NCCL has enough of a particular tradition and ideology on these questions to attract the supporter of anti-discrimination laws in housing and repel his opponent who believes such laws are wrong.

There are, of course, other groups and societies concerned to protect and promote rather abstract social values. Where NCCL differs from these is in the highly political nature of its interests as civil liberties are, in the last resort, to be protected only by the public authorities of police, courts, Government and Parliament. The Council is, of course, concerned at any threats to liberties coming from private organisations and may actively negotiate or remonstrate with such bodies.[1] Any progress which the Council makes in these matters comes from either negotiations or legislation. Thus, if unofficial persuasion fails, the political path to Ministers and Members of Parliament must be followed.

The NCCL is particularly distinguished by the very broad range of its field: so many matters may have a civil liberties element. Indeed, it would not be surprising if the Council sometimes wished it could hive off some of its running interests to new single-interest bodies, such as a 'Police and Community Society', which would examine relations between the two

[1] In 1968 NCCL gave increasing attention to alleged threats to people's liberties and privacy from the activities of detective and other enquiry agencies which attempt to compile dossiers on individuals.

groups, work towards an acceptable complaints procedure, promote public knowledge of police problems and assert the civil rights of policemen accused of irregularities and offences as vigorously as those of citizens who want to complain about police conduct. Another offshoot could well be the 'Lawful Assembly Society', to assert and study the rights of peaceful demonstration and picketing, often against the claims of the authorities to maintain the 'free flow of traffic' against obstruction. There have been real, rather than such fanciful examples of this process in NCCL's history. A very widely involved organisation can serve as an umbrella body covering a topic until a single-issue body begins work to achieve particular progress upon it. Thus NCCL was interested in the legal discrimination against male homosexuals and then saw the Homosexual Law Reform Society take up the cause and work for the required legislation; the recent increase in public interest in the problems caused and faced by gypsies and other travellers (which also included the formation of a specialised interest group) followed several years of concern on the matter from NCCL as part of its long agenda for study and action.

A group which combines this multi-interest character with the sharply political quality of civil liberty issues faces difficulties in presenting either a general public image or a series of clear messages to the public. In the parliamentary context, the NCCL faces a particular challenge since MPs are busy, preoccupied and subject to a wide variety of competing messages which all try to claim their support and sympathy. Everyone would claim to know what 'civil liberties' means but no one sees them as the primary issue—they are the assumed, barely-perceived background for all of the other issues and activities which occupy those most involved with the political process. A body in NCCL's position tends to be most often heard complaining about liberties being threatened or reduced; because the number of potential examples of this is almost as wide as the activities of the political system itself, it is easy for only partially attentive, and possibly not very sympathetic, observers to get the impression that such a body is merely a busybody, sniping at the authorities as the day's events allow, in the name of lofty general principles.

The ideal solution for this problem of presenting the NCCL's many concerns to MPs is the selective approach and personal contact which we have already seen demanded by some MPs themselves. To divide up the organisation's broad interests and present each segment in some depth to those MPs (and other interested people) who share this interest would be the perfect approach. But lack of funds prevents this and a gallon of concerns must, instead, be conveyed to Members in a pint jar.

The general secretary of NCCL, Tony Smythe, was until recently the Council's only official above clerical level, but his duties in the membership and fund raising field are now undertaken by a colleague. Mr Smythe is in charge of the routine functions of its small office and is also on constant call for urgent, or even emergency, cases requiring the immediate help of a friendly lawyer, a conversation with a senior police or immigration officer or the intervention of a sympathetic MP. When all this is done there is the longer-term task of studying policies and building up the crucial political support in Parliament without which neither current issues nor emergency cases could be effectively treated: it is no reflection on the attachment to libertarian principles of the police, the armed services, local government or the immigration authorities to say that their knowledge of NCCL's ability to have Ministers called on by MPs to answer in the House is a factor in the status and attention they are prepared to accord the Council.

A formal link with the House was established in 1963. As is usual with these all-party groups, the formal organisation of these few Members' common interest is not obtrusive. Like other, similar, 'good cause' groups of Members (such as the limbless ex-servicemen's welfare group or the animal welfare group), the Members particularly interested in civil liberties tend to assist the organised body in that field individually on particular cases and problems, and combine with each other only occasionally on some larger policy problem. The officers of the Civil Liberties Group at the time of our survey were Eric Lubbock (Liberal Member for Orpington) chairman, Dame Joan Vickers (Conservative Member for Plymouth, Devonport) vice-chairman, and Joyce Butler (Labour Member for Wood Green) secretary-treasurer.

The Group as such performs some functions although an outside observer cannot easily determine who are the main actors within it and whether most of its actions would not be undertaken anyway by a few keen Members if the Group as such did not exist or could not agree on how to proceed. Deputations to Ministers and public statements are its main tasks: thus in March 1967 the Group met and decided to brief peers to oppose the Government's proposal for majority jury verdicts and, at a second meeting, looked again at the long-term contracts of teenage servicemen and their legal rights to purchase their discharge, with a view to meeting a Minister on the subject.

The limitations of the parliamentary Group appeared later in 1967 when two Conservatives introduced private Members' motions on 'individual liberties' which permitted wide debates on NCCL's interests. The first of these, in July, brought from the Council's newsletter *Civil Liberty*[1] the comment that although three Members had asked for and obtained NCCL briefs for use in the debates if they were called to speak, this did not constitute the 'planned interventions by members of the Parliamentary Civil Liberties Group' which ought to occur. At the end of the year, after the second debate in this field, the newsletter's comment was sharper:

'Civil liberty could have been the focus of the debate. Unfortunately, the party political stance . . . was repeated throughout. Only one MP, Dame Joan Vickers, contacted the NCCL beforehand and as a result was able to make valuable points covering discrimination against women, the erosion of trade union rights, police identification, Grosvenor Square demonstrations, increases in police powers under the Dangerous Drugs Act and majority verdicts. Most other contributions consisted of pious generalities . . . we need debates on civil liberties which would seriously challenge policies, procedures and institutions which are eroding human rights in Britain. It is the task of the Parliamentary Civil Liberties group to ensure that these take place.'[2]

Two observations can be made on this rebuke: firstly to note the variety of 'NCCL topics' in Dame Joan's single speech; secondly to remark NCCL's difficulty in appearing clearly to be an expert body with technical information to offer to MPs. William Plowden also made this point regarding all 'roads' bodies as a whole and the mass motoring organisations

[1] *Civil Liberty*, July-August 1967.   [2] *Civil Liberty*, December 1967.

in particular: when almost everyone in the country is involved in a field it is more difficult to appear authoritative. Although NCCL would not say that an approach to them for briefing is a necessary condition of a good civil liberties speech in the House, there are some fields, notably drugs, which are very technical and which, as yet, have no specialised interest groups to cover them closely from a socio-legal standpoint.

Apart from hoping to brief a reasonable co-ordinated team of MPs when a full debate is in progress, the NCCL tries to reach MPs on more particular matters. Beyond the Civil Liberties Group (whose main purpose, we have noted, is for clearly identifying deputations and statements on issues promoted by the main 'civil liberties' Members) is a panel of 'interested' Members who receive free copies of *Civil Liberty* each month and all Press and public statements by NCCL on current cases and issues (such as, in 1967, teenage servicemen, majority verdicts and drugs). Not many of these 'interested' MPs are paid-up individual members of NCCL. Mr Smythe says that these one hundred or more Members have offered evidence in the past of their sympathy for the civil liberties cause and may be assumed to read what they are sent: thus a sixth of the House is in regular genuine contact with NCCL work. Although recognising the need for selectivity in dispatches to MPs, NCCL (like many groups) see value in occasional full coverages of all 630 Members. Members' interests change and develop and new recruits to the panel or Group may be obtained. There is also thought to be some value in 'keeping the name before Members' even though, in the case of these full mailings, the 'name' is often framed for a fleeting moment in the mouth of a parliamentary waste paper basket. *Civil Liberty* may suffer that fate less frequently because it is concisely written on only one sheet of paper and generally conforms to the standards of good presentation as described by so many of our survey respondents.

On the central issues a smaller number of Members will be circulated with rather heavier material: two dozen Members received an elaborate brief attacking the 'police search' and other clauses of the Dangerous Drugs Bill to which the Council was strongly opposed. On this issue a meeting was planned at the House, postponed several times and then dropped—an example of the great difficulty of assembling Members to consider a technical subject in any depth although this one did not lack immediate political relevance.

Part of the difficulty seems to be that although there are many social groups or topics interesting NCCL which have no other champion (teenage servicemen, demonstrators' rights or the civil rights of scientology adherents) the Council's ambit is so wide that a Member may not obviously feel he must approach them. No Member wishing to introduce a private Member's bill on the reform of divorce, birth control, abortion or animal welfare would be likely to proceed without consulting the reformist groups in those fields unless he already knew their views and was deliberately concerned to propose some different line. It is likely, however, that Alexander Lyon (Labour Member for York) developed his 1967 'Ten Minute rule' bill to promote privacy and defence against intrusion without involving NCCL because he did not automatically see them as the body with specialist experience and opinions to offer in this field. He told us that he saw this initial exercise on the problem of privacy as a stimulant to public discussion and was studying NCCL's published report on the subject as part of that discussion.

If his Council's funds permitted, Mr Smythe 'would love to be down at both Houses one day a week, getting to know Members and peers and learning their various special interests in civil liberties'. This would not be a mere PR exercise on a par with similarly good personal contacts with the Press or other interested parties in the discussion of civil liberties and social problems, but something much more crucial. It is, in essence, the nature of British Constitution which makes the parliamentary links of an almost totally political organised interest group, as we have already said, not merely desirable, but essential. There is no written Constitution, incorporating a Bill of Rights and no constitutional interpreter, such as the state and federal supreme courts in the USA, to whom an interest group can turn for an authoritative legal judgement on a civil liberty issue which may well override and reverse the Government's policy and desires. Where 'responsible Ministers' may decide so much, subject only to the political checks of Parliament and the electorate, the flow of 'information' to Parliament from a group such as NCCL is as important for Parliament as it is for the successful operation of the group itself.

5. TWO ASPECTS OF INFORMATION ON INTERNATIONAL AFFAIRS

(i) *Two expert institutes: the Royal Institute of International Affairs and the Institute for Strategic Studies*

The following of international affairs is a minority interest in the House of Commons. Labour's focus as a party has always been on domestic issues of social welfare and economic control, while the personal knowledge and interest among Conservatives of overseas conditions obtained during service abroad in the armed forces, diplomatic or colonial services or in private business has dwindled in recent years. A few Conservatives have entered the House fairly recently after periods of Government service abroad or in the responsible Whitehall Department (e.g. Peter Blaker, Member for Blackpool South, who was in the Foreign Office, or Sir George Sinclair, Member for Dorking, who had a career in the Colonial Service) whereas the only Labour Members with such experience are Evan Luard (Oxford) who was a Foreign Office official until resigning over the attack on Egypt in 1956, and Donald Anderson (Monmouth), who served at a later date in the same Department.

In post-war politics, international affairs have been closely tied to another parliamentary minority subject: defence. We briefly examine two impartial British bodies which exist to extend knowledge and analysis of international and defence affairs: the Royal Institute of International Affairs (RIIA) (often called 'Chatham House' after its premises in St James's Square) and the much younger Institute for Strategic Studies (ISS). We asked these bodies what work they do from which MPs could benefit and what their parliamentary following amounts to. We already knew from our interviews that the group of MPs who do claim these interests are well aware of these bodies and had either joined them as members, attended some of their activities or were meaning to do so. Both bodies were very favourably mentioned to us in the context of getting good information on international and defence affairs. Their main offering to MPs and other members and guests who are London-based, is their meetings. Expert speakers describe and discuss topics in the two Institute's cognate fields. There are also specialised libraries and (especially at the RIIA) some resident staff experts, apart from the two Directors themselves, to whom an interested MP could have a reasonable amount of personal access, especially if, for example, he was about to make an overseas visit. The two bodies produce both regular and occasional publications which the interested Member would probably file. Both bodies are expert rather than popular, especially the ISS. The RIIA's rules now require that proposed new members be likely to benefit the Institute by bringing some knowledge of international affairs to its common stock. MPS are treated a little differently from this and would always be welcome into membership although their interest in international affairs may be so new that, for a number of years at least, they would absorb specialised knowledge rather than have much to offer. This attitude is typical of any organised group's view of interested MPs: Members have political status, access to major political leaders and they may at a later time become very valuable international affairs specialists in their party—they may also be useful to the Institute itself as an organisation.

1968 membership of Chatham House among MPs compared with 1958 levels was as follows:

1958		1968	
Conservative	53	Conservative	21
Labour	33	Labour	19
Liberal	1	Liberal	1
	—		—
	87		41

In mid-1958 the House had an overall Conservative majority of 55, whereas in mid-1968 Labour had an overall majority of 70. Both parties have therefore fallen away in membership of the RIIA, the Conservatives more than proportional to their losses of MPs and Labour in direct contrast to their considerably expanded ranks during these years. It is possible that the Conservative decline is mainly due to Members leaving both the House and the Institute following retirement or electoral defeat. The Labour record emphasises sharply the even greater concentration on home affairs on those benches.

Figures of the MP membership since 1959 of the Institute for Strategic Studies also indicate modest parliamentary interest in military and strategic affairs, but with some interesting features. For example, Labour's parliamentary ranks were depleted in

1959 but the number of their Members belonging to the ISS rose. It continued to rise by a small amount to reach its maximum of fifteen members on the eve of the PLP's considerable expansion in October 1964 (to be followed by further growth in 1966). But neither of these elections led to a rise in Labour's ISS membership. The proportion of Labour MPs in the Institute in 1967 was thus notably smaller than during the Opposition years of 1959–64. Being in Opposition from October 1964 may be connected with the Conservatives' greater support for ISS during 1964–5: three of the four extra Conservatives who joined during 1964 did so during the last quarter of the year and six Members joined during 1965. The Conservatives in ISS in early 1968 included three shadow Ministers one of whom, James Ramsden, was an ex-Secretary for War and another the then shadow Secretary of State for Defence, Enoch Powell. Backing this enhanced individual Conservative interests in what ISS could offer in information and analysis was the corporate membership of the Conservative Research Department. Six of the twelve Labour MPs in ISS in early 1968 were Ministers, including two Defence Ministers, Denis Healey and Gerry Reynolds, while three more had official Defence positions[1] and a fourth, Christopher Mayhew had resigned from the Government as Navy Minister over a policy dispute. This left only two Members who were simply interested backbenchers: Sir Eric Fletcher and Reginald Paget.

Of course, neither Chatham House nor ISS restrict their information and activity to paid-up members and this liberal approach would be even more definite in the case of interested MPs. Other MPs no doubt attend some meetings and would certainly occasionally see their printed material. The very limited attachment among MPs to these two expert bodies may well be an indicator of parliamentary insularity within the political information network. Alastair Buchan, Director of ISS, told us:

'as to our general relations with MPs, we welcome their membership. But I cannot say we see a great deal of them for the simple reason, which I am sure you come across in other aspects of your study, that they have a time-table which really cuts them off

[1] Raymond Fletcher, a parliamentary private secretary (i.e. semi-official unpaid personal aide) to Defence Ministers; Sir Geoffrey de Freitas and Philip Noel-Baker, chairmen, respectively, of the PLP's defence and foreign affairs party groups.

from civilised life. Some of our meetings are at lunchtime, when we do see MPs but most of them have to be at 5.30 p.m. or later in the evening when Members are rarely available.'

This problem of timetabling outside meetings to attract MPs into a mixed and fairly expert audience (combined with a basic and well-known unwillingness of Members to venture very far from the House) is compounded by any improvements in their parliamentary facilities there, however desirable they may be in themselves. Thus, Kenneth Younger, Director of RIIA,[1] believes the halving of MP membership of the Institute over ten years is partly due to the gradual improvement of the House of Commons Library's services on the international affairs side. He also notes that prominent overseas visitors to London nearly always speak to special meetings of interested Members at the House, and also appear on television, making expeditions by MPs to other parts of Central London, including St James's Square, unnecessary. Mr Younger was Labour Member for Grimsby, and a Minister at the Home and Foreign Offices in the Attlee Governments, followed by a period as a shadow Minister. He is, therefore, very well placed to appreciate the difficulties for MPs wanting to become well-informed on international affairs: the field is vast and the detailed background which it is possible to absorb on any one of well over one hundred states and dozens of international organisations is inexhaustible.

Like virtually every current MP interested in this field to whom we spoke in our interviews, he has a critical view of Parliament's current methods of deliberating on international affairs in the chamber: their unsatisfactory nature combines with the inherent difficulty of the field to limit very severely the number of Members with more than a superficial interest. The political centre of gravity for MPs is firmly fixed in domestic affairs. Knowledge and understanding of international problems is therefore a more difficult communication problem for bodies in these fields. RIIA and ISS certainly have no problem of authority, image or political status, such as the National Council for Civil Liberties must solve; but they do face the

---

[1] We gratefully acknowledge the figures of MP membership supplied by Messrs Buchan and Younger. The ISS's membership lists are published, thus permitting outsiders' analyses.

problem of serving a special group such as MPs while pursuing the highest possible standards of informed technical enquiry within each of their fields. They cannot simply become, even in part, 'educational' bodies which can do very broad introductory work for either a small group, such as interested MPs, or for the general public. They are not designed for this purpose and thus they manage to relate directly to very few MPs despite their very welcoming attitude to interested Members. Something more suitable in its design is required.

The need is for international information and analysis which is tailor-made on the several different levels of potential MP interest: general, broad interests; particular interests (perhaps in a particular country or region); and sophisticated and technical work including strategy and development studies of the kind conducted at institutes such as ISS and Chatham House. The obvious base for such a service (which need not confine the fruits of its labour to MPs) is the House of Commons Library.

(ii) *Printed diplomatic sources*
If all the printed and duplicated material received by MPs is placed in broad classes according to its source, such as trade associations, 'good causes' or other voluntary interest groups, private firms, diplomatic sources, etc., the diplomatic material is clearly the largest. Its volume derives from the regularity and frequency of the main items which are often sent weekly. The overall size of this class of material is not a reflection of the greatly increased number of states in the world: most which have friendly relations with Britain (and which therefore have some kind of representation in London) send nothing, or, at least, nothing regular. Some other governments, which Britain does not recognise, such as East Germany and North Vietnam, do send material. A few states make up most of the total, some of the main contributors being USA, USSR, South Africa, the regime in Rhodesia, Kuwait, Zambia and Spain.

Our featured comments, 'MPs talk about printed circulars and brochures' (see section 2 of this chapter) contain several uncomplimentary references to diplomatic material, sometimes mentioning a particular foreign government to which the Member is especially hostile, but sometimes criticising all of it: 'I rate the diplomatic flow of stuff very low, although foreign affairs is an interest of mine' (Conservative). The longer list from which these comments were drawn had about ten examples in all of Members' comments showing particular indifference or hostility towards these offerings by other governments. In addition, a few Members who told us they look personally through all items received (however routine and uninteresting and even though they may have a secretary) cited glancing at 'even the diplomatic stuff' as examples of their method.

It is only fair to this diplomatic material to recall that most MPs are not, in any case, interested in much beyond the broadest sweep in international affairs so its authors have a hard row to hoe compared with, for example, an organisation which can tell Members, all of whom have statutory tenants among their electors, something new about these people's problems or situation. But when several of the minority of MPs who are interested in international affairs also criticised this diplomatic stuff, we formed the impression that it may not be very good. Two Middle East specialists among our respondents thought little of the Arab countries' offerings: one looks rather more closely at Kuwait's material when it is 'glossy' only because he feels it more wasteful to throw 'glossies' away unseen. Two Members with special interest in East European trade criticised those states' political and cultural PR material: one said, 'It needs patience, because it is so dogmatic'—but it is unlikely to receive much patience from his fellow Members who do not share his personal interest and connections. But some replies to our inquiry about Members' general opinion of the total amount of circulars and brochures received, mentioned diplomatic material in a more friendly tone. A Member, who had said he welcomed circulars generally and strongly supported anybody's right to send things to MPs, instanced the House's debate on the June war of 1967: 'Topicality is important—I've had hand-outs for today's debate on the Middle East from the UAR, Israel and the UN; very useful if one hopes to speak.' This Member is not a Middle East specialist and would presumably not pay much attention to routine material from these states when there is no actual fighting or other grave crisis in evidence. As a fellow-Conservative said, he will throw Kuwait's weekly newsletter away unread for years and then look at it in June of 1967 to learn its official line on the war with Israel.

Just as some Members throw some governments' offerings away in a specially hostile manner, so others like to be in touch with certain overseas matters—a Labour Member, hostile to American policy in Vietnam, finds their material, along with that from Hanoi, very valuable; a colleague of his was reading Zambia's material in 1967 because he had been an official guest there some time before and now saw the country as a new interest. But these particular aversions and attractions to certain overseas governments are details compared with general re-action to diplomatic material as a whole. We observed during our analysis of Members' postbags an even higher rate of dis-carding things unread, and often unopened, than material coming from domestic British sources. It was also plain from this enquiry how little diplomatic material with which the Member does not expect to sympathise is ever read. Again, we see that Members' search for 'information' is practical rather than general: the search for background to existing views and sometimes, quite simply, for ammunition. The Member who had gone on an official visit to Zambia now read that country's news and comment as a sympathiser because he felt a link with them. But another Member may have no such special interest in the country and may therefore simply say critically, as one did to us, 'I'm not against getting, for example, Zambia's PR but I want it to be good PR—for their sake as well as mine'.

Having observed the generally cool reception which diplo-matic material is accorded by Members and seen the quantity and occasional luxury of this flow for ourselves, we naturally wanted to know why it is sent and what result its authors think is achieved. As several Members had complimented the French Government's supply of information on its country's affairs and as Kuwait had also been mentioned as a major source of this material, we discussed the topic with those two embassies.

Like most of the diplomatic missions in London, Kuwait's puts the emphasis of its political links with politicians on the all-party group of MPs and peers which exists to foster good relations between the two countries and which is affiliated to the UK branch of the Inter-Parliamentary Union (IPU). The Anglo-Kuwait Group, whose chairman at the time of our enquiry was Dennis Walters (Conservative Member for Westbury) is not, of course, promoted by the embassy which can only help and encourage an initiative from within Parliament. The most interested members of the Group, whether MPs or peers, then form the embassy's further personal links with a wider circle of their colleagues. As in the case of the all-party groups on civil liberties or animal welfare, the Group as such is secondary to the idea to having some sympathetic Members (preferably of all parties) who can help with wider good relations (by suggesting Members to invite to embassy receptions or to be invited on an official visit to the country concerned during normal times and by lobbying or organising on behalf of the country if difficulties in its relations with Britain arise. The list of these IPU groups is long and involves many Members as their honorary officers and regular sympathetic supporters. Like the party groups maintained by the 1922 Committee and the PLP (which we discuss briefly in Chapter V) these all-party IPU groups have a political role which is at least as important as their purpose of channelling information. When events in the country concerned, such as a *coup d'etat*, produce passionate but differing reactions in Britain, the battles within these groups can be spectacular (as they have been in the Anglo-Greek Group since the 'colonels' coup'). Usually, however, the IPU groups form a very quiet parliamentary field.

Kuwait's regular offering to Members is the *Kuwait Bulletin*— a weekly duplicated newsheet of four to six pages when we surveyed Members, but due to be printed by letterpress in the near future. It goes to about 90 per cent of MPs—all those who have not written in hostile terms saying they do not want it.[1] As no Member has written in non-political terms saying he would prefer not to receive it, and as a Member will occasionally write to ask why the supply has stopped (due to a change of address or similar oversight) the embassy concludes that all 90 per cent want it and assume they must either read or file it for future reference. *Kuwait Bulletin* goes also to about one hundred peers (some of them ex-Members, of course) and to the libraries of institutes and universities. It consists of short, detailed items about Kuwait which the British Press would not cover: ministerial appointments, visits and ceremonies by Kuwaiti dignitaries (particularly, of course, any visits to Britain) and official statistics. It is difficult to feel that even the MP whose entire political activity centres on Arab affairs (and there are not more than two or three in the House) could gain much from such a mixture of unrelated facts and ephemeral pieces of news.

[1] These Members are partisans of Israel's position.

The bulletin is seen by the embassy as background for the interested person who reads it in conjunction with a good newspaper.

The embassy holds to the accepted PR view that 'regular contacts' during normal situations is the true foundation of any influence which may be enjoyed in a special or crisis situation. It is felt that the recipient will not accord much attention to a source he does not already know and trust on a regular basis. Thus diplomatic items sent to MPs such as *Kuwait Bulletin* are felt to have a value as a service, a link, even if they are normally unread: when events bring the Member's attention to the *Bulletin* (as on the June war and Kuwait's position in it) he knows what he is reading and whether it is normally a responsible source.

The difficulty with this argument is the meaning of the term 'regular contact'. If, in fact, the item's regular physical contact is with only the Member's wastepaper basket, perhaps being identified by him or his secretary from its wrapper, the only possible political contact is the Member's knowledge that the item exists and arrives regularly and that it is a potential source for him if he wants it. This is a logical enough position for the sender to adopt, although a subtraction should be made from any positive general image this routine 'service' may help to establish for the negative effects of annoying some Members by helping to overload their postbags. It is possible that a normally uninterested Member who normally throws *Kuwait Bulletin* away (or has his secretary do so) may fail to recognise that a specially important message on Kuwait's attitude to the war with Israel is contained in one particular week's normal-looking edition. He may be generally less hostile and his attention more easily arrested if, instead of fifty bulletins each year, he received two or three special messages.

'Regular contact' is, however, the conventional wisdom of the PR business and may, on balance, be the correct tactic. Outside politics, of course, it often takes the form of fairly obvious presents such as desk diaries or calendars which probably come much closer to meeting the basic aim of keeping the sender's name before the recipient. We suspect that an annual item such as a fairly good diary or calendar would do more to prepare an MP for occasional important political messages from a foreign government than do fifty issues of a highly dispensable and often unread newsletter. The danger of this novel course for the first government to try it would be the fear of being thought flippant. We recorded some complaints amongst Members against the waste involved in sending 'glossies' to Members who do not keep them and one or two suggestions that poor countries, in particular, should not 'waste' money on expensive items to send to British MPs or anyone else. Recalling the Conservative who let his wife look at, and then discard, expensive glossy books and brochures, a good tactical approach may be for governments to send Members diplomatic gifts of ladies' desk diaries.

Kuwait Bulletin is supplemented by occasional publications some of which, according to one of our interviewed Members with Middle East interests, are expensively produced. This material is not designed exclusively for British MPs, of course, but goes, in Britain, to the Press and other interests. Visits to Kuwait are arranged, but mainly for journalists rather than politicians. The Kuwaiti Government runs an exchange scheme for Kuwaiti and British journalists to pay visits: a British journalist, it is believed, is a more effective medium for disseminating his impressions of Kuwait than a backbench MP who is not also a journalist.

The Anglo-Kuwait Group in the House (which had about thirty-six members in 1967–8) has co-operated with the embassy to arrange visits by several Members interested in the Middle East and Arab affairs such as Ian Gilmour, Daniel Awdry, Eldon Griffiths, Mr Walters (Conservatives) and Colin Jackson (Labour). These visits are permitted by the whips only if parliamentary business allows (even, sometimes, when opposed Members are fully paired for voting purposes) and it is quite typical that two Members' trips to Kuwait were cancelled during 1967–8 for this reason. These trips, like all exercises in parliamentary public relations are, of course, partly for information-gathering and partly 'influencing'. We should also note that, at his level and adopting much more personal and private techniques, the head of mission in London of any overseas government is also seeking contacts and influence in order to promote his diplomatic interests: the publicly distributed material and the official visits for journalists and MPs are only the visible part of any government's total diplomatic effort in Britain.

The French Embassy's efforts in this same field of public information and PR 'service' for British people offer several contrasts with Kuwait's, mainly due to the much greater cultural contact between the two countries (such as teaching in many kinds of schools and colleges of French language, literature, history, art and the political system). Cultural links are maintained by the Cultural Counsellor and the four official French Institutes in Britain. The Press Counsellor deals with parliamentary contacts alongside Press-work (as at the Kuwaiti Embassy) but on a larger scale. Naturally, at both embassies Press contact is more professional and workaday than the broader public relations work, including that for MPs.

Two series of publications are produced by the French: a monthly information bulletin and a specialised monthly pamphlet. The bulletin has about eighteen sides of typed foolscap on public affairs in France with a broadly classified contents list on its face, dividing items into political, economic, and social or cultural. There is a lighter touch of 'personality' fare and a brief diary of public events during the preceding month. The listing of the monthly specialised pamphlets is divided into the more generally interesting ones ('A') and the more specialised or technical titles ('B') and distributed accordingly. An example of a 'A' title is 'French Planning'—a fourteen-page typescript with maps and diagrams. Other such fairly recent titles are on French nationalised industries, cinema, education and newspapers. The more narrow 'B' titles include French civil service training, hospitals, chemicals and atmospheric research. The Press and Information Department in London has some independence to produce pamphlets on whichever topics they think are opportune in Britain and other English-speaking countries (for whom they also prepare material). There is, of course, an inverse relationship between their ability to analyse and discuss topics openly in these pamphlets and those topics' political difficulty. On their government's attitude to NATO and to Vietnam the department would either obtain the fullest clearance from Paris before issuing a pamphlet or confine themselves to reprinting French ministerial statements. It was to these monthly pamphlets on particular topics that Members referred when speaking of the quality of the French output.

Their total clientele for this material is broad and well-organised for the selectivity which our interviewed Members stressed so often. When seen from the Press and Information Department, MPs fall into perspective along with other groups of opinion leaders including peers, the party headquarters, professional organisations, over one hundred trade union officials, nearly six hundred unsuccessful candidates at the most recent general election (who responded positively to an enquiry about continuing to receive the monthly items after the election) and a varied group of nationally eminent 'personalities', a few of whom are also MPs.

The distribution to Parliament is based on the large Anglo-French Parliamentary group of MPs and peers which numbers between 150 and 200 (about half of them being Members) whose names are submitted annually to the embassy by the Group's officers. To these names are added about fifty Members who are known followers of French affairs who have not joined the Group (which tends to speak French at some of its meetings and may well thus deter potential members). The onus is on the Member to display his interest by joining the Group or by a speech or Press article, as even such a large embassy lacks the resources to meet each new MP personally on the off-chance that he is interested, or could become interested, in France.

All these groups receive the monthly bulletin and the more generally interesting ('A' list) monthly pamphlets. The 'B' list titles go out according to their field to some of the fifty sub-groups into which the Press and Information Department's mailing list is divided. It is therefore possible to distinguish between sending a specialised item to university French departments or political science departments; or between professional groups and all university contacts. Although the French probably judge it correctly, this sophisticated selectivity can become counter-productive, whether between sub-groups of people outside Parliament or between the 'possibly' interested and the 'rarely' interested MP. As Cdr. Powell is quoted as saying in William Plowden's section of this chapter, to be too refined can cost more than the extra costs of a wider distribution and one runs the risk of offending someone whom one excluded on inadequate evidence. For the French Embassy, however, a further consideration applies: they often distribute limited quantities (perhaps only twenty copies) of a very specialised document, in which case the fifty sub-groups of the total list of nearly six thousand names are very useful.

The French also believe in 'regular contacts' as the basis for any major effort at persuasion and influence which they may need to mount at any time but they modify their coverage compared with many diplomatic missions (of which Kuwait's is one example), firstly by sending any material at all to only a minority of Members and, secondly, by adjusting the dispatch of 'B' list titles to minimise the chance of anyone receiving a specialised item which they do not want. The Press and Information Department does not prepare any documents specifically for MPs nor can they offer any personal service. But people they know or may be introduced to (including MPs) may use their files of French and English material about many aspects of French affairs to make their own notes for speeches and writing.

While examining these matters we were, of course, very interested to gather why overseas governments want to try and influence British MPs by these methods. It is, of course, very difficult to gather from courteous diplomats whether they and their governments really see backbenchers as a highly significant group of opinion-makers or merely as a conventional element among Britain's public notables. Kuwait gives priority to having British journalists rather than parliamentarians go on official visits and the detailed routine of Press relations naturally looms larger than parliamentary PR for the French Press and Information Department. As the mass media develop, it may be that the idea of parliamentarians having some special influence to exercise which is based on their highly significant (albeit inevitably limited) circles of acquaintance will be seen as redundant. If a given country wants some limited concession or agreement from Britain which, she believes, would be more easily granted if British 'public opinion' is 'favourable', whom should she invite on a free trip—six journalists (or one TV crew) or six Members drawn from the three parties? Mr Walters of the Anglo-Kuwait Group believes that the MPs could offer a good platform for the country's case (assuming it to be a strong one which easily convinces the MPs) so long as the invited Members are genuinely interested and know the background. If such Members come back convinced, they will carry weight in the House and with Ministers. What would not help much in Mr Walters's view would be to invite on an official visit 'a random selection of Members in a rather vague PR exercise where a particular country has an axe to grind on an issue and quickly arranges for rushed visits'.[1]

Adapting Mr Walters's phrases to the regular routine of diplomatic material sent to Members, one could say that many governments do send such material at random in a decidedly vague public relations exercise, not because they have an axe urgently needing grinding but in case they may have sometime in the future. The essence of their difficulty is to find something to say about their countries to 630 MPs (who are principally interested in British domestic affairs) which will not bore them so much that they never look at the material, but which will also convey a calm, responsible image against the day when they will want to raise their voice and really carry an important message to the British Member of Parliament. This is close to an impossible task but the French (albeit with their major cultural advantages over more distant countries) seem to have a very sound approach.

6. THE HOUSE IN THE 'NETWORK'; CLUBS—AND THE HOUSE AS A 'CLUB'

We have looked briefly and individually at several sides of the national information network as it would be laid out in a two-dimensional diagram: Members' use of books, journals and television which cover politics, the steady flow of letters and printed items calling attention to many issues; the work of all-party groups in the House linked to outside organised interests (Roads Study Group, Civil Liberties Group, Anglo-Kuwait and Anglo-French Groups) and Members' links with specialist bodies such as Chatham House and the Institute for Strategic Studies. In later chapters we shall extend this sketch of the network by adding the different types of information which come to Members from the Government, from their party headquarters, their sponsoring trade unions and the parliamentary parties' various party groups on particular subjects.

What the observer must do, however, in order to appreciate the actual information situation of the MP is to overlay these various aspects of the network on top of each other rather than set them out in two dimensions. The third dimension of depth is

---

[1] Letter to the authors.

all important: elements or sources in the network often overlap with each other allowing, as we said in the opening section of this chapter, the same messages to come by several routes, although not necessarily with the same emphasis or slant. If there is a pattern to the network it is a very informal one, composed of chance and calculation among those seeking to inform and influence the political office-holders, combined with the design of the Member's own personal links and communications.

Members often mention outside contacts and experts to each other, and may make an introduction to a colleague who faces a particular 'information challenge' (such as results, for instance, from success in the ballots for private Members' motions or bills). A Member may know that a certain outside expert occupies more than one position in the information network and may judge his opinion and analysis in that light. Thus a Conservative Member will note that Professor A is a consultant to the Ministry and a member of official committees, but also writes Fabian pamphlets. A Labour Member notes that Dr B, who is a prominent writer on aviation, also has links with an aircraft company and thus may not see the industry's problems quite as the Member sees them.

Among Members themselves the process of giving and receiving advice and news is traditional. The maintenance of lines of communication with other Members who are normally to be seen as political enemies but who sometimes (perhaps on a single issue) are allies, is a standard device even within a legislature as clearly divided according to party as is the House of Commons. Today's enemy could be tomorrow's friend, especially on one of the non-party humanitarian issues such as the law concerning hanging or male homosexual conduct. For Members to treat each other as sources of information and guidance is natural. For outside organised interests to come to enjoy this position with Members is a goal of parliamentary public relations. It is the same in Washington where the lobbyist's object is to be accepted by Congressmen as a 'service' whose interests and usefulness go beyond the formal limits of the organisation for whom he lobbies. By offering valuable information and advice on the broader field, the lobbyist hopes that his views on his client's real interests will be equally acceptable to the legislators.

Mr Smythe of the National Council for Civil Liberties told us that his object in attending at Parliament regularly (as he would like to do, given greater resources in the Council's office) would be similar to this. He would identify the aspect of civil liberties which interest each Member or peer whom he met and give help and information on that issue: one aspect would lead to another until the Member's civil liberties interests and knowledge were wider and stronger. A particular example of 'multiple contact' is provided by Lt. Cdr. Powell. He is responsible for the parliamentary relations of the British Road Federation (whom he has advised since the War) and also for those of the Society of Motor Manufacturers and Traders. In a personal capacity, he has been Secretary, since its establishment in 1940, of the unofficial all-party Parliamentary and Scientific Committee which brings together MPs, peers and scientists. This personal service to Parliament in a field of great importance and over a long period of time has given Cdr. Powell two parliamentary hats. Those Members who see him at the Parliamentary and Scientific Committee may also have contact with him when he acts for his clients on roads and motor industry matters. This would be a significant overlap even if these two fields were quite unrelated (as, for example, the County Councils Association and Arab affairs). In this case, however, they do relate when the Parliamentary and Scientific Committee holds meetings on roads and road transport questions.

The West End clubs are prominent examples of the overlaying or overlapping of information channels for their members. The informal verbal network of information which has traditionally characterised them is similar to the House's in its operation. We were interested to discover, informally (since there was insufficient time in our formal interviews to raise this matter), how much MPs seem nowadays to be involved in the clubs side of the overall political information network.

Obviously, if an institution brings together for relaxation and social intercourse opinion leaders and decision makers from several parts of the political system and the mass media, there is a considerable potential for the exchange of information of both the 'factual' and the 'opinion' types. If a Member of Parliament is mixing, often on a personal and confidential basis, with civil servants, service officers, sundry senior officials from nationalised industries and many other public bodies, editors and journalists, educational leaders, bishops, barristers and judges, and senior businessmen, he will hear things which Ministers either do not themselves know or which they would not vouchsafe at the dispatch box in the House. Some things which he hears may never enter the parliamentary wing of these oral or gossip networks at all, unless he carries them down to the House himself. Of course, by no means all this potential 'information on public affairs' will be of any particular value to the Member: much of it will be the fine details of intramural rows or talking points within a Government Department, a newspaper office, between two large companies, or even concerning the domestic affairs of the club itself. It does not follow from the existence of a rich and flourishing information system within and between each of the St James's clubs that the would-be well-informed person, including an active and interested MP, ought to join in with it: the things he would learn may be irrelevant to his political needs, trivial, or both.

The notion that the clubs are a potential source of information on national affairs rests on the twin assumptions that their members have some knowledge to impart and that they exchange it freely with fellow members and their guests. However true the first of these points may be, the clubs vary in their attitude to 'open talk' and also in their inherent suitability for it, given the size of their memberships and the design of their principal rooms. Thus, the Travellers Club (a largely Foreign Office club) maintains an atmosphere discouraging to casual conversations: there would be little scope for an MP to gather any political background on his own initiative in such an atmosphere. The Travellers is like the Reform, immediately next door in Pall Mall, in its heavy civil service emphasis, and MPs are rarely seen as members, or even as members' guests, in either club. The impersonality of the Reform is so marked that all but the longest-established members seldom speak to another member to whom they have not been introduced. Members can frequent the club for months and speak only to those whom they already know. If many MPs belonged (and only a few do— one of them, at the time of our enquiry, living there when he is in London for the parliamentary sessions) they would be largely confined to each others' company plus that to which they were gradually introduced over a period of time.

Labour Ministers who are members of the Reform tend not to entertain or do political business at the club, perhaps for fear of compromising the many senior officials there, some of whom may be connected with their ministerial or general Government concerns. Thus, although there is a great deal of arranged meeting between civil servants, businessmen and some university people in these clubs, the informal and spontaneous exchange of information and comment, which is above the level of the merest conversation and which is based on a fraternal trust relying on common membership of the club, is nowadays greatly reduced compared with what it is alleged, at least, to have been in earlier years.

As no questions about the club were put to our sample of Members we cannot be sure what non-ministerial MPs think about them. The younger academic Labour MPs are no more in evidence at the Reform than are their trade union-sponsored colleagues, which may be a sign of changing social and intellectual tastes or simply a lack of funds. One Labour interviewee showed us how his £3,250 salary represented about £2,250 after his share of a secretary, his postage and other expenses had been met but before tax was deducted. He had a London home and was thus more fortunate than a Member who must also pay for board and lodging in London while running a family and home in the provinces. The salary is, of course, without increments (and was announced in 1964 as being intended to stand for a considerable period). This Member therefore had a part-time job which increased his income but reduced his leisure time to a level at which all of it must be devoted to his family: a Pall Mall club would obviously have to offer enormous political fascination to attract either the subscription or the attendance of such a younger Member of Parliament.

In the nineteenth century, before the rise of the Labour Party, Conservative and Liberal MPs were almost universally members of more than one club, even leaving aside the Carlton which performed a particular Conservative Party function. The tradition of spontaneous exchange of information in these clubs, often across constitutional and party lines (such as civil servants, service officers, industrialists and rival politicians discussing together) was based on leisurely meal times and sustained by an assumption of confidentiality and mutual trust, even between overt political rivals.

121

The substitution of the Labour Party for the Liberals as the Conservative's rival weakened this assumption, both by bringing more ideology into professional politics and by physically separating the parties, as Labour people simply did not join the clubs. The rise of the mass media, first newspapers and then television, and the weakening of 'Reithian' assumptions about their 'duty' and function within the political system have further threatened the assumption of 'in-group' confidentiality which the 'club' approach to public affairs fostered. A third factor has been the great growth of both the official and the mass media worlds, covering a greater range of involved people.

If these are reasons why MPs do not often cross St James's Park to the Pall Mall clubs (except Conservatives who are bound for the rather different Carlton and White's Clubs), it remains to ask whether the House of Commons itself is a 'club' in its own right. Seventy years ago the House itself, was of course 'the best club in Europe' and Members were also prominent in other clubs. The rise of Labour has made the House as a whole more insular in this kind of activity. The Labour Movement has never developed a club or centre in London and the committee on the Aneurin Bevan memorial fund, originally concerned with providing one, changed its terms of reference to permit an alternative form of memorial. A few Labour MPs join the Reform, and the more 'cultural' clubs such as the Garrick, Savile, Arts or, rather differently, the Press Club have a few as well.

As the party and election systems are unlikely to produce a major party which is largely composed of social isolates, it is not surprising that the Labour MPs have made parts of the Palace of Westminster into their club. Some Labour Members, notably left-wing journalists such as Aneurin Bevan and Richard Crossman have, in the past, joined in with the largely Conservative *habitués* of the more conventional club atmosphere of the Smoking Room, which is restricted to Members and has its own bar. Members are forbidden by custom, in typical club style, to repeat what they hear in the Smoking Room. The Commons Tea Room is also for Members only and is more of a Labour than a Conservative venue. Years ago, the former Map Room was home to a group of trade union Labour Members. The Strangers Bar in the Commons and the Lords Bar have their sets, with the former's regulars being mainly Labour rather than Conservative Members. The Members' own dining room, which does not admit visitors, is divided to some extent into two evening sittings, with Labour Members eating before the Conservatives come in at about eight o'clock, in accordance with somewhat vestigial outside social customs. This practice minimises the risk of co-partisans having to change the subject or their treatment of a conversation to avoid being overheard by members of the other party. Within these two broad dinner sittings, Members, particularly the longer-serving ones, have their circles and regular dining companions. As in the other rooms and places mentioned, some of the group will be Ministers or shadow Ministers and others with special information: their companions' sources of information on Government and Opposition frontbench affairs will therefore be characterised by what their particular prominent friend knows, what he passes on to them and how he actually puts the points across. Contacts such as these over dinner and drinks are important parts of the means by which information (often 'confidential') is disseminated and general impressions created.

It was clear to us when talking to a total of approximately 120 Members (including some Ministers) in the course of our study that some are immersed in these informal processes and consider themselves well supplied with all the latest information, or, at least, the latest gossip and rumours. Others seemed quite cut off, either because of the amount of their outside work or because they did not mix very much. A younger Conservative told us he did not particularly enjoy the company of his co-partisans in the Smoking Room in the evenings and was therefore faced with an unexciting choice between the largely Labour Tea Room, the rather lonely Library, an even lonelier private office upstairs, or the debate going on in the chamber itself: he thus tended to listen to more than an average number of debates. One of the Labour Members said frankly that virtually all of his information on the Government's affairs and other political talk came from one or two Ministers with whom he regularly dined.

It is, of course, these personal oral contacts which characterise the legislator's life in virtually all political systems. The balance in the House between receiving information by ear and by reading, or watching TV, may change. As in all institutions, it is not only Members' contacts with each other which become institutionalised, but their actual exchanges themselves: people repeat themselves. It is possible that younger Members will try to adopt a different style of parliamentary life involving less of what they may consider to be repetitive gossip and more individual work, but the restraints on this may prove to be severe. The design of the building puts privacy at a premium: the space in which to build more private offices is not easily found, even at the great expense of the recent additions in the Upper Committee Corridors. Even if offices and a good Library are provided as the basic tools of more individual work it is not easy to see what a Member can do with the fruits of his labour, unless he is a journalist or author: he cannot 'get in' to debates easily, he cannot have his findings read into *Hansard*; the standing committee is not, at the moment, designed to receive information and analysis as an aid in considering the clauses of bills and few select committees yet offer a platform or workshop for such studies.

In addition to these restraints may come more of the overt pressure on Members, which was exerted at one point in the 1967–8 session on the Labour side by whips and opinion leaders, urging Members to stay on the main floor of the Palace around the chamber during evening sittings and not to disappear to private offices, thus damaging the 'club' or institutional atmosphere of the place. If the Bridge Street extension of the House is ever built and if party leaderships approve the inclusion in its design of many more private offices for Members, any 'anti-club' tendency among Members would have room to grow and become the dominant parliamentary style—depending on the Members' own wishes based on their personal characteristics and backgrounds. This is very much a matter of fine balance: members of any legislative body are obviously always going to receive a great deal of political information, especially on current opinion and tactics, directly from each other by word of mouth. Many of the Members we interviewed commented, however, that 'talking with colleagues' is a major and highly variegated source on the more short-run or tactical aspects of political information. Compared with some other legislatures, the House's ways encourage this, notably by the largely nocturnal social walking by which the House decides contested issues. But as politics become more complex and Members more full-time we suspect that the House will become less like Pall Mall and rather more like Capitol Hill, with a distinctive 'work' culture based upon the MPS' offices and private or small group activity, but retaining (like both Houses of Congress) a social aspect requiring 'good mixing' and a friendly style of the man who would succeed. The development of the specialised committees (whose American counterparts give Congressmen much of their formal workload) will be the probable determinants of any such changing social practice. But the foundation of such developments will, obviously, be the wishes of Members: we return to this basic question of parliamentary personnel in our concluding chapter.

CHAPTER III

THE MEMBER'S VIEW OF
PARLIAMENT

1. INFORMATION FROM GOVERNMENT AND PARLIAMENT

In common with all other interested observers of public affairs, MPs rely to a considerable extent on official information emanating from the Government and also on material which is published by Parliament. Parliament's own output often presents and comments on information which has been requested from either the Government or from other sources.

One result of the rise during the present century of nationally organised 'interest groups' which negotiate with Government Departments is that Ministers may now control the flow to Parliament and the public of more information about the views of such groups than they did when parliamentary committees or official committees of enquiry more commonly served as public platforms for such groups. Nowadays this information needs to be extracted from Ministers by a parliamentary Question, and the informal understandings of confidentiality between Departments and organised groups rather overlay the constitutional assumption that Parliament should be kept informed of these groups' demands and position. As the role of Government has become larger and more complex Ministers have tended to claim privacy for such negotiations and to insist that neither the Government nor the organised interests can be expected to negotiate in the open. This air of 'diplomacy' when dealing with organised groups on behalf of the public interest is, of course, taken from the world of foreign affairs where the information available to Parliament has always been even more constrained, although erratically so. Peter G. Richards, in *Parliament and Foreign Affairs*[1] notes that many factors, including the personality and political strength of the Foreign Secretary or Prime Minister of the day as well as the intrinsic nature of any key document have affected how much official material Parliament

[1] Allen & Unwin, 1967, pp. 50–1.

126

and the public have been allowed to read regarding Britain's foreign relations.

One hundred years ago the situation in this, as in domestic fields, was relatively 'open' but the trend towards secret diplomacy and the two World Wars of the present century have closed the field considerably. Governments will naturally not publish accounts of incomplete negotiations and this encourages officials and Ministers to see some long-term objectives (for example, current relations with Western Europe or with the states 'East of Suez') rather in these terms. Professor Richards concludes that foreign affairs information to Members is particularly thin due to its often very formal nature, with the actual political issues involved left to the unofficial commentators in the Press and Parliament to deal with as best they can, usually on such 'inside' information and conjecture as they can marshall.

These modern constrictions on the flow of both domestic and overseas affairs information from Ministers to Members and the public deserve serious attention. It should not be forgotten, however, that modern public administration and world affairs are so complex that the flow of material which is published or released by the Government forms a veritable flood.

Regular items which are the Government's responsibility include the annual estimates of expenditure to be voted by the House, the annual reports issued by some Departments, particularly on the social service side, white papers (which are supposed to be official statements of intent) and the new green papers (which are supposed to promote publicity and discussion of their contents prior to Government policy being formed). The Government also issues hundreds of statements of policy each year, often in reply to oral or written parliamentary Questions (which are frequently arranged for the purpose): the Commons or Lords *Hansard* will therefore include them. Ministers also often talk publicly to journalists and interviewers—although often making points they have already made in white papers or to the House, so that the absence of a collated report of such statements does not, at the moment, greatly impede the free flow of such official intelligence.

On a more regular basis and still fully official in status are the periodicals produced by Government Departments. Such publications as *The Board of Trade Journal*, *The Employment and Productivity Gazette* (formerly the *Ministry of Labour Gazette*) or *DEA Newsletter* are not intended as policy statements and Ministers are not seriously expected to stand by every phrase used by the information officials who write them; their statistics and other facts, however, are taken by MPs and other interested people as official. At least one of these journals, *Trends in Education*, was started by the Ministry of Education, as it then was, to provide a channel for publishable facts which were finding their way neither into the Press nor into *Hansard* as the written answers to Questions. As administration becomes more complex and Governments more public-relations conscious the official departmental journal or similar publications may become more common and thus provide Members and others with new sources of information.

The Government also publishes many reports which it has arranged to receive from outsiders who have conducted an official enquiry, although their findings and views are not, of course, official policy and may well be ignored or contradicted at a later stage. Occasionally this kind of material is thought too secret for publication: the Plowden Group on the control of public expenditure in 1961 (which had been given access to certain Cabinet papers) compromised on the matter and published a brief paper claiming to collate several private reports to the Prime Minister, although the Leader of the Opposition, Hugh Gaitskell, had several times asked in the House that the report be published. On this matter, as on much else, there is no rule and Ministers enjoy discretion, subject to criticism of their use of it.

Parliament itself produces a great deal of information on public affairs, either in the form of the official report of all its proceedings in the two chambers and in various kinds of subsidiary committee or in the shape of reports to either House from such committees on some aspect of public policy. Thus, to take an example which brings together Government and parliamentary sources, a Member interested in the future of the coal industry's manpower could apply to the Vote Office of the House for free copies of: successive white papers from the Ministry of Power, successive annual reports and accounts from the National Coal Board laid before Parliament by the Minister, the reports of any outside enquiry set up by the Minister to study the problem, *Hansard* reports of debates and Questions in either House on the matter and any relevant reports from the select committee on nationalised industries or other select committees. The *Hansard* report of what is said in the chamber is, of course, such a rich source for all public matters because the British system requires Ministers, by convention, to give their official information and views to the House before speaking to the Press and broadcasters, and also to answer parliamentary Questions. A comparison with the American Congressional Record shows the difference made by the system of a non-ministerial legislature in making the transcript more valuable as a source of legislators' views rather than these combined with officially produced facts.

MPs rely very heavily on these Government and parliamentary publications, either after getting a free copy from the Vote Office or (more commonly than they used to) asking the House of Commons staff to furnish a photocopy of a particular section. Since 1921 a distinction has been made by the Controller of the Stationery Office who prints, publishes and sells to the public all these documents, between 'parliamentary' and 'non-parliamentary' papers, only the former of which are available free on demand to Members at the Vote Office. Non-parliamentary papers must be requested from HMSO, the Member signing to the effect that he needs the documents for his parliamentary duties. No one, except possibly the Controller, is very sure how this distinction is applied to the great variety of modern documents although it makes little difference to a Member who takes the trouble to ask for an item and can wait for it to come from HMSO. Members can get free single copies of a wide range of HMSO documents and books within certain limits of subject matter and cost: the application form declares that 'historical, technical and scientific works and similar classes of publication are excluded from this arrangement'. Single copies of documents distributed in Britain by HMSO on behalf of international bodies may also be obtained free, although often only after some delay.

The decision in 1921 to divide 'non-parliamentary' from 'parliamentary' was an economy measure to curb the undoubted existing abuse and waste. Its continuation may serve as some guide to the importance which the Government attaches to a particular document (the 'parliamentary' ones being considered, perhaps, more important because more freely available) or may be a symbol of the decline of the MP's importance in official eyes since that date. But, despite the 1921 ruling, Members nonetheless benefit from quite elaborate arrangements to secure their adequate supply of relevant documents.

Ministers are expected to supply the Commons Library, in advance of debates, with a list of official documents which they consider relevant to the discussion. Members may order any item from this list through the Vote Office (plus, of course, any other parliamentary paper which they feel would be useful but which the Minister did not list). If these orders are placed at the Vote Office by 4.15 p.m. on any sitting day the document can be obtained within two hours; later requests may not produce the document until the following morning.[1] The onus is on the Member to select an item from the Minister's list and ask for a copy: this reduces the waste involved in placing actual stocks of these 'relevant' papers in the Vote Office but does little to help HMSO predict likely demand—to be safe, they must reprint a listed document whose existing stocks are low, in case more than only a few MPs call for copies. If an argument over some point in a document developed during the early stages of a debate it is possible for, say twenty Members, to submit requests for their own copies by 4.15 p.m. They could then have these documents by 6.15 p.m. and possibly use them for their own speeches and interventions during the evening period of the debate.

Although some of the documents listed by Ministers are, no doubt, the subject of negotiations with HMSO as to whether their relevance to the debate really justifies an otherwise unnecessary reprinting job, it seems clear that considerable trouble and expense are undertaken to provide Members with adequate documentary support for their parliamentary interests in general and for debates in particular.

The Vote Office of the House holds stocks of the two previous sessions' output of parliamentary papers, any of which

---

[1] For some years before 1966 the Minister concerned was responsible for arranging through HMSO for actual supplies of all papers (statutes, regulations, etc.), which he thought relevant, to be available in adequate numbers in the Vote Office in time for a debate. Some Ministers were unduly comprehensive in their approach to this task, perhaps from a wish to impress Members with their helpfulness. As the Speaker tactfully put it in 1966 when introducing the more reserved modern policy: 'But it has been found that Departments, in order to avoid any risk of failing to fulfil this obligation, have tended to supply such an extensive variety of documents and in such quantities that the normal functions of the Vote Office are being seriously interfered with' (H.C. Deb., February 21, 1966, c. 34.)

Members can pick up at the counter in the Members' lobby immediately outside the chamber. The Vote Office acts as agent for Members' written requests to HMSO for 'non-parliamentary papers'. It also provides an early-morning delivery by messengers to Members' addresses within a three-mile radius of the House of *Hansard*, bills, etc., and any other document which a Minister thinks is sufficiently important. In 1966–7 the Vote Office received from the printers the enormous number of 1·55 million documents, about half of which were delivered on the morning rounds or left at the House with Members' post for them to collect when they came in. A lot of the other half are not, in fact, requested by Members and go back to HMSO after their stay in the Vote Office. It is thus impossible to know the numbers of any particular document which are drawn by Members, much less how many are ever actually read or consulted. Members vary widely in their demands for this free supply of official and parliamentary information as was clear to us from references during our interviews; there is probably a more even spread of total demand across the House's membership than a few years ago which is one of many reflections of the more active role of this Parliament's backbenchers, particularly as the newcomers have gradually come to appreciate what they may receive on demand.

So long as Members may demand free single copies of all but the most costly and politically marginal HMSO publications, the 1921 rule dividing material into 'parliamentary' and 'non-parliamentary' papers has little practical effect; tendencies such as the present Government practice of putting out official reports as HMSO documents rather than as parliamentary papers do reduce the flow of documents through the Vote Office, but are certainly not preventing any interested Member getting a free copy, if he cares to ask HMSO for it, and if he is able to wait a short time for its arrival.

2. MEMBERS' ATTITUDES TO THE COMMONS AND LORDS CHAMBERS AS SOURCES

'Well, it's dead. Nobody attends debates, and this gives a general atmosphere of lifelessness about the whole place. . . .' This notably definite assertion about the House of Commons in 1963 by Humphry Berkeley (then Conservative Member for

Lancaster) has enjoyed some prominence since it was first broadcast as the opening statement in a broadcast television feature.[1] It is a double statement, declaring that no one attends debates and that a near-empty chamber causes general lifelessness throughout the premises. It might be thought that, assuming Members have not left the Palace of Westminster, there must be 'life' wherever they happen to be: in select and standing committees upstairs, in party meetings or groups or even merely in the Tea and Smoking Rooms. We obviously needed to examine the standing of the chamber as a 'source of information' for our respondents: our results suggest that Mr Berkeley was, of course, exaggerating the low interest among Members in debates, but not by more than the amount customarily permitted for public statements designed to be quotable.

Our question to interviewed Members ran: 'On the House itself as a source of information to you. . . . Leaving aside frontbench speeches (opening and winding-up debates) do you often listen to many backbench speeches in a debate?'

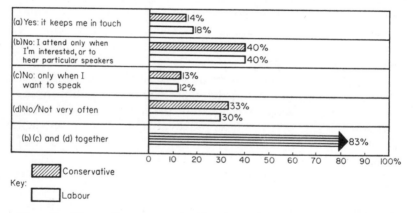

Figure 9. '*Do you listen to many backbench speeches?*' (See Appendix, Table 7.)
(N—105: 55 Conservative and 50 Labour MPs)

This question specified backbench speeches because this seemed to us the test of the chamber as a broad source of information. We excluded frontbenchers' speeches as we knew, of course, that the House thins out considerably after the two

[1] It is quoted by, among others, Anthony Sampson, *Anatomy of Britain Today*, Hodder & Stoughton, 1965, p. 38.

openers have spoken from their dispatch boxes and the first backbencher is called, and then fills up again as the first of the two frontbench speakers who will wind up the debate is preparing to rise (usually at about nine o'clock, the vote being due at ten). As Members often reminded us, the frontbench speakers say a lot which is informative both on 'facts about situations' and facts about the state of opinion on those situations. We feel that for Members to extend this interest to even some backbench contributions would be a reasonable sign of the status they accord debates as an information source.

Only one respondent in six told us that they often listen to backbenchers speaking. Two-fifths replied that they were selective as to the subject being discussed and who was speaking. All Members are selective to some extent, of course: these Members differ from the 17 per cent who said they often listen to backbenchers in being less likely to enter the chamber on the off-chance of hearing an interesting speech. A small but significant minority were even more restrictive and said they would attend only when they wished to speak in the debate and nearly a third simply replied 'no'. These responses are coded by us in Figure 9 from a range of remarks which means that an element of rather arbitrary classification is present; the simple negative answers (d) are not alternatives to (b) since all Members want themselves to speak at some time, which requires their attendance to hear at least some of the other speeches out of both courtesy and prudence. It is not wise for a Member to risk being accused in debate of not listening to others. Members often explain in their speeches that it was a prearranged appointment or the pressing need for tea which drew them briefly and reluctantly from the chamber while another Member was speaking. Members also have to bear in mind that the Speaker uses his list of those who have asked to be called fairly flexibly. This preserves his independence and enables him to judge the balance of debate as it progresses. It also helps to prevent Members spoiling the debate by behaviour often described by Charles Pannell (Labour Member for Leeds West) as 'blowing in, blowing up and blowing out'.

This rather strongly negative response could not be redressed by including Ministers and Government whips among the respondents. Ministers are particularly specialised attenders at debates, often coming in only for their Department's business (when they may well be due to speak) or, like most other Members, for the climax of the debate before voting. Ministers do, of course, turn out in strength for the opening of major Government business and, individually, when a constituency interest comes up. Senior Ministers sometimes spend time in the chamber as an escape from the great pressures of work in their Departments and some junior Ministers do so for the opposite reason. Government whips, of course, listen to debates a great deal, and a whip always attends on the frontbench of each party to support the Minister or shadow-Minister whose business or field is being debated: their official role marks them off from the backbencher who can stay or go as he pleases.

There was no significant party differences in these responses: the slightly higher proportion of Labour Members among the 17 per cent of respondents who said they often listened to backbench speeches is merely a reflection of the fact that more of the newer Members, who are mainly Labour, answered in this way. Generally, longer-serving Members were slightly more likely to be uninterested in backbench speeches: those in this group who were ex-Ministers were most likely to say that they seldom or never heard them and not one claimed to listen to such speeches often. Although the 1964 and 1966 entrants, taken together, were more likely (in 1967) to react positively on backbench speeches, nearly one-third of the 1966 entrants gave the strongly negative response (d) rather than the weaker (b). The key factor appears to be education. Those with only an elementary education were far more likely to say they listen to backbench speeches frequently and this applies to a lesser extent to those with a background of non-graduate further education. Members with a full secondary education, and especially those who subsequently became graduates, were far less likely to attend other backbenchers' speeches.

Some of the more strongly negative responses sometimes carried the caveat that a particular Member's name coming up on the annunciators (which tell the Members in various parts of the House who is speaking) would make the respondents interrupt what they were doing, if possible, and enter the chamber to listen. Out of several dozen Members who either volunteered a name or who were informally asked by us whether they had such a favourite, all but one mentioned Michael Foot. All Labour Members and most Conservatives mentioned him first, with most Conservatives, but fewer Labour Members, then also mentioning Nigel Birch. Mr Foot was described by all those who made the comment as the perfect House of Commons speaker for both humour and effect, while Mr Birch received praise from fellow Conservatives for his 'splendid sarcasm' and bite. No other backbencher was at all widely mentioned. Frontbenchers are rather different as they have, in the evenings at least, rather captive audiences who are waiting to vote; but Reginald Maudling was mentioned by a few Conservatives. Other Members said that they would always go in to hear a 'rebel', or for any ministerial resignation speech.

It was clearly right for us to judge how far Members go in catching up with other Members' views by looking at *Hansard*: 'When you're not able to listen to much of a debate in the House for yourself, about how often do you read or look at the *Hansard* report of it?'

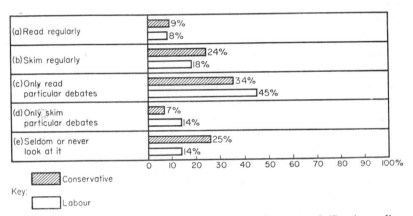

Figure 10. *Respondents' use of House of Commons* 'HANSARD'. (See Appendix, Table 8.)

(N—104: 55 Conservatives and 49 Labour MPs)

Less than one-tenth of our respondents said that they regularly read *Hansard*, although a further fifth skim it regularly. Nearly half, however, read or skim particular debates (with most claiming to read rather than skim) while the remaining fifth seldom or never use *Hansard*.[1] There are some party

---

[1] These responses refer to frontbench as well as backbench speeches; it was not practicable to ask Members to distinguish between backbench and frontbench contributions when looking at reports and debates.

differences: slightly more Conservatives read or skim *Hansard* regularly, whereas Labour Members are more likely to read or skim particular debates. On the other hand twice as many Conservatives seldom or never use *Hansard*, so that the overall picture is one in which Labour MPs make rather more use of it than do Conservative Members. There are some differences related to parliamentary service, although there is no regular trend of increasing or decreasing use with length of service. The 1964 and 1966 entrants tend to be more selective in their approach to *Hansard* and more than half said that they read only particular debates. This seems to be a reflection of these newer Members' more specialist approach rather than a sign of their rejecting *Hansard* altogether. A much smaller proportion of the 1964–6 entrants than of longer-serving Members said that they seldom or never used *Hansard*. It is likely that this is a result of these newer MPs gradually accustoming themselves to the use of *Hansard* in their particular fields of interest and showing less inclination than their longer-serving colleagues to abandon it altogether.

There are, once more, differences according to the educational background of MPs: the more extensive a Member's education, the more selective his attitude towards *Hansard*. The shadow Ministers we interviewed are less likely to use *Hansard* than the backbenchers although, when they do use it, they favour reading particular debates as would be expected in view of their shadow jobs.

Members with addresses within three miles of the House receive the free delivery of *Hansard* during the early morning and can thus see it over breakfast. Most Members live further out than, for example, the Zoo or Kensington Palace Gardens and must therefore rely on the Press for such breakfast reading. We asked our respondents: 'Do you normally look at the Press coverage of Common's debates?'

86 per cent do look at the debate reports in one or more newspapers. Most of these Members (three-quarters of the total) tend to make do with these reports, while a small group of 10 per cent use the Press only as a prompt for reading a speech or item in *Hansard* itself. As Figure 11 shows, Conservatives make up most of this group of 'prompted' Members who prefer to see a speech in its full version: otherwise there are no party differences on this matter although there are educational differences.

Following the trend on attitudes to debates, there is some evidence that reading debates in newspapers decreases with more extensive education and with longer parliamentary service. In respect of parliamentary service, however, the trend was irregular and there was a difference between ex-Ministers and current frontbench spokesmen the latter being more inclined to follow debates in the Press.

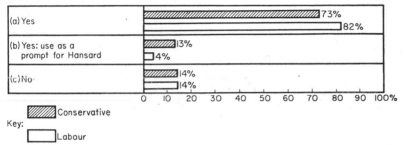

Figure 11. *Respondents' use of Press reports of Commons' debates. 'Do you normally look at the Press coverage of Commons' debates?'* (See Appendix, Table 9.)

(N—104: 55 Conservative and 49 Labour MPS)

These simple questions on our respondents' habits for discovering what goes on in the chamber prepare the way for their judgement on its value as a source of information. The business of the House which is done in the chamber is much too varied to permit a general enquiry, so we asked Members to give an opinion of its value in a field of special interest where they feel reasonably able to judge the quality of what they hear: commonplace or original, thoughtful or superficial, experienced or lightweight—'Your attending debates in the chamber or reading *Hansard* is obviously linked with your own special interest. How would you assess the chamber as a source of information in one of your own special fields of interest?'

Only one-third of Members replied that the debates in the chamber in their particular field of interest are a valuable source of information, although nearly another fifth said that, within a wide variation of quality, they sometimes heard or read valuable contributions. Thus, taken together, this positive response represents half (52 per cent) of our respondents although we should report that the tone of those who mentioned variation of quality was equivalent to the theatrical euphemism that a play received 'very mixed reviews': their emphasis was

137

usually on the uncertainty of finding a worthwhile contribution from a fellow Member.

Some Members, mainly Conservatives, made comments on the House's quality in their particular fields, often saying they wished that the other side could put up a better showing to improve debate generally. This criticism was made by Conservatives of Labour speakers on agriculture and City finance, although others said Labour had improved considerably as a result of the 1964–6 intakes in their ability to offer what these Conservatives regarded as reasonably informed speeches on aviation, economic policy, defence and international affairs.

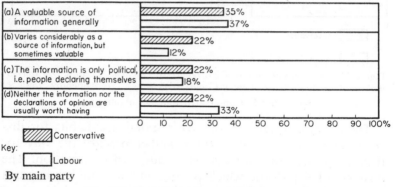

Key: Conservative
      Labour

By main party

(N—104: 55 Conservative and 49 Labour MPs)

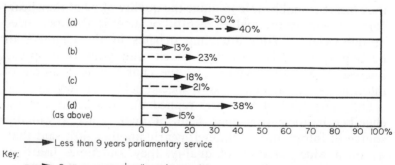

Key: ────▶ Less than 9 years' parliamentary service

      ──▶ 9 or more years' parliamentary service

By length of service

(N—107: 55 Conservative, 49 Labour and 3 Liberal MPs)

Figure 12. *Respondents' views of the chamber as a source of information in a field of special interest—by main party and length of service.* (See Appendix, Table 10.)

138

For their part, some of these Conservatives (several of whom have outside jobs in industry) wished their own party was stronger on industrial relations and factory-floor problems.

Another fifth of our respondents drew a distinction between what we have called in this study 'facts about situations' and 'information on people's opinions on those situations'. They made comments close to our coded response (c) in Figure 12 but should not, we think, be taken as dismissing information on people's opinion as unimportant or of a lesser order than 'factual' knowledge of the 'real' situation outside the House: that would be an extremely odd thing for a politician to do, as we stress in our Introduction. Some situations are, in any case 'internal' to Parliament and the Government: the question in 1940, and again in 1963, was whether the Conservative Prime Minister of the day had lost the confidence of enough of his former supporters to jeopardise his position as Leader of his party and head of the Government. Leo Amery and Nigel Birch made their expulsive speeches which expressed or caused (or both) a draining away of support from Chamberlain and Macmillan. On these occasions there was nothing to be stated by any Member except his reasons or feelings on the question of confidence. The famous speech by Enoch Powell in 1959 in the debate on the beating to death of prisoners by guards at the Hola Camp in Kenya also offered no new information on the case itself, but rather Mr Powell's reasons why he felt his party's Government should reconsider the adequacy of their official reaction to it.

On less stirring or tragic occasions backbench Members (and even, sometimes frontbenchers) often give a debate an added flavour or twist by not saying quite what may have been ex-pected of them on the issue, given their party and position. The Members who gave response (c) are not denying this attractive attribute of the House's debates but suggesting that it is rare. For them, the reiteration of expected or already known posi-tions is the main political 'information' offered in debates, par-ticularly, of course, by backbenchers who have no Government or Opposition position to outline. Unlike their colleagues who responded under (b) in Figure 12, these Members do not, even 'sometimes', find valuable statements of a 'factual' kind; but also unlike the remaining 28 per cent of our respondents, they did not reply in phrases which could be entered under our response (d)—that neither the 'factual information' nor the 'political declarations' in debates are usually worth having.

Approximately the same proportions of Conservative and Labour Members subscribe to the view that the House's debates are a valuable source of information (response (a)) although there is a considerable difference between the two parties on the view that the value varies considerably, with about double the proportion of Conservatives saying this compared with Labour. The opinion that only declaratory or 'political' information is available from debates is about equally shared while rather more Labour Members than Conservatives (33 per cent against 22 per cent) took the clearly negative line of response (d).

These views of debate are much more strongly linked to Members' years of service than to their party. More favourable views are associated with longer service, with a sharp dichotomy among Members around the nine-year point. Nearly two-fifths of the Members elected during or since 1959 gave the clearly negative response (d) compared with only one Member in seven of the pre-1959 intake. Conversely, two-fifths of the longer-serving group regards debates in their particular fields as valuable sources against less than a third of Members with fewer than nine years' service. The longer-serving Members were also more likely to give the middling response that these debates vary greatly in their value. The diversity of views among Members with a more extended education which we have noted in other contexts reappeared on this point: MPs with only an elementary education were the group most favourable to debates as sources for information, those with a secondary or non-graduate further education background the least favourable, while graduates fell between the two.

The parliamentary Question has received a comparatively large amount of attention from scholars[1] and is well known as a weapon of political battle as well as a source of information for Parliament and the country. At the time of our survey Members were divided in their attitudes to Mr Speaker King's policy of 'speeding up Question time' which had resulted in the Question's author receiving only one opportunity to put a

---

[1] See D. N. Chester and N. Bowring, *Questions in Parliament*, an historical and documentary study, and N. Johnson, 'Parliamentary Questions and the conduct of Administration', in *Public Administration*, 39 (1961), pp. 131–48.

supplementary question and other Members, who considered themselves equally involved with the subject of the Question, often none at all. Comments supporting or criticising Dr King's policy and contrasting it with the different approach of his predecessor Sir Harry Hylton-Foster, often led Members to say say what they thought Questions are 'for'—a topic with strong partisan overtones depending on a Member's position on the Government or Opposition side of the House.

We wanted a fairly quick 'image response' on Questions made up of various replies which we could allot among several coded entries in Figure 13. We therefore simply followed our questions about the quality of debates by asking, 'What about oral and written answer Questions in this field?' We arranged four responses on the use and perception of Questions themselves and two on reading of the printed results in *Hansard*. The multiple response results are in Figure 13.

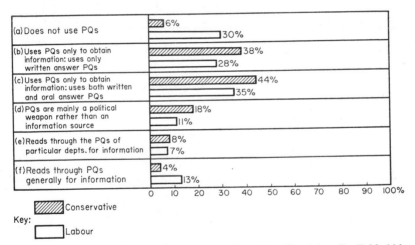

Key: Conservative / Labour

Figure 13. *Respondents' use of parliamentary Questions.* (See Appendix, Table 11.)
(N—96: 50 Conservative and 46 Labour MPS)

The figure shows that a small but not insignificant minority of more than a sixth declared they never used either oral answer or written answer Questions. It was among this group that the most hostile attitudes to the modern state of the Question were expressed: the thing was a farce, greatly abused, a self-publicity machine, etc. These very critical opinions on the way Question time is treated were shared by some of the one-third of our respondents who said they never bothered with oral answers, even for requests for information from the Government, but used only written answers for this purpose. But other Members in this group advanced a practical reason for sticking to written answers: they often received an answer more quickly as they did not need to join such a long queue as for the oral answer Questions. The relative speed of the written answer was worth the loss of the chance to ask a supplementary question.

A further two-fifths of respondents claimed to use Questions for both oral and written answer but only to elicit information. These three responses demonstrate the elasticity of the word 'information' in politics: responses (a), (b) and (c) in Figure 13 are, of course, mutually exclusive in that a Member can follow only one of the three courses described. Yet together they total 90 per cent of our respondents, leaving the other 10 per cent, presumably, to ask all the 'political' and 'point-scoring' types of Questions. The asking of oral answer Questions is indeed con-centrated on a relatively few Members but not to this extent: Members were clearly tending to assume that all their own Ques-tions are objective searches after truth and it is the other fellow who uses the system to score political points.

Most of the Members responding (a) or (b) said that, argu-ment about the mistreatment of Question time apart, they got better results by approaching Ministers privately, usually by letter. Letters are now the main channel from Members to Ministers and carry some political advantages as we have noted in the next chapter. Some Members also take up con-stituency cases concerning Government Departments with the local managers of branches of employment exchanges, the driving test service or the Supplementary Benefits Commission as they feel this helps both efficiency and good relations with local officials. Other Members always write to the Minister on local matters as a demonstration of his ministerial responsi-bility for the service concerned and, perhaps, also of their status at the centre of the system.

The general wish to settle questions privately would naturally be stronger on the Government side whereas Opposition party Members would not deliberately avoid publicity on a case which might merit a Question, even though they may not deliberately seek it. The sharp party contrast in Figure 13, where about one-third of all Labour respondents, compared with only

6 per cent of Conservatives said they did not employ either type of Question, must be closely linked with this political attitude of the Government supporter. It does not at all follow that these Labour Members never question or press Ministers on either constituency cases or national policies. But when in Government the pressures towards allowing the Minister to change or develop his thinking out of the public eye are great. Question time is widely seen by our respondents—not only those who replied that it is mainly a political occasion—as a part of the general challenge to the Government from the Opposition. Some Opposition Members make it their main parliamentary occupation. When asked the question of Figure 13 one Conservative replied, 'I ask the most Questions—or, at least, if not the most, then I'm certainly in the top ten', and this political approach is shared, to some extent at least, by more Conservatives than Labour as the results on response (d) indicate.

Not more than one respondent in seven said that they read the Questions and their oral and written answers printed in *Hansard*. More Members than this probably do so but the fact that no more than this proportion mentioned the fact during our exchanges about Questions may suggest that they do not do so regularly or thoroughly. Labour Members were more inclined to say they read the Questions sections in *Hansard*, either generally or for particular Departments.

The overall function of parliamentary Questions, the best way to organise them, the full costs to the Government of handling them and the benefits which the present system generates are all political and procedural matters lying outside our study. One Conservative ex-Cabinet Minister was quite clear on the matter: Question time was particularly related neither to information-gathering by backbenchers nor to ministerial responsibility and the control of the Executive in the constitutional sense of those terms. Speaking in an *ex cathedra* tone he asserted, 'the purpose of Question time is to train the Minister: to train a quick mind and a discreet tongue'. If this is counted as a benefit of the system, the practice of one Labour lady Member is, no doubt, to be seen, as a cost: 'If the written answer I have asked for or the reply to my letter is delayed, I telephone the Minister and remind him or his principal private secretary—and if the answer is unsatisfactory when it comes I ring them again and ask them whether they really meant to send such a poor thing in reply.'

To ask the members of one house in a two-chamber legislature whether they gathered any useful information from the proceedings of the other is a natural question. The House of Lords is unique in several respects, of course, not least its world-record size of over one thousand members and its majority hereditary membership. Our interests centred on a third peculiar feature: its very small modern residue of formal power and the consequent role with which it is often credited of being a legitimate and valuable national debating society, enjoying special authority in those fields of public policy such as social and 'moral' questions which the major parties choose informally not to fight over as organised armies under their customary leaders. A second chamber of this kind might be thought to hold some special interest, on certain topics at least, for the members of the politically senior house.

MPS can receive neither influence nor information from the Lords if they do not follow that House's proceedings, so we asked our respondents: 'About the House of Lords ... About how often do you go up and listen to a Lords debate?'

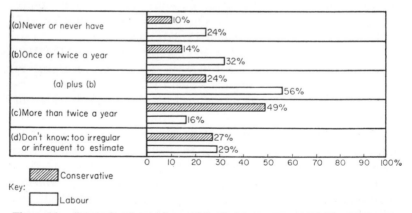

Figure 14. *Respondents' attendance of Lords debates.* (See Appendix, Table 12.)
(N—87: 49 Conservatives and 38 Labour MPS)

The design of Figure 14 shows that there were insufficient reports of hearing the Lords debate much more often than twice per year to justify a separate grouping within the data of these more frequent visitors. This factor, combined with a high number of 'don't knows', whose visits are presumably too irregular or infrequent to permit even an approximate estimate, gives the responses a negative air. About one respondent in six said they never went to hear the Lords, or that they never had. Our 1966 entrants had been in the House about fourteen months when we spoke to them and they showed a higher rate of saying 'never have'. The 1964 entrants were less likely to say this and we presume that, within the context of generally very low M P interest, it takes time for a Member to come across an occasion when he wants to go up to hear the Lords.

Nearly a quarter of our respondents said they go about once or twice a year and often mention particular speakers who had attracted them: the current case at the time of our interviews was Lord Avon (formerly Sir Anthony Eden) speaking on the June war of 1967. A further third indicated that they went a little more often than twice a year but, as we have noted, we had insufficient candidates for a further group of MPs who claim, for example, a monthly visit on average. The remainder could not estimate, saying they only attended when a debate on their special interest was held. We gathered that this in effect put these Members close to the 'twice a year' group rather than to any more interested group within the response (c).

It is no surprise to see a symmetrical design in Figure 14 indicating a significant party difference. One-half of the Conservatives, against one-sixth of Labour Members, claim to attend the Lords debates more than twice a year. One quarter of Labour Members 'never' went there compared with only one Conservative in ten—although the size of this group has probably declined in the period since we met them as the Lords have had more potentially attractive events with which to tempt these Labour newcomers up the corridor on what will probably become an approximately annual visit.

With regard to Members reading Lords debates in *Hansard* or the Press, slightly more Members (one-fifth) said they 'never' see the Lords *Hansard* than 'never' attend their debates. Only two Conservatives and one Labour Member out of ninety respondents on this topic claimed to read or skim it regularly; the other 77 per cent replied that they looked at it only when interested. It would therefore seem that Members do not go to the Lords *Hansard* looking for general information or to see

145

what peers as a whole said on a range of topics: they will pick up a copy at the Vote Office when it contains a particular speech which they have heard described or seen in the Press, or when the debate was on a personal interest which draws them to see if anything interesting was said.

The overall tone of these responses was distant and unenthusiastic. Members replies to our question, 'Do you normally read or look at the Press coverage of the Lords?' went some way, however, to fill this rather empty picture of the Lords as a source of information to the Commons. Over half (54 per cent) of all respondents said they do normally read or look at the Press reports. A further 10 per cent said they regard looking at the Press report as a prompt for getting the Lords *Hansard*, while 36 per cent said they very rarely or never look at the Press coverage at all. Again there were no differences, even party ones in this case, and the 1966 entrants were again less likely to pay any attention to the Lords.

These findings of a very modest intake among all MPs of both the 'factual' and the 'declaratory' kinds of 'information' publicly offered by peers will be no great surprise to people who know the Commons. MPs are in a unique 'information position' and probably feel they can manage their work without regularly following the proceedings of the politically junior chamber. MPs are very far from being like the general public in the matter of political information and it may be that public attention and apparent respect for the Lords' proceedings is much higher.

Evidence of what members of the House of Lords themselves believe to be the degree of interest in their debates maintained by MPs is provided by the survey of peers' opinions conducted by Peter Bromhead and Donald Shell in 1967.[1] Peers were asked whether they thought either the Government of the day or MPs as a whole 'pay attention to speeches in the House of Lords', 'regularly', 'occasionally' or 'very rarely'. Just under one half of all peers thought that the Government regularly pays attention whereas only one peer in ten believed that this was true of MPs. Labour peers were more optimistic than Conservative peers with regard to the current (Labour) Government but even more pessimistic regarding MPs. The peers who had

[1] P. A. Bromhead and D. Shell, 'The Lords and their House', *Parliamentary Affairs*, Vol. XX, No. 4 (1967).

themselves served in the Commons were rather more likely than the others to say that MPs very rarely pay attention to Lords debates. All types of peer seemed to be clearly of the opinion that the Government takes more notice of them than do the members of the other House.

3. THE SPECIALISED SELECT COMMITTEE

'Either one specialises in this place or one goes mad'—Eldon Griffiths (Conservative, Bury St Edmunds).

'Does not your memorandum give the impression that avoidance of axial shuffling is possible only with a $7\frac{1}{2}$ inch diameter? Would you care to correct that impression'?—Eric Lubbock (Liberal, Orpington). Select Committee on Science and Technology: *Report on U.K. Nuclear Reactor Programme:* oral evidence, Question 881, to E. S. Booth (Member for Engineering, Central Electricity Generating Board).

(i) *Members' Views*
When we interviewed our sample of Members in the summer of 1967, the first two 'specialised' select committees of the House—on science and technology and on the work of the Ministry of Agriculture—had existed for only about seven months and had produced no reports. The attitudes of our respondents towards the idea of specialised committees and these two particular groups were quite strikingly favourable, but before presenting them a brief background note may be useful.

The modern House makes less use of select committees which conduct *ad hoc* enquiries than was the rule in the middle and late Victorian period. In the first edition of *The Reform of Parliament*, Professor Crick traced the decline of such activity to its present, almost vanished, state. On the other hand, the regular select committees which carry on their scrutiny of Government activity as a standard annual routine (although with memberships which often change) have grown in importance since Victorian days and, indeed, have added most to their stature and their numbers in quite recent years.

These established select committees each do a particular type of work across the entire field of Government: the Public Accounts Committee examines efficiency and regularity of

Government accounts; the Estimates Committee has, since 1945, established itself as an examiner of current administration; the Committee on Statutory Instruments offers a technical legal scrutiny to legal rules made by the Government; and the Nationalised Industries Committee has, during its first fifteen years, studied the work of these industries (as they were defined after the post-war period of nationalisation Acts, although the committee obtained a broadening of this definition in the 1968–9 session).[1]

Formally speaking, none of these committees is allowed to venture into matters of 'ministerial policy'. In fact, the Estimates Committee has plainly done so on several occasions,[2] and the Nationalised Industries Committee has also become involved in very weighty official questions. Because the NI Committee is concerned with public corporations (for whose 'day-to-day' operations Ministers are not legally responsible) it has always enjoyed some latitude on the controversial question of whether committees of MPs should be allowed to deal with Government 'policy'. It has used this latitude over the years to explore the true extent of Government control over the nationalised industries which took it well into the 'ministerial policy' ambit; this was achieved with such authority, however, that no formal official rebuff was ever received. Instead, the ground was being laid for the establishment of select committees whose terms of reference would allow them to deal with policy matters within Government Departments, for which Ministers are fully responsible. As it had long been suggested that such committees should follow the affairs of one Department, or one topic, these newer groups are usually called 'specialised committees' to distinguish them from the established select committees.

[1] There are also the domestic Services, Privilege and Procedure Committees all of which, of course, deal with some matters of public political interest. For exhaustive analysis of the Nationalised Industries and Estimates Committees see, respectively, D. Coombes, *The MP and the Administration* and N. Johnson *Parliament and Administration* (both Allen & Unwin, 1966).

[2] How close the modern Estimates Committee has sometimes come to obvious 'policy' matters not deriving from any financially-based 'efficiency' approach is shown, for example, in the 1967 enquiry on prisons and borstals conducted by a sub-committee chaired by Mrs Renee Short. The resulting report of the full Estimates Committee included the recommendation of conjugal visits between carefully selected men prisoners and their wives. It is not surprising that, either through error or journalist's shorthand style, a reporter referred to this Estimates Committee report as having come from 'The Parliamentary Select Committee on Prisons' (*Sunday Times*, January 7, 1968).

Select committees are of obvious interest to a study on MPs' sources of information; the new specialised committees hold particular promise as new sources of additional knowledge for the House. Any large, deliberative body naturally looks to sub-committees or other small groups of its members to conduct all detailed work, whether of administration, negotiation or information-gathering. Those MPs and other observers who have long wanted the House to search out more information on public affairs have therefore emphasised the importance of the characteristic select committee method: gathering evidence, discussing the issues and, finally, agreeing and publishing a report, to which most of the evidence is appended.

Although, when we interviewed Members, the two new specialised committees had existed for only a few months, and had not reported, many of our respondents had heard something of their progress. They had picked up some of the current talk around the House both about the rows developing between the Committee on Agriculture and the Foreign Office over the Committee's wish to travel to Brussels to take formal evidence from officials and also the suggestion that this fuss was a mere cover for the political clash over British entry into the Common Market between the Foreign Office, under its very 'pro-entry' Minister, George Brown, and the 'anti-entry' element on the Labour side of the committee. Some Members mentioned these matters in passing. This serves to emphasise that we were asking our respondents to give an opinion not only on the general theory about having specialised committees but also on two actual committees, one of which already found itself in some choppy political waters.

We asked two questions, one general and one particular, about the extension of select committee work, notably the prospects offered by Members for the two new specialised committees. To obtain a background perception of the 'information position' of Members we asked: 'Speaking generally, do you think MPs *feel* they're adequately informed about the many administrative acts of the Government and civil service?' The results were as in Figure 15.

The general view is clear enough: only 8 per cent of our ninety-eight respondents believed that MPs as a whole feel adequately informed about Government administration and

149

only one Member felt unable to generalise in this way. The others replied 'no' in the manner shown in the Figure 15. Although their numbers involved are small, there was a tendency for the newer MPs to declare even more often than their longer-serving colleagues that Members as a whole feel inadequately informed: none of the 1966 entrants and only two of the 1964 entrants to whom we put this question disagreed with this view. Apart from this particularly strong opinion among the 1964-6 intakes, however, there was no general tendency for the belief that MPs do feel adequately informed to increase with longer service in the House.

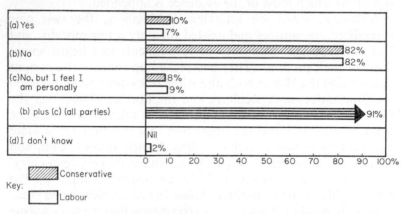

Figure 15. *Respondents' perception of whether MPs as a whole feel adequately informed on Government administration.* (See Appendix, Table 13.)

(N—95: 51 Conservatives and 44 Labour MPs)

Note: the three Liberal respondents replied 'No' and are included in the aggregate of 91 per cent.

A slight difference of perception was found between Members when considered by frontbench experience rather than by party. Slightly more of the backbenchers who lacked any frontbench experience said MPs did feel adequately informed compared with those with such experience (i.e. the ex-Ministers of either party and the current Conservative shadow-Ministers). But the group with frontbench experience was divided, internally, no current Conservative shadow-Minister, current Conservative whip, or ex-whip of any party saying that MPs do feel adequately informed (or even that, although MPs as a whole do not feel adequately informed, the respondent was himself satisfied with his own position). Somewhat against this simple negative perception, the twenty ex-Ministers of both parties were diverse in their reactions but only two of them thought that MPs felt adequately informed. Looking at graduates as a whole, rather more of them (86 per cent) than the non-graduates (78 per cent) replied that MPs had no such feeling. This massively negative answer on the state of MPs' knowledge about the work of the Government carried no significant party distinction: 82 per cent of both Labour and Conservative Members said MPs did not feel adequately informed. Naturally, Members would have differing notions of what constitutes 'adequate' information, but this almost unanimous negative reply suggests that (no matter how Members define the word) they were seeking an improvement in the situation. We therefore asked whether the further development of select committees (whether of the 'traditional' or 'specialised' types) was a scheme which appealed to our respondents. We wanted to take account in our responses of any Member who supported more activity by 'traditional' but not by 'specialised' select committees. We asked a question which would admit this viewpoint and proposed to code it separately. In fact (as Figure 16 shows) it did

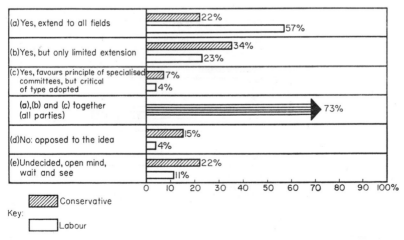

Key:
▨ Conservative
☐ Labour

By main party

(N—102: 55 Conservative and 47 Labour MPs)

Note: Two of the three Liberal respondents are included in the aggregate of 73 per cent.

Figure 16. Part One

151

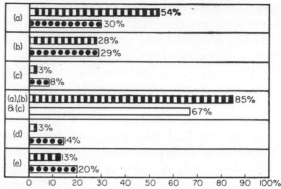

Key:
▮▮▮▮▮ Local Council experience

●●●● None

By local council experience

(N—105: 55 Conservative, 47 Labour and 3 Liberal MPs)

Figure 16. Part Two

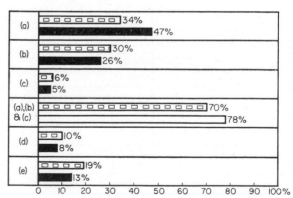

Key:
▢▢▢ Graduates

▬▬▬ Non—graduates

By university experience

(N—105: 55 Conservative, 47 Labour and 3 Liberal MPs)

Figure 16. Part Three

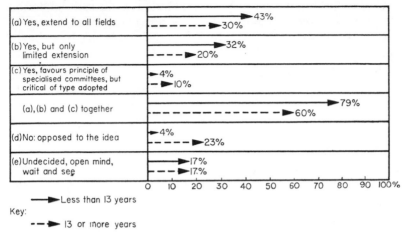

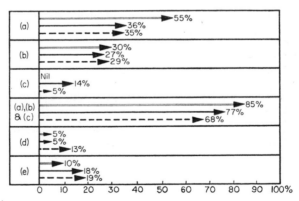

By length of service

(N—105: 55 Conservative, 47 Labour and 3 Liberal MPs)

Figure 16. Part Five

Figure 16. *Respondents' attitudes to extending the system of select committees on Government activity—by main party; local council experience; university education; and length of service.* (See Appendix, Table 14.)

153

not emerge, this question being answered exclusively in terms of the specialised committee idea. The actual question ran: 'And again, speaking generally, do you think more parliamentary select committees like Estimates or these two new ones on Science and Agriculture are going along the right lines to help with the problem?' The results were striking. Figure 16 sets out their analysis by party; by university education; by local council experience, and by length of service (both thirteen years and by 1964–6 entrants).

More than 70 per cent of respondents favoured the principle of specialised committees which can consider ministerial policy. A few disapproved of the design of the 1966 innovation while supporting the principle. The rest (just over two-thirds of the total) did not voice such criticism and favour the extension of such committees either across the board (39 per cent of the total) or to certain further fields (29 per cent of the total).

We did not record all Members' reasons for adopting the more cautious view that the extension of these committees should be limited: we can therefore offer only an impression on why they felt this way. It seemed to us that the most common reason being offered was the practical one of 'manning' a considerable number of new groups. These Members often stressed that although they wanted to see a wide range of these committees, they feared the value and penetration of their enquiries would suffer if a lot were established quickly and the available Members thus went on to committees less out of interest in their fields than from the pressures and persuasions of the whips. Other Members advanced the view that some policy fields (notably economic, foreign and defence policies) were too contentious, too confidential or simply too important to be legitimate subjects for specialised committees to study.

Not quite one Member in ten was against the idea of specialised committees and about one in six preferred not to express a view, nearly always pointing out that neither the Science nor Agriculture Committees had yet produced their first reports: these Members often stressed to us that they were quite pragmatic on the matter and would judge the first reports with an open mind. Now that several reports have emerged from these committees which have been welcomed by those Members with special interests in the fields covered, it may well be that at least some of these 16 per cent of our 1967 interviewees have since moved into the ranks of supporters; some, no doubt, have moved into opposition to these committees. Thus the opposition to the specialised committees among non-ministerial MPS was numerically very weak.

Important party differences emerged in the analysis (see Figure 16.1): in general there was greater support for some extension of specialised committees among Labour Members than Conservative (80 per cent as against 56 per cent) and more outright opposition among the latter. Similarly, over 20 per cent of the Conservatives were undecided compared with little more than one in ten Labour Members. Among those favouring specialised committees, Labour Members more often supported a general extension whereas Conservatives were more likely to prefer their extension to only a limited number of fields. This is part of a more basic Conservative-Labour distinction in which Labour Members appear, not surprisingly, to be more radical in their opinions and the extent of the changes they favour.

There was no survey made during the 1959–64 Parliament of Conservative Members' attitudes to specialised committees, so no formal comparison with our data is possible. We suspect, however, that there was then less support for the idea than we found in 1967. If 63 per cent of all Conservative MPS in that period had favoured some experiment (as they did in the summer of 1967) their Government would probably have allowed one. From the way Conservatives spoke to us on this topic we formed the strong impression that Conservative opinion has moved since their party left Government office and not merely as a reflection of the turnover in their ranks since before their 1964 defeat. Individual Conservative Members, some of whom were in the House well before 1964, had changed their minds (as some of them told us) and this new situation shows in our results.

Probably this shift was to some extent a partisan reaction to the Conservatives' new situation: new committees which will enquire into the activity of the Government may prove politically useful to the Opposition. But the fact that Conservatives were less enthusiastic about specialised committees in 1967 than were Labour Members suggests that, although the partisan consideration favouring the new departures may well have been present, a more general Conservative caution regarding innovations proved the stronger factor.

As a final party breakdown we may note that the Liberal Party is, of course, the one party which has for some years supported specialised committees as official policy: their 1966 manifesto proposed them on foreign, defence, economic and scientific affairs. Two of our three Liberal respondents favoured extending them to all fields while the third was undecided on such committees.

Looking at the graduates as a group, they were slightly less keen on the specialised committee idea than the non-graduates, not so much as a result of any hostility than from having a higher proportion undecided (see Figure 16.3). An analysis by Members' length of service produced a significant dichotomy at the point of thirteen years of service (see Figures 16.4 and 16.5). Strongest support for the new committees was found among the 1966 entrants of whom over half favoured a comprehensive extension and over four-fifths a comprehensive or limited extension, with only one Member opposing the idea altogether. This compared with just over one-third of 1964 entrants favouring a full coverage by these committees and about three-fifths of them wanting either a full or limited extension. Only just over one-third of Members who were in the House before 1964 favoured a general extension to all fields with almost as many again preferring the limited approach, thus producing about two-thirds as being in favour of some extension. The main difference between the 1964 entrants and their longer-serving colleagues was that a higher proportion of the longer-serving Members (one in twelve as against only one in twenty) opposed the specialised committee idea altogether.

Looking at these figures according to Members' frontbench experience, the strongest opposition to specialised committees came from ex-Ministers, a number of whom were particularly concerned with the effect on the 'doctrine' of ministerial responsibility and with the possible burden on Ministers of frequent attendance at committee meetings to give evidence. But when ex-Ministers did favour the idea they tended to favour a general, rather than a limited, extension. None of the current Conservative frontbench spokesmen whom we interviewed, on the other hand, were opposed to the principle of specialised committees, although they tended to favour only limited extensions. They are too small a group for anything more than tentative analysis. Backbenchers who had no frontbench experience tended to favour a general extension of these new committees.

Finally, we analysed these responses in terms of Members' experience as local government councillors or aldermen (Figure 16.2). There are strong historical and political reasons for doing so going back to Fred Jowett's 'municipal' scheme for parliamentary reform (which would have placed the management of Government Departments under parliamentary committees and which had a long run as a reformist proposal between the Wars). A Member of Parliament who has been involved with the committee system of local government may have significantly different views on parliamentary committee work.

We found that although the views of these Members who have sat on local councils is linked to their party allegiance (since considerably more Labour Members than Conservatives have this experience and since Labour Members are more favourable to these committees than Conservatives), the difference between the views of the two groups appearing in this Figure are not entirely attributable to their party. In particular, the division between those who favour a general extension and those who would prefer to see a limited extension of these committees does not run along party lines. There does appear to be some evidence that those Members who have actually shared responsibility for local government services through functional (or 'specialised') executive committees of their councils see value in having parliamentary committees with similarly devised ambits of interest (although not necessarily, of course, the same executive tasks). Only one Member with council experience was against the idea of specialised committees in the House. In our general context of identifying and studying the flow of 'information' to Members, we should note that the local council's main source of information on its own administration is the regular report to the full council of each functional committee, such as education or health. Leaving out of account the executive functions of local authority committees, one can still see the 'municipal' model which may be in some Members' minds on which they base their view that the House should receive regular reports from specialised committees, telling it about aspects of current Government administration. Such a view need not be a 'municipal' inspiration of course. As Professor Crick's study served to remind us, the Victorian

House was concerned to receive information through select committees in a purely 'parliamentary' manner (before the modern local government system existed). One could also support such a view by a study of certain overseas legislative practices—'committees' (as R. A. Butler liked to call them, in his classic dismissal of such doubly alien devices) '*à l'Americain*'.

MPs Talk about Specialised Committees

(In response to the question: 'Do you think more parliamentary select committees like . . . these two new ones on Science and Agriculture are going along the right lines to help with the problem [of informing MPs about Government administration]?')

'Yes. We should have a Defence specialised committee. The whips could select it to avoid possible security risks being chosen.' (Labour—ex-Minister)

'Yes. Very much. We're already going deeper into things than Questions allow, e.g. the Chairman of CEGB gave the Science Committee up-to-date costs on Hinckley 'B' which the minister said in reply to a Question were not available.' (Liberal)

'Too soon to be certain, but I think yes. They must be kept small: six to seven well-informed MPs are better than a large group. But these committees should not be used just to keep MPs busy.' (Labour)

'Whatever a committee's formal powers it's best to pitch in until you are stopped by someone. Cosiness could be a problem of the specialised committees: a little "secret" knowledge leads to sealed lips.' (Labour)

'Yes, let's have everything out in the open.' (Conservative)

'I'm a bit worried . . . the principle is that Ministers are responsible to the chamber of the House and to the mass media and no select committee should pre-empt this.' (Conservative)

'Yes, I am sympathetic. I used not to be.' (Conservative)

'No: they should keep off policies. Only the Public Accounts Committee is effective because it has an official and staff: the Nationalised Industries Committee should have the same.' (Conservative ex-Minister)

'I am very much in favour but they must evolve slowly.' (Conservative)

'Yes, there's not nearly enough pre-legislation discussion with the Government supporters, e.g. the Steel Bill, like much else, was offered on a "take it or leave it" basis.' (Labour)

'Yes, but it would be a mistake to assume we can go as far as the USA: the floor of the House is and still will be the place to bring the political challenge against the Government.' (Conservative)

'Yes, but we don't want "committee interests" developing which tend to remove issues from party politics.' (Conservative)

'I am against the formulation of public policy in collaboration with political opponents since *less* gets done that way rather than more. Having extra facts and figures may be a good thing.' (Labour)

'I am very much in favour since there are too many extra-parliamentary bodies which are dealing with information currently denied to MPs.' (Labour)

'Yes, we need several more at least. Civil servants should give factual evidence and Ministers policy evidence: MPs can tell the difference and would question each in an appropriate manner.' (Labour)

'I am not sure they are a good thing. I am not really in favour of developing Parliament since our Constitution is Cabinet dictatorship subject to instant dismissal.' (Conservative ex-Minister)

'No, they are a waste of time: I don't see the point since they will gather no extra information one doesn't get now in the chamber itself.' (Conservative)

'Yes, I strongly favour them and don't mind if the Agriculture Committee is rather anti-Common Market when I am not: let one hundred flowers bloom.' (Labour)

'Yes, I support a Defence Committee although Ministers are reluctant. If the whips selected the Defence Committee it would get round the security problem by keeping out the Labour leftists.' (Conservative)

'The principle of them doesn't offend me because the Government is not obliged to answer, especially in public sessions: Mr Dulles once told me he'd had 185 sessions with congressional committees in one year which would be intolerable.' (Conservative ex-Minister)

'Yes, I welcome them if it helps Members get out and about, away from the confined Westminster atmosphere.' (Conservative)

'No, they will produce no new information but merely weaken the Executive: I am quite prepared to see any Government made to look foolish, but I am strongly against weakening the Executive.' (Conservative)

'I am not happy unless they have American organisational powers and a seniority rule since this works against patronage and placemanship.' (Labour).

'I was rather against at first, but now feel a long, continuing look, especially on agriculture, would be a considerable help.' (Conservative)

'They should not be extended to controversial issues since this would increase the number of coalitionites.' (Labour)

'You'll soon have so many committees that only the deadbeats can be found to man them.' (Conservative ex-Minister)

(ii) *Developments since 1967*

Rather more than two further parliamentary sessions will have elapsed between the gathering of our responses from Members in the summer of 1967 and the publication of this study. In this period the choppy water in which the Agricultural Committee already found itself in July 1967 has spread to other committees and the Agriculture Committee itself has, indeed, disappeared. Some observers believe that this, the major 'Crossman reform' of 1966 has begun to list badly and may yet sink. A brief résumé of events may help to bring the survey results of the previous section of this chapter into a 1970 focus.

The Agriculture Committee pursued its wish to visit Brussels in connection with its enquiry into the relationship of the Ministry's work to the British application to EEC and a compromise was reached with the Government on the form which this trip

160

would take. In its first report the Committee recounted its side of the dispute and criticised the Government. Its substantive report on British agriculture and the EEC did not become an open issue in its own right.

The Government's reaction to this stormy first year of the Committee's life was to propose at the beginning of the 1967–8 session that the House increase the Committee's size from sixteen to twenty-five members, thereby, perhaps, diluting its militant flavour. One of the former sixteen members, John Mackintosh (Labour Member for Berwick and East Lothian) has recounted the result: '. . . at the first meeting, the new members were asked if they had actively sought to be included. The reply was that the whips had pressganged them. So they agreed, with one exception, to stay away, leaving the original group to continue with the work.'[1] The Committee proceeded to its second main enquiry, agricultural import-saving, which may also be seen as a rather controversial matter of Government policy, although not one of the two subjects (EEC and the British annual farm price review) which the then Minister of Agriculture, Fred Peart, was said to have indicated to the Committee would be unacceptable to him as subjects for their enquiries.

A year later, at the start of the 1968–9 session, the Government moved against the Committee. On November 7, 1968, the Government (with Mr Peart now serving as its Leader of the House) announced the intention to re-appoint the Committee's twenty-five formal members but only for the remaining few weeks of 1968, when the Committee would die.[2] Following protests that work in progress could not be completed within this period, the Government granted a two-month reprieve. The Committee thus lasted rather longer than two years.

The other original committee, on Science and Technology, avoided major disputes with the Government, although its work has involved delicate and important policy matters. Its first major enquiry concerned the future technical and commercial policies of the atomic reactor industry in which the

[1] John Mackintosh, 'The Failure of a Reform: MPs' Special Committees', in *New Society*, November 28, 1968. This alleged packing of the Agriculture Committee was mentioned, but not denied, in an attack on Mr Mackintosh's article by a fellow Labour member of the former committee, Alfred Morris (*Sunday Times*, February 16, 1969).

[2] H.C. 772, c. 1205–12 (November 7, 1968).

6   161

Government (notably through the UK Atomic Energy Authority) is, of course, the major element. The Committee made majority recommendations in its first report which, although very controversial at the administrative and technical level, are not matters of major party dispute.

During the course of this atomic energy enquiry, the Government moved that the House refer to the Science Committee the matter of coastal pollution and the official actions to combat the oil from the wreck of the *Torrey Canyon*. Not wishing to see its work on atomic reactors interrupted, the Committee set up a sub-committee on the new topic (a technique it was later to develop until, by January 1969, it had four). This sub-committee proceeded to prepare a very critical report on the *Torrey Canyon*. Although the Government may well regard arguments over this chapter of its record as being more administrative and technical than of a 'policy' nature, it is ironical that the one report to date from a specialised committee which has offered a detailed attack on an aspect of the Government's performance came from the most settled and secure of the new committees. Moreover, this report was called for by the Government itself, possibly against the will of the Committee (which was concerned not to be diverted from its major enquiry on atomic reactors by a Government-allotted task not of its own choosing).

The coastal pollution report does not appear to have disturbed good relations between the Science Committee and the Government. As its second major enquiry (following the controversial but not highly partisan report on atomic reactors) the Committee chose scientific and research establishments run by the Ministry of Defence, including such secret establishments as the chemical and biological warfare stations at Porton Down, Wiltshire and the underwater weapons centre at Portland.

The third of the specialised committees (on the work of the Department of Education and Science) had a quiet first session investigating Her Majesty's Inspectorate of Schools, although it produced a fairly bold report. The fear that the Government's doubts and hostilities to specialised committees ran beyond the Agriculture Committee developed in November 1968, when the Government moved to re-appoint the Education Committee. The proposed terms of reference stated that the Committee should report to the House 'this session' rather than the usual phrase 'to report from time to time'. Members asked whether this indicated that the Government intended to kill off the Education Committee in October 1969 after a two-year career, along the lines of the Agriculture Committee. The Minister would not say,[1] although it later became clear that a limited life for the Education Committee was indeed intended.

Since the original two specialised committees were set up by Mr Crossman, as Leader of the House, in December 1966 the Government has been under various pressures from Members (mainly Labour) to allow additional groups to function: the regional problems of East Anglia and of northern England have been nominated and pressure for a specialised committee on Scottish affairs (presumably in addition to the existing Scottish Grand Committee which is a debating committee) continued until the Government granted a Scottish Committee in early 1969. At the same time, a new committee on Overseas Aid and Development was announced by Mr Peart, apparently as a substitute for the Agriculture group. A specialised Committee on Race Relations and Immigration had been established earlier in the 1968–9 session as a by-product of the Government's emergency legislation on Kenyan immigration in the previous session.

A word should be added on the affairs of two other select committees—the Nationalised Industries Committee and the new select committee on the work of the Parliamentary Commissioner for Administration or 'Ombudsman'. The PCA does not have legal authority to question the 'merits' of an official decision and may report to his select committee on only those aspects of cases which appear to suggest maladministration. This is broadly conceived as any illegal or improper conduct by officials and any failure to follow the normal rules and procedures. The PCA's first clear attempt to establish and criticise maladministration on a significant matter concerned a small group's long-standing claims to compensation as former concentration-camp victims.

For years the Foreign Office (which administered these funds from the West German Government) held that these claimants had been confined, not within Sachsenhausen camp itself, but in an annexe which had afforded significantly different conditions. Upon representations from Airey Neave (Conservative

[1] H.C. 773, c. 537–8 (November 14, 1968).

163

Member for Abingdon) the PCA's investigation led to his official view (sustained by his Select Committee) that Foreign Office officials had not been as open to information and representations on the matter as normal standards require. The matter came to the House and flared briefly when the Foreign Secretary, George Brown, showed anger at some Members' reluctance to view his assertion of 'ministerial responsibility' on the Foreign Office's decision not to pay compensation as the last word on the subject, even though he had read all the papers himself and had reluctantly concurred in the established policy. As this Select Committee was the second to run against Mr Brown on matters of ministerial responsibility in just over twelve months, it may be necessary to count his attitude and personality as a significant factor in the narrative of these committees' careers in the 1967–9 period.

Mr Brown left the Government soon after his speech on the Sachsenhausen affair and one cannot, of course, know whether that case contributed to any general hostility to select committee activity in ministerial or senior official circles. The campaign by the Nationalised Industries Committee to broaden its terms of reference was less dramatic than the brief Sachsenhausen case and ended, after protracted negotiations, in a compromise. The Select Committee, led by its Labour chairman, Ian Mikardo (Poplar) and its Conservative vice-chairman, Claude Lancaster (South Fylde) wanted to extend its ambit to cover not only the traditional list of 'nationalised industries', run by public corporations, but also all other commercially-involved bodies over which the Government has actual or potential control. The Committee did not wish to assert claims over any organisation whose public nature already made it subject to scrutiny by other House committees such as Estimates or Public Accounts. Eleven bodies, notably the Independent Television Authority and the (formally 'nationalised') Bank of England, were claimed for their scrutiny by the Select Committee. When negotiation was at last complete, the Government moved, in February 1969, to reappoint the Nationalised Industries Committee with new terms. Authority to investigate the ITA, Cable and Wireless Ltd, and the administrative levels of the work of the Bank and of its relationship to the Treasury was granted; scrutiny of British Petroleum and three firms in the aviation field was denied. Messrs Mikardo and Lancaster tried to substitute for the Government's careful formula a grant of authority to their select committee to investigate 'other bodies in which the state has a controlling interest', but were defeated on a division.

If we set these events of the period between July 1967 and early 1969 against our survey's responses from Members on the general subject of specialised committees we may be led to ask several questions. Why has a Labour Government been able to kill a specialised committee to which it was hostile, when opinion among Labour backbenchers was found by our survey to be so favourable? A lot of these Labour Members supported not only the general idea of specialised committees but declared they should be established across the board. Why has the Nationalised Industries Committee obtained only about half of what it claimed as its extended territory? If the specialised committee idea has turned sour, how could it have done so against the background of positive support shown in our 1967 data?

If this tenor of questioning is allowed, for a moment, to stand unchallenged one can offer fairly obvious responses. It may be, for example, that, although the Members who gave us these responses in 1967 were genuinely keen on the idea of specialised committees they did not consider them salient issues in their parliamentary working lives; perhaps the newer Labour Members were moved by an enthusiasm which has since abated—and (on the demise of the Agriculture Committee) some Members on all sides may feel that the Committee was reckless and thus paid the price. If it is assumed that Ministers have cracked down on the specialised committees since 1967 in exactly the way they wanted, then it would seem either that the expressions of enthusiasm for the committees which we recorded in 1967 were insincere or that the Government has ridden roughshod over both Labour backbench views and general House opinion and has done so without serious challenge on the subject.

In fact, we would question the assumption that Government action on these committees has been untouched by the need to compromise. Outside observers cannot know for certain, but it would be, at the least, unusual if the Government could have acted quite freely in this area of its parliamentary relations. It is

165

at least possible that hostile Ministers see the steps taken by the Government as the best they can expect in a House which offers broad support to the idea of a more vigorous committee system.

Perhaps the questions on these events since 1967 should, in fact, be reversed. Why did the Government try to 'pack' the Agriculture Committee as a means of achieving a more docile group which could have been allowed to survive? Why did the Nationalised Industries Committee get about half of what it wanted and why did the Home Secretary, Mr Callaghan, feel that an offer to the House of a new specialised committee on race relations would aid the passage of his legislation to curb Kenyan immigration? The perspective one adopts must depend on one's estimate of what the Government would have liked to do in this field if opinion among its supporters had been different from the actual situation. We would claim to have caught accurately in our survey the main features, at least of that positive attitude among Members towards specialised committees.

This is not to say that opinion among both Labour and Conservative MPs in 1969 is the same as that shown in our data. Only a re-examination of our sampled Members would establish these facts, but we would speculate that our respondents have developed more particular opinions on the different aspects of specialised committees and the controversies concerning them. Thus a Member may not be greatly disturbed by the demise of the Agriculture or Education Committee, nor greatly surprised by the Government's ability to have its way in the division lobby on virtually any issue it chooses to pursue that far: he may, however, be as keen a supporter of the idea of policy-oriented select committees as he was in 1967 and may, for example, have developed a strong admiration for the work of the Science and Technology Committee.

As the specialised committees have become part of the regular parliamentary process, it is likely that Members' views have diversified away from the inevitably rather general and hypothetical positions which they adopted during our interviews in 1967. Concluding our speculation, it seems to us that Members will now adopt a pragmatic view of these committees' affairs and willingly support Government curbs on their activity only when a case can be made by Ministers in terms of the accepted current

166

conventions of the relationship of the House to the Government. If, for example, the Government moved in 1970 to abolish the Science Committee on what appeared to be merely general grounds that the specialised committee 'experiment' had 'failed', there would, we suggest, be a far greater row than followed the verdict against the other committees. Some of this hostility would flow from the Opposition front bench, as the Science Committee was the only one in which the Opposition leadership was positively interested during the negotations on this subject between the main parties in the summer of 1966. The reaction from the backbenches of both parties would probably also be strong, however, because of the style and dedication of the Science group and the widespread view that its field stands in need of much more illumination in the minds of Members and the public.

As well as political troubles with the Government, some specialised committees have had other difficulties—largely shared with the established select committees. Problems of 'manning' and obtaining a quorum at meetings are considerable, although this latter point is more serious for some of the established select committees (the Estimates Committee's various meetings attract on average, only about one-third attendance).

Several Ministers have appeared before specialised committees to make statements and respond to questions. This exercise has so far avoided the whips entering into the picture, probably because no Minister has yet been involved in a major altercation when performing this task. MPs will, no doubt, continue to look to the official or outside expert witnesses to give them the solid information they seek, while the Minister deals with the broader sweep of political or administrative policies. The forebodings of Herbert Bowden, when Leader of the House, that Ministers would undergo excessive political strain when appearing before a small and fairly well-informed committee of backbenchers have not, so far, materialised: Ministers can, on the whole, look after themselves. They can also stand firm, as when Cledwyn Hughes, the Minister of Agriculture, declined to tell the Agriculture Committee which committee of the Cabinet dealt with his Ministry's affairs. It should be remembered, however, that it has never been part of the case for establishing specialised committees that they would discover and reveal state secrets.

CHAPTER IV

THE MEMBER'S VIEW OF HIS
CONSTITUENCY

FOREWORD

In this chapter we present those findings from our survey which describe the flow of information to the Member from his constituency and the local communities which it contains. First, however, we set out a background of some survey knowledge of the British public's apparent general attitudes towards politics and elected political leaders. How people feel about these things will obviously help to shape the behaviour of the politicians who deal with public affairs: if the British public appears to feel familiar and confident towards the country's political processes it is likely that they will freely call on their representatives to assist them to press any claim they may have on the authorities. We shall then approach the constituency aspects of the Member's overall need for information on public affairs by two avenues. The first is his postbag of letters and other communications coming from his constituency, taken together with his meetings with constituents who attend any regular 'surgery' or 'advice bureau' he may hold. After presenting our survey findings on Members' estimates of their constituency postbag and their reports of their surgeries we shall discuss the modern Member's so-called 'welfare officer' role. The second avenue is his links with local institutions which may serve as channels of more general information on what is going on in the constituency—his local political party supporters, local authorities and the local newspapers. Finally, we add a note on the MP who becomes involved with a local public issue.

1. WHAT DO THE BRITISH EXPECT?

A BACKGROUND NOTE

In 1963 two American political scientists, Gabriel Almond and Sidney Verba, published the results of a major British attitude survey conducted for them by Research Services Ltd as part of a five-nation study, *The Civic Culture*.[1] The regional and social class distribution of approximately 1,000 people interviewed (59 per cent of the sample) conformed closely to the national pattern. They were asked first, 'About how much effect do you think the national Government in London . . . has on your day-to-day life?' They replied: 33 per cent 'Great', 40 per cent 'Some', and 23 per cent 'None', thus showing that, for all their geographical compactness and political and cultural homogeneity, they had rather less belief in the Government's importance to themselves than the American respondents who are spread over a vast and federally governed country. But America apart, Britain ranked quite highly among the five countries on this point and similar results occurred in the case of local government. As to whether the national Government (however close its doings are felt to be one's day-to-day life) is a beneficial device, three-quarters of the British supported the statement that, 'Our national Government improves conditions'. Despite this favourable verdict the British respondents claimed to follow British affairs through newspapers and broadcasting less than some other countries; the British buy more newspapers than other nations but political fare in the most popular ones is strictly limited.

Asked what things, taken from a list, made them feel proud of Britain, these people chose 'Governmental and political institutions' comparatively often (46 per cent, compared with the Americans' 85 per cent and the other countries' lower figures) and 'social legislation' fairly often (18 per cent, the highest return on five countries). Pride in these things rose with a person's education. This feeling of pride was, as it were, put to the test when the respondents were asked whether they expected their British Government officials and policemen to treat them equally (as compared with any other citizen) and with considerateness (by asking, for example, to hear their side of the story or pointing out regulations fairly and so on). Imaginary examples of visiting the tax office or being accused of a motoring offence were offered. The British showed the greatest expectation (over 80 per cent) of both equal and considerate treatment to themselves and other citizens from both central or

[1] G. Almond and S. Verba, *The Civic Culture: Political Attitudes and Democracy in Five Nations*, Princeton University Press, 1963.

169

local government officials and from the police, the police rating even higher than the officials. The most educated respondents had the highest expectations, although the differences among the British were very small and over 80 per cent of each group (elementary, secondary and university) expected equal treatment from officials and police. They were slightly less sure about considerate treatment, but still ended with an average of 78 per cent of all three educational groups in the four cases of equal and considerate treatment by both officials and police.

People with these expectations are presumably likely to assert themselves when dealing with the authorities on personal matters like taxes and minor offences. Will they be equally moved on a matter of public interest? Almond and Verba asked them to imagine a proposal being considered by the House of Commons (or by the local authority) which they felt to be unjust and harmful: what did they expect they could do?; would they expect to succeed?; how likely was it that they would actually try? The British were comparatively confident that they could and would try to influence affairs if they felt strongly, especially on a local authority issue where more than three people in four felt they could do something. But confidence fell away on national matters to only 57 per cent who felt able to act on both local and national levels. There was a correlation between these people and those respondents who had actually become involved in some issue in the past: it would be important to know exactly what the others in this confident group—those who were confident but lacked personal experience —thought they could do, since any general rosy optimism could quickly disappear at the first setback. For example, their idea of 'doing something' may be merely to sign a stereotype letter, or even just a petition, to their MP with no wish to go further when that appeared to have no affect.

An aggrieved or upset citizen can attempt two kinds of action: gathering support and co-operation from others, or acting alone. Almond and Verba found that on both local and national matters very few respondents in any country rated the existing, formal organs (such as the trade union, church or professional groups) to which they already belonged very highly for this purpose: the *ad hoc* group, public meeting, petitition or group letter to the authorities was far more popular. On national political matters, the American and British respondents emphasised the appeal to the political leader (Congressman or MP) or to the Press (not separated out). The spread of respondents' beliefs that they could influence unjust or harmful Government policies if they tried between the least and the best educated groups was smallest (14 per cent spread) in Britain out of the five countries and greatest in America (35 per cent)— a further indicator of the comparative homogeneity of the British in these matters, which must have its effects on the attitude to the public of both politicians and permanent officials.

These British respondents seem clearly to be fairly proud of their 'governmental and political institutions' and to expect proper treatment by the authorities. They feel they could, if necessary, take part in a local public issue, and less commonly, in a national one too. They have a strong preference for taking their views to elected officers (local councillors and MPs) and to the local and national newspapers. Given this background, the British MP can expect to be kept fairly busy. But we should remember that the above results, while true for the nation as a whole, do contain significant differences of outlook as between working class and middle class citizens, and that this image of the generally optimistic and confident person requires closer scrutiny to perceive even the comparatively modest differences between British social groups.[1]

In 1968, the British Gallup Poll conducted an enquiry for the *Daily Telegraph* with apparently different results. A sample of people were asked, 'Do people like yourself have enough say or not enough say in the way the Government runs the country?' 68 per cent said 'Not enough', 19 per cent 'Enough', and 13 per cent 'Don't know'. (There was no provision for the reply 'Too much'.) This response was the highest of the list which included nationalised industries and local government (which followed with virtually the same returns of 67 per cent and 64 per cent). Other fields, in descending order of the dissatisfied answer ('Not enough') were BBC and ITV television programme outputs, childrens' schooling, work conditions, trade unions, shops, banks, etc., newspapers' output and employers' policies.[2]

[1] Almond and Verba's questions to British people in their feelings of competence to join in a public issue which roused them were repeated by Eric Nordlinger whose *The Working Class Tories*, MacGibbon and Kee, 1967, contains confirmatory results.

[2] Windsor Davies, 'The gap between "Them" and "Us"', *Daily Telegraph*, July 13, 1968.

It is possible to reconcile, at least in part, the optimistic and confident air of the responses to the 1963 study with the alienated and dissatisfied tone of Gallup's 1968 poll without necessarily claiming that there was no change at all in British politics and people's perception of the system during the intervening years. Granted that the pressure for more 'participation'—in Gallup's words, for 'more say' by 'people like ourselves'—may well have increased between these two dates, we should nevertheless note that the two polls did not ask quite the same thing of their respondents. It is quite possible for a person to declare that he could, if the need arose, participate with some effect on a local policy issue while maintaining that people like himself are not normally given enough say in the way local councils handle things. This mental division between normal times and crises or challenges to his own interest is presumably enforced by his strong belief that if he does get involved the paid officials will treat him equally and probably fairly or considerately as well.

The Member of Parliament may, in these circumstances, receive even more complaints and cases since the background of acceptance of the political system (which would itself bring work to him as an important feature of that system) is overlaid with dissatisfaction at the lack of participation. If government is felt to be important, but distant and vague, the MP is likely to be a target for claims since he is fully official, yet rather closer to people (or at least more visible to them). He is one single person who carries the official keys to all the labyrinthine suites and wings of the mansion of public authority. As Ronald Butt puts it, one of the great advantages of the MP is his ambivalent position as an 'insider' who is also an 'outsider'.[1]

[1] Ronald Butt, *The Power of Parliament*, Constable, 2nd (rev.) ed., 1969, p. 338.

THE 'WELFARE ROLE'

2. CONSTITUENCY POSTBAGS AND SURGERIES

We have seen that, according to the Almond and Verba survey of 1963, the British people often do feel competent to raise their views on a problem or issue, and have a preference for doing so with an elected representative such as a councillor or MP. How they do this may well depend on their normal habits and customs, some writing a letter while others try to speak to the representative and explain matters personally. The letters received by an MP from his constituents are obviously likely to prove a principal source of his information on both the views and affairs of his constituents and perhaps, by inference, on those of people all over the country.

We sought to establish first the volume of post which each interviewed Member estimated he received from his constituency in normal circumstances, during an average week. We then asked how much of his parliamentary time was taken in dealing with all of his post, including non-constituency letters; (we could not, unfortunately, establish the time spent by Members on only their constituency post). We then asked: 'What do you think about spending this amount of your parliamentary time in this way?' The answers to this open-ended question almost entirely revolved around the idea of the modern Member being seen by the public as a 'welfare officer' or 'case worker' to whom they can take their problems or complaints concerning public authorities of all kinds, or, sometimes, concerning private firms or bodies, their neighbours, or their own family.

We present first our findings and a discussion on the letters from Members' own constituencies and follow with a similar treatment of surgeries. We then present our respondents' opinions on the 'welfare officer' role and a discussion of this side of Members' duties, based on what they think about spending the amount of time they do in dealing with their postbags.

'First, on the post you receive as an MP ... How many letters do you receive from constituency sources (i.e. individual constituents, firms and organisations in the constituency) in an average week?'

Looking first at the total figures for all parties, only about one Member in ten among our respondents claimed to receive either less than 25 or more than 100 letters per average week from their constituency. Just over 80 per cent said they received less than 75, and over half said they got less than 50. There are some differences between the parties; approximately the same proportion receive less than 50 constituency letters per week but more Labour MPs receive between 50 and 74, while more Conservatives get 75 or more. These differences are not great, and may be attributable to factors other than party label.

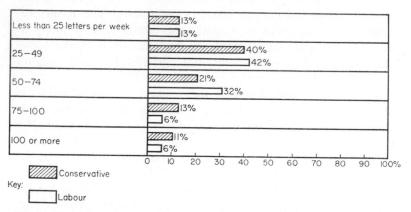

Figure 17. *Respondents' estimates of the average weekly number of letters received from their constituencies.* (See Appendix, Table 15.)

(N—99 (excluding 5 'Don't know's): 52 Conservative and 47 Labour MPS)

One such factor is the differing sizes of Members' electorates. As is to be expected the size of an MP's electorate does affect the volume of his constituency postbag. As Figure 18 shows, all four Members with electorates of fewer than 40,000 received less than fifty letters per week, whereas those with much larger electorates were rather more likely to appear in the higher bracket. But other factors were involved: the urban Members claimed to receive fewer letters than those representing rural seats, despite the fact that the electoral system has deliberately made rural constituencies less populous (traditionally because of the view that more difficult communications in country areas entitles their inhabitants to a rather more generous allocation of MPS). (See Appendix, Table 17.)

174

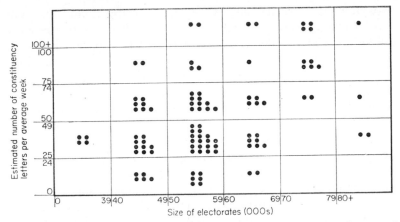

Figure 18. *Comparison of estimated weekly number of constituency letters and the size of respondents' electorates.* (See Appendix, Table 16.)

(N—101: 52 Conservative, 47 Labour and 2 Liberal MPs)

Note: Each dot represents a Member.

Having looked at party label, size of electorate and the rural-urban division in an attempt to discern a pattern within our Members' estimates of constituency postbags, we turned to two other possible factors: the size of their majority and their length of service in the House. Both these scales showed a wide dispersion among Members in the same postbag brackets for both majority size and length of service. Neither showed any clear correlation with the Members' estimates on constituency postbags. This may seem rather surprising, since it is widely thought that newer MPs try to 'dig themselves in' to a seat, especially when their majority is precarious. Whether Members do appear to think in these terms we shall consider below, when seeking a pattern in these findings on constituency postbags in the context of the 'welfare officer' role of Members of Parliament.

In our examination of Members' postbags (see page 50, footnote 2) we noticed that every one of a very varied group of constituencies produced more letters raising personal cases and problems than offered opinions on local or national issues. These personal case letters also exceeded, in each instance, the number of letters of all kinds received by the Member from outside his constituency. The most common personal cases were about social security and housing, especially in mainly

175

working class constituencies. Where housing conditions and overcrowding were particularly bad there was no greater flow of letters and people who were apparently experiencing such conditions did not figure prominently, let alone proportionately, in the Member's postbag. Almost all of the letters we saw were very articulate and some complaints did not involve personal deprivation such as over-crowding but rather the delay in fitting a telephone or the refusal of planning permission on land owned by the constituent. From what we saw it would seem that writing to one's MP is primarily a middle-class custom and that working class people write only under grave provocation, preferring if possible to visit the Member's surgery.

Turning now to consider the characteristics of the Members' estimates of postbag volumes presented above in Figures 17 and 18, we may first ask whether one reason why urban Members, as a group, claim to get somewhat less constituency post than rural Members is the greater frequency with which urban Members offer themselves at surgeries. Labour Members, as a group, also do this more often than the Conservatives, and nearly all Labour Members sit for urban seats (forty-four out of fifty-two among our respondents). A further small influence in this direction may be the fact that the urban constituents of London seats can and do telephone their Member at the House without great expense, or go and seek him out there, rather than write a letter.

The constituency postbag is a topic, like many others in our survey, which we are looking at through only the Member's eyes; we have no figures on what kinds of constituent write most or least letters to their MP, since we lacked the resources to interview a representative sample of constituents. We were offered a few informal impressions by Members, such as the view that working class country people are less ready to write to their MP than similar people in towns. Several Members sitting for constituencies which are, in whole or part, deeply rural, mentioned 'rural illiteracy', by which they mean that village and farm folk are, in their experience, particularly reluctant to take up the pen and thus particularly glad to tell their Member their troubles at his surgery or at some less formal moment when they meet. At the same time, we have some reason, based on our impressions when analysing twenty actual postbags, to believe that the rural or semi-rural 'middle classes' (that is, in modern usage, everyone except the working class) are so comparatively prone to write to their MP that their efforts rather more than make up for the rural working class and place rural Members under a generally rather heavier burden than urban Members. There are quite a few rural seats with a traditional attraction for retired middle class people who may be the source of some of this effect. The 'literate retired' are not confined to rural areas, of course: several Conservatives sitting for resort and spa towns and prosperous city suburbs particularly mentioned this element while giving us rather high estimates of constituency postbag figures. 'I have a highly literate constituency' ... 'nothing much else to do but write letters' ... 'mine is a very good quality constituency', were among the comments we had. Civil service, colonial and military pensions, plus the 'animal lobby' were said to be prominent features of this kind of correspondence.

A second question deserving some thought is the lack of a common pattern of constituency post among marginal, safe, new and established Members respectively, and we may ask whether 1964 and 1966 entrants, particularly, were not 'digging themselves in', during the early summer of 1967 when we spoke to them, by the traditional means of serving both constituents and constituency, and getting publicity credit for it in the local newspaper. This does, of course, go on. One 1964 Labour entrant was willing to describe his careful plans for relating his Westminster activity to his constituency's newspaper's deadline; another newcomer allowed his co-partisan fellow-newcomer, sitting for a seat which also fell within his local newspaper's circulation area, to step forward and take the lion's share of local publicity to help him become established in his extremely marginal seat. At least two of our interviewed Members are convinced that they held on to their seats in the elections of 1959 and 1964, when their respective parties did badly, because of the personal reputation for 'welfare' they had built up in their constituencies. And although these beliefs may well be irrational (and younger Members seem to have a greater awareness of the impersonal swings which electoral studies have shown to be the dominant elements of general elections) no Member, however well-versed in psephology, would deny that his personal reputation could, theoretically, tip the scale in his favour. In 1966 seven Labour and nine Conservative Members were elected with fewer than the 500 votes proverbially set as the limit of any candidate's 'personal vote' serving as their majority. The numerically largest of these sixteen majorities (George Younger's Conservative majority of 484 in a straight fight at Ayr) constituted only 1·2 per cent of the total poll. One or two of these younger Members told us in the privacy of our interviews that they certainly were deliberately 'digging in' by the well-tried methods of 'welfare officer' work and local press publicity, when they would find it politically embarrassing to declare this publicly and intellectually dubious to claim that they would have any real chance of 'beating the swing' at the next election, if it moves against their party. It is not only marginal new Members who feel a need to establish themselves in their seats: younger Members of both parties (more often Conservatives) who hold safe seats, told us privately that they would like to build up a good credit balance of personal and constituency service to draw on when they disagree with elements in their local party on a bitter national issue. The memory of Nigel Nicolson, pushed out of a safe Conservative seat after opposing capital punishment and the Suez invasion, lives on. As one younger Conservative in a safe seat put it: 'My taking a firm stand against the warble fly may help me to take a similar attitude to Ian Smith.'

Whether a Member trying to become known and accepted is in a marginal or a safe seat, his main device is personal contact with people when he can show interest and concern in their lives and problems. The idea of a Member deliberately building up his constituency postbag must imply that he can generate letters from constituents if he wants to, or, alternatively, by inference, discourage them. Getting about in the constituency (with the local Press photographer following) and writing in, or being written about in, the local paper, are the obvious ways. Publicly inviting letters and surgery visits, is, of course, an even stronger course. One new Member displayed a poster in his constituency: 'In Trouble? Ring or Write to X', and, at about the same time, when making a regional broadcast on a certain topic, invited listeners (not just his constituents) to write to him if they had a problem in that field. Between them, these two actions led to a five-fold increase in his mail which went well outside the topic specified in the broadcast, and which lasted for a considerable time.

Such deliberate generation of mail is rare and is usually linked to a Member's active concern to gather evidence, or demonstrate popular support, on a national political issue of the kind we discussed in Chapter II. We found only one Member in each main party among our 111 interviewees who said they had deliberately generated constituency mail in an attempt to bolster their electoral position. They are the two Members mentioned above who said that their bacon was saved by this device in the elections of 1959 and 1964. A much more common attitude which we discerned during both the interviews and our work on postbag analysis is that, whereas the Member does not look for extra constituency correspondence, he does what he is asked as best he can, in the knowledge that his letters to constituents may pass from hand to hand and the news of his helpfulness may spread through family, neighbours, local pub, and factory canteen, until dozens of other people know something of it.

Most Members do not deal with 'personal case' correspondence from outside their own constituency: a long-standing convention exists whereby such letters are passed to the writer's own Member, although this is often ignored when the Member addressed is glad to help directly, or the writer mentions a personal or party dislike of his own Member. Among our interviewees, one Labour newcomer and one established Conservative mentioned that they received personal cases from their party's supporters in neighbouring seats held by the other side, who want to deal with one of 'their own' Members. One long-established Labour Member said he got such letters from people who lived in the same Conservative constituency as himself, and who saw him as a 'shadow Member'. Liberal Members receive extra post of this kind, including the personal case work, from Liberal supporters throughout the country; those we spoke to agreed it formed an extra burden, although a useful source of knowledge on affairs and problems in parts of the country which lack a Liberal representative. Another small group who attract a national correspondence on personal problems are the 'public figures' among MPs—the television stars, newspaper columnists and journalists, and ex-Ministers. We did not meet enough of these either in our interviews or during our postbag analyses, to gather how they reacted to this aspect of fame. It is possible they distinguish in their minds

179

between getting letters of opinion (which indicate their effectiveness as communicators even if their correspondents do not always agree with them) and personal case letters which ought strictly to be directed to the writer's own Member. We mention these few 'star' MPs as they are good examples of the only explanation of the pattern of Member's constituency post that offers itself—that it is Members' individual personalities and the conduct which flows from them, which determines the level of their constituency post. We have seen that party, size of electorate, urban or rural character have only partial influence with a widespread fluctuation between individuals in each case; we found marginality and length of service similarly unhelpful. It is plainly possible both to build up and to minimise constituency correspondence compared with any existing base. A Member can develop his surgery work in addition to receiving letters, or try to keep both written and oral communications from his constituents down to the minimum level possible, given his constituency's social characteristics.

It is important to note that there is no logical difference between constituents with problems of various kinds first approaching their Member by letter or telephone on the one hand, and by turning up at his surgery on the other. It may be true that better educated constituents will tend to write a letter while people who prefer to explain their problems orally (perhaps from a lack of self-confidence in their letter-writing) will tend to come to the surgery, but there must be many cases where the choice of approach to the Member is random as between these two courses. Quite often, Members receive either a brief note from a constituent saying he has a case to raise and asking to meet him, or a long, but none too clear, letter setting out the story as seen by the constituent, and asking for the Member's help. In either case, the Member will ask the person to attend during or just after normal surgery hours to hear the story and to try to unravel it if necessary. It would be easy to understand why the Member often tries to question a constituent for himself in as systematic a way as possible to sort out the facts of a case presented to him in the style of this imaginary, but fairly typical, example of a letter to a Labour Member which concerns a dispute or misunderstanding between a private landlord and his statutory tenant:

Dear Sir,

I hope you will allow me to write to you as a lifelong resident of the town and who has been in the union and dyed-in-the-wool Labour all my life and so are my children too because this new landlord is enough to make a saint swear and my wife gets so worried every time they send this chap round to find fault and it upsets her so she worries about the doctor telling her to take it easy as well as the thing about the house and the rent.

The rent tribunal told us in 1948 and we went to them again about six year ago that we were in the right about them putting in a larder but now he says it's an extra 2/6d a week for the bath although we said years back we would take on the decorating side if they'd put us in the bathroom.

And now this new chap he's a bit more civil than the other one was says it's all to do with a letter we got last Christmas from a solicitor but we never did and we've got no dog to eat the letters up before we get to them. So please help me tell this new company what I told the other landlord about this because if it goes on like this my wife can't stand it and I don't know what'll happen.

We defined the surgery as a regular, open session at which the Member makes himself available to anyone without a prior arrangement being necessary; we take regularity and the possibility of talking to the Member without notice as the mark of a true surgery, since some Members often see people in their constituency, but only by appointment, usually following an advance to the Member by letter or via his agent. These arranged interviews often take place in the constituent's home, which Members who adopt this practice often believe is greatly preferable to the possibly impersonal atmosphere of the local party offices or other common surgery venue. But Members who do run surgeries in the usual way have often stressed to us that constituents may feel inhibited during a domiciliary visit especially if their problem is connected with their spouse or children: Members sometimes get divorce and other family matters, including birth control and abortion problems, raised at their surgeries. In rural areas, domiciliary visits may be very difficult because of 'village gossip' and social relationships. One rural constituency's Conservative Member has bought a caravan to use as his mobile surgery (and his campaign vehicle at election-time) partly because he can display his name across it but also because he feels village people would not feel comfortable discussing their affairs at home or in a neighbour's front parlour, even in a private talk with the Member. 'When my 'van stops in the street it's neutral ground as between neighbours.' Holding these surgery sessions in one fixed place is not a necessary feature of a surgery: rural seats may require, and often have, a regular circuit surgery programme shared between the various towns and villages.

We felt justified in not pursuing the matter of surgeries very vigorously within the limited scope of our interviews compared with other topics of interest because of Robert Dowse's postal survey of a sample of 100 Members (including Ministers) in 1963 which attained a response rate of 69 per cent, biased a little towards Labour Members.[1] As well as asking the obvious question whether our Members did hold a surgery, we re-used his questions on the frequency of surgeries and whether the Member felt his surgery work helped him to get the 'feel' of the electorate.

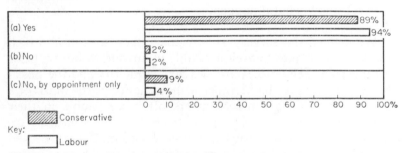

Figure 19. *Proportion of respondents holding constituency surgeries.* (See Appendix, Table 18.)

(N—105: 53 Conservative and 52 Labour MPs)

All but a tiny handful of non-ministerial MPs were holding regular surgeries for their constituents in 1967. Only two Members out of the 108 who answered this question were not, while a further eight Members (7·4 per cent of the total) held irregular surgeries or other kinds of interview by appointment only. This result of 91 per cent of Members offering regular surgeries to their constituents is somewhat higher than that

[1] R. E. Dowse, 'The MP and his Surgery', *Political Studies*, XI. 3 (October 1963), pp. 333–41.

found by Dr Dowse in 1963. There are two possible reasons for this: he included Ministers in his sample of 100 MPs and although he states that frontbenchers of both parties responded proportionately as a group, it is possible that the pressure of official duties had reduced their constituency activity and thus placed them in his 'No' column; secondly, there may have been a genuine extension of the surgery habit between 1963 and 1967, particularly in view of the considerable turnover among Members during those years. Nearly 40 per cent of our respondents entered the House in 1964 or 1966 and the proportion of MPs in this group who hold surgeries was found to be about 5 per cent higher than the average of all Members and nearly 10 per cent higher than Members elected before 1964. This practice of the 1964–6 entrants may account for the Labour-Conservative difference detected in our study (5·5 per cent against only 1·2 per cent in Dr Dowse's enquiry) since the great majority of the new Members are Labour. We then asked how often the surgery took place.

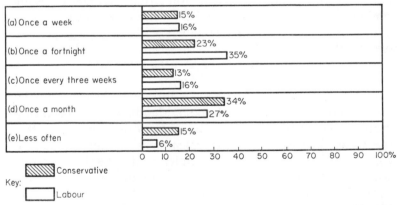

Figure 20. *Frequency of respondents' surgeries.* (See Appendix, Table 19.) (N—96: 47 Conservative and 49 Labour MPs)

The frequency with which different MPs hold their surgeries varies considerably (as Dr Dowse's study also clearly showed). The most popular intervals, found by both studies, were the fortnight and month; similar proportions of Members in both studies had favoured the weekly, fortnightly, and monthly surgery. But the earlier survey found considerably more Members (nearly 25 per cent) holding surgeries less often than monthly compared with ours (10 per cent). This more common offering by Members of a rather more frequent surgery is, almost certainly, a reflection of the higher proportion of Labour Members in 1967: as Figure 20 shows, Labour Members hold more frequent surgeries than do Conservatives and the party difference on the frequency of surgeries was more significant than on the previous question of whether they hold surgeries at all.

Party lines are crossed, however, if these responses on frequency of surgeries are studied with regard to years of parliamentary service. Although there were no differences according to length of service in the holding of a surgery, those Members with less than nine years' service reported a notably greater frequency than their longer-serving colleagues, and this tendency ran across party lines. Among those with less than nine years' service the Members who had won their seats as 'gains' from another party held surgeries even more frequently than the others. Also running across party lines was the tendency of non-graduates to hold surgeries more often than graduates and similarly in the case of Members with experience on local authorities compared with Members without such experience (see Appendix, Table 19). As we have already noted in the discussion of constituency postbags, urban Members held more frequent surgeries than rural Members, although this result, like the local government point, is little more than a function of the party division, since Labour Members as a group have more local council experience and more of the urban seats than the Conservatives. From the constituent's point of view, of course, this rather lower rural frequency of surgeries is emphasised in its importance by the very common circuit surgery in rural constituencies: if a Member runs a surgery, say, once every month, but in different parts of the constituency in turn, it could be several months before he comes to a particular village or part of the constituency again.

The frequency of Members' surgeries is worth attention not only for any differences which may emerge between parties and between types of Member and constituency, but also to illuminate the differences between Members' estimates of the number of constituency letters they receive. It may be that holding a surgery more frequently tends to reduce the flow of letters. We have seen that rural Members claimed rather higher constituency

postbags than urban Members and reported rather lower surgery activity. To discover whether this relationship existed
among our respondents as a whole, we cross-tabulated postbag
estimates and the frequency with which Members held surgeries. This showed that those who claimed a higher volume of
post tended to hold more frequent surgeries. This would
suggest that rather than being alternatives surgeries and constituency post are complementary, so that the Member who has
a constituency which generates a great deal of post may find
it necessary to hold frequent surgeries, while his surgery activity
may itself stimulate letters from his constituents by giving the
Member a reputation as a 'good constituency man'. In either
case it seems likely that both the volume of constituency post
and the frequency of surgeries is in part a reflection of the incidence of personal problems in particular constituencies.

Our final question to Members about their surgeries was:
'Do you think your surgery work helps you get the 'feel' of the
electorate?'. Our results were rather vague on this deliberately
rather vague question, designed to identify the Member's
general 'image' of his surgery work. Nearly 75 per cent of all
our respondents answered 'Yes', compared with 17 per cent
who said 'No', and 8 per cent who were unsure. There were
some party differences (see Appendix, Table 20): although
similar proportions of Conservative and Labour respondents
(18 and 16 per cent) replied that their surgeries did not give them
the 'feel' of the electorate, more Labour MPs replied that it did
(80 per cent against 69 per cent), and Conservatives were more
likely to be uncertain (13 per cent against 4 per cent).

We were particularly interested to observe the views of Members who had had local council experience, as they ran across
party lines, and even went against them. Despite the facts that
more Labour than Conservative Members had been councillors
and that a higher proportion of Labour Members did think that
their surgeries helped them to get the 'feel' of the electorate, our
analysis showed that MPs with no local council experience were
more likely to say that they did obtain the 'feel' of the electorate,
while MPs who had served on councils were more likely to say
that they did not.

This contradiction of the party division may be explained by
the terms of the question: Members were not asked whether
they thought their surgery 'useful', or whether they welcomed

or accepted this duty, but whether they got the 'feel' of the electorate from it. A number of Members replied in fact that, although their surgeries had great value to both their constituents and themselves, it did not help them, as Members, to get any 'feel' or general impression at all. It is possible, therefore, that MPs who are or have been councillors may, more often than other Members, see the surgery as a problem-solving device because they have had more experience of the local government services which are often involved in these problems. Their view may be specific rather than general— case-oriented rather than directed towards an assessment of a local or national issue.

It appears that the typicality or wider significance of the information which Members receive from their surgery visitors is very much a matter of individual opinion, with some Members more ready than others to extrapolate general trends from particular cases. (Thus, two Conservative ex-senior Ministers, both in the social services field, gave equally emphatic but opposite answers on this question.)

Taking information received from their constituency post-bags and at surgeries together, it is worth emphasising its great variety. MPs deal with a wide range of problems and disputes involving housing, pensions, roads, education, local amenities or transport. This work brings them into contact with private firms and voluntary bodies as well as the local authorities, Government Departments and nationalised industries which provide public services. All these matters could be roughly organised along a spectrum from the most individual kind of constituent's problem to a matter which clearly has wider significance. Often, the individual problem (such as helping an elderly person obtain a supplementary pension) brings very little new information to the Member, who sees it as a simple, routine service. Other cases may appear highly significant to the Member and make him think at once about raising a policy point with the local authority or Government Department concerned. An example of this would be his discovery that the local Social Security office is interpreting a rule in a way which the Member believes to be contrary to Parliament's intention when it was first introduced. Cases which throw light on local or regional issues, such as race relations in certain cities or Welsh language-teaching in Wales, fall between the individual constituent's problem and the potential national policy issue on this spectrum of MPs' constituency casework.

Every item from the Member's constituency postbag or surgery, however routine it may be, offers him some extra information or experience. Each case adds at least quantitatively to his impression of how common a problem seems to be in his constituency. Dealing with routine cases also maintains his knowledge of important background matters, such as how helpful and efficient the local Social Security office or the council's housing department seem to be.

This considerable variety of types of constituency casework explains the different interpretations which the Members we interviewed placed on this aspect of their parliamentary duties— notably on the 'feel' of the electorate obtained at surgery sessions. Members can choose on which end of the spectrum, from individual problems to potential public issues, they will put their emphasis. We suspect that Members make this choice largely in terms of their own personalities and attitudes to individual and public problems. It is clear from the following selected comments that some Members tend to see public policy questions in terms of individual cases, while others perceive policy questions on a general level and regard individuals' problems as an inevitable, but subsidiary aspect of the constant search by public authorities for the optimum policy which best suits the times and conditions in each field.

Partisan philosophy does, of course, play a part in determining which of these tendencies a Member follows. Several Labour Members, but no Conservatives, made remarks about Government officials' alleged attitudes on this matter very similar to this one: 'Although in normal times I believe most, if not all, one's surgery visitors are the "social casualties", it would still do senior civil servants from Whitehall a world of good to attend the surgery every other month. They would see their administrative schemes working out through local officials to local citizens—and they would be less remote from real life as a result.'

MPs talk about their surgeries

'My surgery's completely unorganised; people visit my house at any time and I'm available at Labour Hall. No need to advertise: they know where to come.' (Labour, Northern England)

187

'I'm a local man who lives there so I know what's going on, but one can be too available, e.g. asked to help with income tax returns.' (Conservative, Southern England)

'I don't hold a surgery. I discovered after a short experience that the complaints were in the main trivial or of local council concern. There was no reaction when I stopped it.' (Labour, Scotland)

'I get the feel of official administration rather than of the electorate. I learn not where the party political shoe is pinching but the social shoe, e.g. Is the Supplementary Benefits Commission any better than the old National Assistance Board? It's clear from my surgery that people need a "sense of service", not just rules and regulations, and I am as unimpressed with SBC as I was with NAB.' (Labour, London)

'I have to hold my surgery in the local party HQ because the council won't let me use the Town Hall.' (Labour, Northern England)

'I do get the feel of my electorate . . . but of only a section of the electorate: the most deprived.' (Conservative, London)

'. . . surgeries tend to be a pulse of what issues are disturbing the public; also a criterion of how far a Member breaks through a political barrier to personal problems.' (Labour, Northern England)

'I find the surgery very useful but it's much too inconsistent to be a reliable guide to the feel of the electorate.' (Conservative, Southern England)

'. . . most complaints have nothing to do with me.' (Labour, Scotland)

'Surgery does not give one the feel of the electorate. They are all personal cases. Usually (as with those who write to their MPs) spiritual bankrupts whose case has already been rightly turned down by the appropriate authority and who are turning to the MP as last resort.' (Conservative, Northern England)

'An MP's help is clearly necessary even though the responsibility is local councillors'. I have a councillor with me at surgery just to listen: I prefer to do the job myself to make sure it's done.' (Labour, Midlands)

'I see people on their own without councillors since people are more frank if on their own.' (Conservative, London)

'All my local councils are so corrupt that people are afraid to write to them for fear of victimisation. So they see me about it.' (Conservative, Southern England)

'My predecessor as MP used to have not merely a local councillor sitting in on his surgery but a local reporter as well. When I did not follow this practice on what should be an entirely confidential interview the Pressman said, "Is it a secret session, then?" I said, 'Of course it is you daft ha'porth."' (Labour, Northern England)

3. THE 'WELFARE OFFICER'

The answers we received on the size of constituency postbags and the holding of surgeries prepared the way for the key question of Members' attitudes to these matters. We thought it wise to avoid asking a direct question, such as 'What do you think of handling constituency case work?', by establishing instead the Member's estimate of the time his postbag usually took to deal with and then asking him what he thought about spending this time in this way. As we have already noted, this estimate necessarily covered all kinds of mail requiring any answer, since Members deal with all kinds at one sitting and, we found, could not separate out the constituency element for our benefit. We feel this matters very little, since we know that few Members claim to receive any significant number of letters from outside their constituencies which require an answer. It was clear that nearly all Members in our interviews answered the key question of what they felt about this use of their time in terms of only their constituency postbag, this being, at a guess, 90 per cent of their total requiring an answer.

The difference between the main parties (and between Conservatives and Labour-plus-Liberals, if our three Liberals are representative of their fellows) is clear. Twice as many Conservatives as Labour Members claim to deal with their post in the equivalent of one hour a day or less, while twice as many Labour Members as Conservatives estimate two hours a day or more. The range of replies was between one quarter of an hour

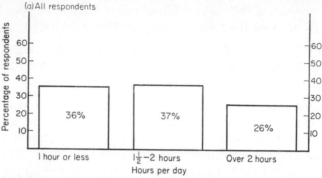

(N—99 (excluding 7 'Don't know's): 48 Conservative, 48 Labour and 3 Liberal MPs)

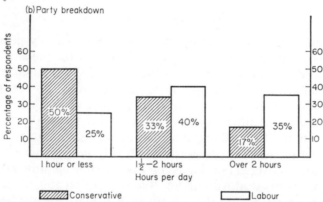

(N—96 (excluding 7 'Don't know's): 48 Conservative and 48 Labour MPs)

Figure 21. *Respondents' estimates of the average time they spend in dealing with their postbags—all respondents and by main party.* (See Appendix, Table 21.)

per day and six hours. Five Conservatives and one Labour Member (all of them with outside jobs) said that they would have to spend more time on correspondence if they did not have such good secretaries, who can deal with routine matters. One Labour Member's secretary 'opens and sorts the post and then deals with some such as sending a telephone complaint to the GPO and showing me the answer when it arrives'. Less fortunate are two other Labour Members, who told us they did everything themselves by hand. Both said that this entailed a full morning or afternoon's work each day, although one claimed his handwritten replies gave his constituents a better impression. Both these Members gave rather low postbag estimates.

We saw in Chapter II, when examining Members' estimates of non-constituency mail, that Labour Members claim to get rather more printed circulars, etc., and more individual letters from people outside their own constituency than do Conservatives. These factors could make their total postbags rather bigger than the Conservatives' and thus more time-consuming, taken as a group. But, against that, we have already noticed that urban Members claim, as a group, rather less constituency post, which must largely apply to the Labour side. In considering why Conservatives spend less time dealing with their post it is very likely that these factors are trifles compared with the different levels of secretarial assistance used by Conservative and Labour Members. Apart from having less secretarial help in general, Labour Members are far more likely to employ a part-time secretary, who is often not on duty, compared with the Conservatives, more of whom share the services of a full-time secretary with one or more colleagues and thus have more flexible access to this kind of help.

Figure 22 gives the main results of our questions about Members' secretarial help.

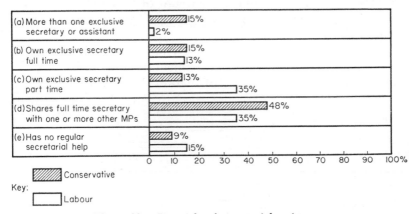

Figure 22. *Respondents' secretarial assistance.*
(N—106: 54 Conservative and 52 Labour MPs)

We also found that there were significant differences in respect of parliamentary service and the time Members spent on their postbags. There was a clear tendency for Members elected during and since 1964 to say that they spent more time dealing with their post than did their longer-serving colleagues. This was in part linked to party differences on secretarial assistance in that the post-1963 Members are overwhelmingly Labour. Further analysis also showed that more recently-elected MPs are less likely to employ a full-time secretary or share a secretary with only one other Member, probably because the Member is uncertain of how much help he needs and can afford. Clearly, less secretarial assistance would tend to increase the time spent by a Member on his post and it is also likely that newer MPs spend more time dealing with mail at least until they have become familiar with the volume of post and the various problems arising from it.

Nearly all our respondents spontaneously answered the question of what they thought about spending 'this' amount of time on their post by giving their view of the 'welfare officer role' arising out of cases found in their constituency postbags. But, as we are approaching this key question from the topic of secretarial assistance, we may note here that a few Members said that their view of the welfare role was influenced by their desire to have some secretarial help or a desk, or room at which to do this work, e.g. 'I find this amount of time too much, but only because I need a secretary's help: I'm not against the welfare work'.

The responses to the question, 'What do you think about spending this amount of your parliamentary time in this way?', are displayed in the four parts of Figure 23: by party, length of

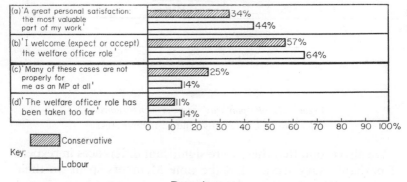

By main party

(N—106: 56 Conservative and 50 Labour MPs)

Figure 23. Part One

192

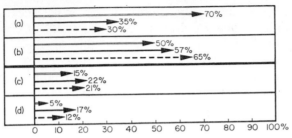

Key: ➤ 1966 entrants
    ➤ 1964 entrants
    ➤ Pre–1964 entrants

By length of service

(N—109: 56 Conservative, 50 Labour and 3 Liberal MPs)

Figure 23. Part Two

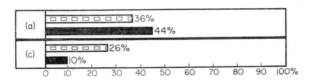

Key: ▢▢▢ Graduates

    ■■■ Non–graduates

By university education

(N—109: 56 Conservative, 50 Labour and 3 Liberal MPs)

Figure 23. Part Three

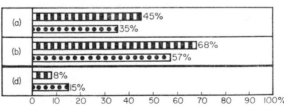

Key: |||| Local Council experience

    ●●●● None

By local council experience

(N—109: 56 Conservative, 50 Labour and 3 Liberal MPs)

Figure 23. Part Four

Figure 23. *Respondents' attitudes to the time spent on their postbags (i.e. the 'welfare officer' role)—by main party; length of service; university education and local council experience.* (See Appendix, Table 22.)

service, university education and experience as a local councillor. They are drawn from the variety of comments made by our Members in response to this open-ended question. The four quoted responses are the most common ones (one pair 'favouring', and one pair 'doubting' the welfare officer role) which we identified from hearing answers which often became brief conversations.

The results are interesting. Nearly 40 per cent of our 109 respondents felt that the time they spent on their post was the most valuable part of their work as MPs, or that it gave them great personal satisfaction, while the role of the MP as a welfare officer was welcomed or accepted by 60 per cent. But 20 per cent say that many matters are not really for them (usually local government responsibilities) and nearly 12 per cent feel that the welfare role has been taken too far.

There were significant differences between the major parties (Figure 23.1): more Labour than Conservative MPs expressed great personal satisfaction in this aspect of their work; while more Conservatives complained that they received requests to deal with problems which were not really their concern. It is no surprise, therefore, to find that rather more Labour Members than Conservatives are prepared to accept the welfare officer role, although slightly more Labour Members than Conservatives feel that this role has been taken too far. Although the numbers involved are relatively small (Figure 23.2), more of our respondents who entered the House in 1966 regard their constituency post as giving them 'great personal satisfaction' than any other group (70 per cent of the 1966 entrants expressed this view compared with 35 per cent of the 1964 group and 30 per cent of the pre-1964 entrants). But notably fewer of these 1966 entrants—only half of them—also said that they 'welcomed or accepted' the welfare officer role; 57 per cent of the 1964 entrants and 65 per cent of the longer-serving Members made this response. That the newcomers of 1966 certainly did not reject the welfare role is shown by their very meagre support for the hostile statement that it has been 'taken too far': only 5 per cent of them thought this compared with 17 per cent of the 1964 group and 12 per cent of the longer-serving members. Our impression of the 1966 entrants was that they welcome constituency welfare work but were not attracted to any idea that this should become their entire or principal parliamentary role.

It should be noted that these responses came from the 1966 entrants between twelve and fifteen months after their entry into the House: whether more of them would now be willing to settle for a more 'welfare-based' and less policy-oriented parliamentary role must remain speculation unless these same Members are questioned again on these matters.

Analysis by university education (Figure 23.3) showed the greater diversity of views among graduates on a given topic (which is a feature of our survey, as of many others). But two differences are worth noting: more graduates than non-graduates (26 per cent against 10 per cent) made the fairly anti-'welfare' response that much of their constituency post was 'not really for me at all', while rather fewer of them (36 per cent against 44 per cent of non-graduates) claimed 'great personal satisfaction' from the handling of their constituency postbag. There was no particular difference between graduates and others on the other two responses, nor was there any pattern to be seen when these 109 Members were divided according to front-bench experience (as an ex-Minister or current Opposition spokesman) or the lack of it.

There was a clear difference in attitudes towards the welfare officer role of the MP between those Members who had been members of local councils and those who had not (Figure 23.4). A higher proportion of the Members who were current or former councillors replied that their constituency work gave them great personal satisfaction (45 per cent against 35 per cent) and a similar division of views was found in the extent to which these Members welcomed or accepted the 'welfare officer' role (68 per cent against 57 per cent). Conversely, slightly more of those respondents who lacked local government experience felt that much of the post they received from constituency sources was not really their concern. Moreover, nearly twice the proportion of these same respondents said that the 'welfare officer' role had been taken too far compared with those who had served on local councils (8 per cent against 15 per cent). There was no significant difference in the proportions giving other answers to this question.

Although all our respondents' replies were analysed according to whether or not they had attended public schools, in almost every case this appeared to make little difference to their attitudes. On this question of attitudes to the welfare role, however,

195

we found a meaningful difference, which may well be a reflection of the differing class backgrounds of these two groups of respondents. Considerably fewer public school Members (30 per cent) than other Members (50 per cent) said that this work was a great personal satisfaction to them. It is important to note that this holds true for both major parties: 31 per cent of Conservatives who had also been to public schools registered this satisfaction, against 50 per cent of other Conservatives; while 31 per cent of Labour public school men expressed the same view, compared with 49 per cent of other Labour Members.

Conversely, more public school respondents as a whole (25 per cent against 13 per cent) said that much of their constituency postbag does not concern them as MPs and should be directed to the authority concerned, although the public school distinction on this point was less sharp on the Labour side than among the Conservatives. This same party difference applies to the very small margin by which all public school men were more likely to make the stronger comment that the welfare officer role has been taken too far: every MP making up the 11 per cent of Conservatives who made this comment has a public school background.

Having presented our findings on Members' experiences, behaviour and opinions in the matter, we should now consider the issues involved in the welfare role. That the British public assumes that MPs should be available to help their constituents in personal cases is beyond doubt; the evidence of the extent to which Members now share this assumption is set out in this chapter. It is an important part of modern British political culture or, in Peter G. Richards's phrase, 'an established social custom', in which the Member acts as, 'a sort of Citizens' Advice Bureau-cum-preliminary court of appeal'. Often the citizen does not expect a Member necessarily to achieve whatever the citizen wants, although he does expect him to try; in Professor Richards's words, 'The Member is thought to have done his duty if he takes a sympathetic interest in the troubles brought to him and communicates with the appropriate authority'.[1]

How long has this 'social custom' been established? Several Members had a word to say about this when answering our

[1] P. G. Richards, *Honourable Members*, 2nd (rev.) ed., Faber, 1964, p. 169.

questions about their constituency postbags and surgery duties. As a younger Conservative, who has experienced these demands in both an urban, marginal seat, and in a traditional, rural one, said, 'Older Members tell me that this is the biggest single change in Parliament compared with before the War—and it's certainly the biggest demand on us. We're glorified Welfare Officers.' As a number of Members, mainly Conservatives, made similar historical comparisons implying that the welfare role is largely a post-1939 development, it is worth pausing to consider the evidence that exists on the point. Writing in 1962, Chester and Bowring trace the habit of Members writing letters to Ministers about personal constituency cases back to at least the turn of the century.[1] One Member, speaking in the House in 1902, is quoted as saying that whereas he put down only about one formal parliamentary Question each year, he often asked a Minister to examine a constituent's case, as set out in a letter—a practice which was supported in the same debate by Joseph Chamberlain. These authors suggest that over the sixty intervening years, most Members have taken up most of their personal cases with Ministers in this private manner; the modern scale of these requests from the public has now resulted in these private channels carrying far more traffic than the public device of the Question.[2] The private letter to a Minister is attractive to the Member as he can expound a person's case history at length and is not bound by the strict rules governing the design of Questions; he can also pass on in good faith what proves to be a misguided or unfounded complaint, and receive a courteous private answer putting the matter straight with no public embarrassment.

A select committee on Members' expenses in 1920 heard one Member (J. M. Hogge) estimate that the average Member had to reply to about fifty letters a week in his public capacity; a distinction between those from within and outside his own constituency was not made. Mr Hogge also said that during

[1] D. N. Chester and N. Bowring, *Questions in Parliament* (Oxford U.P.), 1962, pp. 104–5. Asking a Member of Parliament to intercede with the authorities was hardly a novel procedure, of course: patronage and honours, such as Government jobs and pensions, titles and awards, and appointment to the magistracy were very commonly solicited through Members during the eighteenth and nineteenth centuries. Individual preferment has now given way to universal entitlement in modern political conditions.

[2] Chester and Bowring, p. 103, quoting K. E. Couzens, 'A Minister's Correspondence', in *Public Administration*, XXXIV, pp. 237–44.

the First World War, when he had become interested in military pensions, 'My correspondence went up very rapidly, and it never was at any period of the War less than 1,000 letters a week, from people who had, in many cases, no real business to write to me' (that is, presumably, they were not his own constituents).[1] If his recollection is even remotely accurate, it is striking evidence that the welfare function of at least some MPs was well established many years before 1939, at least during the unusual conditions of wartime. We cannot know, of course, what kind of people contributed to this very high figure; officers, their widows and other relatives may have made up the greater, or at least a disproportionate part of it. The rise of the Labour Party brought working class Members into the House, together with their radically minded co-partisans of middle class background. These Members, whatever their personal class background, were in politics to improve the lot of the majority of people and a welfare role would have been natural to them. The Labour-held seats of those days were mainly working class in their social make-up and oral, rather than written, communication was the rule.

If any figures existed from the inter-war period of letters sent to MPs by constituents on personal or local matters, they would need to be examined in the light of this 'face to face' tradition, where the Labour Member was close to his constituency (perhaps a native) and relied on his eyes and ears to gather knowledge of both local problems and personal cases. We can, however, only speculate whether more than very few working class people in the '20s and '30s ever wrote to their MP of their own volition about some personal or family problem involving the authorities. We asked John Parker, who now sits for Dagenham, to recall his pre-war and wartime years (1935–45) as Member for Romford—a seat which then included the four towns of Romford, Barking, Dagenham and Hornchurch, and which had an electorate of 207,000 in 1945, the biggest in the country, when it was divided.

'I think more of my pre-war correspondents probably came from the middle class and Tory areas of my constituency, although from Labour people there who were pleased to have a Labour MP. In those years, most constituency correspondence

[1] H.C. 255 of 1920, Q. 363.

was from individuals rather than local organisations, which more frequently asked one to address them at the relatively numerous public and other organised gatherings of those days on such subjects as "The Work of an MP". Compared with today, one got many letters from very illiterate people, especially women, who could not spell and found it difficult to express themselves. The "surgery" was less developed then, although I always had one before and during the War, taking the four towns in turn. People did not write about national issues such as Spain or the Fascist danger from Mosley, which were dealt with at meetings, although Munich was an exception to this.

'My biggest correspondence was in the latter days of the War, when people had got used to it, and were keen to assert themselves and voice their grievances. I don't think Attlee's "welfare state" increased my correspondence after 1945 save when new schemes (such as that on National Insurance) first came in, and many people were unsure whether they were covered. Until the schemes were working smoothly one had many "successes" in getting cases included which had been marginally turned down by local Ministry officials.'

Looking at the years before the Second World War, it is probably right to say that a considerable amount of welfare work was being undertaken by Members, although often without the aid of a constituent's letter or a Member's formal surgery, especially on the Labour side, where Members were more often in their constituency, and thus open to personal approaches. Although we asked no historical questions on the point, we formed the general impression, when listening to older Conservative Members, that the wartime rise in constituents bringing personal problems involving public authorities to their MPs, and the further strengthening of the habit in the post-war years, came as a novelty more to the Conservative Members of the day than to the Labour ones. Then, as now, Conservative electoral strength was concentrated in rural areas, which usually follow urban fashions after some delay, and in the most prosperous districts and suburbs of cities where constituents more often had the financial and personal resources to look after themselves when dealing with authority. Against this, the very large National Government majority of Conservatives and their allies meant that plenty of the mainly working class constituencies were represented by Conservative Members before 1945.

We were not, unfortunately, able to ask the broad range of Members, including Conservatives, to cast their minds back to this aspect of their duties before the last war. We did note, however, that some Conservatives to whom we spoke in our interviews, feel that this constituency case-work aspect of Parliament has been developed deliberately by Labour candidates and Members for partisan reasons, and that this process began during and just after the Second World War.

Whatever the earlier history of the welfare function of MPs, it was clear by 1945 that public demands were growing. A select committee of 1946 was told that 50,000 items of mail had been delivered to MPs in one week, in December, 1945: an average of nearly eighty per Member.[1] This aggregate figure included printed circulars of many kinds on national affairs, few of which delay Members long, as well as personally directed letters on non-constituency matters.

Although Mr Parker, as a Member with a long-term record of welfare work, has the impression that the Attlee Government's innovations did not permanently add to his case work burden, many of our interviewed Members with whom we had some brief discussions on the point had no doubt that the general rise in Government and other official activity since 1939 has largely created the modern demand. As an ex-Member, Nigel Nicolson, said in a letter to us, 'I don't quite see how the MP . . . could avoid the role of welfare officer, once we had a welfare state. Their grievances were a legitimate concern of Government, and hence of the MP.'

Professor Richards takes a similar view. The growth of welfare work is, he writes, 'a product of the philosophy of the Welfare State: it is now assumed that the processes of public administration should provide for those in need'.[2] There cannot be the slightest doubt in the mind of anyone familiar with twentieth-century British politics that this Welfare State philosophy has been 'mutually' generated by both public opinion and radical political parties, such as Labour, over the last seventy or more years. Taking the social security field alone, from the original Old Age Pensions to the current campaign for a guaranteed income for all disabled persons, the idea that

[1] H.C. 93 of 1946, Q. 120.　　　　　　[2] P. G. Richards, op. cit., p. 171.

where there is want the Government ought to do something about it lies at the heart of 'Welfare Statism' and the welfare role of the Member which has developed as one of its attributes. This idea makes the majority of Members (who welcome or accept the welfare role) sometimes use phrases such as 'We must know, and must tell the Government, where the shoe is pinching'. This phrase occurred quite often in our brief exchanges with our Members; for some, it seemed to carry the relatively weak sense of Members learning through their welfare work where the existing machinery of Government may be failing in some officially established aim (e.g. the low 'take-up' of free school lunches by poor parents). For others, it carried the stronger sense of Professor Richards's phrase: 'that the processes of public administration should provide for those in need' (including needs which no official provision yet meets, such as that of disabled housewives). Among the minority of our interviewed Members who in some sense doubt the legitimacy of the welfare officer role, there was little criticism of this general background situation. No Member positively declared that it was not his business how social or economic legislation is working out in practice, although a few felt that a local constituency social worker or similar kind of aide could well handle the details of cases, while keeping the Member informed of the trends and difficulties of the moment.

The Members' roles in this situation of welfare politics may be defined, in ascending order of vigour, by a list drawn from Professor Richards's account:

1. to offer the constituent sympathy and consolation short of any action being possible.
2. to assist the citizen to shape his claim or complaint most effectively for any or all of the purposes below.
3. to discover, by enquiry and challenge, a plain mistake.
4. to challenge a decision in order that the Minister may personally learn how the case was treated, even though no challenge to current policy is necessarily being advanced in this case; (in this way an 'image' or 'climate' of opinion may be built up in the Minister's mind with a view to making a challenge on policy at a later stage).
5. to challenge a discretionary decision on a case to make that case admissible under current policies or rules

201

(these are the 'successes' referred to by Mr Parker, above) without necessarily challenging the policy or rules themselves.

6. To make a definite claim that the administrative rules or procedures concerned are wrong on the evidence of this case, and should be changed.

It was rather the other attribute of their welfare work which came in for criticism from some of our Members who were doubtful or hostile to the welfare role, namely, the constituent's possible belief, that, by raising a problem with an MP, he would get a more favourable result in his claim or case against some public authority. Professor Richards feels that this belief on the part of constituents must, presumably, be part of the reason why they approach MPs. Lord Attlee's criticism of the MP's welfare work stressed this point: 'I think the present practice whereby many MPs spend the bulk of their weekends dealing with constituency cases is a bad one . . . Government Departments deal, I think, with cases on their merits, and intervention by an MP is often quite unnecessary.'[1] One Conservative ex-Minister we interviewed asserted that it should be held a corrupt electoral practice for any Member to be asked to help an elector to receive some favourable decision from Government authority: it is a kind of political bribe if the Member does it or promises to try to do it. 'I represent my constituency in Westminster—not the other way round', he declared. But this Member admitted that, 'of course', he does himself take up local housing cases and other matters outside the MP's formal ambit since not to do so, while every other Member does, would lay him open to attack from his rival candidates at the next election or from their parties writing in the local Press before the election falls due. He also said that he keeps his constituents' complaints against the local authority's domestic refuse collection within manageable proportions by conducting a blitz on the subject every six months or so. This senior Conservative's proposal on corrupt electoral practices was offered, of course, with a touch of humour born of his realistic appreciation of the chance of seeing the reform implemented in modern political conditions. More seriously, he looked back to his time spent on the receiving end of thousands of routine constituency complaints

[1] Lord Attlee, *Fabian Journal*, November 1957.

and claims (he was one of the four Conservative ex-Ministers in the social service field whom we were particularly glad to have among our respondents, for the ministerial view they could offer). It was quite wrong, he said, for either the constituent or the Member to suppose that the routine business of sending local authority matters, such as council housing cases or planning development control matters, to the Minister made any difference. The Member sends to the Minister a printed letter supplied by the House: 'I shall be grateful if you will give the enclosed communication from Mr X your attention and send me a reply which I can forward to my constituent. Please acknowledge.' When the official reply arrives, the Member sends it to his constituent with another printed note: 'I took up with the authorities the matter about which you wrote to me. I have now received a reply, which I enclose.' Of course, as Chester and Bowring point out,[1] Members often take a more personal interest in such cases and may try to press the responsible Minister hard. But our ex-Minister insisted that for the great majority of cases the Minister is forced by modern conventions to appear to help the Member to go through the motions of taking up a case with the Government and thus impressing his constituent.

Nigel Nicolson described to us in correspondence his view of the process based on his experience:

'Most MPs welcome (the welfare role) since it brings them in touch with manifold experiences and enables them to pose as father of their people. And it was really very easy to deal with these cases, by dictating a note to the responsible Minister, from whom a detailed reply would eventually come. You would forward this to the constituent, who was no doubt impressed by the notepaper with "Dear Charlie" at the beginning, even if he wasn't impressed by the arguments it contained. Some MPs just refused to do this. I know of one case where all "welfare" cases were dealt with by his secretary, who forged his signature. The "Dear Charlie" letters came back just the same.'

Professor Richards's conclusion on the matter raises the problem of the wastefulness of these processes. He explains how a Member's letter to the Minister is processed differently

---

[1] Chester and Bowring, op. cit., p. 100.

from the public's communications. The ordinary person's letter will be sorted and seen first by a Clerical Officer and then possibly by an Executive Officer or Higher Executive Officer for a decision on how the case relates to the rules. The letter which arrives with a Member's note attached goes at once to the Minister's private office in the Department, where his private secretary (a Principal, or, if the Minister is a Secretary of State, an Assistant Secretary) becomes responsible for its treatment. From the private office it goes to the HEO, whose section deals with the topic, and then up to his superiors until an Assistant Secretary (the grade above Principal) approves it for submission to the Minister. The Minister will probably sign the letter without question but may express dissatisfaction—it is at this point that the process may be effective in bringing home to the Minister how his policies are working out in practice and giving him food for thought. While it is 'a strict tradition that the Minister's letter does not call for a different decision to that which would be given to any analogous case, unless very rarely it induces a Minister to initiate a change of policy . . . possibly the greatest advantage of a Member's letter is that it suffers no danger of receiving a stock answer that is inappropriate to the case'.[1] Our Conservative ex-Minister contradicted this view and suggested that the formal routines robbed the process of even this advantage. The truth surely lies between the two: the complaint taken up by a Member suffers some chance of an inappropriate stock treatment but less than that of an ordinary person's letter. As Professor Richards says, each such case consumes much expensive, senior administrative manpower. Departments and sections of Departments vary. A sudden *cause célèbre* may lead to many letters which cause inattention to policy formation on that or other issues that should be dealt with in that section. 'Yet while the cost of trying to satisfy Members is heavy, it must be borne, since it forms another means of making the executive reconsider and justify its actions. . . .'[2] But, as the Fulton Committee on the Civil Service has since pointed out, Parliament should 'take fully into account the cumulative cost (not only in time but in the quality of the administration) that the raising of minutiae imposes . . .'.[3]

---

[1] P. G. Richards, op. cit., p. 174.   [2] Ibid., p. 178.
[3] *Report* of The Committee on The Civil Service, Cmnd. 3638, Vol. 1, p. 93.

THE LOCAL COMMUNITY

4. THE LOCAL PARTY

We asked Members to say exactly how they received information on local affairs from elements of their local constituency party. Members quite often actually made, or implied by their tone of voice or brevity of answer, a reservation, such as 'Insofar as my local party is a source of local information to me at all. . .'. Some Members replied quickly that their local party was not a source of information to them: 'On the contrary, I tell *them* things about what's going on.' These are, therefore, a rather muted set of responses; we shall describe later how the local party compares with other sources of local information, such as constituency postbags and the local newspapers. 'I'm interested in your local constituency party as a source of information to you on *local* affairs. . . . How do you receive information from them?'

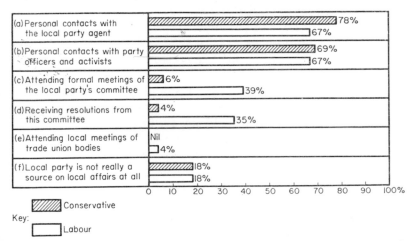

Figure 24. *Respondents' views of their local constituency parties as sources of information.* (See Appendix, Table 23.)

(N—106: 55 Conservative and 51 Labour MPs)

The most important local party source of information on local affairs for the great majority of our respondents is the official agent, although he is closely followed in importance by the contact which Members have with local party officers or other prominent and active members. Rather greater emphasis was laid on the agent by Conservative Members (78 per cent to 67 per cent) while each party's MPs laid the same quite considerable stress (69 per cent Conservative and 67 per cent Labour) on their picking up of facts and opinions from prominent party activists. The somewhat different stress laid on the agent is no doubt due in part to the simple facts that more Conservatives than Labour Members have an agent at all and that the Conservative agent is more likely to be a full-time official who has had, or who may look forward to, quite a long period of service in the job and, moreover, in that particular constituency. As our Labour Members sometimes said on this point, this happy situation of having a professional long-term agent is much less often enjoyed among their ranks. The ideal situation was enjoyed by one south-coast resort Conservative Member for over twenty years: he had a professional agent, who knew the constituency's affairs inside-out, working alongside the Member's own private secretary who looked after the welfare casework and made all the arrangements for the Member's local appearances from the same office.

Apart from the Conservative and Labour agents, whose supply and conditions of employment are largely matters of money, there were other, more interesting, differences between the parties. Conservative MPs tend to lay much greater stress than Labour Members on informal contacts with both agents and party activists, as opposed to formal appearances at official business meetings. As Figure 24 shows, Labour Members give considerable minority indications of these more formal processes. Very few Conservatives indeed (6 per cent) mention going to formal committee meetings where they might hear discussions of local (or, of course, national) issues. Conservatives do attend annual general meetings of their local party's main committee where they will, like any other MP, make a speech and talk informally after the meeting: but this is often their only official 'business' meeting link. Of course, if he has a fairly rural seat, as do many Conservative Members, he may well attend the AGM of each branch of the constituency Conservative Association, which can be a tall order. One Member told us that he has about fifty village branches, each holding an AGM between March and June, and that he attends them all, at the rate of about three a week. (We suppose that these affairs are small and informal with a strong social element and would not, therefore, press too far the distinction between 'business' and 'social' activities especially among the Conservatives where the two probably run rather closer together than on the Labour Party.)

As a part of this style of local political organisation, the Conservative Association very rarely passes resolutions on local matters. Only 4 per cent of our Conservative respondents registered receiving local information through this practice, against 35 per cent of Labour Members. Conversely, Labour Members are much more likely to receive copies of resolutions passed by their local executives; they are much more likely to attend local party meetings on a regular basis, and a few attend local trade union meetings from time to time. The very nature of these contacts emphasises the more formal and yet more integrated relationship between the Labour Member and his CLP. The Conservative MP tends to have a less formal approach and yet is, in a sense, more distant from his local association: many more Conservative than Labour Members stressed that they do not 'interfere' in association affairs. The areas of emphasis are strikingly different and reflect differences between the local bodies of the two parties: the Conservatives' essentially social approach, as against the Labour Party's more political outlook on local organisation. Despite these differences, however, it is an interesting footnote to observe that the same proportions of Members in both parties (rather less than one-fifth) do not regard their local constituency parties—even the agent or chairman—as being sources of information on local affairs at all. One Labour Member, who gives regular pub lunches to his activists to exchange points on affairs in general and on local matters in particular, sometimes finds it mildly difficult: 'I want them to talk about the constituency, but they want me to talk about national and overseas issues.'

These rather low-key findings should be put into context. British MPs are often not natives of the constituency they represent and, as a result, have frequently been unfairly dubbed with the pejorative American name of 'carpetbaggers'. Leaving out Ulster, and with some Scots, Welsh and local English exceptions, there is generally a fair chance of a national market in available candidates being allowed to operate by the more than 1,200 local Labour and Conservative parties. Even when an 'incumbent' local party, which has seen its previous candidate become first the local MP and then rise to great ministerial and national party responsibilities and fame, now decides that it would like its next MP to be a more attentive, if less brilliant, 'constituency man', it does not exclude strangers of the right type from its consideration. There are more than a few Members today who were selected on this principle, while not being local men. It is part of the conventional wisdom offered to the new Member that if he is not a local man, he should keep his distance from his local party's and his local councillors' squabbles. If he is a local man, who rose to the nomination, and thence to the House, from these very ranks, he should gradually withdraw from a partisan role in any disputes. This frees his mind for his parliamentary duties, gives his local party supporters and local government co-partisans a potential arbitrator in case of serious dispute, and avoids his making enemies within local Conservative or Labour circles.

Every Member would like his local party to be a smooth and efficient electoral machine and most would also be pleased if it served as a lively (but not too lively) political forum between elections. But every Member knows that the potential conflict of 'loyalty' on some issue to his own conscience, to the view of his local party and to that of his parliamentary party can become an actual conflict at any time. Whatever the outcome, the fact that his local party's view is only one element in his political judgement will encourage the Member to at least stand back a little from his local party. When his local party and his parliamentary party at Westminster take different views, the prudent Member supports at least one side: he does not seriously alienate both at the same time, if he can avoid it. But for every Desmond Donnelly who loses his party ties at Westminster and seeks to survive as an MP on a raft of local party and local public support, there are dozens of Members who go flatly against their local party and prefer to support their parliamentary leaders, especially when they form the Government. Their pleas to their local stalwarts to be allowed to put intra-parliamentary party loyalty before loyalty to local party views or conference resolutions are usually granted and the tradition of their political independence from those who nominated them for the House thus maintained.

The reasons for this tradition are partly social ones and stem from the strong, although not exactly similar, strains of social and political deference which each party cultivates and preserves. In part, also, MPs may be reluctant to see their local party as a typical expression of wider public opinion on an issue. A national opinion poll's findings may confirm a Member's suspicions on this point, or he may find evidence in his constituency while meeting people other than local party members. Considerations such as these, in our view, explain why the answers set out above came across to us in a rather minor key.

5. THE LOCAL AUTHORITY

Each Member of Parliament has only one local constituency party, although it is worth remembering that many consist of more than one town or village parties which are, in fact, the real centres of activity. Most Members have more than one local council, however, which presented us with a more complex background for any questions we might ask about them. We asked the Member to choose the local authority which he felt most important to most of his constituents and answer our question in respect of this one. (A few respondents whose constituencies lie wholly within a county borough's borders had, of course, only the one authority to talk about.) We asked, 'In what ways do you get information from this local authority?' (A further prompt was usually necessary, including to those Members who replied 'I don't', often followed by a critical remark.)

As with local parties, Members lay great stress on their personal contacts with local authorities and, although a minority of Members do arrange regular meetings with local councillors (always of their own party) the vast majority rely on *ad hoc* contact to deal with problems as they arise. Only three of our respondents were currently members of local authorities in their constituencies, but more than one-third had been local councillors or aldermen in the past. There is an important party difference here, however: considerably less than one-third of the Conservatives but nearly half the Labour Members had been on councils. This may account for the closer contact that many Labour Members appear to have with their local authorities. For instance, Labour MPs are noticeably more likely to receive, and to say that they read, council minutes; they are more likely to approach the appropriate chief officer of the local authority department concerned with a case (e.g. the Housing Manager on a council house tenant's case) rather than deal formally through the Clerk; they are more likely to hold regular discussions with their co-partisan councillors. Of course, a Member will tend to be much more involved with his municipal co-partisans when they control that particular council: there is scope for policy planning on such major issues as comprehensive schools or the sale of council houses to their tenants, on which the Member's parliamentary links with national party policy may offer the councillors a valuable source of advice. We were unable, within our survey's bounds, to pursue a systematic analysis of our Member's links with councillors, according to party control, since many Members have many authorities in their constituencies among most of which 'party control' is a very vague, or at least subtle, concept. The point was often mentioned, however, especially by urban Members, whose constituencies have a more clear and developed system of party control in their local authorities.

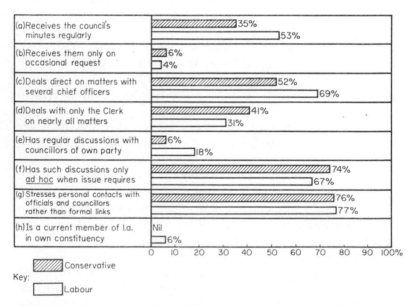

Figure 25. *Respondents' views of their local authorities as sources of information.*
(See Appendix, Table 24.)

(N—105: 54 Conservative and 51 Labour MPs)

210

In reply to our question asking what Members thought of this local authority as a source of information on local affairs, only 12 per cent of our respondents expressed dissatisfaction: they usually wanted more discussion with councillors or officers, or both, on the background to policy problems. One county borough Member felt, for example, that the Council's minutes on education, or even those of the Education Committee itself, did not illuminate the real problems for her as fully as would the internal briefs from the chief officer and his colleagues (such as the Medical Officer of Health) to the Education Committee. She would like privately to discuss long-term policy problems with chief officers. Several Members, including 'satisfied' ones and from all parties, characterised their local authorities as typical of the whole local government system in its disregard for proper public relations and information work and looked forward to major reforms which should drastically reduce the number of separate authorities with which MPS have to deal. We formed an impression, talking to our respondents, that an important deterrent to their becoming more closely involved as observers of local government work is the fear that 'If I do it with one, I'll have to do it with them all': and that there are simply too many of them. There was no significant difference between the parties on 'dissatisfaction' (see Appendix, Table 25) although older Members appeared more satisfied—no Member of 56 years of age or over expressed dissatisfaction.

The significant distinction was, in fact, between those Members with and those without personal experience on a local council (see Appendix, Table 25): 18 per cent of those Members without this experience expressed dissatisfaction with the local authority as a source of local information, compared with approximately 3 per cent of those who had had that experience. This would suggest that serving on a local council gives a Member a much better idea of what information is available from the local authorities in his constituency and how it can best be obtained. He is, perhaps, more likely to appreciate the many problems with which local government officers are faced and may be more tolerant of the delays and difficulties that sometimes occur in the provision of information. This difference between the respondents with council experience and those without is not a reflection of a party division since no significant difference was found between the two major parties. This emphasises the relevance of having been a member of a local council.

At the same time, the probable context of this generally overwhelming satisfaction with the information received from local authorities should be stressed. Many Members pointed out that, from their point of view, local authorities are primarily agencies from whom they can seek help or official decisions in solving welfare cases and local problems, rather than mere sources of information. Information from the authority is very often directly concerned with individual constituents' problems or with very local issues, such as the parking of heavy vehicles in a residential street or complaints about refuse collection.

The problem-solving nature of the council's relationship with a Member is most clear in the poorest areas of his constituency. Where social deprivation (basically in housing conditions but spreading to all other social fields) is greatest, the MP can often make the least impact on the council's officials and committees with any given personal case, such as overcrowding. The council's first reaction, especially to a new Member who is not a local man with council experience, will be to show him their general housing list and some other similar individual cases to impress upon him that for every deserving case which happens to come to his attention they have on record dozens of others. He will naturally continue to do what he can for those people who come to him but circumstances force him to move his thinking from the case-work to the policy level and try to help the Housing Committee to obtain funds and consents for their programme. But he must be careful. He may take up the case of a person or family who seem to be very deprived and deserving in their housing needs and be told, routinely, by the Housing Manager that this case is normal and is receiving full and proper consideration within the local context of widespread need. It is only by persistent questioning of both sides that the Member may discover unusual features of the case suggesting official prejudice or even victimisation of the claimants, perhaps because of their rule-breaking in the past or because they make louder claims for the provision the law may allow than do most people—writing letters to councillors, local papers and their MP. When so many people in a locality lack adequate provision (especially in the field of overcrowded housing) it is easier for an official's injustice or even illegality against a claimant to be missed. In this situation the conscientious Member becomes an impartial 'investigating magistrate' rather than a welfare officer and can exercise his considerable political and public status, especially in those rare instances where local authority officials are found breaking rules and legal provisions. One Member mentioned to us in an interview (and several others confirmed) that there is a widespread belief that an MP can direct a local authority (and also, incidentally, a nationalised industry). If this Member's impression is accurate it would go some way to explain the popularity of approaching Members with personal claims on local authority services such as housing; that this widespread belief is formally unfounded does not seriously alter the case since the perception of an MP's high local status on which it is based is accurate. The problem for the claimant who brings damaging evidence against the local council to his MP's attention is that although the MP possesses the status to attack and seriously damage the council's reputation in the field in question, he may pause to consider very carefully the costs to his other contacts with the council in equally important policy fields over the years ahead of exposing them publicly on this current malpractice.

Outside these problems of local authority public services, Members tended to emphasise to us that local authorities are merely one of a variety of channels by which they keep in touch with local affairs. With only one exception, for example, every Member mentioned his local Press, and it was virtually impossible to find a Member who did not also ascribe a great deal of the local information he receives to personal contacts. A 1966 entrant would obviously tend, when we saw him in 1967 after only one year in the House, to stress his dependence on the Press and local authorities for his information, as he would lack a network of personal contacts in the constituency (unless he was himself a local man). Several Conservatives of longer standing emphasised to us that their contacts ranged well beyond our list of local party, local authorities and local Press: local and county business people, traders and doctors (the only professional group mentioned) were cited as those whom Members approached, if need be, to get information 'from the horse's mouth' rather than from official intermediaries. Labour Members, however long standing, did not make this emphasis so

213

strongly and specifically; the attraction among Conservatives for going for information to the man on the job, who is expected to know from his practical experience, is a strong one.

MPs talk about Local Councils and Councillors

'I used to take housing cases to councillors as being the proper thing to do. Now I go to the Housing Manager for efficiency's sake.' (Labour)

'I'm a local man myself: I shop, drink and live there. I have a big correspondence with the County Council who have opened a special department to deal with me.' (Conservative)

'I have a mass of local authorities which will all, quite rightly, be merged in the next few years.' (Conservative)

'I am not an established local man so we are not close.' (Labour, 1966)

'I liaise with Conservative councillors as we are trying to build up a strong Conservative group.' (Conservative)

'I don't interfere with local politics and don't support local Conservative candidates.' (Conservative)

'The County Council is more distant and more officious but I have good relations with the district councils.' (Labour, 1966)

'I'm not really interested in local affairs—more Commonwealth and foreign affairs.' (Labour)

'As sources of local information for me my seven district councils vary from very good to zero.' (Conservative)

'I don't interfere with local government. I'm satisfied.' (Conservative)

'A good local authority runs its own affairs.' (Conservative)

'My Town Clerk runs the borough and for a time tried to run me. The standard of all local councillors has declined a lot over the past ten to fifteen years because businessmen no longer have the leisure to go in for it, since business is tougher now. You get pettiness: Labour suffers from the lower calibre of councillors more than do the Conservatives in my constituency.

I have only ever met one properly competent committee chairman in twenty-two years.' (Conservative)

'I'd like a bi-monthly report from the majority Conservative group but they are rather parochial at the moment. The new GLC system should improve this gradually.' (Conservative, London)

'On the really tough problems such as local unemployment one deals with officials and Government Departments—the councillors are too low-calibre to help.' (Labour)

'I'd welcome a quarterly meeting with Labour councillors so long as I didn't get involved politically.' (Labour, 1966)

'I wouldn't want a regular meeting. It wouldn't be wise to get too closely identified with the Labour group in case they do something silly.' (Labour, 1964)

'On balance I find it's helpful to be a local councillor as well as an MP. I find no problems as to rank or status at Labour group or full council meetings.' (Labour, London)

'I don't get a thing from them. They are all corrupt, all graftful and all victimise people.' (Conservative)

'I read in the local Press that one of my local councils has raised a matter with me: three weeks later, the letter arrives.' (Conservative)

6. THE LOCAL PRESS

We introduced the local Press as a source of information on local affairs into our interviews by asking Members to place it in order of importance together with the three sources we had covered with them: the constituency postbag, the local party and the selected local authority. A fairly large minority of Members found this rank order impossible, usually on the grounds that each of these four items produced its own kind of information which was not comparable with the others. The postbag is information on personal cases, the local council produces information on local public issues and problems while the Press offers general news and unofficial information on public issues and problems, plus some news on personal cases.

But nearly two-thirds of those seventy-one Members who did attempt a rank order of importance put their constituency's local newspapers first (often emphatically so, with the postbag, local party and local council coming well behind). A further quarter of our respondents put newspapers as second in importance. Only two Members thought them the least important of the four items and one of these was moved by the political argument that the paper was so anti-Conservative as to not report his local doings, so he ignored it.

More than a third of these Members stressed that, for them, the local Press is an important source not only because they read it, but because of their personal contacts with the editor and reporters which, they said, are equally or even more significant, especially for 'inside' or background information which would not appear in the paper itself. These Members felt they often told the journalists things as well as learning from them. Woven in with this 'information' relationship between MP and local journalist is the 'news-publicity' relationship: the Member wants publicity from the paper and the paper wants news from the Member. How far each serves the other as an information source depends on how happy they are with this more crucial 'news' side of their relationship, so we should consider for a moment the Member as an information source for the journalist as well as *vice versa*.

Some Members write regular columns or occasional articles for their local papers, while others are confined to getting their publicity in the form of news items about their activities. Some provincial newspapers have their own correspondents in the parliamentary lobby at Westminster, while others share a lobby man as a common service to them. These journalists constantly ask the Members whose constituencies come within their papers' circulation areas for advance news and background on activities such as Questions, adjournment debates and party disputes, especially where local affairs are involved. Although Members do give some news to lobby journalists it is usually 'personal': what the Member is doing or thinking about a topic. The 'public' news usually flows from the journalist, who is, as a result, a significant source for the Member. Thus a provincial newspaper's lobby man will ring up a Member from his paper's area and say, 'The Government are going to announce (or have just announced) that they will (or will not) give the

much-awaited ship-building contract to a yard in your constituency's area: what do you think?' The Member then replies
off the cuff. The lobby man may well also say, 'I suppose you
think it quite right (or wrong) and (if wrong) that you'll be putting
down a Question and even considering leading a delegation to
the Minister?' One ex-lobby journalist told us that this leading
of Members by journalists, based on giving MPs news, is very
common among lobby journalists, especially the provincial
papers' men who know 'their' group of MPs so much better than
the national papers' correspondents can hope to know the
whole House.

Journalists with different jobs will co-operate to feed news to
Members and share the fruits of the Member's reactions. Thus a
national paper's lobby man may discover a fairly hot item of
advanced news on which he would like some parliamentary
reactions. He may tell the news to a lobby colleague on a provincial newspaper and ask him to gauge reactions from his particular group of Members (who may react more frankly and
openly to their familiar local man than to the national journalist
whom many of them would not know well). The two journalists
would then compare notes, the provincial man offering political facts on Members' reactions and the national man perhaps
helping his colleague with the national meaning and interpretation of the news item itself. This trading may be separated
into two parts concerning different stories.

If the local paper is not actively hostile to a Member's party
and if their 'news-publicity' relationship is fairly satisfactory
to both sides, there is no doubt that the personal links between
a Member and his local newspapers' staffs will probably be a
valuable source of local knowledge for him in addition to the
benefit to be gained from merely reading each issue of the paper
carefully, as most MPs appear from our results to do.

MPs talk about their Constituency Newspapers

'They are the only source of information on local affairs.'
(Conservative)

'They're probably the most important single contact at local
level.' (Labour)

'They keep me in touch with local trends—talking to journalists
is useful.' (Conservative)

'They're really only an initial source of information.' (Conservative)

'I read three local papers every week.' (Conservative)

'Information in the local Press always needs checking.' (Conservative)

'It's often inadequate and politically biased.' (Labour)

'It's a very anti-Conservative, pro-Liberal paper: they send me a complimentary copy but the wrong area edition for my constituency and I have nothing to do with them.' (Conservative)

'It's useful for general contacts but they're left-wing and give me no direct help at the personal level.' (Conservative)

'The local paper tells me what the local Tories are up to. It's also useful for general information which I need: I learned recently from the local paper that a Labour stalwart had lost a son and was able to write a letter of sympathy.' (Labour)

7. LOCAL ISSUES

We have noted that the local newspapers offer general views and information on issues and problems, with additional news on personal cases which come to their attention and which they consider worth publicity. Either deliberately or unconsciously, the local papers therefore tend to become one of the most important means by which local demands are generalised or aggregated ready for some official political response. Individual cases are presented as news and local officials and elected persons both on the council and in private associations are asked for their views on them. An editorial line on the subject may also be offered to the papers' readers. It is not, of course, difficult for a paper to 'start something' and it is correspondingly easy for people in responsible public positions to react with the opinion that an issue is 'all got up by the Press'—particularly when they feel, as, for example, many local Labour Party councillors and leaders feel, that the newspaper is permanently hostile to their interests. The Member of Parliament may share the view that a local demand is being created rather than aggregated by the local paper particularly if he himself knows of no examples of the individual events or cases which presumably form the basis of the matter. But, like the doctor or social worker,

218

the MP receives his caseload largely as a result of others' initiatives, whereas the reporter goes looking for evidence on a fulltime, although short term basis. It is true that, unlike the doctor or most social workers, the MP may well canvas or call on constituents as part of his general constituency work and thus pick up new cases and information, but, on the whole, he is sent or given such knowledge while the reporter actively seeks it out. Members are therefore wise not to dismiss too readily the local Press's claims on alleged new issues or scandals since they are not themselves regular investigators of local affairs. Members nonetheless do form ideas on local issues for themselves without, or well ahead of, local Press reaction.

Local issues did not bulk very large in our survey either in our interviews or in the individual Members' postbags which we analysed for four weeks each. Among the few letters about local issues which did appear in these postbags the most common topics were local roads problems, railway services and aspects of education (although not secondary reorganisation). In our interviews the Labour Members representing mainly working class seats quite often volunteered the fact that they received virtually no letters on either national or local issues. This was not to say that their working class constituents lacked opinions, but they needed to be identified in other ways: at surgery sessions, through the local party stalwarts or in pubs and clubs. Some of these constituencies are in any case very quiet, old places with little new development or the community changes it produces, compared with the newer suburbs or towns. When asked how he kept in touch with local opinion on issues (as opposed to the welfare role of helping personal cases) one Lancashire Labour Member replied that, in common with most Members for similar seats, he had never received letters from the constituency giving views on issues except for a few from 'cranks' and a certain amount in 1967 on abortion. Asked specifically about keeping in touch with local issues he replied 'my constituency has no local issues', a remark which could not, we suspect, be drawn from a Member from a South-East or Midlands seat, however deprived or affluent its constituents. It is the relative quietness of community affairs in this Member's seat which interests us: he is certainly not saying that his constituency has no local problems—but in that social setting they do not emerge as issues.

Local issues are not sharply distinguishable from personal casework. A series of cases may make, or contribute to, an issue such as a series of local authority tenants who want to see the rules changed to allow them to keep cats and dogs in their homes and who obtain a little publicity in the local paper and approach the MP as a means to their end. Or a personal case may be presented to an MP (or interpreted by him) in issue terms, such as a particular child (and thus all children) who has to go down an unlighted path on winter evenings after attending the youth club. Both these examples are local council matters and serve to remind us how closely involved with councillors' responsibility MPs can become and how many Members try to keep their distance from such matters, at least when they reach the level of local public issues. As we have seen, some Members insist that local government must, as a matter of principle, be left independent of MPs and Whitehall and others frankly declare that they do not wish to be splashed during altercations at the parish pump even in support of their co-partisans and councillors.

For these reasons, Members usually adopt an impartial and inquiring position when asked to involve themselves in disputes between local interests. All the warring factions may well be constituents and Members will not lightly offend one side in order to placate the other unless, of course (as with some aspects of local secondary education reorganisation) the local fight is a mere reflection of national politics and the Member is playing out a clear partisan role (thus one Conservative told us he had made a strong defence of local grammar schools and his local Conservative Association had passed a resolution supporting him). Where a local issue is less of a dispute between groups in the community and more of a challenge to authorities on behalf of one group, the sympathetic Member feels less hesitant about advocating rather than judging their cause. If these people's loss or injury is the gain of only the 'public interest' (as decided by the officials or elected leaders of some local council or nationalised industry) and there is no local group urging support for this official policy then the MP can go into battle on behalf of a 'united local public opinion'. Thus Peter Kirk and Stan Newens (Members for Saffron Walden and Epping) could battle for the anti-Stansted Airport views of the North-East Essex and East Herts Preservation Society because the opposing pressure group (the Stansted Development Association) was so weak both as an organisation and, apparently (not certainly) as a vessel of local opinion. Likewise Terry Boston (Member for Faversham, including Sheppey) could champion the anti-Sheppey Airport campaign of groups such as the Faversham Society because (so far as a non-resident can tell) there was no local organised group at all in favour of having the airport on Sheppey. The Stansted Development Association apart, these three Members were much freer to take an advocate's line than are, for example, Members for towns which are designated as New Towns or Expanded Towns (or which negotiate overspill agreements with authorities such as the GLC or Manchester); or Members who represent beautiful rural areas and who must deal with the common tensions between the 'locals', who often favour development, jobs and liveliness and the people who have bought property in the area because they wish to enjoy the unspoiled and peaceful beauty during their retirement or their weekends. We have not conducted any systematic enquiry into these two possible roles of the Member in local issues: the wary judicious listener to both sides of a community dispute and the battling advocate of an apparently united local public opinion. Such a study would be part of interesting research into the nature of the Member's public and political status.

One aspect of Members' involvement in local issues which has interested us informally, however, is the particular problem of their getting and grasping the information necessary to play a part in a local issue about a technical subject. Technical subjects are those where the political matters of good policy-making, and even the tactical or partisan appreciation of which interests stand to win or lose by some proposal, depend for their answers on technical facts and estimates. They contrast with simply amenity questions, such as bungalows on cliff tops or petrol stations in villages, by being difficult to judge without some attempt to follow the technical reasons behind them. Power lines, super grid sub-stations, natural gas terminals, gas holders, the lines of motorways and noise problems are common examples of technical local issues offering an 'information challenge' to Members whose constituencies are due to be adversely affected in the view of some local people. One such issue interested us particularly: the problem of aircraft noise over London, especially Chelsea.

Aircraft noise is a completely technical subject. London Airport being where it is, it is certain that planes will pass over certain places at certain heights with their engines running in certain ways. These facts flow from current methods of landing and take-off which themselves depend on current passenger aircraft design in general (not yet, for example, vertical or short take-off and landing) and the design of their engines in particular. There is some flexibility in handling the aircraft but, as we shall see, it is held by those responsible to be very limited. Noise over these places is therefore inevitable. It can be moved to other places and reduced in frequency by reducing traffic, but not reduced at its source given present aircraft design. Its effect on the people underneath can be reduced by insulating homes and other buildings at a range of costs for a range of returns in extra quietness.

Marcus Worsley (who sat as Conservative Member for Keighley from 1959 to 1964, returning to the House as Member for the safe Chelsea seat in 1966) came under some public pressure from constituents on the aircraft noise issue in 1966–7. Looking at the history and background of the problem, he believes that when London Airport was developed twenty years ago it was never thought that such distant districts as Chelsea would be affected. But now aircraft follow the flight path for landings up from South London over Battersea Park and turn for the final run over Chelsea. As the aircraft are banking at this point, their power, and thus their noise, is increased. The problem is particularly bad in the summer when the airport is running at capacity and night flying (particularly holiday charter flights) is at its peak, while people on the ground want to keep their windows open in the evening and at night. But Chelsea's daytime problem is also made worse by the large number of people working at home, in studios and offices, often on creative work needing a maximum of concentration.

Public complaint took the form of letters to Mr Worsley and activity by the Chelsea and Kensington Action Committee on Aircraft Noise, founded by two Chelsea ladies. This group got up a petition which Mr Worsley was to pass on to Douglas Jay, then President of the Board of Trade, and also arranged at least one public meeting which Mr Worsley attended. So the MP is confronted with a local group complaining about noise and wanting him to get it stopped or reduced or ameliorated. How can he relate this simple political demand to the complexities of the technical problem?

There is a variety of types of local issue as we have already noted; one functional distinction of great importance for the Member is that between issues on which the authorities are helpful and sympathetic towards what is an obvious problem and those where they deny or minimise the importance of the complaint. In these cases the Member, like the organised protest group or sympathetic local newspaper, must take on the role of David against Goliath and hope to count as his first victory the recognition by the authorities that a problem even exists. Mr Worsley believes that aircraft noise is emphatically not one of these cases: the Government and its various agencies, such as the British Airports Authority (BAA) which runs the airports, are sympathetic and helpful. Mr Worsley visited the Board of Trade twice in 1966 to obtain official information and views. A technical briefing from an official was arranged by a Minister and an all-party delegation called on the President of the Board of Trade to press the case at the policy level. There had been an aviation debate in the House in November of 1966 in which Mr Jay had discussed the problem. Mr Worsley had visited London Airport as one of the Conservative Members' party committee on aviation affairs when two-thirds of the time talking with the BAA officials had been spent on noise problems. He was also in touch with two anti-noise pressure groups, the Noise Abatement Society and the British Association for Control of Aircraft Noise (BACAN) and, through a Conservative colleague, also became familiar with the views of an organised interest in the field, the British Airline Pilots' Association (BALPA).

Access to information on the problem presented no difficulty; if there had been a dearth of factual background Mr Worsley would have turned to the House of Commons Library for impartial help. As it was, his information came easily, although always tied to some policy position, however loosely. The Board of Trade, BACAN and BALPA are all responsible sources of information. But in public affairs involving controversy there is no 'pure' information: Members and other interested persons must always judge each source and its basic interests when receiving its offering of information or facts.

Mr Worsley's main sources of technical background were his briefing from a Board of Trade official and his visit to the airport authorities. The letter from the Minister which came from J. P. W. Mallalieu, Minister of State, in reply to Mr Worsley's presenting the petition from the Chelsea and Kensington Action Committee was itself a valuable source. It also serves as an example of the letters Members receive from Ministers in reply to their advances about constituency cases and local issues, and shows the effort which Ministers require their officials to put into drafting correspondence with MPs. This particular letter was in reply to a petition and one would expect the Minister to appear sympathetic and concerned following such a demonstration of public opinion. But fairly solid as it is, this ministerial letter is by no means the most elaborate one we have seen in the course of our study; some very detailed replies, running to greater length, concern individual welfare cases or small matters of administrative policy having no weight of demonstrable public opinion behind them.

Board of Trade,
London,
S.W.1.
17 January, 1967.

As I have now taken over from Roy Mason duties in connection with Civil Aviation, the President has asked me to reply to your letter of 20th December enclosing a petition signed by a large number of inhabitants of your constituency, on the subject of aircraft noise. This is clearly a matter of deep and understandable concern to large numbers of people, and as you will have gathered from his winding up speech in the Aviation Debate on 21st November, the President has a great deal of sympathy for them, and is taking a close personal interest in the matter.

I understand that you recently had a fairly detailed explanation from our officials of the air traffic patterns which affect your constituency, so I will not repeat here the explanation of the reasons why aircraft fly over the area. But I can tell you that we are examining the possibilities of changing these patterns to some extent, though it would be wrong to give you the impression that anything which would significantly improve the situation in your constituency is likely to prove practicable in the near future.

Turning to the specific proposals in the petition, I must say at once that, as Roy Jenkins indicated over a year ago, we do not regard proposals for the closure of Heathrow Airport, and its replacement elsewhere, as a practical proposition. We have indeed been led to believe that the Noise Abatement Society, to which the petitioners attribute this proposal, have in fact now abandoned it.

The majority of civil jet aircraft operating today are already fitted with some form of noise suppressor (or 'silencer'). Substantial reductions in the noise of aircraft at source seem, in the light of the discussions at the recent International Conference on this topic, likely to depend on development of new aircraft which are basically quieter. The Conference indicated that technical progress in this field, had now reached the point where development of such aircraft were within the realms of possibility, and the idea of including noise criteria in the certification of new aircraft, which the President mentioned with approval in the Debate on 21st November, and which was strongly endorsed at the Conference, should enable such development to be assured.

In suggesting that the 'air highways' be re-aligned over less densely populated areas, I imagine that the petitioners have chiefly in mind the present arrangements whereby a high proportion of the aircraft coming into land at Heathrow have to pass over Central and West London. This is primarily the result of the siting of the airport up wind of the Metropolis, and the fact that present day aircraft have to carry out at least the last 8 miles of the approach in line with the runway. Under present air traffic control procedures, some have to be sent out even further to the east than this, in order to achieve safe separation between arriving aircraft.

Consequently these routes are closely related to the alignment of the main runways at Heathrow. The petitioners ask that the 'north/south runways' at the airport be brought to constant use, no doubt with this object in mind. In fact, the only other pair of parallel runways available at Heathrow are those on a north-east/south-west axis; as Roy Mason said in reply to your question in the House on 8th December, to bring these up to the same standard as the east/west ones would be very costly and large numbers of people would still be disturbed.

J. P. W. Mallalieu

Marcus Worsley, Esq., MP,
House of Commons,
S.W.1.

This official letter concentrated on the air traffic control and aircraft design aspects of the problem. Mr Worsley obtained an authoritative statement of the air safety side of the problem from a copy of the letter from Philip Warcup, then General Secretary of BALPA, sent to Mr Worsley's colleague, Cranley Onslow (Conservative Member for Woking), at his request as secretary of the Conservative Aviation party group. Mr Onslow then offered this BALPA statement to any interested Conservative who would appreciate knowing BALPA's view of the private Member's bill on aircraft noise currently before Parliament sponsored by Hugh Jenkins (Labour Member for Putney) whose constituency is affected similarly to Chelsea and other London seats.

BALPA,
Hayes, Middlesex.
11th November, 1966.

Cranley Onslow, Esq., MP

Noise Abatement—
Proposed Change to Legislation

The draft Bill calls for a maximum noise level of 100 PNdB and within the five years of the Bill coming into force this is to be reduced to 90 PNdB. The current requirement for London (Heathrow) is 110 PNdB by day and 102 by night and in the United States the requirement is 112 PNdB. In the UK statistics show that the noise levels are exceeded on approximately 5 per cent of all take-offs so it seems that it would be almost impossible to meet the target of 100 PNdB in 1967 without being unduly restrictive on the operators or requiring unsafe procedures by the pilots.

While no specific accident can be laid at the door of noise abatement procedures, there are at least two that have

226

occurred in the New York area to large jet transports where such procedures could well have been a major contributory cause. We in BALPA are positively against any operating techniques that reduce safety below the present level and our representative will be expressing these views at the International Noise Abatement Conference in London later this month. The proposed 90 PNdB level is even below what was achieved by a large number of piston engined aircraft, and we feel, and our American cousins in ALPA agree, that this figure will be impossible to achieve without a major technological breakthrough.

I have mentioned safety standards and it might be as well to elaborate on these. Present noise abatement procedures require pilots to throttle back on power even below their cruising power shortly after take-off, they are required to climb at a speed much nearer to the stalling speed than they would like, they are often required to make quite steep turns thus reducing the margin above the stall, and finally, they often are forced into taking off on what would not be the best runway for the particular occasion, i.e. they sometimes have to take-off with a strong downward or cross-wind component, which again must contribute to a reduction in safety.

The whole question of noise abatement would seem to hinge on which part of the community deserves the greatest protection. Is it the airline passenger whose safety should be paramount, or is it the person who lives within the vicinity of the airport and who has been most likely drawn to that area because he has some connecti onwith the airport? This decision must be the responsibility of the legislators.

For our part, we feel that it would be nonsense writing into any legislation the figures of 100 PNdB and ultimately 90 PNdB if there is little hope of these levels being achieved. We have had numerous examples where legislation has required operators to equip their aircraft with things like flight recorders, weather radar and transponders and where the mandatory date has had no chance of being achieved and dispensations have had to be given by the authorities.

We would support any move to reduce the noise levels around an airport but any action must ensure that safety standards are maintained and that the crew and passengers are not put to any additional risk. In this respect, of course, an accident occurring near to London Airport would almost be bound to cause casualties to the civilian population as the area is so heavily built up.

P. E. Warcup

This letter shows how technical information and judgements nearly always come to Members mixed with some policy implication or presumption, such as Mr Warcup's point that the resident 'within the vicinity of the airport . . . has been most likely drawn to that area because he has some connection with the airport'.

A third document conveying information to Mr Worsley was a report from the Heathrow sub-committee of BACAN which had met under the chairmanship of a representative of the Harlington Residents Association (adjacent to London Airport) to examine the Government's 1965 scheme whereby the Airports Authority would pay local householders grants towards sound-proofing their homes or channel the money to them through local councils. The sub-committee's report spelled out four reasons why the scheme had not been widely employed during its first year: poor publicity, poor administration, public apathy and the costs remaining to the householder even when one of the 50 per cent grants was payable. After commenting on each reason (and claiming that public apathy was a public lack of faith in the sound-proofing devices rather than a lack of concern about aircraft noise) the group called for a 70 per cent grant, a removal of alleged anomalies such as purchase tax on some sound-proofing items and a cheapening of the scheme by a bulk-purchase approach to its materials and labour. BACAN warned that if an adequate sound-proofing scheme was not introduced, public pressure to reduce airport use would become irresistible and the public resources poured into London Airport therefore under-used.

Information sources such as these helped Mr Worsley to answer constituents' letters, speak to the meeting organised by the Action Committee, deal with the matter in the House and local Press and generally to handle the issue. Like many Members coping with the local manifestation of a national problem, he gathered a good deal from colleagues, some of whom, such as Anthony Royle (Conservative Member for Richmond, Surrey) or William Rootes (then the Conservative Member for

South Kensington) had more experience of the problem. To a considerable extent on a matter of this kind there is co-operation with interested political opponents, such as in this case Mr Hugh Jenkins and Sidney Bidwell (Labour Member for Southall) who also count aircraft noise among their local issues. But there is often a certain amount of rivalry between parties who try to stop each other gaining a monopoly of publicity on a popular cause: Members therefore do certain things, such as formal deputations to the responsible Minister, on an all-party basis, but certain other things (such as confidential discussions with the BAA or with co-partisan GLC councillors) on a party basis. Aircraft noise over London would, of course, be a topic interesting the two separate London groups of Labour and Conservative Members.

Some Members, as we have said, receive no overt pressure from their constituencies on anything except rather special events such as Roman Catholic views on the Abortion Act of 1967. Mr Worsley considers Chelsea to be surely one of the most articulate of all, although the very range of local, national and world issues which interest an unusually high proportion of his constituents may limit the impact of each individual effort. The Chelsea and Kensington Action Committee on Aircraft Noise was the specialist group on this subject and the local London Borough Council passed a resolution supporting Mr Jenkins's Anti-Noise Bill. But neither Mr Worsley's local Conservative Association nor any other established body approached their Member on the issue: the matter rested on the Action Committee and on the newspaper coverage.

Even though Chelsea's grievances on this issue were not deafening, they were, at the time we are examining and are likely always to be, considerably louder than some other areas because of differing social class structures. There is a story (which almost has to be apocryphal) of a Chelsea resident who invited friends to dinner in the summer of 1966 after which they were to play some chamber music together. In view of the warm weather and the usual problem of aircraft noise this gentleman telephoned the London Airport authorities, explained his position and asked if the flight path could be moved for an hour or so to allow the quartets to be fully enjoyed. This was agreed and the planes moved for the period specified. Requests of this kind from Fulham are probably less frequent. Whether this story is true or not, it would be very interesting to lay a map of the aircraft stacking areas and flight paths to London Airport over maps of constituencies and socio-economic class distribution and study the strength of openly-expressed public opinion against the noise. Even the incomplete sequence of Putney, Battersea, Chelsea, Fulham, Southall and Hayes and Harlington gives an idea of the variety which may be expected in local protest groups' pressure on each of the Members, the local Press coverage, etc.

Members can, of course, influence these things just as they probably can encourage or discourage the flow of individual welfare casework: Mr Jenkins of Putney was sufficiently concerned about the problem to introduce a bill under the 'Ten Minute rule' and, having taken that step, was obviously interested in publicising the issue and making his case against the current levels of noise. For a Member in this clear posture on a local-cum-national issue of this kind all public outcry is valuable ammunition and the Member will try to encourage its flow. A Member who is faced with local demands to take some line on which he is doubtful or hostile, however, will do the minimum necessary on the issue to avoid trouble and will judge how strong, how effective, and how closely connected to his own partisan basis of support the complainants appear to be. Members of Parliament, like the rest of us, tend to be rather deaf to messages they do not welcome and this might distort the results of any broad study of the varied strengths of public opinion across several constituencies. But no one is in favour of aircraft noise and a comparative study of Londoners' protests would at least illuminate the roles of MPs as recipients, reflectors and creators of local public pressures.

We have seen in this chapter on the Member's sources of information on his constituency that the messages and pressures which he receives are of several kinds. In the case of letters from constituents and visits to his surgery, our broad conclusion has been that the Member himself could well be the main determinant of how may people will bring their troubles or their opinions to his attention. It is relatively easy, over a period, for a Member to establish a reputation as a keen welfare officer and even easier for him to set a fast pace in the local newspapers, with his views and comments on political issues of all kinds. Conversely, a Member who requires his constituents to take the initiative in consulting or lobbying him with only a minimum amount of stimulation in terms of local reputation as a 'welfare' type of MP, or who seeks no publicity for his views and activities, may depress such advances from the public to the lowest possible level within the socio-economic framework of his constituency. Given that middle class people tend to be more vocal in the community than working class people, it is possible for the level of advances to a Member sitting for a mainly working class constituency to be very low indeed. This notion of a Member influencing the volume of requests and messages which he receives should not be exaggerated, but its presence may be quite marked in certain cases. In particular, the Member can normally control his public 'visibility' by developing either a close or a distant relationship with his constituency's news media.

A second conclusion on information for Members about their constituencies concerns its overlapping or 'network' nature, when seen through the Member's eyes, similar to the national political 'network'. A Member comes to appreciate that a local issue is forming, or that a new problem is facing some of his constituents, by a variety of channels. He absorbs these various messages in a rather random sequence and forms an impression or view as the evidence builds up. Thus, for example, on a Saturday in his constituency, he may begin by reading constituents' letters sent to him at the local party office and catching up with items in the local Press. He then perhaps, discusses party organisation and local matters with his agent before holding his surgery. Lunch may be with his agent, a group of party stalwarts, a local businessman, or the Clerk of one of the constituency's local authorities. The day could then continue with some afternoon canvassing or a tour of several villages and farms. There may be a social function to attend in the evening involving further conversations and exchanges to add to the day's already considerable total number.

Throughout this day of reading and talking the Member will receive news and comment on all kinds of topics, not all of them local matters. He could claim to be gauging 'public opinion' on anything from local street lighting to Herr Willy Brandt. But, taking constituency matters alone, it is clear that no one channel of information, such as constituents' letters or talking with his agent, will normally hold a monopoly of the messages he receives on a given topic. It is, no doubt, this experience of overlapping information, or a 'network' effect, which led Members to stress to us the importance of their personal contacts in the constituency and, often, to find it impossible to put into a rank order of importance their sources of local information gained from their postbags, local parties, local authorities or local Press.

CHAPTER V

THE MEMBER'S VIEW OF HIS PARTY

1. INFORMATION FROM PARTY HEADQUARTERS

The results of our survey on Members' links with their local parties appear above in Chapter IV. In this chapter we refer to any information or assistance which they receive from the national party organisations. All modern Members of Parliament are nominated, supported and financed by a close partnership of the local branches of national parties (which nominate them, partly finance them and do the local grass-roots electioneering) on the one hand and the national headquarters of these parties (which oversee and supervise both nominations and organisation and may also help financially) on the other. The three main parties' headquarters are thus elements of parties which are systematically organised down to individual constituency level; the Member's local party is indubitably part of the national party, pays funds to it and enjoys constituent rights at its regional and national annual conferences. There is not the brief quadrennial gathering of fifty fairly separate state parties of American party politics nor the complex movement of elected legislators between party groupings of some continental Parliaments.

A British MP is nominated and elected on a party ticket and he behaves as a party man at Westminster: his party's national headquarters exists to organise the party and has the right of veto when he is first nominated as a candidate for the party. Although the personal relationship between a backbench MP and his party headquarters officials may be distant or nonexistent, their formal political relationship is clear. He is one of the party's MPs and participates in the affairs and decisions of the parliamentary party (which include the election of the national party's Leader) while having a special relationship with one of the constituency parties. What expectations flow from this situation and, in particular, what 'information relationship' do Members appear to expect with the national offices of their party?

The Conservative, Labour and Liberal Parties each maintain party headquarters in London (all three, at the time of our study, in Smith Square, Westminster about 400 yards from the House of Commons). Each organisation has departments concerned with information and research on public affairs. We tried to establish the importance to Members of these facilities and their opinion of any arrangements made by the parties for information services to their MPs; we wanted also to establish and explain any differences between the two main parties. We also considered Smith Square as a possible potential source of further information for MPs. We first set out our respondents' views on their party headquarters as information sources and then give the detailed responses of Labour and Conservative Members, together with accounts of their parties' organisations for research and information.

As with other topics in our survey we asked our Members to weigh the importance to them of different sources of information by answering the question: 'May we turn to national affairs?... About your party's headquarters.... Would you say your party's headquarters offers backbenchers a major source of briefing and information?' The 'chalk and cheese' distinction between Conservative and Labour Members shown in Figure 26.1 is most striking: 80 per cent of the Conservative, compared with 18 per cent of the Labour Members, saw their party headquarters as a major source of information. Moreover,

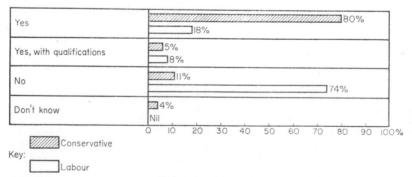

Figure 26. Part One
'Do you consider your party headquarters a major source of information?'
(N—105: 55 Conservative and 50 Labour MPs)

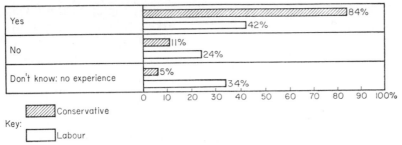

Figure 26. Part Two
'Could you obtain an individually written brief or research report from your
party headquarters?'
(N—105: 55 Conservative and 50 Labour MPs)

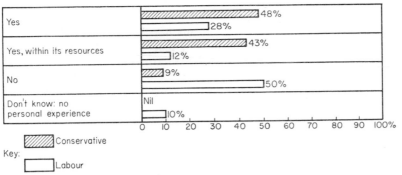

Figure 26. Part Three
'Are you satisfied with the research and information provided?'
(N—104: 54 Conservative and 50 Labour MPs)

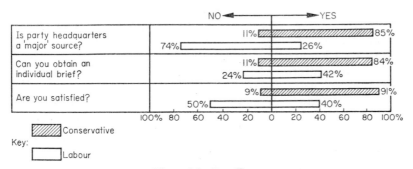

Figure 26. Part Four

Figure 26. *Respondents' views of their party headquarters as sources of information.* (See Appendix, Table 26.)

these proportions were scarcely affected by the provision for a qualified positive reply. We then asked (Figure 26.2): 'Can backbenchers in your party personally obtain an individually written brief or research report from your party headquarters?' 84 per cent of the Conservatives, compared with 42 per cent of Labour Members, replied 'Yes'; 11 per cent of Conservatives, compared with 24 per cent of Labour, replied 'No' while 5 per cent of Conservatives and 34 per cent of Labour did not know, usually because they had never themselves tried. Our third question (Figure 26.3): 'Are you satisfied with the research and information provided to backbenchers by your party head-quarters?' produced a 91 per cent general affirmation by Conservatives (compared with 40 per cent on the Labour side) with 9 per cent of Conservatives and 50 per cent of Labour Members expressing dissatisfaction. All Conservatives expressed a view on this while 10 per cent of Labour Members said they did not know whether to feel satisfied. These results taken together offer the most party-polarised picture of all our survey results.

The Labour Party

Only one Labour Member in four among our respondents was prepared to describe Labour's national headquarters as a 'major' source of briefing and information, even within the context of some qualification on their answer. Whether the three in four Members who replied 'No' were dissatisfied or critical about this situation is another question, however, since Figure 26.3 shows that the ratio of *satisfied to dissatisfied* respondents was only 5 to 4. Threequarters of the dissatisfied Labour Members were elected in 1964 or 1966 although rather more of the 1964 entrants were dissatisfied compared with those who entered the House in 1966. Similarly there was a heavy concentration of dissatisfied MPs among the younger elements of our respondents.

Further analysis suggests that these differences between the 1966, 1964 and pre-1964 entrants are related to what help they expect to receive and what help they would like to receive from their party headquarters. The pre-1964 entrants appear to have low expectations and low aspirations: not only were they more likely to say that Transport House is not a major source of information and that they could not get individual briefs, but they were generally satisfied with this situation. The 1964 entrants appear to have low expectations, but high aspirations: they agreed with their longer-serving colleagues that Transport House was not a major source and that they could not get individual briefs, but were generally dissatisfied. Finally, the 1966 entrants seemed to have somewhat higher expectations and high aspirations: of the three groups they were the most likely to say that Transport House was a major source and that they could get individual briefs, at the same time expressing some general dissatisfaction with the Party headquarters. The fact that the 1966 entrants found the gap between their expectations and aspirations less wide may explain why they were less dissatisfied than the Labour Members elected in 1964. There is some evidence to support this view: Members elected before 1964 were more likely, and 1966 entrants least likely, to say that they were satisfied 'within the resources available'. This would suggest that the Members elected in 1964 or earlier were, because of their longer experience, more aware of permanent limitations on headquarters imposed by lack of resources and the accepted constitutional position of the Research Department. Thus Members first elected in 1966 may still have felt that certain services, including the provision of individual briefs, were available: one Labour MP elected in 1966 said that he had received a notice informing him that MPs could get individual help from Transport House. Their longer-serving colleagues, however, while often aware of such help, regard it as minimal, unimportant and certainly not amounting to the provision of individual briefs; and whereas the pre-1964 entrants were satisfied with this state of affairs those first elected in 1964 were not.

The extent to which Labour MPs were dissatisfied with the services by Transport House is even clearer if the strength of phrases used is considered: unfavourable comments outnumber the favourable by 3 to 1 and even those who made favourable comments were hardly showing any great enthusiasm. The most favourable remark was, 'they get quite a lot of criticism but they're pretty good'. Another Member, one of the 'don't knows' said, 'they have capable people there', while the most another was prepared to say was that Transport House was a useful rather than a major source of information. Two other MPs remarked on the excellent Press cuttings library at

Transport House, but complained that Members were not encouraged to use it. Some of the more critical remarks speak for themselves: 'hopeless—very, very poor'; 'they don't exactly badger MPs with help'; 'peddling well-known stuff'; 'I can't imagine them being able to help'; 'they have no ideas or useful research to offer'; 'Transport House stuff is often ill-timed and indiscriminate'; 'they appear to give MPs a very low priority'.

In addition to criticisms of either the intrinsic quality of the Research Department or its policy on priorities there were some claims that ideological barriers exist and that the Department had no independence or objectivity of view. One Member asserted: 'Left wing views are an obstacle to obtaining information and that which is provided is not particularly useful . . . I would not trust the information received from them . . . they are too much under the control of the leadership.' Similar complaints were made by a number of MPs, mostly, but not all, Left wingers. One Member, for instance, had asked for information on the Common Market: he was not a Left winger and is, in fact, in favour of Britain joining the EEC but he felt that a balanced statement on the advantages and disadvantages would be useful. But this was refused, he told us, and he was offered only ministerial statements instead. Similarly a Welsh Member asked for information about Labour policies for Wales and was simply given ministerial statements. These two examples may have practical rather than political explanations based on a simple lack of resources to do anything more than send a Member a copy of a Press release already done on a ministerial speech. If they do have political reasons behind them, however, they may reflect the need for the Research Department to dispense only the official Government line (or official Opposition line when Labour is out of office) while privately pressing the NEC and party leaders (whether Ministers or Opposition spokesmen) to change the line. If the Department is involved confidentially through the NEC in trying to influence a policy, it is natural that it should avoid any charge of divisiveness by putting out for public use anything other than the strict official position. It is also understandable, however, for Labour MPs who do not know of these exchanges going on between Transport House, NEC members and their parliamentary leaders to conclude that a flat repetition of the official line is all that the Department is capable of.

What is the background to these striking views from Labour Members? How are Labours affairs arranged so that the combination of remoteness and hostility which our backbench respondents revealed to us has come about? The well-known and controversial view of Robert McKenzie is that despite formal appearances the distribution of power in each of the two major parties is very similar. Regarding their professional headquarters organisations he writes:

'Thus while the Labour Party can justly claim that its professional organisation is subject to the control and direction of the democratically elected executive of the Party, it can with equal justice be pointed out that the parliamentary leaders of the Party have been able to wield very nearly as much influence over the activities of the professional organisation of the Party as have their opposite numbers among the leaders of the Conservative Party.'[1]

In some respects it is undoubtedly true that Labour Party Leaders and other prominent members of the PLP have exercised considerable influence over the work of Transport House. Professor McKenzie shows this clearly in respect of Ramsay MacDonald and Arthur Henderson.[2] A great deal depends, however, on the personalities and party background of these leading personalities and the current political situation. A Leader who is seen as politically strong in general will enjoy more effective power and influence within the National Executive Committee of which he and his Deputy-Leader are, of course, formally only two ex-officio members among twenty-six others. Unlike the Conservative Leader, he does not enjoy the power to select and reject the Party's Chairman and Vice-Chairman nor the formal Conservative power to hire and fire any of the Party's full time officials. He is not head of the Party's organisation, nor the sole source of authoritative policy, nor the exclusive agency by which official policy-making and research may be conducted: the NEC and the Party's annual conference are these things. Yet the political authority of the Leader within both the PLP and the NEC is so great as to modify this formal constitutional situation into one of considerable

---

[1] R. T. McKenzie, *British Political Parties*, 2nd (rev.) ed., Mercury, 1963 p. 560. [2] Op. cit., pp. 560–6.

ambiguity if not quite to the position parallel with the Conservative Party which Professor McKenzie detects. Thus annual conference, Party headquarters in Transport House and the PLP are all in an ambiguous or interpretable relationship with one another on many issues of Party affairs.

In particular, the PLP's powers under the Party's Constitution to decide the tactics and timing of the implementation of Party policy could be held to imply a share in policy work, involving in turn a claim on the Transport House research facilities (which would otherwise be devoted to the policy functions of the NEC and conference itself). With a complex formal situation, the informal influence of personalities can find considerable scope in Labour's affairs: when those personalities or other factors change, the machinery may permit a rather different formal interpretation based, or rationalised, on a different internal political situation. A study of the formalities, therefore, offers little guidance as to what demands for research and information Labour MPs may in practice make on Transport House and we found this ambiguity reflected in our Members' responses.

Each department at Transport House is responsible to the NEC, usually through one of its sub-committees. For instance, the Press and Publicity Department is responsible to the Publicity sub-committee and its Director acts as the sub-committee's secretary. Each sub-committee consists of NEC members with a possible addition of a number of co-opted members (usually MPs) and one or two Trades Union Congress representatives on such committees as Home Policy and Overseas. The responsibility for regular party propaganda and political education lies with the Press and Publicity Department and some of this material will normally reach Labour MPs, although it is not specifically prepared for them. The only publication which is primarily prepared for, and made available to all members of the PLP is *This Week*, a short broadsheet, usually about eight pages long, providing concise facts and comment on current issues, forthcoming by-elections, local elections and so forth, and generally providing MPs with material with which they can attack the Opposition and defend the Labour Party's record as a Government. It is edited, not by the Publicity Department's staff in Transport House, but by the Parliamentary Press Liaison Officer, Gerald Kaufman, who is located in the Prime

Minister's office in 10 Downing Street and is available to all members of the PLP to advise them on relations with the Press and on publicity in general. With the exception of his editorship of *This Week*, however, Mr Kaufman's job is to give advice and help rather than political information.

The responsibility for research at Transport House is divided between two departments, the Research Department[1] and the Overseas Department under the direction of Secretaries (Terry Pitt and Gwyn Morgan respectively, at the time of our study). Each is responsible to a sub-committee of the NEC, the Research Department to the Home Policy sub-committee and Overseas to the Overseas sub-committee. These sub-committees normally appoint additional committees and study groups to examine particular policy areas. For example, there are four committees working under the auspices of the Home Policy sub-committee: finance and economic affairs, science and industry, social policy, and local and regional government. Each of these committees consists of NEC members together with a number of co-opted MPs. Since 1964 these Members have often been junior and middle-rank Ministers. In addition there are always several *ad hoc* study groups whose membership is normally drawn from a rather wider circle comprising members of the NEC, Government representatives (usually junior Ministers), backbenchers and outside experts who are members of, or sympathetic towards, the Labour Party. In 1967 there were seven such groups of which four were studying industrial democracy, North Sea gas, race relations and regional planning.

The work of these study groups on aspects of home policy and the servicing of the NEC and its sub-committees form major parts of the Research Department's responsibilities and receive considerable emphasis. Between the 1966 General Election and July 1967 the Department produced some two hundred papers for these purposes. Mr Pitt sees the Department's main task as contributing to party policy formation which would, of course, make a regular information service for Labour MPs or party members a subsidiary concern. The difficulty is that the Research Department lacks the staff and budget to do more policy research work. The staff of the department in 1968, in addition

---

[1] The Labour Party's Research Department should not be confused with the Labour Research Department which is a separate body with no Labour Party connection.

to its head, was fourteen research assistants, eight clerical workers and eight in the Party's library which the Department runs. The Conservative Research Department had thirty research staff and forty supporting staff, all on higher salary schedules than obtained at Transport House.

Labour's Research Department does offer some service to Labour MPs. An 'Information Series' of briefs relating to current or future political issues is produced and made available to all Labour Members. These documents have been produced with any frequency or regularity only since the Party's return to power in 1964. Between that date and mid-1967, fifty-two briefs in this series were produced with a concentration in 1966 which saw the appearance of twenty-nine of them. These Information Series briefs are not, however, specifically prepared for the use of MPs in debates, although they are often occasioned by particular matters of current interest which are also the subject of debates in the House of Commons; they are, in fact, available not only to Labour MPs, but to local parties and party members. This means that the Labour Party produces nothing that is exactly similar to the briefs prepared by the Conservative Research Department for Conservative Members.

The Information Series are foolscap typescripts whose length varies with different topics, although they are never very long. Since 1964 they have naturally had the defensive tone of a party in office and often lean on plain statements of Government policy at least for their introduction, followed by an account of Government action and a note on its results so far. The Party's opponents and critics are less often attacked directly in these briefs than in *This Week* or in the Research Department's recent addition to its generally published output, *Economic Brief*. The statistics in the Information Series are, however, often based on a pre- and post-1964 distinction, to emphasise Labour's record as Government. Nonetheless, the approach is generally positive, emphasising and justifying what has been done and what the Government intends to do and this serves to offset the somewhat defensive tenor.

These briefs are designed for varying purposes: a relatively full note was produced as an urgent brief on devaluation in late 1967 and the Government's 'package' of public expenditure cuts in January 1968. At other times a shorter brief will cover a topical issue as occurred on cotton policy and the fees charged to overseas students. There is an occasional purely background offering such as the affairs of the drug industry, the Government's holding in private industry or the problems of the social services. Some are mere reading lists on particular topics such as the Labour Party and British politics, comprehensive schools or trade unions. Many of these Labour briefs are drawn from a single source rather than bringing together a range of materials into one document. Examples of these weaker efforts were a 1966 brief on transport, which was in fact a ministerial speech by Barbara Castle and a similar 1967 example which was a speech by Anthony Greenwood, Minister of Housing. A more valuable type of single-source brief are those conveying new information to Members such as the 1967 briefs offering digests of the evidence to the Royal Commission on Local Government in England and of the PEP report and survey of *Racial Discrimination in Britain*.

The briefs prepared by the Research Department are made available to Labour MPs through the Labour whips' office at the House and the number provided for distribution varies according to the Department's estimate of the likely demand. Their availability is mentioned on the Labour Member's weekly voting timetable which the whips' office produces (which is also called a 'whip'). Between about fifty and three hundred copies of each brief are sent over to the House: there is no arrangement for direct delivery of particular briefs to Members who are known to have a special interest in that field.

As the provision of generally available briefs to all Labour Members is rather limited, it is not surprising that the provision of specially prepared briefs or reports for individual Members virtually does not exist. Only very occasionally will the Department undertake to do an individual job for one backbencher. They do try to help the average of three or four Members who inquire each week, usually by sending them a letter. This letter, however, is often little more than a reference to existing sources, sometimes merely telling the Member where he could secure the information he wants. Members who ask are permitted, but not encouraged, to use the Party's library and extensive Press cuttings collection.

In addition to its research work for the NEC on present and possible future policies and its regular briefing tasks for MPs and others, the Department must perform routine servicing functions for the Home Policy sub-committee and its offshoots and process the annual tide of resolutions submitted to annual conference by the constituency parties and affiliated trade unions ready for the NEC's declaration of its official view on each one. Between conferences the Department similarly examines and comments on many resolutions on current issues sent into Transport House from the same sources, to which other headquarters departments make a reply. There is a continuous flow of enquiries of all kinds (about 100 each week) by letter, telephone and personal callers. Leading party spokesmen (nearly always Ministers or NEC members) require briefs and drafts for speeches or make enquiries in this connection; these have run at about three or four each average week in recent years with the demand no less since the party's return to office in 1964. A good deal of publicity or propaganda work, such as writing or preparing party publications and preparing or checking Press releases is also done in the Research Department rather than in the Press and Publicity Department for purely traditional reasons. Since, as in any office, the routine jobs are often also the urgent ones, they take up most of the Department's time leaving a fairly small portion—perhaps less than one-fifth—for research of a broader and longer term nature.

This proportion is obviously unsatisfactory for an office called a 'research department' but the lack of Party money is a permanent problem. If more was found and spent it would probably be wisest, from the viewpoint of policy research and the concept of a policy-making NEC, to relieve the graduate researchers of some of the routine information and publicity tasks (by hiring non-graduate staff who can be trained in this more simple work) but without cutting off the researchers from the flow of politics and events. It would represent a considerable improvement for these researchers if they could spend even half of their time on longer-term, sophisticated work which may form the foundation of party policies a few years hence.

If at some future time the Research Department and other Transport House departments come to enjoy bigger budgets they may well be spent in other directions than to meet the needs of Labour backbenchers. One function enjoying an enhanced priority from a better-equipped Department could well be the briefing of party spokesmen (whether Government

Ministers or shadow Ministers in a Labour Opposition) and covering their speeches both within and outside Parliament. As John Mackintosh has noted when comparing the parties on this point, 'the Labour Party has always expected its leading members to do more for themselves . . .'[1] This was evident when Denis Healey, now Secretary of State for Defence, was shadowing Sir Alec Douglas-Home (then Lord Home) as Foreign Secretary and was asked after a lecture how he kept up with foreign affairs. He replied that he cut lots of newspapers, including overseas ones, and filed them; he had no help with this, whereas Lord Home no doubt had them placed in front of him, ready marked and filed, by civil servants. Now that Sir Alec is himself a shadow Foreign Secretary, his position contrasts with Mr Healey's in 1961 as he has the services of at least one research officer at the Conservative Research Department. Although Mr Healey said at the time that he suspected doing this routine job for himself helped him to remember the items which he cut out and read, it is possible that Labour's leading spokesmen will demand more research backing in the future, and be in a position to persuade the NEC to provide it as a priority over backbench needs.

Another possibility for research growth at Transport House would be the research servicing of the party groups of Labour Members within the PLP whose work is outlined in the final section of this chapter; if the House as a whole develops more specialised committees which examine major issues of public policy, the party groups of Members on both sides will tend to become the party caucuses of these new official parliamentary committees. In that case, a clear demand to the NEC for full Transport House servicing would be a natural consequence, and may be met as the importance of these new committees becomes clearer. A further development within a better endowed Transport House could be a mass party policy education enterprise similar to the work of the Conservative Political Centre and the several post-war Conservative offerings to their national membership of 'two-way exchange of ideas'. Whether such very large-scale exercises in obtaining political 'feedback' from a national party are genuine attempts at participation or mere public relations routines, their existence on the Conservative side probably predicates a certain issue-centred or, at

[1] J. P. Mackintosh, *The British Cabinet*, 2nd (rev.) ed., Stevens, 1968, p. 525.

least, discursive approach to constituency politics which changing political style may come to require of the Labour Party.

To sum up the Labour side: the Party's Members are currently offered a minimal information service and virtually no research support by headquarters. Most Labour backbenchers recognise this fact and some are bitterly critical, while their colleagues are resigned to the tradition that the Party's policy-making processes are so shaped by the customary interpretation of the Party's Constitution as to direct the efforts of a very modestly staffed Research Department towards the NEC and its subsidiary committees and groups and the party's front-bench leaders, leaving almost nothing over for backbenchers to use. If more money flowed into the Transport House organisation the Research Department could be improved in several other ways than offering to Labour backbenchers the kind of service which, as we shall now see, Conservative backbenchers receive. The Department need not, for example, alter its present terms of reference at all but merely hire extra subsidiary staff to allow its graduates more time to read and write and even travel in pursuit of their special subjects, and thus to improve their value to the NEC's policy-making function. Or, as we have noted, the Department could take on new tasks of political support for the leadership or political education among the mass party. If Labour MPs want better servicing, either as a whole or in their party groups or individually, they will have to press for it in competition with other claims, all of which have stronger footholds in the councils of the NEC than do Labour backbenchers as such. They might be well advised to turn their attention towards officially provided information services in the House of Commons Library and Chapter VI offers evidence that this is in fact the trend among the more active Labour Members.

The Conservative Party

The Labour Members appeared so hostile to, or at least separated from, their party's research arrangements that we thought it best to present their views before an account of Transport House situation. On the Conservative side, however, we have seen from Figures 26.1 and 26.3 that opinions are much more favourable and will therefore discuss them after an account of the party research organisation and services themselves.

Three organisations constitute the Conservative Party headquarters: the Central Office, the Conservative Political Centre (CPC) and the Conservative Research Department (CRD). Central Office is the least important in the research and information field and the Conservative Research Department the most important. Central Office is the administrative and financial arm of the Party concerned with the constituency and electoral organisation, party finance, propaganda and public relations. The various departments dealing with these routine matters liaise with the voluntary organisation of the Party through the National Advisory Committee of the National Union of Conservative and Unionist Associations, although they are not responsible to them. When Conservative MPs require help and information about these internal Party matters, Central Office will supply it but general political information is the specialised concern of the Conservative Political Centre and the Research Department.

The Conservative Political Centre, like the departments of Central Office, is linked but not responsible to the National Union by a National Advisory Committee. The CPC is, as Professor McKenzie has described it, 'not primarily concerned with providing party members and speakers with ammunition for use in immediate political controversy. Its purpose is rather to provide background information and to encourage the study of long term problems.'[1]

The pamphlets published by the CPC provide MPs with useful information about the trends in Conservative thinking and policy, although these pamphlets are of course personal and recommendatory rather than official statements, often representing only the view of the author. Useful as such commentaries often are to MPs, the CPC is not a body from which Members can expect a constant flow of information nor one upon which they can call from time to time for specific assistance.

This more general service, either to all Conservative MPs or to individual Members is one of the several functions of the Conservative Research Department. The Department had its origins in the 1920s,[2] under the impact on Conservative affairs of the two minority Labour Governments. Viscount Davidson and Neville Chamberlain were particularly involved and

---

[1] R. T. McKenzie, op. cit., p. 283.
[2] R. T. McKenzie, op. cit., pp. 284–6.

Chamberlain tended to use the new semi-official organisation as his personal office. R. A. Butler built up the Department after the war, when he served as its chairman, and established its modern position. Since 1948 the Research Department has been dependent on Central Office for virtually all its finance, and has therefore been under its broad administrative control. In 1964 R. A. Butler ceased to be chairman and Sir Michael Fraser (then Director of the CRD) was created deputy chairman of the Party Organisation (and secretary to the shadow Cabinet), 'with special responsibility for the Conservative Research Department'. This meant that the link with Central Office became closer, but not entirely formal and the CRD retains a semi-autonomous status. Thus, unlike the departments of Central Office and the CPC, the CRD is not linked to the National Union by means of a National Advisory Committee, but does work closely with the Advisory Committee on Policy, which includes representatives of the National Union. The CRD is, furthermore, responsible to the Leader of the Party.

According to the party publication *Party Organisation*, the Research Department has four functions:

'to undertake long term research and to assist in the formulation of the Party policy; to provide official secretaries for the parliamentary committees of the Party and to prepare briefs on issues coming before Parliament; to provide Members, candidates, speakers and all party workers with information and guidance on current political affairs; to assist all departments of the Central Office with factual information.'[1]

These last two functions of servicing Party activists and the departments within Central Office obviously bring the Research Department into close co-operation with Central Office and its Publications Department which produces and distributes party literature, much of which is prepared by the Research Department. In this, the Conservative practice is similar to Labour's and pre-empts some of the working time available to the Research Department for less propagandist and more original work.

Inevitably, different priorities are given to these various functions: first priority is given to research into future policy, second to parliamentary briefing, third to the preparation of party

[1] *Party Organisation*, 1961, p. 16.

publications and fourth to the servicing of Party activists. Our interest in the Department's work is confined to its parliamentary work: Professor McKenzie offers a broader account of the various functions listed above.[1]

The Research Department is situated in two historic houses in Old Queen Street (one owned by a retired MP) and about the same distance from the Commons as Central Office itself. Its physical separation from Central Office is a reflection of its semi-autonomous status within the Party organisation. The staff consists of a Director and thirty research officers specialising in particular policy fields. The majority of the research officers work closely with the shadow Ministers (or other frontbench spokesmen) appointed by the Leader. In addition the Department has forty supporting staff who provide research and clerical assistance.

Just as the Research Department has priorities concerning its work in general so it has priorities concerning its parliamentary work in particular. These are, in descending order of importance, servicing the shadow Cabinet, assisting *individual* shadow Ministers, servicing the parliamentary committees to party groups of Conservative MPs, providing general briefs for all Conservative MPs and, finally, undertaking individual work for backbench MPs.

The Director of the Department, Brendon Sewill, estimated that about one quarter of the Department's time is devoted to original research and the analysis of materials designed to help form Party policy. At the same time his research officers are each concerned with day to day tasks as well as longer-term studies, as are their opposite number on the Labour side. But these tasks are more clearly parliamentary in character than in Labour's case: the research officer's first duty is to the Leader and his frontbench colleagues, especially when the Party is in Opposition and the leadershiplacks Civil Service backing. Once these demands have been fulfilled priority can then be given to the party groups in Parliament. These groups receive policy outlines and briefs from the research officers, who act as their secretaries, with clerical assistance also being provided by the Research Department. The servicing of backbench Conservative MPs as a whole and, still less, the provision of individual assistance to backbenchers are not therefore regarded as its

[1] R. T. McKenzie, op. cit., pp. 284–6.

most important task by the Research Department. Nonetheless, they are regarded as important and it is important to bear in mind that they must, in the nature of things, be carried on simultaneously with the other tasks allotted to the Department and may sometimes be regarded as more urgent than these.

When the Party enters Government office this order of priorities does not change; the emphasis shifts, however, since the frontbenchers, now Ministers, can obtain Civil Service support, thus leaving rather greater leeway in the Research Department from which MPs may benefit. We formed the impression that some Conservative respondents answered our questions about Party research in the pre-1964 context of greater facilities being available to themselves. We interviewed them some thirty-two months after their party lost office and some Members gave very complimentary answers which they then modified or updated to conform with existing conditions: this 'lag' may well make our Conservative responses a little too rosy, although we were careful to record the modified answer in such cases. When the Party is in power the principal contact between the Research Department and Conservative Ministers, apart from the Department's continuing responsibility for long-term policy projects, consists of providing the political touch to Civil Service briefs especially in Ministers' public pronouncements and for Party political occasions.

When the Party is in Opposition the link between the Department and the frontbench spokesmen is very strong: each shadow Minister is appointed chairman of both the Party's policy group and the party group of Conservative Members in the House which relate to his shadow responsibility, while the Department's relevant research officer continues to be secretary to both groups. Moreover, the research officer acts as a personal assistant to his shadow-minister: some senior shadow Ministers, such as for foreign affairs or economic policy, enjoy the services of more than one research officer. The main routine job of each research officer is to provide his shadow Minister with briefs before debates in the House (copies of which go to the frontbench spokesman who is winding up the debate). In a more general sense the research officer acts as a focal point in each policy area for ideas on particular subjects. He tends, with experience, to build up a range of contacts allowing him to draw upon a considerable variety of sources in serving members of the shadow Cabinet and acting for the relevant policy and parliamentary groups.

The role that the Department plays during those periods when the Conservative Party is in Opposition has two disadvantages, both stemming from the concentration of its sources on servicing the frontbench spokesmen. First, long-term policy planning and research comes under greater pressure of time and second (of particular importance to our study) the services available to backbenchers are curtailed. It is therefore important to bear this in mind when assessing the current usefulness of the resources of the Department to backbenchers.

The services available to backbenchers are of two kinds: those offered to all backbenchers and those offered to individuals. Backbenchers receive a considerable amount of party literature, much of which is prepared in the Research Department. All Members receive *Weekend Talking Point*, which many Members use as a basis for constituency speeches on current matters and *Weekly Newsletter* which is a more general publication. 80 per cent of Conservative Members pay a subscription for *Notes on Current Politics*, which provides them with factual ammunition and comment on a great variety of current issues equivalent to Labour's *This Week*; there are also less general publications offering rather more comment such as *European and Overseas Review*.

Apart from these items of Party literature, MPs may also receive briefs on specific matters which are before Parliament or which are of current political interest and likely to be raised in Parliament. The exact circulation of these briefs varies according to the nature and breadth of the topic. Overall, and as a result of both greater resources and a rather different attitude towards the parliamentary Party, this Conservative briefing operation is larger and of better quality than on the Labour side. Occasionally, on major matters every Conservative peer, prospective parliamentary candidate and agent throughout the country, as well as every MP, receives a copy. Each significant bill attracts a brief for its second reading debate and major political legislation such as the annual Finance Bill or nationalisation measures would call for additional detailed briefs covering all clauses at their committee and report stages. Other topics attracting a brief would include regular political events such as the publication of the Government's annual farm price review and current political problems such as family poverty, or the *Torrey Canyon* wreck and the Government's treatment of the oil pollution which followed. Unlike the 'Information Series' produced by Labour's Research Department the majority of Conservative briefs are prepared for particular debates, and even those briefs prefaced by a phrase such as 'a political controversy is arising . . .' are usually in anticipation of a possible debate.

Some of these briefs are placed in the Conservative whips' office for Members to pick up (and Members notified on their weekly timetable whip). In May of 1967, for example, all MPs were offered a brief on rates in preparation for a debate on the subject on a private Member's motion moved by Julian Ridsdale (Conservative Member for Harwich). In other cases, however, where only certain Members are likely to be interested, the brief will be sent to selected MPs. All Conservatives representing rural constituencies, for example, will receive a brief on agriculture; all Scottish Conservative MPs will be sent briefs dealing with Scottish legislation; if the brief is concerned with details of the committee stage of a bill then the Conservative side of the relevant standing committee will receive a copy. There may be two briefs on a topic offering two levels of detail. Thus the team of about twenty Conservatives who dealt with the Transport Act of 1968 in all its stages received much fuller briefing than that offered to Conservative Members as a whole. But even this level of detail may not compare with that offered privately to shadow Ministers. On the Government's 'package' of cuts early in 1968, several hundred pages of typescript were produced for the Opposition frontbench.

Nearly all of this material is the Research Department's own product. When the Party is in Government the Research Department is most likely to produce all of its output itself since the major organised interest groups deal directly with Conservative ministers through their civil servants. In Opposition, however, some of these groups are attracted to the Party's Research Department as an avenue for influence during disputes with a Labour Government. During the prolonged period when the steel industry was faced with re-nationalisation the industry's trade association, the British Iron and Steel Federation, took over much of the briefing function of the Conservative side of the debates in the House notably, of course, at the detailed committee stage. The Research Department naturally relied on the Federation for much about the industry and therefore conveyed the Federation's material to its MPs after approving it for general political emphasis and removing any detailed Federation proposals (such as on precise compensation terms) to which the Conservative Opposition did not necessarily wish to be committed.

Since the revitalising of the Research Department under R. A. Butler's chairmanship after the war it has produced an annual average of about one hundred and twenty briefs for the parliamentary Party. They are usually foolscap typescripts, sometimes containing photostats of other material. Even the generally available briefs can be quite long, such as the forty-three pages on the 1967 Defence Estimates, but the average length of an informal selection of briefs which we saw between February and May 1967 was twelve pages; some, such as those on decimal currency and teachers' salaries, had only four pages. Nearly all of these briefs are severely practical documents symbolising the Research Department's routine service for its MPs while in Opposition: the provision of effective background information coupled with reliable facts to assist their effective parliamentary performance as opponents of the Government. The design adopted for this purpose is a factual introduction to the topic in question followed by more detailed information, including statistics, from a variety of sources. Extracts from Labour and Conservative speeches and pronouncements and quotations from expert authorities may then be offered before, occasionally, some suggestions for further study. The majority of briefs are prefaced by the words, 'it is hoped that Members may find the following notes useful . . .', thus seeking to demonstrate that in no way is the Research Department trying to impose its views on backbenchers nor conveying a Party leadership line.

Conservative Members may also make use of the Party's Press cuttings library, which was run by the Research Department at the time of our survey. This library is situated in the Central Office building in Smith Square: in July 1968 responsibility for it was transferred to the Press Department in Central Office. Mr Sewill described it as the most comprehensive in the country (and, in particular, notably better than that offered in the House of Commons Library which is based on only one national daily, *The Times*). Some twenty years' supply of cuttings are cross referenced by their topic and the name of any MP mentioned in the text. It would seem, however, that most Conservative MPs either do not know they can use this service or do not feel the need for it, at least to the extent of going over to Smith Square, since Mr Sewill found it underused by MPs—a situation he regretted. Our interviews with Conservatives on Party research services sometimes revealed ignorance of the Central Office cuttings library and one Member declared that such a collection that he could use was plainly needed at Party headquarters. In our section in Chapter VI concerning Members' attitudes to the House of Commons Library we shall show how Conservatives appeared less aware of the Library's provision and more inclined not to answer our various detailed questions, pleading lack of experience and knowledge of the House's Library services: in one case Conservative 'don't knows' were one quarter of their party's responses. This more passive approach to reference services which require some activity by the Member himself may be part of the explanation of Conservative Members not fully using the cuttings at Central Office.

In addition to the service offered Conservative Members on a collective basis all Conservative backbenchers may ask the Research Department for individual help, possibly involving a special brief or report. This service continues when the Party is in Opposition although it is attenuated in practice, as Members themselves seem on the whole to recognise in their answers to our questions. Examples of this extra facility which some Members gave us usually concerned local constituency issues of special complexity of the kind we discuss in the final section of the previous chapter. In Opposition conditions a particular specialised research officer will meet such individual requests as he can. He may be able to offer something highly satisfactory to the Member because he is currently involved (perhaps with his shadow-Minister or a Party policy group) with that very topic; he may agree to offer a document at a later date, or he may be obliged to decline all help beyond a telephone conversation giving the Member sources to follow up.

It was clear to us from our inquiries that some manners of approach and perhaps some particular individuals at any given time will receive the minimum formalities of assistance compared with their colleagues: the line which the Department keeps in reserve against being put upon is that their first priority is to the Party rather than any individual outside the leadership. The Department keeps no separate record of inquiries from Members—they form part of the approximately one thousand inquiries by letter and telephone received each average week including approaches by Party candidates, activists and agents in the constituencies and by the general public.

As we have shown in Figure 26.1 85 per cent of our Conservative respondents regarded their Party headquarters as a 'major' source of information. The small minority of 11 per cent (six Members) who said it was not tended to be the longer-serving Members (a characteristic among Labour Members as well). None of these six had been in Parliament for fewer than eight years, two had been MPs for over twelve years and three for more than seventeen years. All six were over forty-five years of age and four were over fifty. Thus, in our sample, this negative view was confined to longer-serving and older Conservatives. Over 80 per cent of our Conservative respondents told us that they could 'personally obtain an individually-written brief or research report' from the Conservative Research Department. Again, only 11 per cent (six Members) denied this, five of them being pre-1964 entrants; three Members said they did not know or had never tried—two of them were also in the House before 1964.

There is, we suspect, a little difficulty with this question. Despite great care in drafting and putting the question, it is possible that Members took the point in more than one way, their answers thus depending on what one means by an individually-commissioned job.

Bearing in mind this problem of method we should note that what may have been ignorance of the services available from the Research Department was not confined to recently elected Members. It is reasonable to suggest that these Members have been convinced, as a result of various experiences, that they cannot obtain individual briefs and that only the general briefs are available. Some of these who replied in the negative may never in fact have tried to get an individual brief because they have always believed that no such service exists. Others probably tried, received what they regarded as a negative response and concluded that the Research Department was not willing to

255

supply individual briefs. Finally, some Conservative Members were convinced that the Department was already overburdened with frontbench responsibilities that rendered it unable (perhaps unwilling) to provide backbenchers with individual briefs. There is a sense of hierarchy and proper approach to the Research Department which is a rough equivalent to Labour's 'Left wing problem': as one Conservative put it when asked this question about getting individual jobs done, 'it depends on your importance: if you're genuine and not a nuisance they will help'.

We have seen from Figure 26.3 that 91 per cent of Conservatives were 'satisfied with the research and information provided to backbenchers by party headquarters'—(a result which is not, we believe, particularly influenced by the fact that a small group of our Conservative respondents were frontbench spokesmen, who enjoy priority at the Research Department and who were not, therefore, speaking for themselves in reply to this question about backbenchers). But only about half of these Members (48 per cent of all Conservatives) expressed unqualified satisfaction, the rest indicating satisfaction with the CRD 'within its resources'. This qualified reply indicates a natural wish for a bigger and better Research Department, with which probably no Member would disagree, rather than any agreement with the tiny handful of Conservatives who felt that the information they received from the Research Department was poor or even, as one single Member described it, 'useless'.

There was a widespread belief that such deficiencies as existed had far more to do with the budget within which Party headquarters had to work than any possible desire by the Conservative leadership to deprive Conservative backbenchers of information or to restrict Central Office and the Research Department to working exclusively for the frontbench. (The remark that a Member who is not 'important' needs to be 'genuine' and 'not a nuisance' should be borne in mind, however). Some Conservatives (as with some Labour Members) commented that better research for their Party's MPs should enjoy higher priority within the party budgeting and one Conservative frontbench spokesman sharply criticised the Party's mass advertising campaigns of recent years as an alternative to spending more on research and information work. Further analysis of the responses to this question showed that the more recently elected MPs were considerably more likely to give a qualified positive reply, whereas their longer serving colleagues were more likely to express an unqualified satisfaction. There was also some evidence that such dissatisfaction as existed, whether outright disapproval or qualified approval, was rather concentrated among graduates as opposed to non-graduates. There does not seem to be any significance in this beyond the fact that the more extensive a person's education the more diverse and more conditional his opinions.

The number of favourable comments, both about the Party headquarters in general and the Research Department in particular, far outnumbered the unfavourable ones. Some Members were entirely uncritical, offering the frequent comment that the services provided were 'first class'. Others, however, were less eulogistic: praising the work of the Party's headquarters but recognising the limited financial resources. One such MP remarked that the help he received was 'very good as a routine service', another (a senior frontbencher) said, 'they do the best they can with the available resources'; a third simply said 'they do their best'. These were general remarks: rather more particular praise was found for the briefs prepared by the Research Department and distributed through the Conservative whips' office. These were variously described as 'excellent general briefs', 'good circularised stuff' and 'good standard briefs'. One Member linked these briefs to his own approach: 'I'm no highbrow going deep into politics—their general briefs are good enough for me.' A frontbench Opposition spokesman described the individual briefs done especially for his speeches as 'usually of a high journalistic level'. Another, more senior, frontbench spokesman felt it 'inevitable and unfortunate that the research officers of the Research Department are rather chair-borne—a pity they can't get out and about more'.

In a sense this was a plea which found an echo among a number of backbenchers: in their cases it took the form of a demand for a wider experience among the staff of the Research Department which would better fit them for undertaking research into policy in depth and making policy recommendations to the Party. Some of these Members felt that too much attention was paid by the Department to immediate tactical considerations in Parliament and not enough time or energy was devoted to research in depth. This view occasionally crystallised into suggestions that the Department should 'act as a civil service for backbenchers', although it was not always clear how far the needs of individual backbenchers and the party groups in Parliament could both be met by the Research Department. The granting of priority in Party research services to frontbench spokesmen and to the party groups of Conservative Members, with individual backbenchers coming behind, was freely acknowledged and supported as was the fact that the leadership needs more support from the Research Department when the Conservatives are in Opposition than when serving as the Government.

Our questioning of the five Scottish Conservative Members and one Ulster Unionist among our respondents did not reveal a very different situation in the services available from the offices of the Scottish Conservative and Ulster Unionist Parties in Edinburgh and Belfast. The shadow Ministers on Scottish affairs enjoy a similar priority within a naturally much smaller overall size of operation. These offices confine themselves to Scottish and Ulster affairs and these Members turn to the Research Department in London for other things. The Ulster Unionist told us he has more contact on his Ulster information needs with the Northern Ireland specialist at the Conservative Research Department than with the Ulster Unionist headquarters in Belfast: after the CRD he turns direct to the Northern Ireland Government Departments (which are, of course, controlled by his party).

The overall pattern is therefore one of general satisfaction often with some limited reservations. Conservative MPs generally appreciate the services provided by Central Office and the Research Department even though many regret that more help is not available. This generally favourable view covers Party propaganda (which a number of our respondents found useful) the general briefs (which came in for little criticism) and the special briefs made available when possible to individual MPs (for which a number of Members had particular praise).

The Liberal Party

Two of our three Liberal respondents said that their Party's headquarters in Smith Square was a 'major' source of information for them, the other saying that it was not. This Member, however, is one of the handful of MPs who has provided himself with personal research and administrative assistance from his own resources and is therefore not comparable with the other two respondents.

The obvious difference between the Liberals and the two main parties is size: their headquarters organisation is tiny and very hard pressed financially, but they have, on this side of their responsibilities, to deal with only twelve MPs, including the Leader. These Members all do a 'frontbench job' by speaking for the party in the House: thus, for example, John Pardoe (North Cornwall) spoke on social security, Richard Wainwright (Colne Valley) on economic affairs and Michael Winstanley (Cheadle) on health policy at the time of our survey. Within very limited resources, their researchers in Smith Square must try to treat each Member as the main parties treat their frontbench leaders. A natural result of these specialised links between each MP and Liberal headquarters is that Members are very hesitant about asking the Party's researchers for jobs which fall outside their official demands as Party spokesmen.

Despite their roles as Party spokesmen in the House, Liberal headquarters is obliged to give the MPs a lower priority than the other, more taxing, functions of policy-making research and the writing of Party propaganda and publications. On these matters the gap between what the Liberal Party on the one hand and the two main parties on the other have to accomplish is not so wide since, for example, a well researched election manifesto calls for a similar amount of work from both a large research office and a very small one. To prepare such a document well is an enormous challenge to a department as small as the Liberal Party's. The resources of the modern Liberal Party have always been more limited than those of its major rivals. During 1968 the Party was faced with a financial crisis in which its budget was cut by a third, involving a loss of two senior officials, six junior staff and the reduction of the headquarters establishment from fifty to thirty-six. These drastic cuts did not affect the Research Department because it is 'financed mainly from a bequest about which the Party never gives details.'[1]

The Research and Information Division of the Liberal Party is headed by a Director, Ron Arnold, and has two sections: the Research and Information Departments. The Information

[1] *The Daily Telegraph*, June 10, 1968.

Department consists of an information officer and two assistants who are responsible for a Press cuttings collection, the Party headquarters library and the compilation of day-to-day, factual information and routine policy background briefs. The Research Department comprises four research staff (normally graduates) and two secretaries. Like the two main parties this Department has a threefold priority which, although different from both Labour and Conservative practice, also places MPs in the third and lowest position. The Department's first priority is the needs of the official Party panels and committees producing policy proposals; they require briefs and drafts and also routine servicing like their equivalent bodies in the two main parties.

The second Liberal research function is more individual to the Party—a bi-monthly pamphlet which goes out to the Party for discussion and information. This more discursive or 'background' kind of job falls to the official party researchers because the Party has no regular, unofficial body producing new material of its own volition. Although the Liberal 'Unservile State Group' has published on Liberal philosophy and policy, the Party's research and information Director cannot concentrate on hard 'manifesto issues' knowing, as his opposite numbers in Transport House and Old Queen Street know, that this kind of discursive or analytical work is going on elsewhere. Thus the Fabian Society, certain trade union and TUC research officers, and occasionally *Socialist Commentary* on Labour's behalf, and the Conservative Political Centre, the Bow Group and the Institute of Economic Affairs for the Conservatives, are continuously organising and publishing useful material which will nearly always illuminate Labour and Conservative policy-making problems and sometimes influence and contribute to the papers which the research departments of the two main parties themselves will submit to their respective party policy-making authorities.

The third priority of the Liberal researchers is to service their MPs and prospective candidates. The twelve Members receive the fortnightly *Campaign Bulletin* which is designed for speeches and political work like its rivals, such as *This Week* or *Notes on Current Politics*. The Party's small size leads to all of the MPs being on one or more of its policy groups which are serviced by the Research Department. This participation in party policy discussion by all Members removes the alienated feeling we observed among Labour and Conservative Members who were not themselves included in party policy study committees set up by the NEC, the NEC and PLP jointly, or by the Conservative Leader and which led them in our interviews to manifest, on the Labour side, some hostility towards processes they saw nothing of and, on the Conservative side, a possibly somewhat deferential acceptance of the importance of these affairs.

Before the General Election of 1964 the Liberal Research Department devoted most of its time to the consideration of long term policy and relatively little to the servicing of the parliamentary Party. When the Labour Party secured power in 1964 with a very small majority and the Liberal Party felt itself to be almost in a position of holding the balance, much greater priority was given to the Liberal MPs. This state of affairs continued until after the election of 1966 but the earlier pattern gradually reasserted itself and long-term policy has again taken first priority. Within this plan, every reasonable effort is made to help the Liberal Members prepare for debates and other aspects of their parliamentary work, but the Research Department freely acknowledges that it encourages Liberal MPs to use the Research Division of the House of Commons Library whenever possible, especially where the matter on which they require assistance is outside their responsibility as Party spokesman. Our three Liberal Members stressed the problems faced by their headquarters and said that although they could have individual work done it would nearly always relate to their official spokesman job. Liberal Members also appear to ask each other for help a good deal, based on their spokesmanship and other known interests and support each other as a team: they have a convention that all will leave a job elsewhere in the House to help fill the Liberal bench when one of them is on the Speaker's list to speak for the Party in a debate. Our respondents praised their Research Department's staff ('they are very devoted and will work all night to prepare for a debate'), although one disapproved of the priority afforded MPs by headquarters policy and what he felt is a poor distinction made there between long term policy research and the provision of more regular information.

This Member's fairly mild criticism of the arrangements

apart, our Liberal respondents conveyed the impression that they fully sympathised with headquarters' problems, accepted the resulting priorities and tried to work within these limits as best they could. Naturally, if limits can be overstepped, so much the better: one of our three Liberal Members had, on previous occasions, failed to get information he needed from his own headquarters and had successfully telephoned both main parties' research departments and asked them. He was unsure whether he had benefited from traditional British fair play or from the more humdrum reality that assistants in the main parties' headquarters probably do not know the names of all their own party's Members and took him for one of their own.

What should be the research service offered by their parties' headquarters to backbench Members who do not speak officially for their party? It is clear from our survey results that all Members in the three parties would like the situation in which some organisation, possibly their party in Smith Square, was willing to be a general factotum giving them facts, quotations, documents, briefs and speech notes quickly upon request. But Members did not particularly demand that this ideal situation should be brought about by their party: the feeling of being poorly or well-equipped for information was not logically linked in their minds with a failing of their party to the exclusion of other resources such as official parliamentary facilities—the House's Library—or physical facilities such as offices, secretarial help or personal research assistants.

Having studied the three research departments alongside our respondents' views, we share the feeling that beyond a certain natural distinction between 'propaganda' and 'information service' there is little logical reason why one agency rather than another should provide help to MPs. The partisan element must obviously come from the party itself: we asked Members who told us they were dissatisfied with their party headquarters, 'What advantage would (more of) their work have which other sources lack?' Most Members who were asked this were Labour, since many more of them declared their dissatisfaction, but quite a number of Conservatives made the same comment in passing: the universal reply was that only party headquarters could select, emphasise and bring together facts and arguments ready for political battle. No other source, not even a quasi-partisan or friendly source such as a trade union or trade association which is fighting a particular issue with or against a given party, can offer the Member the political cutting edge and clear party line which his own party's officials can provide. The other special function of the party is to produce simple propaganda or 'political education literature' in which the Member can share as a party man. Nearly 60 per cent of our respondents who said they were dissatisfied with the research and information provided by their headquarters (mostly Labour) also said that the straight partisan material which 'packed a political punch' (as some put it) was well done.

Although asking the parties to do the partisan work for Members seems to us the limit of their logical function, there have been some voices urging a much greater burden on the parties. A few Members (and also, we have informally gathered, some senior civil servants) believe that official information services in the House of Commons Library should be severely attenuated on the grounds that the parties should pay for any sophisticated information service Members may demand. One journalist completed an account of the constituency case-work of Eric Lubbock (Liberal Member for Orpington) with the straight assertion that because Members need help with the complexities of this casework it is the business of their party to provide it.[1] This opinion presumably rests on the perception that the parties send these Members to Westminster and should therefore look after them. This is a tenable view but no more so than that which stresses that it is the electorate that returns MPs to Parliament and then proceeds, quite properly, to make political and personal demands on them. Therefore, on this argument, the public should provide for their general information needs through official agencies, such as the House's Library (while duties concerning constituency casework and local issues could also be publicly supported, either by the taxpayer or locally by the ratepayer).

The parties are private associations which are free to spend their money as they think best. We have seen that on the research and information side of their work the individual needs of the single Member come lowest in their priorities. With the Liberals running a minimal service, with Labour hard-pressed

[1] Mary Holland, 'What your MP can do for you', *The Observer*, September 22, 1968.

to expand even modestly the size and conditions of service of its small research staff, and with even the comparatively well-endowed Conservatives[1] under pressure (at least while they remain in Opposition), it seems clear enough that the parties would each use any extra money either to do their present jobs rather better or to expand the work they can do for groups of clients, particularly formal committees or teams of their MPs. A group approach reduces the chance of a researcher rehearsing material to several individual Members and is generally more efficient.

We suspect that the gradual growth of the omnibus, individually-based information service offered to all MPs by the House of Commons Library will lead the party research departments to scale down their regular information work (including, perhaps, the present Conservative and Labour 'whips' office briefs'). This would allow them to concentrate on policy work, the servicing of party spokesmen and the basic partisan and propagandist material which only they can produce. These matters are very much questions of opinion: in our view such a division of the task of assisting Members and their leaders to operate the party and parliamentary systems would be a reasonable one.

2. INFORMATION FOR SPONSORED LABOUR MEMBERS

Most MPs are associated, formally or informally, with outside organised interests. In some cases this involves the payment of a retainer and the recognition by the group concerned that the Member is its official spokesman in Parliament. For instance, James Callaghan was spokesman for the Police Federation before he became a Labour Minister in October 1964 when he was replaced by Eldon Griffiths (Conservative Member for Bury St Edmunds). Similarly, MPs drawn from both major

[1] In 1967 the Labour Party's expenditure from its General Fund (i.e. all national expenditure excluding by-election expenses) amounted to £404,214 (NEC Report, 1968, pp. 44–6), whilst Conservative national expenditure amounted to £1,085,000, including £191,000 on research alone and a further £37,000 on parliamentary services (The Times, January 5, 1968). A further contrast is seen in the fact that the salary range of research personnel at Transport House is £985–£2,115 (these salaries were under review at the time of writing), compared with personnel in the CRD who receive salaries which range from £1,000 to a figure at present considerably higher than the Labour ceiling.

parties act as spokesmen for the National Union of Teachers, receive information from the NUT and ask parliamentary Questions on its behalf. In the case of the NUT the MPs concerned are usually ex-teachers and their link, like many of the less formal relationships, reflects a long-standing interest on the part of the Member.

Many of the informal associations that MPs have with interest groups do not involve any payment or financial assistance to the Member: sometimes the Member's interest pre-dates his election to Parliament, sometimes it develops after his election, and sometimes a group will actually approach a Member to represent it in Parliament. The vast majority of interest groups, however, do not usually seek parliamentary representation through the selection processes of the political parties; they rely on the accident of selection to provide a House of Commons in which they will find one or more MPs sympathetic to their interests.[1] The essential relationship that develops once the Member has been elected is normally between that Member and the interest group and not between the group and one of the political parties.

There are, of course, two important exceptions to this rule: the trade union 'sponsored' Labour candidates and those who stand as Labour-Co-operative candidates. Thus the unions and the Co-operative Party actively seek selection by Constituency Labour Parties (CLP) of candidates they have already themselves chosen and whom they are willing to sponsor financially. If their candidate is selected the CLP will receive financial assistance with election expenses and, quite often, a further grant to help run the local party. So the unions and Co-operative Party seek representation through the establishment and maintenance of a parliamentary group of 'their' Members who are also, of course, Labour MPs and full members of the Parliamentary Labour Party.

It is true that the NUT does give electoral grants to the all-party panel of MPs which assists the NUT in the House (the National Farmers' Union gave similar grants to some Conservative MPs before the War) but the NUT is not aligned with

---

[1] A group may lose their single spokesman through death or electoral defeat and recruit a new one. The Pharmaceutical Society had one of its own members as spokesman in Sir Hugh Linstead (former Conservative Member for Putney) and now have a barrister, Ivor Richard (Labour, Barons Court). Some Members perform such services, and receive fees, without their connections being announced.

any party, nor does it try to secure the selection of sympathetic candidates by constituency political parties. Even where several MPs are associated with one outside organised interest such as the NUT, they form a rather looser group than the union or Co-op groups of sponsored Labour Members who have nearly all shared the experience of selection as a sponsored potential candidate before they were adopted by a CLP, and who also serve as bridges between their sponsor and their CLP across which the financial grant passes. In addition to the sponsored union Labour MPs and the Labour Co-op Members there are, of course, many other Labour Members who are ordinary individual members of trade unions and (less commonly) of the Co-operative Party: we are not concerned here with them since our interest is in the various groups or panels of union-sponsored and Co-op Labour Members as possible sources of political information to the Members concerned.

About two-fifths of the Labour MPs at each post-War general election, and about one quarter of the Labour candidates have been sponsored either by a trade union or by the Co-operative Party. The union attachment has been the more common: more than one-third of Labour Members have been sponsored by a union and about one-fifth of Labour candidates. A general Trade Union group (comprising all union-sponsored MPs) exists within the PLP. It is, in effect, a backbench group similar in function to the groups of Labour MPs for Wales or Scotland. But we are concerned with the relationship between sponsored Members and their own particular unions, as revealed by their information links, rather than with the role within PLP affairs of the aggregate grouping of all union-sponsored Members.

At the time our sample was drawn, there were 132 union-sponsored MPs in the House of Commons, of whom a hundred were backbenchers and thirty-two Ministers or whips. The largest individual trade union groups were the National Union of Mineworkers (NUM) and the Transport and General Workers (TGWU), each with twenty-seven Members, followed by the Amalgamated Union of Engineers and Foundryworkers (AEF, formerly the Amalgamated Engineering Union) with seventeen, and the General and Municipal Workers (NUGMW) with ten MPs. A further twenty-three unions had representatives in the House of Commons, ranging from the Shop-workers' eight Members

(USDAW) to those like the Steel-workers (BISAKTA) and Draughtsmen (DATA) each of whom had one representative. In these latter cases the union's one MP has to deal with all the union's business in the House, but the larger unions all have viable groups which meet from time to time and share the work of representing the union in Parliament.

Eleven of our sampled Labour respondents were trade union-sponsored Members, and one further Member had formerly been sponsored by his union, but had retired from the parliamentary panel, and is now an unsponsored Labour Member. We asked each of these respondents how far his union provided him with information on public affairs, what other assistance it gave him and to what extent he found his association with the union useful in his role as an MP. In addition to this, a particular study was made of the AEF and its group of seventeen MPS.

The AEF is one of several unions which have expanded their parliamentary representation since 1945 in a conscious effort to increase their influence in the PLP: the seventeen Members in the union's parliamentary group in 1966 contrasts with four in 1945. This is also true of the two general unions, the NUGMW and the TGWU, particularly the latter, and the AEF's policy may be seen as part of its modern trend towards being a general union despite its craft origins. The AEF is now the second largest union in Britain and one of the most active in the field of sponsorship. It selects union members to go on to its parliamentary panel (which makes them eligible to be sponsored candidates if a CLP offers a parliamentary nomination) by a extensive system of examinations and interviews. The extremely interesting concept of consciously training them to serve as parliamentary candidates and, hopefully, as Members of Parliament, is already well-developed.

Like most of the larger unions, the AEF maintains a research department whose resources are available to members of the union's parliamentary group. At the time of our study in 1967, this research department consisted of a research officer and three research assistants, together with some clerical help.[1] The AEF is, of course, first and foremost an industrial organisation

---

[1] Two of the research assistants at this time held Diplomas in Economics from Ruskin College, Oxford, and the other was an economics graduate. The department has to face a fairly high turnover among these staff.

and its research department's first priority is to serve the industrial needs of the union rather than the political needs of its parliamentary group. Moreover, the location of the department at the AEF headquarters in Peckham does not facilitate frequent and informal personal communications with their MPS.

Of the seventeen Members in the AEF group in January 1967 two were Ministers and three were officers of backbench party groups of the PLP. In addition to these a number of peers associated with the union also attend the group. The group does not meet regularly or particularly frequently: the frequency of meetings depends on the issues before the group and on average it meets about once every six weeks. There is no steering committee and the secretary of the group (currently David Watkins, Member for Consett) deals with any routine matters, including contacts with the union's chief officers.[1] From the union's point of view, the parliamentary group is primarily a means of applying political pressure to solve its problems or secure information which may not otherwise be available or is at least more readily available through Parliament. Thus members of the group are often asked to raise matters on behalf of the union, to write to a Minister or to ask a parliamentary Question. Although these matters may include highly contentious national issues, such as prices and incomes policy, they are usually to do with specific union interests—very often particular individual cases or grievances arising from the AEF officials' routine services to their membership.

The assistance that the sponsored MPS receive from the union takes a rather wider form. Members of the group receive copies of most union publications, while the union's research department provides the group with briefs on particular matters from time to time. Members of the group may also obtain individual briefs from the research department, but these are almost invariably on union matters in which the particular MP has a special interest or on matters which are of general interest to the union. In general, however, the research department has little direct contact with individual AEF MPS and

[1] Liaison between the group and the union is carried on through the group's secretary, who sits as a non-voting member of the political sub-committee of the AEF executive. This sub-committee meets twice a year. Finally, three times a year there is a joint meeting of the AEF executive and the union's parliamentary group.

approaches to the researchers by the Members normally have to be made through the General Secretary.[1]

Our five AEF respondents generally felt that their contacts with the union provided them with useful information. But this was almost exclusively on issues directly affecting the union. They also said that their link with the AEF gave them a useful connection with a large section of industry, but there were complaints that insufficient general information was available from the union, that information was too often related to specific cases, and that it was seldom presented in a form useful to MPs. For instance, information would be oriented towards specific wage claims rather than provide a broader picture of wages in the industries represented by the union. Nevertheless, each respondent stressed that he found the information provided by the union on particular issues most valuable.

Apart from these reactions there was the further criticism from one respondent that political barriers existed in the union. This Member acknowledged that he held strong Left-wing views and alleged that he had been denied information for this reason. In the light of AEF politics, with the constant clash between Left and Right, this does not seem surprising. The effect is achieved by the General Secretary who keeps a tight rein on the relations between the union's MPs and the research department. Moreover, AEF officials did not deny to us that an MP might be refused any briefings on an issue on which he held a view which clashed with union policy. Our respondent has since told us that the situation has now changed following the election of a Left-wing President of the union, Hugh Scanlon. But this union seems to be untypical in this line, since we found no evidence among other unions' sponsored MPs of any 'information sanction' against Members who disagreed with the unions' official policy.[2] In general therefore the information

[1] One subsidy or service from their union which may help their information-gathering tasks is the £1,000 annual grant offered to the AEF MPs for a secretarial pool.

[2] The twenty-seven sponsored TGWU Members, some of whom appeared among our respondents, appear to have very little pressure put on them: the union's campaign for a £15 weekly minimum wage was not pressed, even informally, and there has been remarkably little pressure on the union's Members (some of them, such as Anthony Greenwood and, formerly, George Brown collectively responsible Cabinet Ministers) about 'prices and incomes' on which, ostensibly, the union's chief official, Frank Cousins, resigned from the Cabinet prior to vigorous opposition to this aspect of Government policy. In July 1968

which the AEF supplies to its sponsored Members is almost exclusively related to union affairs and any dissatisfaction expressed by MPs in the group stems principally from the view of the group's role which is apparently held by the union's leaders. The complaint from some of this union's MPs seems to be: 'We are here; we are willing, but we are not used enough.'

Turning from the AEF to other groups of union-sponsored Labour Members, we found a very similar picture of information received from unions being also on a fairly narrow basis, usually concerned with the union's own particular routine work. No union provides its MPs with a comprehensive information service going beyond immediate union interests. For example, help would normally be offered on a private Member's bill only if it was related to the union's own industry, like the Shops (Early Closing Days) Act, 1965, sponsored by the late Richard Winterbottom of the Shopworkers' Union (USDAW). Clearly some of the matters which concern the unions are of major political importance, such as prices and incomes policy, minimum wage legislation, particular industrial disputes of national importance, transport policy, the nationalised industries and so on; but all are looked at specifically from the union's point of view when information and briefing are offered to their sponsored MPs.

The unions which have sponsored groups of Labour MPs do not use them as their general spokesmen on the bigger issues of the day because they do not need them. Each main union enjoys national standing within the particular bargaining machinery of each industry where it has membership, and this status is confirmed when the Department of Employment or the Prime Minister become involved in any tasks of conciliation. Away from actual industrial disputes each main union has its influence, and often its man, within the General Council of the TUC, if not also within its key Economic Committee. This inner group enjoys direct access to the Chancellor and the two economic Secretaries of State as well as to the Prime Minister himself and shares with Government and business leaders the membership of the NEDC and countless other consultative bodies involved with national economic problems.

---

the TGWU passed a resolution 'declaring in effect that its twenty-six sponsored Labour MPs risked losing union financial support if they did not back union policy on prices and incomes' (*The Times*, July 17, 1968). A review of the panel has since begun.

It has become a commonplace of discussions about major interest groups that they prefer direct, private access to government to indirect and publicised representations made on their behalf in the legislature. Some additional, although comparatively minor, reasons why union-sponsored Labour MPs are asked to perform only modest political tasks may be mentioned. The unions are more often divided on political policy questions than they are united: the divisions appear both on very broad national questions of foreign and social policy and on economic policies such as prices and incomes. They may be 'Left versus Right', in normal Labour Party terms, or craft union versus general union. When a union's very existence is felt to be threatened by industrial reorganisation (as the locomotive men, ASLEF, and even the railwaymen, NUR, are said to feel about Government plans for the transport system) the inter-union hostilities can be considerable, especially if, as in the transport field, another particular union (the TGWU) is thought to be poised for a takeover of membership. In such a potentially bitter atmosphere it is far more attractive to the rival unions concerned, and to the movement as a whole, to air grievances and wash any dirty linen inside the relatively private offices of the TUC or in their own two or three respective union headquarters. Their respective groups of sponsored MPs could, perhaps, be schooled as gladiators for their unions but their battles would be too public and not very relevant to their Westminster background. The MPs would not want this aggressive task, as their profession is to be Labour MPs, with all the normal implications this has for conciliation and party loyalty when inside Westminster and impartial public services to the constituency and other elements of public life when outside.

All MPs lead very general political lives. The union-sponsored Labour Members, who meet, as we have seen, in the big Trade Union group have many problems in common as parliamentary trade unionists. At the time we spoke to some of them in 1967, for example, they faced the continuing problem of prices and incomes policy, a Royal Commission sitting to consider the future of the unions and the apparently rapid social changes in the PLP which may jeopardise trade union representation in the political wing of the Labour Movement in the years to come. With fish to fry in common of this importance, they have very little spare fat for spilling in public on rows between their

271

unions' executives. They risk almost no trouble with fellow union men on the Labour benches if they as MPs go on performing useful technical services to their unions. The unions can then fight their battles or take different views on issues in relative privacy with those persons, such as presidents, general secretaries and executive members, who carry responsibility to the membership (as the MPs do not) for handling their unions' arguments and tactics.

Like the similar small successes which all MPs can win in their constituency work, sponsored Labour Members may well get more satisfaction from performing limited, uncontroversial services for their unions, since they may often succeed in getting what they want in the Government Department concerned. If the Department knows that the trade union Members' requests will remain at this non-political level, they may be willing to offer concessions. For their part the Member and his whip know that party loyalty and the Member's record in the division lobby will hardly ever become involved in such a limited matter, and the Member is free to pursue it, on behalf of his union, through the normal stages of correspondence, deputation and Questions to the Minister. The union has its parliamentary spokesman; the Member performs his service; the whip sees no threat to discipline, while the Minister, especially in a Labour Government, has an acceptable channel for granting limited concessions in the administrative rules after full discussion and representations.

Although the Labour Party's relationship with the trade union movement as a whole is, of course, vital to the Party's existence, it is essentially a series of bilateral relationships with a large number of individual unions who each affiliate to the party and thus provide at least 50 per cent (and perhaps as much as 70 per cent) of its income. Because these unions are seldom completely united it is possible for the party (and less certainly, also for a Labour Government) to alienate them more sharply than if the unions formed a united group. It is the tacit recognition of this situation, and the related perception of their sponsored Labour Members by union leaders as somewhat distant allies who are not really part of the union's policy-making process, which restricts the flow of union-produced information and briefing to the Members to a modest level of both content and volume. The unions do not need, and their sponsored Members do not want to become, single-minded spokesmen for their unions in the House of Commons, with all other priorities as MPs and as Members of the PLP down-graded in consequence. To paraphrase the well-known aphorism concerning Communist deputies in the French National Assembly, it may be said that there is more in common between two Labour MPs one of whom is union-sponsored than between two members of a union one of whom is its sponsored MP.

It may be wondered why the unions with sponsored Members bother to use them to extract factual information, consideration and concessions on their memberships' problems from Government Departments. With these bigger unions moving into a closer relationship with Government, through the Department of Employment, the TUC, NEDC, etc., it would probably be possible to devise a common service bureau to take up individual cases from unions about employment exchanges, industrial diseases and injuries, and other social security matters with which the unions' MPs now deal individually and on a piecemeal basis. Perhaps even the wider problems of local unemployment, pit closures or union recognition by a certain employer could also be dealt with centrally. The sponsored Member would in that event have almost no duties to his union and would need no information from them. His special position as a sponsored candidate (and the union money involved) would then have become an almost wholly political and psychological demonstration of the continuing integral role of the trade unions in the political wing of the Labour Movement. But to throw attention on to this role in present circumstances would be risky, particularly if a Labour Government is committed, in the cause of its economic policy, to legal impediments on the basic process of collective bargaining.

It is likely, therefore, that sponsored Labour MPs will continue to perform their limited but useful tasks for their unions, although their individual impact on Government Departments may not be the best way for the unions as a whole to go about this kind of work. Its value is that it gives the MPs a role to play for their unions and the unions a visible and apparently practical purpose in continuing to sponsor candidates. The flow of information and briefing to these Members will thus remain appropriate to their political relationship to their unions.

The Co-operative Party is the political wing of the Co-operative Movement and roughly nine out of every ten co-operative societies in Britain are affiliated to it. This gives the party a nominal membership of over eleven million, although its individual membership is only about 18,000.[1]

In the public mind, however, the Co-operative Party is closely identified with, if not indistinguishable from, the Labour Party, although, like the Trades Union Congress, it is not directly affiliated to the Labour Party. The most important link between the Co-operative and Labour Parties has therefore been a series of electoral agreements, the first of which was conclude in 1927. Under this and subsequent agreements members of the Co-operative Party are allowed to seek nomination as Labour candidates with the financial backing of the Co-operative Party and, if selected, to stand as Labour and Co-operative candidates.

Relations between the two parties have been somewhat stormy: the Labour Party has tried to persuade the Co-operative Party to affiliate on the same basis as the unions and there have been a series of bitter disputes over the number of candidatures that the Co-operative Party should be allowed to support.[2] In practice, there have never been more than thirty-eight Co-operative candidatures at a general election and the present limit is thirty, which will normally produce about twenty Co-operative Members of Parliament. At the time of our survey in 1967 there were in fact eighteen. Five of them had been appointed as Ministers and four others held office in the party groups of the PLP. In addition to the eighteen MPs there were three Co-operative peers, who normally attended the monthly group meetings: like the MPs, they may be called in to the weekly

[1] As a constituent part of the Co-operative Movement the party is responsible to the Co-operative Congress, the governing body of the Co-operative Union. However, since the Congress meets only once a year, liaison between the Co-operative Union and the Party is carried on through the Union's Parliamentary Committee, which consists of representatives drawn from both the Union and the Party itself. See the *Constitution of the Co-operative Party*, the *Organisation of the Co-operative Party*, Co-operative Union, 1951 and 1953 respectively; and T. F. Carbery: *Consumers in Politics: a history and general review of the Co-operative Party*, Manchester University Press, 1969.

[2] See G. W. Rhodes, 'Co-operative- Labour Relations, 1900–62', *Co-operative College Papers*, 1962; Barbara Smith and G. N. Ostergaard, *Constitutional Relations between the Labour and Co-operative Parties: an Historical Review*, Hansard Society, 1961; and M. D. Rush, *The Selection of Parliamentary Candidates*, Chapter 7, Nelson, 1969.

tactical meetings of the elected steering committee when they have special knowledge to offer.[1]

The Co-operative Party's separate organisation includes a small research department, which is available to assist members of the Co-operative group in Parliament after its main duty of meeting the research needs of the party as a whole. It is responsible for a great deal of the material found in party publications and for undertaking research into the various policy areas in which the Co-operative Party has a special interest. The relationship between the Co-operative group and the Co-operative Movement is two-way, like that between the unions and their sponsored Members. The Members offer service to the Movement and, in turn, receive help in their parliamentary duties.

The use made of the Co-operative MPs takes a variety of forms. As a matter of routine, resolutions from local Co-operative parties and societies are passed on to the group by the Party headquarters. Any action to be taken on such resolutions is normally a matter for discussion between the group and Party officials. At a higher level initiative may also be taken by the Co-operative Union, by the Party headquarters or by individual members of the group. This is normally on matters directly affecting Co-operative interests, of which a recent example was the introduction of the selective employment tax (SET). Here the Party, as one of our respondents put it, 'operated a healthy pressure on the Government' and subsequently claimed some success.[2] In cases such as this the Co-operative Union supplies the Party in general and the group in particular with factual information, while the political tactics are left largely to Co-op Party headquarters working in close conjunction with the group.

Quite apart from special cases like the SET, the party keeps a

[1] The Secretary of the Co-operative Party is secretary of the group and meetings are also attended by the Party's assistant secretary, by the secretary of the Parliamentary Committee of the Co-operative Union, and the Party's research officer. No other MPs attend, except by special invitation, e.g. Paul Rose (Labour Member for Manchester—Blackley), who is a barrister, has attended meetings at which the law affecting the Co-operative Movement was to be discussed. Two members of the group are appointed to the National Committee of the Co-operative Party.

[2] For an account of the Co-operative Party's response to SET see the report of the National Committee of the Co-operative Party, 1966, pp. 11–12 and 19, and Ian Aitken, *The Guardian*, May 11, 1966, 'Co-op Tax Rebellion is over': 'The Co-operative MPs capitulated yesterday to the Chancellor's new payroll tax . . .'

watching brief on parliamentary business to ensure that forth-coming legislation or any other Government action affecting Co-operative interests is carefully scrutinised; and considerable use is made here of the special interests of individual members of the group. The group may also be used to urge Government action, either privately through representations to Ministers or publicly through such devices as parliamentary Questions,[1] while the group frequently takes the initiative itself by introduc-ing private Members' bills.[2] Extensive use is made of the close contact that members of the group have with Labour Ministers, and of oral and written Questions, to elicit information which is of use both to the group and the Co-op Party outside.

For its part, the Co-operative Party helps its MPs both col-lectively, as a group, and individually on request. They receive both Party[3] and Co-operative Union publications, together with various private reports prepared by the Party's research department. This includes what one of the five Co-op MPs we interviewed described as 'a first-class monthly statement of forthcoming legislation with a consumer or Co-operative interest, plus a digest of minor changes in the law on consumer matters'. Another respondent said he receives 'a large dossier' each week from the Party. Naturally, there are certain priorities in the provision of the individual briefs requested by the MPs. The needs of the group as a whole come before those of indi-vidual members and Co-operative matters take precedence over other fields. Most of these individual briefs are concerned with Co-operative matters, but the department also supplies back-ground information of other topics, particularly for use at Co-operative political meetings.[4]

---

[1] See *Co-operators in Parliament: The Work of the Parliamentary Co-operative Group, 1959–64*, London, 1964; and the *Report of the National Committee*, 1966, pp. 10–12 and 17–21.

[2] E.g. in the 1967 session the group, through one of its members (W. T. Williams-Warrington) successfully sponsored the Licensing Act (Amendment) Act, 1967, whilst two others introduced private Members' bills (A. Morris—Manchester-Wythenshawe: The House-buyers' Protection Bill; and Mrs Joyce Butler—Wood Green: Labelling of Food Bill), although these did not achieve second readings.

[3] This includes the Co-operative Party's monthly newsletter *Platform*, and *Co-operative Party Notes*, which deal with particular issues (e.g. consumer protection, SET, The Parliamentary Commissioner or 'ombudsman') together with occasional pamphlets (such as the 1966 series on 'Co-operators in Local Government') and leaflets.

[4] One Co-operative MP, for example, secured a brief on Vietnam for use at a Co-operative function.

Our respondents felt that they received a great deal of useful information from their various Co-operative sources. One Member said that he generally received 'more information from the Co-operative Party than the Labour Party' and there was general praise for the quality of the information. Any complaints stemmed from the perennial problem of inadequate money and facilities rather than any unwillingness to help and there seemed little doubt that, as one Member said, 'if the information is there it is given to the MPs.' The relations between the group and the Co-operative Party were described as 'very good' and one respondent felt that the influence of the group in Parliament was 'quite out of proportion to its size'. The situation of the group within the wider PLP, however, has its difficulties.

The group, at eighteen MPs, is much smaller than the aggregate of all the union groups which amounted in 1967 to 132. The Miners and the TGWU each have groups bigger than the Co-operators and, in 1967, the AEF group had only one fewer Member. The Co-op group should therefore be compared with those bigger individual union groups rather than with the entire trade union contingent. We see the Co-op Members performing services for their patrons which are similar to the trade union case, although with less of the individual membership casework which the unions put to their MPs. Like the unions' researchers, the research department of the Co-operative Party also does work for its MPs only after meeting its main commitments to serving the national organisation. Looking at the Co-op group, we can also see a range of ideological positions in Labour's normal 'Left-Right' terms and ought therefore to ask the same question as we have about the various larger union groups: in what sense does the group represent the Co-op Party and is this political relationship responsible for the volume and nature of the information it receives from the Party's office?

The SET case shows that although the political impact of the group is not great, its members are at least capable of standing together to make the Co-op Movement's point. As relationships between group and Party are said to be good, it is probable that the rather higher quality of information reaching Co-op MPs is a reflection of their rather higher status as part of the Co-op Movement's political wing compared with that accorded the sponsored trade union Members. To this political interpretation should be added the more practical suggestion that Co-op MPs get better and broader information support because the Co-op Party is a political organisation which takes positions on all kinds of public issues (although it does, of course, have a strong trading and consumer affairs bias). Each main trade union's research department, on the other hand, is able to leave such wider questions to the researchers at the TUC and at Labour Party headquarters and concentrate on the union's own field. Exactly why the Co-op group fares rather better for information and briefing than the various union groups is probably a mixture of these two interpretations, political and practical.

3. PARTY GROUPS IN THE HOUSE AS CHANNELS OF INFORMATION

The PLP and the Conservative and Unionist Private Members Committee (the '1922 Committee') each sponsor a long list of subsidiary groups of MPs which interest themselves in particular aspects of public affairs. The Conservatives call theirs 'party committees' while Labour's name is 'subject groups': we shall call them all 'party groups' to distinguish them from the House's official committees on the one hand and from the very varied collection of other groups of Members in the House pursuing certain interests on a quite informal and often non-partisan basis on the other.

These party groups attract our interest because they can certainly be sources or channels of facts to Members both on situations themselves and on people's (and especially fellow Members') opinions about those situations. We will say something about each kind of information. The following party groups existed in 1968–9. They are arranged here side by side only for easy visual comparison of the two parties' lists and not as an implication that they necessarily exist in pairs across party lines or that one party's apparent 'failure' to match a group on the other side is a necessary indication of less interest: that topic may be covered by that party within another group's ambit.

The parties' full meetings, through their elected officers and the parties' chief whips, keep control of the number and disposition of their party groups and seek to prevent too many springing up and vying for Members' time and attention. The basic reasons for this discipline are those of effective party management. The whips and the senior elected Members who head the main parliamentary parties' organisations would agree that, although specialised group activity by Members has value to the Members (and also has its uses to the party managers themselves), it would not be wise to allow an unchecked proliferation which could provide many different (and perhaps competing) foci for the formation of opinion and possible opposition to the parliamentary party's policies or wishes. In our particular context of the effective flow of political information

Labour 'Subject Groups'	Conservative 'Party Committees'
Agriculture, Fisheries and Food	Agriculture, Fisheries and Food
Arts, Cultural Activities, Leisure and Sports	Arts and Amenities
Aviation	Aviation
Commonwealth Affairs	Commonwealth Affairs
Communications	Broadcasting and Communications
Consumer Protection	
Defence and Services	Defence
Economic Affairs and Finance	Finance
Education	Education
European Affairs	
Films	
Foreign Affairs	Foreign Affairs
Forestry	(Forestry sub-committee of Agriculture etc.)
Health Services	Health and Social Security
Home Office	Home Affairs
Housing and Local Government	Housing and Land
Legal and Judicial	Legal
Overseas Development	
Parliamentary Reform	
Power and Steel	Power
Prices and Productivity	
Public Works	Public Buildings and Works
Science, Technology and Atomic Energy	Science and Technology
Shipping and Shipbuilding	(Shipping and shipbuilding sub-committee of Trade)
Social Security	
Transport	Transport
	Labour
	Trade
Total: 26	*Total: 19*

Figure 27. *Party groups of the Conservative and Labour Parliamentary Parties 1968–9.*[1]

[1] We gratefully acknowledge the Conservative Research Department and the Secretariat of the PLP as the sources of this list.

279

to Members it could be argued that the undue proliferation of officially designated party groups would be harmful. The trend, however, especially on the Labour side, is for the list to grow although probably no more rapidly than modern politics and Government activity has extended its scope, particularly under the Labour administration since 1964: the Labour list has expanded from seventeen groups before the new Government came to power to twenty-six in 1968–9.[1]

We did not include any questions concerning activity in or opinions about the party groups because we knew they were too complex a subject to accommodate in an interview which also covered other matters. The forty-five full groups listed above (together with their sub-committees, some of which operate fairly independently) would be a formidable field of study even if they all performed one function, such as information gathering. In fact they perform several functions only some of which fall within the scope of our interest in 'sources of information'.

Looking first at these groups as a means of gathering information on the facts in their field, one or two groups put their emphasis on this kind of activity. These tend, perhaps, to be those covering the least partisan of topics such as arts and amenities and forestry whose supporters, indeed, do most of their visiting to places of interest and some of their listening to outside expert speakers at the House in a bi-partisan gathering. If an issue arose on which Labour and Conservative Members who are active in these groups were agreed, they would mount a joint effort to persuade their respective leaders: thus the two arts and amenities groups successfully joined forces a few years ago to persuade the then Chancellor, Selwyn Lloyd, to have the Government buy the land beside the National Gallery for any possible future gallery extension.

Generally, however, the two different party groups which, as the list shows, exist on most political topics, do not co-operate very much even on occasions which may, to the outsider, seem devoid of partisan conflict and purely informative in purpose. Thus the semi-regular visits to London Airport of

[1] For previous sessions' lists of these groups see (for session 1958–9) B. R. Crick, *Reform of The Commons* (Fabian Society, 1959); (for session 1962–3) P. G. Richards, *Honourable Members*, 2nd (rev.) ed., Faber 1964, pp. 101 and 104–5; (for session 1966–7) B. R. Crick, *The Reform of Parliament*, 2nd (rev.) ed., Weidenfeld & Nicholson, 1968, pp. 102–3.

the Conservative and Labour Aviation groups are separate and their hosts, the BAA, deploy their information and arguments on current problems twice. This is to allow each group of Members to pick up and interpret points in a potentially partisan way if they wish and to try out ideas on their hosts without their opponents being present. This reasoning applies in the aviation field to apparently non-controversial technical problems such as aircraft noise and most certainly applies to potential partisan issues such as the uncertain costs and benefits of the *Concorde* as a prototype and a production aircraft. The practice of separate visits to places and separate, repeated, lectures at the House by outside speakers is an example of the point we stress in Chapter I: most information desired by Members is expected to serve an immediate purpose and to be closely related to opinion on practical policies. Members naturally react to facts in a political way and prefer to draw out experts in the company of only their co-partisan colleagues.

For these reasons, attendance at a party group will tend to be lowest when an outside speaker is due to give background information not closely and obviously related to a current policy issue lying between or within the parties. Even closely involved visitors of high expert standing, such as heads of nationalised industries or of major companies or nationally-known professional leaders from the worlds of health or law, may find themselves speaking to a fluctuating and changing audience of four to six Members in the course of an hour's meeting, to the considerable embarrassment of the Member acting as host. This is partly a timetable problem, with the visitor's talk having been arranged well before the evening's business is known. Also several party groups try to catch the best time of the parliamentary week (around 5 to 7 p.m. on Tuesdays and Wednesdays) and so emasculate each others' meetings. But it is also partly a reluctance among Members to remove themselves from the busy flow of their varied parliamentary lives and go with an expert into the deeper background of a social or political problem.

The Conservative groups are offered some assistance with the problem of ordering their fields to help the Members grasp the politically salient points. As we noted in the first section of this chapter the Conservative Research Department services the Conservative party groups in the House with their graduate research staff and supporting clerical assistants. It is the third main priority of the CRD research officer in a given field (after his servicing of the Party Leader and his frontbench colleagues and the Party's policy groups outside the House) to attend the meetings of the party group in his field of interest and act as their research assistant and adviser. His tasks may include preparing briefs and papers and generally acting as the group's 'eyes and ears'. He does these things at the request of the group's chairman and will also co-operate closely with the group's vice-chairman and honorary secretaries. When in Opposition, both parties arrange to have the party's shadow Minister placed in the chair of the relevant party group. Thus the CRD research officer's links with his shadow Minister are even further strengthened by his work for the party group which is called for by his shadow Minister acting as its chairman.

The fact that the research officer will perform these tasks upon request should not lead to an exaggeration of the regularity or importance of these functions: some Conservative groups rarely ask for any systematic tasks from their man, and their chairmen, the shadow Ministers, are in a position to appreciate the pressures on CRD and also their own position as one of the research officers' higher priorities. The groups have no formal policy function, of course, this being confined to the Leader and those persons and teams which he designates on an *ad hoc* basis. The favourite term among the Conservatives for describing these groups' function is 'sounding board', and this requires little special research effort which is not already made on Conservative Members' behalf by the well-developed system of generally available briefs which we have described above.

For the same reason (that the party groups in the House have no policy function for either the Labour Party or the PLP) the Research Department in Transport House does nothing for the Labour groups—several of our critical and dissatisfied Labour Members thought the Department should, even though it may not be equipped to do much work for individual Labour Members. As a result, the Labour groups' efforts to gather knowledge about situations is almost entirely self-supported and they naturally vary very much both among themselves and over time. With scarcely basic clerical functions provided (by the very small staff of the PLP's full-time Secretary, Frank Barlow) and no other help on hand, it is even more likely that a group's information-gathering will flourish or stagnate according to the energy and enthusiasm of only one or two of its officers and regular attenders.

The period since 1964 (like the similar period following the large Labour intake of 1945) has seen considerable activity, with Labour Members gathering facts and drafting papers and recommendations: the increase in the number of groups since 1963–4 is one sign of this energy. A striking, but untypical, example of one such enterprise was the 108-page original research report, containing sixty recommendations to the Government, on the Government's potential economic power as a purchaser of goods and services from the private sector of the economy, written by outside researchers under the commission of Robert Maxwell (Member for Buckingham). He was chairman of a working party of the Economic group of the PLP and presented the report to the full group in late 1967 when it was also published.

Usually, information-gathering or research by the active supporters of any particular group is of the unassisted, 'working party' type, by which busy Members try to put together a document with the help of outside contacts or perhaps, the House of Commons' Library. As we mentioned above in the context of the party headquarters' research departments, if the trend towards specialised select committees of the House continues, the party groups may to some extent serve as party caucuses of these official House committees. In this event they may come to merit a higher priority from the respective party leaderships and headquarters and so considerably expand their present limited capacity to absorb 'information about situations'.

Turning to information about peoples' (and especially Members') opinions of these situations, we see the system of party groups in a different light. The most vigorous and authoritative groups may constantly be factors for the party leadership (whether Ministers or shadow Ministers) to reckon with. The Conservative Agriculture committee is, and has been for many years, a group of this kind. Other groups on both sides do not successfully influence any Minister or party leader in his policy because their group view is too weak, too incoherent or too plainly sectional: this last characteristic is often ascribed, whether justly or not, to the Labour Transport group which is said to be too 'railway-minded' because some of its regular attenders are ex-railwaymen.

Our interest in these groups is as channels of information to Members and, although knowledge of other Members' opinions is an important part of parliamentary information, it does carry us into the realm of the political 'sounding board'—controversy and even rebellion among Members and their leaders and all the tactical business which goes with intra-party disputes. On the political side, in short, having heard the front bench view, these groups generate political information rather than receive it. As gatherers and organisers of information about situations most of these groups are not very important: they are not designed or equipped to be so. They may, of course, all be perfect sounding boards and crucial instruments in conveying opinion between back and front benches. There is some evidence (such as a virtually unanimous complaint from the Labour groups' chairmen when they had the Prime Minister to dinner in May 1968 that they could not attract decent numbers to their meetings)[1] that the groups, in fact, fall well short of that ideal. But however well or badly they perform it, that is their central function.

[1] *The Times*, May 7, 1968, reported that the Labour Party groups' chairmen were disturbed at the lack of communication and information between Ministers and their groups and intended to tell the Prime Minister so at their dinner for him that night. They were also said to have decided to meet monthly to review the situation. For accounts of the systems of party groups see P. G. Richards, op cit., pp. 97–107 and B. R. Crick, *The Reform of Parliament*, pp. 101–4. Further comment may be found in A. Hill and A. Whichelow, *What's Wrong with Parliament?*, Penguin, 1964, which is criticised by J. P. Mackintosh, in *Political Studies*, XVI, 1 (Feb. 1968) p. 116. Mr Mackintosh had already said in print that he found the PLP party groups less useful than he had expected as an academic observer of the House before his election. Of Hill and Whichelow's suggestion that influence on Governments has now passed to full party meetings and party groups meeting 'upstairs', Mr Mackintosh wrote 'Yet as a member of four of these committees, I have found no evidence of any such influence, the meetings being irregular with no minutes kept, there is no fixed membership and no concerted conclusions or action'. Elsewhere ('What is wrong with British Parliamentary Democracy?', *Westminster Bank Review*, May 1968) Mr Mackintosh sketched a comparison: 'When the Conservatives are in office their backbench "subject groups" on agriculture, defence, foreign affairs and so on have some influence; but, though such groups also exist on the Labour Party side, they are less active and influential.'

The only detailed study of the political influence of party groups is in Ronald Butt's *The Power of Parliament*, in which his considerable access as a lobby journalist was brought to bear on the details of the bitter internal Conservative battle over the abolition of resale price maintenance, which was waged with two rival Conservative party groups (finance and trade and industry) serving as armed camps.

CHAPTER VI

THE MEMBER'S VIEW OF
PARLIAMENTARY INFORMATION
AND RESEARCH SERVICES

FOREWORD

This chapter constitutes the core of our study and interest in 'the Member of Parliament and his information'. It contains the responses to our interview questions to Members about their use of existing parliamentary information services and their attitudes on the matter, which are presented together with background commentary of the kind found in previous chapters. This topic being at the centre of our research interest, however, this chapter will range rather more widely in its discursive sections as we attempt to outline a policy for the growth and development of parliamentary information and research services to Members.

Any collective information service provided for MPs by the House itself must be of considerable potential importance, not only because of the obvious convenience of its being on the spot, but also because it would be designed for the Members' needs and free of any bias which may attach to material coming from the Government, a political party or an organised interest group. The staff of such a service would be committed to serving Members in the best possible objective manner within the limits of the existing resources. If objectivity and accuracy are accepted as the prime values in such a system there will be a limit to this service's usefulness to MPs, as the politician always needs, at some stage, to add value judgements to his factual knowledge in order to determine his political position on the matter. But, even though scrupulous objectivity remains the central policy of a parliamentary information service, there is no doubt that, in modern conditions of great complexity in public affairs, MPs could receive elaborate and carefully designed streams of factual information from a service of this kind.

We speak at this stage of 'parliamentary information services'

285

rather than the existing provision of the House of Commons Library because we wish to maintain, as far as possible, a functional, rather than an institutional, approach to these matters. This perspective, we believe, aids understanding of the purposes of these services and also sets the existing Library facilities into a proper context.

We shall, firstly, ask what 'parliamentary research services' amount to at Westminster at the moment and quickly concentrate on the Commons' Library. After an outline description of the Library's development and present services (Section 1) we shall present our survey results on Members' use of and attitudes towards these existing provisions—plus their conceptions of the proper role of the Library's Research Division (Section 2). This is followed by a review of the well-known proposal that MPs should, in some manner, be offered personal research assistance (on which we also have some survey results—Section 3) and a note on the current tendency for the Library to become more closely involved with the work of select committees (Section 4).

Having presented our survey data and reviewed the existing provision of services we attempt (in Section 5) to sketch two models or designs for a parliamentary information system. The first is a simple functional model which identifies the types and flows of information from the system's 'store' to its 'clients'. The second is developed into a sketch for what we regard as an 'ideal-type' parliamentary information system with a computer store and a reasonable number of specialised information staff. Finally, we consider how the existing Library services compare with the ideal-type system and discuss priorities for advance.

The context of the House's Library
The term 'parliamentary information and research services' includes any form of information-gathering or analysis which may be made available to Members by any branch of Parliament's own organisation or by means of any other device which Parliament may be willing to provide or support. The far more elaborate organisation in this field which exists on Capitol Hill includes two sources of legislative, or 'parliamentary', research which could also be conceived for the House of Commons. One is the staff maintained by the standing committees of both Houses of Congress, who produce a vast amount of information

and analysis each year for the particular benefit of Representatives and Senators and the general benefit of the interested public. The other exists within many of the 535 individual office organisations of Representatives and Senators, which contain a senior official acting as 'legislative counsel' or 'analyst', who is researcher and adviser to the congressman on his committee work and legislative activity as a whole.

A third possible source of service may be the lobbyists for outside organised interests who seek to help congressmen with favours which can include doing some research or analysis without charge. This may be a 'pure' service in that it is outside the lobbyist's own field. Thus the American congressman receives relevant information from the committees he sits on, from his own office staff and, possibly, from a friendly lobbyist who, is glad to do a favour as part of his good relationship with a congressman—without yet approaching the 'official' or specialist agency for such work, the very large Legislative Reference Service, which is, of course, a major source of general research effort for Congress.

What traces of these may be found at Westminster? Standing and select committees of the Commons each have a share of the available time of at least one clerk, who services the committee with its papers and (in the case of select committees) undertakes correspondence with the Government Departments and other bodies or persons from whom the committee has decided to seek information, often arranging personal appearances before the committee by witnesses. Any MP serving on a committee of the House is free to consult the clerk on these matters, although the clerk's duties are decided by the committee or its chairman, in consultation with the Clerk of the House, rather than by individual Members' preferences.

The clerk is a member of the staff of the Clerk of the House, and parliamentary procedure rather than a knowledge of the fields currently interesting his committees is his speciality: this is most obviously the case on a standing committee considering the clauses of a bill but remains broadly true on a select committee such as Estimates, Public Accounts or Nationalised Industries, which are examining Government administration and affairs in their respective ways. In a select committee's case, however, a clerk is inevitably drawn quite far into the field of interest itself and becomes well informed, at least within the perspective of his committee's approach to the matter. It would thus be possible for a Member to learn certain things on some public affairs from a committee clerk who is, or who has been, studying it as the 'eyes and ears' of his select committee.

Procedure, rather than the substance of affairs, however, is the clerk's forte. Whether serving a standing or a select committee his main task is to guide his chairman and members in their task as expressed in the committee's terms of reference and to warn them that a certain action or proposed section of their report to the House would, in his interpretation, exceed their brief. Whether the committee heed any such advice, is, of course, a political matter beyond the clerk's responsibility. Clerks' knowledge of procedure is an important source of information for Members who, naturally, wish to work the procedural machine for their political purposes. Thus the clerks in the various sections of the Clerk's Department who accept from Members proposed parliamentary Questions, proposed amendments to bills, proposed motions and other procedural devices are Members' main source of guidance through the extremely elaborate array of rules which force the Member's political initiative into a regularised and controlled form.

It is always important, when studying any legislature, to remember that the procedural rules are almost as much a part of the political terrain for which the organised parties fight as are the substantive issues such as economic and foreign policy. It is, in consequence, correct to count the expert and impartial advice on the technicalities of procedure given to Members by the clerks of the House as an important part of the parliamentary information services available to Members. This expertise is not duplicated in the House's Library which passes any procedural questions received from Members to the appropriate branch of the Clerk's Department.

If 'committee staffs' at Westminster are tiny in number and restricted in their ambit compared with the corresponding officials on Capitol Hill, the equivalent among MPs of the personal staffs of congressmen is an even more minute trace. We believe, on the basis of what we heard during our interviews, that in 1967 only about six or seven Members in the whole House had even a share in the services of a personal assistant (other than a secretary or a good constituency agent); only one

Member, to our knowledge, employed an aide with similar experience to that of a legislative counsel of the congressional type.

Taking the Westminster equivalent of the third possible source of information service apart from the Library of Congress itself—the friendly lobbyist—we have seen in Chapter II that outside organised interests are pleased to offer briefs or other material for speeches to sympathetic MPs, if their resources permit. Such briefs are not, of course, 'parliamentary' in their source and are not equivalent to the Washington lobbyist who offers free service within his own or his organisation's office to a congressman on a topic outside his own field out of calculated friendliness. So far as we know there is no equivalent at Westminster to the American lobbyist who is physically about the place on a daily basis, seeking influence and offering any such service to Members: if MPs do receive favours of this kind it would probably be done discreetly, since it is against the present political culture of the House for Members to be seen dealing with interest groups' representatives on anything other than an *ad hoc* basis linked to the House's current business.

The verb 'to lobby' implies, in the Westminster context, the earnest discussions in the Central Lobby, or in a meeting room, between Members and their visitors, whose visits' *ad hoc* and temporary nature is symbolised by the fact that they tend to keep their overcoats and raincoats on. In Washington the word is more often used as a noun (the 'oil lobby', 'the trucking lobby') and its agent is a permanent full-time 'lobbyist'—a term which does not exist in Britain.[1]

With the committee clerks and other clerks concentrating on procedural and committee management matters, with no personal research staff, and with no obliging and well-endowed lobbyist to do him favours outside the immediate field of the lobby's interests, it is natural that the Member's ideas on 'parliamentary information services' should be based squarely and almost exclusively on the House of Commons Library.

[1] The term, 'the Roads lobby', taken by William Plowden in Chapter II from Professor S. E. Finer's writings, is the exception which proves the rule: as Mr Plowden shows, it is not, in fact, a cohesive lobby at all. The popular current tendency among certain foreign governments, and would-be governments, to hire firms to conduct political PR among British MPs may lead to the word 'lobbyist' gaining a wider usage, especially if attempts to require such agents to register with the British Government are successful.

We have drawn attention to these three other parliamentary sources before discussing the Library itself partly because of our general interest in potential, as well as actual, sources of information for MPs and partly because we wish to return to the matter of select committees, and to Members' personal assistants later in this chapter. At the present stage of the House's affairs, however, the term 'parliamentary information services' is 95 per cent synonymous with the work of the Library. Having established its primacy we should now turn to its description.[1]

1. THE HOUSE OF COMMONS LIBRARY

The Library of the House was established in 1818. Before it was twenty years old the first Reform Act had brought into the House over two hundred new Members whose attitude toward Parliament may not have been unlike that of the large Labour intakes of 1945 and 1964–6. In those days the House's Librarian was the principal adviser to the Speaker and other Members on the printing and publishing of parliamentary reports and papers —the famous British institution of 'blue books'. This aspect of his duties involved him in the preparation of items for printing: it is not historically certain that report-writing select committees of the House have always looked to the Clerk's Department for this kind of assistance. Apart from this, Thomas Vardon, who was Librarian at this time, told a select committee on the Library in 1835 that, 'there is no subject connected with parliamentary business on which I am not called upon to afford instant information', and, moreover r,also claimed to be involved in research tasks for select committees for the House.

As the Victorian period passed, the number of the 'blue

---

[1] Our passages on the Library of the House are indebted to the accounts published by three of its senior officials: David Menhennet, 'The Library of the House of Commons', in *Political Quarterly*, July–September 1965; Dermot Englefield, 'The House of Commons Library, London' in *Library Services to the Legislature: A Symposium*, Sydney, New South Wales Parliament, 1965; and David Menhennet and John Poole, 'Information Services of the Commons Library' in *New Scientist*, September 7, 1967. We also gratefully acknowledge the assistance of the Librarian, David Holland, of his predecessor, Strathearn Gordon, of the Lords' Librarian, Christopher Dobson, and of several other Commons Library staff in addition to those already mentioned. We acknowledge the co-operation of the Library sub-committee in agreeing to permit our examination of examples of individual Library work for Members by arrangement with the Members concerned. Our descriptions and discussions of Library affairs, are, of course, entirely our own responsibility.

books' and, in particular, of select committees of enquiry into public affairs grew steadily, yet the 'research' side of the Library's function does not seem to have kept pace, perhaps because of a more vigorous approach to clerking duties by the House's clerks. The impact of the Reform Act on the House also faded away and the club-land atmosphere of the later nineteenth century built up. Furthermore, public affairs could be followed without great difficulty by means of conversations and parliamentary proceedings themselves, backed up with *The Times* and *Morning Post*, and other periodical publications for gentlemen, together with the blue books for occasional reference.

Some eminent politicians had young men serving them as private secretaries (or 'research assistants' as they would now be called) and many other young men (including Nicholas Nickleby) wrote letters soliciting such openings, often seeing them as apprenticeships for a political career of their own.[1] 'There is firm evidence', writes Dr Menhennet, 'that the average "country gentleman" Member of the nineteenth century, far from resenting the leisurely atmosphere and the basically passive role of his Library, actually approved of such a policy.'[2]

For whatever political and social reasons the demand for an information service of the swift and comprehensive type described by Thomas Vardon in 1835 did not mature and the House's Library was, by the turn of the century, clearly a repository of official documents and other volumes on the one hand and a quiet refuge for the reading of books and periodicals, which may or may not have been concerned with public affairs, on the other. The rise of the Parliamentary Labour Party caused very little disturbance to this situation until Labour Members first constituted a majority of the House in 1945. Many of the early Labour Members were working men, with a background in adult and extension education, who could, no doubt, have been attracted to use a library information service which was presented with some skill and appreciation of their needs. But none was offered and it is not surprising that they seemed to have let the matter go. The middle and upper class Labour Members, who provided many of the party's spokesmen, also seemed to turn elsewhere for their information needs, notably

---

[1] This custom persists today, at least on the Conservative side, and led, in one current case, to the Member engaging the applicant as requested as a personal research assistant.　　　　[2] D. Menhennet in *Political Quarterly*, op. cit.

to the various bodies of the Left, such as the Fabians or ILP, or to the Webbian tradition of individual research (which nowadays seems, from our findings described in the next section, to be rather more characteristic of Conservatives).

Sir George Benson (former Labour member for Chesterfield and chairman of the select committee on the Library 1945–6)[1] was one pre-1945 Labour entrant who reacted against what he found in the Library: 'As a backbench Member in 1930 I was appalled to find the House of Commons served by a Library which had hardly progressed since 1850. It seemed inadequate, unbalanced and in many ways inefficient . . . Latin and French classics still occupied front row space in the exact positions where they had been originally placed in 1852. . . . There was no research. . . . The atmosphere was that of a country gentleman's private library.' It would be fair to say that the library Sir George was describing had a much stronger political and 'reference' emphasis than almost any country house library of any period but his correct judgement of its atmosphere as opposed to its stock is beyond question: its flavour is preserved today in the House of Lords Library, although there is nowadays some access for peers to the individual information services of the Commons Library.

The post-War Labour Government set about the modernisation of the Common's Library following the report of a select committee of 1945–6, although not to the extent recommended by the Committee or the Librarian-designate, H. Saunders. In their first report[2] the Committee offered its definition of the Library's proper function (paraphrasing Thomas Vardon's far-sighted statement of 1835) which has been often quoted since: 'Your committee think that the essential purpose of the House of Commons Library is to supply Members with information rapidly on any of the multifarious matters which come before the House or to which their attentions are drawn by their parliamentary duties. . . . Skilled advice upon choice of books and possible sources of information', should be available.

The committee had heard oral evidence from S. J. Taylor, MP, a medical doctor with wartime experience in the Ministry

---

[1] His own interest in parliamentary enquiries was manifest in his long membership of the Public Accounts Committee whose chairman he was in 1952–9. His remarks are quoted in D. Menhennet, *Political Quarterly*, op. cit.

[2] November 1945. H.C. 35 of 1945–6.

of Information who outlined many possible innovations for a service based on his threefold analysis of the Library's job: a reference bureau, a law library, and a full record of parliamentary proceedings and papers. The committee also grappled with the accommodation problem (which has been and is likely to remain the principal practical obstacle in the way of developing an adequate and efficient service) taking evidence from the only architect-MP of modern times, the late Alfred Bossom, on the feasibility of redesigning the tall and spacious rooms of the Library suite overlooking the river, to make extra floor space— a topic still under discussion in 1970.

The committee's first report recommended two posts of Assistant Librarian to begin a 'research' side of the Library. The posts would require 'very special qualifications ... including a wide knowledge of the social and political sciences'. They should not be connected with routine Library matters but should offer specialised assistance to Members in every possible way. A rather high (1945) salary of £800 (x£25–£1,000) was recommended. In their second report, four months later,[1] the select committee advanced their recommendation by saying that two of these 'research assistants with special qualifications in the social sciences' would not be enough to cover all fields. 'Your committee feel that the House of Commons Library can and should be made into a unique organisation'—it should be far more than a repository of books and parliamentary papers and should aim at providing precise and detailed information on relevant subjects.

The Librarian-designate, H. Saunders (who took up his post in 1946 and served until 1950) offered a rather closer appreciation of the Library's needs if this level of service was to be expected of it. Two of his proposals, offered to the select committee in evidence have so far come to nothing: the prospect of funds for official overseas travel by senior Library staff, and similar official support for the commissioning by the Library of *ad hoc* research projects to be pursued in depth by outside experts, such as university scholars. Mr Saunders had visited the Library of Congress and seen this latter policy followed with great benefit to the Legislative Reference Service staff there. He also observed that in his view the Library of the House should have access to all available political knowledge of the day.

[1] March 1946, H.C. 99—I of 1945–6.

293

Following these reports the Government found what was a good deal of money for the times to modernise the Library's stock and prepare for the shift in emphasis to an information service rather than a conventional library. To make extra space, unwanted books were given away and cellars and rooms (including the former ceremonial kitchens under the Speaker's large official residence close to the Clock Tower) taken over. Books on 'twentieth century subjects' such as economics, political science, the USSR, the Commonwealth and modern history were bought and two 'research assistants' added, in part fulfilment of the select committee's proposal, to make an establishment of four senior staff plus some clerical support. The decision was taken to catalogue the Library according to the London Library's system. The Library's organisation was divided into three sections, Parliamentary (or 'main' Library), Reference and Research, and a separate reference room for quick answers on Members' questions was established. This room also contained the International Bodies Desk (now the International Affairs Desk) which held UN and other international documents. The first research or reference staff now having arrived, the slow growth of this side of the Library's work began.

A memorandum from the Librarian of December 1953 reported progress.[1] Between 1946 and the end of 1953, seventy-nine bibliographies, nine research memoranda and twenty-four statistical memoranda were prepared by the small staff involved —usually in anticipation of the forthcoming business of the House. The bibliographies were periodically revised and copies were often requested for reference by other libraries throughout the country. The scholarly side of parliamentary librarianship, however, was by no means neglected: the complete guide to early debates, diaries etc. was now done, as was the collation of texts of Lambarde's treatise on procedure. This historical effort was not distinct from the 'working reference' side of the Library's tasks, declared the memorandum: an index of parliamentary papers, 1900–50 was to be started. The senior staff were to specialise (as do the grades in the British Museum, to which they are tied for pay and conditions) each Library clerk

---

[1] *Report* of select committee on House of Commons Accommodation, May 1954 (Appendix 'D', Memorandum (December 1953) from the Librarian on amenities provided to Members.) H.C. 184 of 1954–5.

matching his special field of university training with a parliamentary field: the Constitution, law books, debates, parliamentary papers, books about Parliament, etc.

This interest in historical research on Parliament was not, fortunately, the mainstream of such Library work in the first seven years of the post-War period (and its importance has rather declined since); the reference and research sections were gathering knowledge and experience based on a growing demand among Members for information on current political affairs, as intended by the 1945–6 select committee. The four calendar years 1950–3, inclusive, registered a steady growth in the numbers of non-statistical enquiries put to the Library's Research Department—169, 128 (lower because of time lost to the election of October 1951) 207, 219. Comparing the winter period of 1953–4 with the same period one year earlier showed a 27 per cent increase in statistical and a 40 per cent increase in non-statistical enquiries. In addition, both kinds of enquiry (but particularly the statistical ones) were becoming more complex and demanding so that the non-enquiry work of preparing bibliographies and statistical digests was threatened.

Selected examples of the enquiries received by the Research and Statistics Departments at this time included (on the non-statistical side) recent published references to the possibility of a recession in the US, on the features of the recently introduced new Belgian rifle and books about the pre-War working of the Liverpool Cotton Exchange. Of a less bibliographical or 'Press cuttings' type were requests for material on Commonwealth broadcasting, a parliamentary topic concerning the historical use of select committees on bills and a memorandum on the origin and nature of the Burnham Committees on teachers' salaries—the only 'report-writing' job quoted in the list. Statistical enquiries included a seven-part enquiry on road taxation, and an enquiry on income tax whose full answer would require the presentation of at least 130 separate figures in an elaborate table.[1]

Throughout the Fifties the Library's gradual growth as a reference bureau continued uneventfully. As we believe is clear from our survey findings, described below, the largely Conservative intake of 1959 was in fact fairly demanding and ambitious

[1] These 1950–3 details are taken from Appendix 'M' of H.C. 184 of 1954–5: paper (Spring 1954) from the Librarian on statistics of enquiries.

in these matters of Library support but did not raise the kind of campaign, or at least the climate of opinion, which pervaded the Government backbenchers after the Labour victories of 1945 and 1964–6—these 1959 newcomers discovered the extent of available Library services in the usual way and, no doubt, added the weight of their numbers to the growing demand for individual information services.

By the end of 1963 it was possible to look back and observe that the annual average of enquiries from Members during 1959–63 was almost 50 per cent greater than that for the pre-ceding four years. Despite time lost in October 1964 to the election, the 1964 figures were to show a further 42 per cent in-crease over the annual average of 1959–63. The benefits of addi-tions to the research and statistical sections' staffs of these years had been quickly absorbed in the rising level of enquiries so that the essential longer term, or 'housekeeping', tasks of any information bureau or library had to be performed on a very slim margin of the staff's time.

This slow increase in the Library's resources and the steady increase in its duties received a certain shock in March 1961, when the Estimates Committee of the House published the report of one of its sub-committees on the growth of the resources being employed on the Library's work which could reasonably be described as hostile. At that time the Library staff were res-ponsible to the Speaker through an advisory Library Committee of Members: they did not have as their supervisor a select committee of the House itself (as they now have in the form of the House's Services Committee acting through its Library sub-committee). It was therefore necessary for Members who wanted publicly to take the Library's part in any argument over its value and duties to speak up individually, as some did. Arguments went on over the constitutional propriety of a select committee of the House investigating an organisation which was responsible to the House, through the Speaker, and not to a Minister, perhaps as a cover for a certain amount of backstairs politicking, not entirely confined to Members themselves, about the House's overall organisation.[1]

---

[1] See Estimates Committee, 'The House of Commons Library', H.C. 168 of 1960–1; 10th Special report '. . . (Observations of Mr Speaker's Advisory Com-mittee)', H.C. 246 of 1960–1; and procedural exchanges during a debate on the Estimates Committee's report (H.C. 640, c. 1554).

The adventure passed off into history as what the Prime Minister of the day would have described as 'a little local difficulty' and the Library was neither impeded nor damaged, so far as outside observers can judge, in its progress and growth. It is probable that it was supported by the high opinion held by Members as a whole of the value and personal attitudes of its staff which seems, from both informal observation and the several surveys and enquiries touching the matter (including our own), to have been a permanent feature of the Library's place in the House since the War.

The Library's role was also strengthened by the rising level of criticism and concern about Parliament's capabilities (and those of other public institutions) which was making itself felt by the spring of 1961, and which often saw 'better information' or 'better facilities' as part of the solution of the problems perceived. This reformist and expansionist school of thought, notably within the Study of Parliament Group, has brought unprecedented attention to bear on the proper modern role of a parliamentary information and library service within the context of a parliamentary system of the British type. As we have noted in our Introduction, this effort by these observers most closely interested in these matters began in 1963-4 in the hope that wider reform of Parliament would follow the 1964 election.

As part of the general reformist activity of 1964-5, the House Services Committee was established and control of the Library transferred from the Speaker to the new committee, acting through its Library sub-committee. This sub-committee began a comprehensive review of the Library's work as had the *ad hoc* select committee of 1945-6 in the similarly reformist atmosphere of those years. Only one report from the sub-committee has appeared to date and, although this did recommend the appointment of additional Library staff, the recommendations were 'designed to prevent a breakdown in existing standards and to provide for immediate needs and in no sense to introduce wholly new services'.[1]

The most recent figures describing the staffing and budget of the Library convey the result of twenty-two years of slow growth since the 1946 reforms. In 1968-9 estimated annual expenditure was £87,000 for staff and £14,000 for purchasing and binding

---

[1] H.C. 76 of 1966-7. If and when a further Library sub-committee report is published it will probably be a valuable addition to knowledge of this topic.

of books, periodicals and other material. (This latter figure does not reflect the value of the great deal of material received free—all British official and parliamentary documents, the output of international bodies of which Britain is a member, etc.). The staff establishment in 1968–9 was fifty-three (forty-eight the previous year) of whom twenty were graduates in the senior grades of Library clerk and above. Their distribution was:

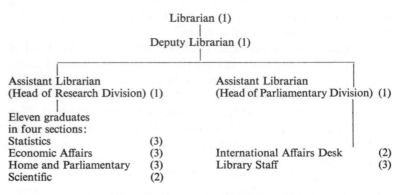

Figure 28. *Graduate staff in The Library, 1968–69.*

In addition there were six staff equivalent to the civil service executive grade (HEO and EO) and eleven equivalent to the clerical officer grade, together with secretarial and other supporting staff up to the total of fifty-three. The staff of the Research Division consisted of twelve graduates, one executive grade post, two office clerks, one personal secretary and three shorthand typists.

The population of 'non-Ministers' from which we drew our sample for interviewing comprised 531 Members,[1] which, divided by the twelve graduates staffing the Library's Research Division, produces a ratio of 44 Members to each graduate. This ratio has, of course, steadily improved as the size of the Research Division has increased over the years to serve a House whose number has remained at 630 since the electoral redistribution of the mid-Fifties. If the graduates of the Parliamentary, or 'main Library', Division are included in such a calculation, the ratio of graduates to the 531 MPs is nearly 1:30 and this is a fairer calculation

---

[1] On the population from which our sample was drawn see Chapter I and the Appendix.

in that it includes the two graduates manning the International Affairs Desk.[1]

The Parliamentary Division is the side of the Library's services most visible to the Member. The staff of this Division maintain the Library counter in the Oriel room where the Member may ask questions concerning the identity or availability of a document or some other item of information. His personal impression of the Library is gained at this point and our survey figures show both how much stress Members put on these approaches to the Library staff and how good an image they have of their helpfulness. Some of the points put orally to the staff at the counter are in fact properly to be directed to the Research Division, and the counter staff then convey them to their colleagues. As we shall see in the next section of this chapter, this system may be thought likely to make the Research Division staff seem to the Member to be rather remote, but this could hardly be the case with the counter staff themselves.

Routine duties at the Library counter include the issuing and receiving of books (which are often loaned to the Commons Library by other libraries, such as the London Library, but which are never loaned out from the Commons Library) and the receiving of parliamentary and non-parliamentary papers from HMSO. A major job is the guiding of Members to the index, catalogue, directory or file they need for the answer to their point—it may be anything from the Glasgow telephone directory to a Press cutting on pesticides held in a filing cabinet in the adjacent Reference Room. The counter is almost surrounded by the various 'visible strip' indexes of current and recent Questions and other proceedings of the House which are kept up to date with new entries; the catalogue of 100,000 volumes in the Library arranged by author and subject (unfortunately according to the obsolescent London Library system, which makes for problems among more modern fields of interest); and an annotated and updated copy of the 'statute book', giving Members the latest version of any Act.

[1] Although such a ratio is a useful measure of provision, it should be remembered that Ministers and Government whips have always been among at least occasional clients of all branches of the Library's service to Members. It is not unknown for a Minister to use the Library to discover something about another Government Department which he does not wish to ask about directly and openly.

The Reference Room contains the most-often used of the 120 newspapers (including the principal regional papers demanded by Members for their own constituencies' areas) and the 1,600 periodicals taken by the Library. The most-used of the one thousand directories taken, plus the encyclopaedias, dictionaries, telephone directories, maps, atlases, etc., from many parts of the world together with standard reference works on many subjects are also held in this room.

A recent addition of 1966 was the series of cabinets containing *The Times* Press cuttings service, which brings to the Library by 3 p.m. on the day after publication, 'an automatic supply of comprehensive cuttings at an annual cost of £2,800 which includes the cost of one additional office clerk'.[1] We have some findings below on the use of this service (which was continued in 1968 after its initial trial period of two years). Contrary to what some Members seemed to believe when we spoke to them in 1967, the Library had a small home affairs Press cuttings collection before the arrival of *The Times* service the previous Autumn.

The four main rooms of the Library suite contain the most used books with the emphasis on the House's *Hansard*, its journals and the law collection. Apart from these reference sources, books on history, biography, travel and the political and social sciences make up the bulk of the stock. There are some literary classics or standard authors but little modern fiction, except that specifically bought for recreational reading. The Library is occasionally asked by several Members at once to supply copies of the latest allegedly pornographic book which someone (perhaps another Member) wants to see banned. In these cases it is difficult to assist Members in their duty to judge the matter for themselves as all other libraries from whom the book may usually be borrowed are, in the nature of the case, receiving multiple demands themselves following the publicity.[2]

Over recent years the Research Division has tried to overcome its lack of visibility to Members by using the Library suite as an outlet for some of its work. The 'reference sheets' which

[1] *Report* of the Library sub-committee of the Commons Services Committee, 'The Library', June 1966; H.C. 76 of 1965–6.

[2] Apart from these transitory cases, one long-serving Member (a French scholar) assured us that the Library's collection of classic light French erotica is 'useful', although no evidence of other views on this branch of the service emerged from our survey interviews.

the Division has offered for some years are one example of this. These typescripts sheets cover particular topical or semi-topical subjects and are available for any Member to pick up. They are rather more than reading lists: as the head of the Parliamentary Division, Dermot Englefield, has written, these sheets 'represent the next logical step in processing (acquired material) as they gather together material from the subject catalogue, the visible-strip indexes and from elsewhere'. As companions to the sheets themselves, the Member is offered the use of 'green boxes' containing documents referred to on the sheets. 'Often, of course, he will need further guidance from the staff and may ask probing questions based on the material handed to him'.[1]

These reference sheets and the accompanying items contained in the green boxes are, like the statistical memoranda produced for many years by the statistical section of the Research Division, a general service whose authors can obtain only an outline idea of its acceptability and value to Members—how quickly copies of a reference sheet or memo disappear, or how often it comes to the authors' attention that more than one Member wished to consult the green box at one time, are some guide to their popularity. The individual information enquiry is, of course, a more definite matter and the number of requests can be counted, although, as we have seen, simple numbers of enquiries are little guide to their very varying difficulty or detail.

The release back to Library use of the fourth room in the suite by the present Speaker in 1966 allowed a general rearrangement of facilities and permitted the desks of some Research Division staff to be stationed in the Library suite, thus making the Division far more visible to Members (and, incidentally, seriously challenging the 'club room' atmosphere with the air of the 'workshop'). With signs on the desks indicating the recently designated broad 'specialities' of the researchers (included in Figure 28 above), it became much plainer to Members that individual information jobs can be done and that they can explain their needs direct to the person responsible. Any disadvantage lies with the staff who are rather exposed to interruptions when working in the Library suite and also (as one concerned Member whom we interviewed pointed out) to disturbance from Members talking or snoring loudly in nearby arm chairs.

[1] D. Englefield in *Library Services to the Legislature*, op. cit.

The service which has always been accommodated in the main Library through which Members pass, and which is run as part of the Parliamentary Division, is the International Affairs Desk. It receives most of the overseas material of the Library, notably the full range of United Nations documents. All other papers from bodies of which Britain is a member are held ready, together with treaties and conventions, etc. It has maintained a select overseas Press cuttings service for some years, equivalent to the home affairs collection which pre-dated the arrival of *The Times* service. It accepts individual information enquiries similarly to the Research Division and now has two graduate Library clerks to deal with them: three other staff maintain routine aspects of the Desk's duties. Over two hundred enquiries classed as 'research' were received in 1967—an increase of about 70 per cent over 1966. In 1968 the number rose to about 450. The second graduate Library clerk at this Desk arrived only in June 1967—a good example of how the Library staff increases, but in the context of rapidly growing demands.

There are, perhaps, three broad types of question which Members may ask the International Affairs Desk: the 'pure overseas interest' question (e.g. one-party governments in ex-British colonies); the 'comparative interest' question (e.g. Danish abortion laws or American university enrolment, for comparison with the British situation, which is in fact the Member's actual interest); and the 'chance' question (such as the one quoted by Dr Menhennet of a Member whose constituency's regional gas board is proposing an underground gas storage scheme and who finds that by chance, information on the matter happens to have been published by the UN Economic Commission for Europe, thus requiring an approach to the International Affairs Desk to obtain it).[1]

The desk gets all three kinds of question and it is thus difficult to judge how much interest in other nations' affairs 'for their own sake' is exhibited by Members in this way, but it is probably a minority of all these types. This functional question is of some importance as the total establishment of the Library builds up, since, in the gas storage case for example, the topic and the UN document is rather more 'technology' than 'international affairs' and a Library 'information specialist' in the fuel and power policies of the advanced nations would naturally know

[1] D. Menhennet in *Pol. Quart.*, op. cit.

about it. The same would be true of two of the enquiries which were put to the Desk during our survey period, and which we examined: they concerned tree surgeons in other countries (because the Member is interested in the treatment of trees, notably—or notoriously—by some British local authorities) and the law in certain European countries controlling cigarette advertising.

On both matters the Members were looking for comparative facts to use as background (and possibly as ammunition) for their public arguments favouring a certain course for British law and public affairs, rather than exhibiting an intrinsic interest in the affairs of the foreign countries concerned. It would seem that as the range of information specialists in the main fields of British public policy available to Members from the Research Division is built up, many of these merely comparative enquiries concerning how matters are ordered overseas will fall within these specialists' knowledge, leaving the International Affairs Desk to offer a more sophisticated and specialised service concentrating on actual international affairs, international law and relations and, perhaps, on strategic studies. This, hopefully, would help to raise the present modest amount of serious interest among Members in these complex matters by bringing particular skill to their presentation.

The special need for care in presenting international affairs material requires even more stress than usual on the staff discussing a point and its sources personally with Members whenever possible. The lower level of knowledge and interest among Members in international affairs almost certainly means a poorer familiarity with the established sources in the field, and the offering to a Member of a bibliography or selection of substantive materials is even less likely to be satisfactory in this field than elsewhere.

The Scientific Section of the Library's Research Division shares this problem of presenting (and, in some respects, even 'translating') its information for Members who lack the technical background or the personal feel for scientific and, possibly also, numerical material. The Section had a long gestation in the inner workings of what the then chairman of the old Library Committee, Sir Hugh Linstead, described in the House in July 1964 as 'antique machinery'.[1] Over two years later in the

---

[1] Debate on the Palace of Westminster, July 13, 1964, H.C. 698, c. 898.

303

autumn of 1966 the section was at last brought forth and after a year of life consisted of two scientifically qualified Library clerks, an executive grade assistant and clerical support.[1] The Select Committee on Science and Technology was established about the same time.

Despite its long-delayed establishment the proposal to introduce a qualified scientific section into the Library had some public support. The unofficial Parliamentary and Scientific Committee, which has brought politicians and scientists together for the consideration of science policy for some thirty years, had recommended 'an expanded library and reference service with scientific staff' as an essential support to the specialised select committee on science which they had called for in July 1964[2]; the Labour Party's Standing Conference on Science which had organised Labour's 1963–4 mission to university staffs and similar audiences (conducted mainly by Richard Crossman and Tam Dalyell), had also served to emphasise the importance of science policy to a future Labour Government—and science was the only specific field which the Conservative Opposition said they wished to see occupied by a specialised committee when these new groups were discussed between the parties in the period following the 1966 election. The delay in establishing the Library Scientific Section does not encourage hopes for the further development of such specialist sections in the Research Division in fields which lack the long-standing, bi-partisan support for more vigorous parliamentary activity which 'science' enjoyed.

Recognising their problem of interpretation of information to Members, the Scientific Section quickly produced a further extension of the Library's slow general move towards a 'positive' or 'processed' information service which is aimed at a particular section of Members. The typescript 'Science Digest', of which fourteen issues were produced during 1967, the Section's first full year, is a newsletter rather than the traditional bibliography or reading list, although it is squarely based on current published sources in the scientific field. It may, for example, take an article in a recent issue of *Nature* or *Scientific American* and convey its gist in a few paragraphs. It is thus an embryonic abstracting service based on the staff's judgement of what is worth covering, given the Digest's very small size. By early 1968,

[1] A qualified librarian has since joined the section.
[2] *The Guardian*, July 31, 1964.

130 MPs were being sent personal copies of each issue of the Digest direct from the Library; a year later about 90 Members confirmed to the Library their wish to continue to receive it. Other Members can, of course, pick up copies in the Library on an *ad hoc* or a pure impulse basis.

The number of scientific enquiries to the Research Division's new section rose steadily throughout 1967 (as did those to the established Statistical Section) to contribute to a record total of enquiries from Members to the Research Division as a whole of about 1550 to which should be added the more than 200 enquiries of a 'research' nature handled by the International Affairs Desk to produce a figure of nearly 1,800 enquiries from Members. A further approximately 200 enquiries from non-Members (peers and Members' constituents, both of which groups are accommodated whenever possible once Members' needs and other essential functions have been satisfied) brought the 1967 total of enquiries answered to around 2,000.[1] It will be noted that this work load was carried in 1967 by about thirteen graduate staff, assisted by two or three others plus a modest amount of clerical support. This represented a rough ratio of three enquiries in 1967 to each graduate per calendar week, in addition to their reference, filing and bibliographical duties and their general pursuit of personal background knowledge in their various extremely wide fields of personal responsibility. The average weekly case-load during parliamentary sessions themselves is, of course, much higher.

2. MEMBERS' ATTITUDES TO THE LIBRARY

We felt throughout our study that Members' attitudes to parliamentary information and research services was probably the central topic we had to investigate and therefore put our main emphasis on it in our interviews. To gain an idea of the general familiarity of Members with the Library we asked how often they visited or otherwise contacted any part of the Library's facilities during parliamentary sessions.

It is clear from a glance at Figure 29 that non-ministerial Members claimed to be very frequent visitors to the Library. Between

[1] In 1968, this total rose to just under 2,400 made up of 1,782 enquiries to the Research Division from Members; 155 from peers and others; and some 450 enquiries to the International Affairs Desk. This increase in work load was accompanied by a small increase in staff.

about two-thirds and three-quarters of our respondents said they went there at least once every sitting day and well over four-fifths visit it at least three times a week; those who 'seldom or never' go there were a mere handful. The two main parties' Members were about equally unlikely to say 'seldom or never' or to visit the Library less often than once a week. But there is a marked difference (9 per cent Conservatives against nil Labour) among those few Members who visit it on an average once a week. The difference is, of course, a reflection of the Labour 'lead' among those who visit the Library much more often which is seen in the Figure.

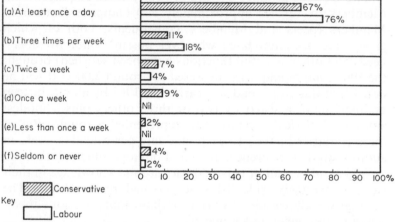

(a) At least once a day	67% / 76%
(b) Three times per week	11% / 18%
(c) Twice a week	7% / 4%
(d) Once a week	9% / Nil
(e) Less than once a week	2% / Nil
(f) Seldom or never	4% / 2%

Key: Conservative / Labour

Figure 29. *Respondents' estimated average frequency of visits to the House of Commons Library.* (See Appendix, Table 27.)

(N—106: 56 Conservative and 50 Labour MPS)

Going to the Library is also linked with Members' length of parliamentary service, since the longer-serving ones claimed to go there less often. Whereas three-quarters of our respondents who had been in the House for less than thirteen years said they visited it every day, less than two-thirds of those with thirteen or more years' service did likewise. The response to this question also shows that all parties' backbenchers who had no frontbench experience seem to go into the Library more than current Opposition frontbench spokesmen, although these spokesmen themselves appeared to go there more than those ex-Ministers of either party who now sit on the backbenches.

Before describing 'Library purposes' of Members' visits to

the Library suite, we shall firstly deal quickly with 'non-Library' ones. Quite a lot of Members still use the Library suite as a writing room for their correspondence or other private work. This function seems to have declined as some Members spoke of it in the past tense, and now use their private room (or desk in a communal desk room) where, as they said, they are beside the telephone and their filing cabinet of papers on, say, constituency case-work or some current special interest. Up in these new rooms they do not have to work out of their brief-case, as they do in the Library. Against this, the Library is nearer the Chamber and division lobbies and easier as a place to find colleagues and be found; it is, some Members mentioned, a nicer place to work, and is less lonely, especially at night, than private and desk rooms which are upstairs or in buildings over the road and as far away as opposite the Cenotaph. So some Members who have recently been given other, more private, places to sit still use the Library as a writing room.

A second use, which does not directly relate to Library services, is the law library function. Many of the practising barristers and, to a lesser extent, the practising solicitors among our respondents emphasised this aspect of the Library before all others. The Library is strong as a law collection, and the even stronger Lords law library is available when necessary. The lawyer MPs generally prepare their cases by themselves, with little reference to the Library staff. Another largely private activity is the writing of books by Members (although we did not knowingly interview any current authors who used the Library in this way), while a daily visit to the Library after lunch for a nap places at least one Member in our 'daily' column in Figure 29. Similarly, several others pointed out that they go to the Library to relax, particularly at night, with a magazine such as *Punch* or *Country Life*.

Figure 30 shows the main 'Library purposes' of our respondents' visits. Taking all Members together, it is clear from these responses, that all the main services of the Library were being fairly widely used, at least if all kinds of 'reference questions' to the staff (the most widely mentioned purpose of visiting the Library) are taken together as one undivided class. Nearly two-thirds of our Members sometimes borrow books, and about 60 per cent read newspapers and journals (which include many of the regional newspapers from Members' constituencies).

More than half said they used the 'visible strip' indexes of Questions and debated topics displayed on the Library counter.

Rather more than half of our respondents answered positively to our prompt on *The Times* Press cutting service, which had been installed about nine months earlier, in 1966. Its existence was unknown to several Members, while others knew of it but had not used it as yet. Several Labour Members felt the choice of *The Times* was wrong as, they believed, it was no longer the 'newspaper of record' it had once been, and should therefore be supplemented by the *Daily Telegraph* for the best general news coverage and the *Guardian* for certain coverage and comment which they felt they would be most likely to use.

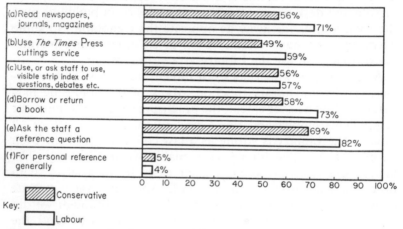

Key:

Figure 30. *Respondents' estimates of the principal purposes of their visits to the House of Commons Library.* (See Appendix, Table 28.)

(N—106: 55 Conservative and 51 Labour MPs)

Turning to a party breakdown, important differences may be seen. In general, Labour Members appear to makes greater use of Library services; in only one instance (using, or asking the staff to use, the visible strip indexes) did Conservatives register approximately the same use. Except for these indexes, and leaving aside the equal handfuls of each party who neither volunteered nor responded to particular activities (and whom we classify in the Figure as 'personal reference generally') a rather higher proportion of Labour Members used each service.[1]

[1] There were differences in the priorities of the two parties: both regarded asking the staff as their most common activity, but below that the Conservatives

The use of *The Times* service claimed by Members is interesting as it was a new device at the time. The Library circularised all Members when it began in 1966, but we got the impression that Conservatives, who as a party responded 49 per cent on this were less likely to have heard of it. We established that many of the 59 per cent of Labour Members who claimed to use it were the 1964–6 intake and it may be that they told each other about it in general newcomers' discussions on parliamentary matters more quickly than would longer-serving Members. It is of particular benefit to Members who practice journalism, some of whom pressed for its introduction, and their use of it would emerge through the Labour figures where journalists are more commonly found.

Examining these accounts of Library use in terms of length of Members' service produces a clear trend. Except for the handful of Members who were able to reply only that they used the Library for 'reference generally' (all of whom were in the House before 1964) all the other services offered by the Library were used more extensively by Members elected at or since the General Election of 1964, as these figures show:

	Pre-1964 Entrants	1964 Entrants	1966 Entrants
(a) Read newspapers, journals, magazines	55	75	70
(b) Use *The Times* Press cuttings service	46	63	70
(c) Use, or ask staff to use, indexes	57	54	60
(d) Borrow or return a book	62	67	70
(e) Ask the staff a reference question	68	92	80
(f) For reference generally	8	—	—

(percentages of three entry groups)

Figure 31. *Principal purposes of visits to the House of Commons Library—by length of service.* (See Appendix, Table 28.)

(N—109: 55 Conservative, 51 Labour and 3 Liberal MPs)

In 1967, when we conducted our interviews, 1966 entrants may still have been showing the temporary effect of asking Library staff where things were kept or how they were arranged, which would have increased these contacts under response (e);

---

put newspapers, strip indexes and book-borrowing virtually on a level (56, 56 and 58 per cent) with *The Times* cuttings registering 49 per cent. Within their generally higher figures, Labour Members followed asking the staff with newspapers and book borrowing at one level (71 and 73 per cent) and the indexes and *The Times* cuttings on another (57 and 59 per cent).

the even higher figure of 92 per cent among the 1964 entrants, however, shows that a lasting trend in Members' use of the staff may be under way. It is also worth noting that, although the 1964–6 entrants did form a definite grouping in their behaviour, they were joined on some matters by longer-serving Members. Thus, respondents with between four and eight years' service consulted newspapers and periodicals in the Library as much as their more recently-elected colleagues, but thereafter use of these facilities tends to decline with service. The same effect may be seen in these results regarding the use of Press cuttings, the sharp drop in usage occurring, in this case, after twelve years of service. It is evidence of this kind, showing distinctions between different groups of Members based on their years of service which lead us to consider in the final chapter the significance of 'parliamentary generations' among Members.

Moving towards our central interest, we next asked: 'Do you ever ask the Library's Research Division to do an individual research or fact-finding job for you?' (i.e. something you ask for and they send in written form after an interval). As this was a question of general practice, using the word 'ever', we were not surprised that 81 per cent replied 'Yes', and only 18 per cent 'No'.[1] The two main parties were virtually equally placed, with Labour 2 per cent higher on the 'Yes' answer. The significant division within this generally positive response was on length of service: Members with less than thirteen years' service were much more likely than their longer-serving colleagues to ask for these jobs. Another point of interest was the very high positive response from the small group of Conservative shadow Ministers.

The four-fifths of our respondents who said that they did put requests to the Library's Research Division were asked for some indication of average frequency.[2]

More than a third of our respondents who did make such requests and who were able to make an estimate of frequency, claimed to make them on average at least once a fortnight. Putting them with the next highest claimers produced nearly two-thirds who said they ask for a brief at least once a month.

[1] The other 1 per cent represented a single 1966 Labour entrant who did not know of the Library's individual information service.

[2] Pressing respondents for a numerical answer, rather than a word such as 'often', was worthwhile: two Members whose first response was 'often' explained it as meaning, respectively, about three times a year and almost every week.

Of the nine Members who said they had only ever made one or two such requests, five were 1964 entrants, with less than three years' service, so this small portion of the result may well have been a temporary feature. An unusually high proportion (22 per cent) of those eighty-nine Members who had said they did, on occasion, make requests, were unable to say how frequently they did so, which, unfortunately reduced the base for our responses on frequency. We believe this inability probably indicates a low actual average frequency, since the Members who made middle and lower range claims on our scale such as 'at least three times a year' or 'only once or twice ever', had no difficulty making their answer, after some thought.

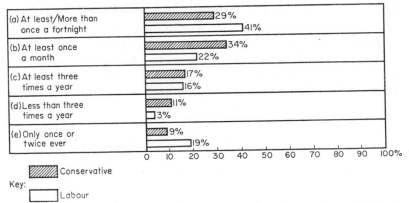

Figure 32. *Respondents' estimated average frequency of requesting an individual reference or fact-finding job from the Library's Research Division.* (See Appendix, Table 29.)

(N—67 (excluding 20 'Don't knows'): 35 Conservative and 32 Labour MPs)

Looking at the party breakdown of these claims, we see from Figure 32 that Labour Members again 'led' the Conservatives, as they did on other aspects of the Library's services.[1] We realised when conducting our interviews that Members had varying ideas of what kind of request to the Library should be covered by our phrase 'individual research or fact-finding job'. It was therefore no surprise that our translation of these estimates into the equivalent of monthly requests made by all 531

[1] The result is made sharper when we notice the probably temporary effect of six Labour Members, against only three Conservatives, replying that they had asked 'only once or twice ever' since four of these six Labour Members were 1966 entrants and another was first elected in 1964.

non-ministerial MPs produced a total claim on requests to the Research Division which was well above the figures of actual requests published by the Library itself. Members obviously overclaimed, the probable reason the problem of definition, despite our spelling out our question in some detail.[1]

Until recently the process of putting a request to the Research Division involves a Member either writing a letter setting out the task or speaking to the staff at the Library counter who took a note and passed it to the Research Division staff. Now that some of these staff occupy desks in the Library suite itself, Members can put their requests direct to the person who will do the job or to their immediate colleague—a closer contact for which the Librarian hoped when making this change in 1966–7. But, even so, the MP and the staff members often do not meet: he puts in the letter and receives a letter containing the response. The staff may ring the Member's private room to elucidate the request or the Member may ring them to offer further guidance before the job is finished or to comment on the completed job. But, short of these contacts (which have grown since around 1966–7 with staff sitting in the Library suite and with more Members being accessible by telephone in their newly-built private rooms) the basic system may be rather impersonal. We therefore asked what was intended as a general 'image' question but which proved in fact to be more useful as a prompt for particular opinions about the staff of the Research Division:

'Some MPs who generally admire the Library's Research Division, say they find the system makes the staff seem rather detached and impersonal to the Member: What's your experience of this?'

Looking at the immediate response, we see at once that an overall majority rejects the suggestion of remoteness or impersonality in the established system for putting in requests to the Research Division. Several Members mentioned that they felt they knew the Division's staff (by telephone at least, although

[1] These 'inaccurate' responses have positive value by showing that Members do not appear to maintain a clear mental distinction between fairly routine information points, whose answers they obtain orally, and the more demanding reference questions which go to the desks of the graduate staff for written answers. It is necessary for the Library to organise itself around this division of tasks but, as it grows larger and Members become more familiar with the service, the Library will be able to make this staffing distinction clearer to Members.

often not their names) while rather more said that they always felt free to ring up the staff and were themselves willing to be called on any point. Figure 33 shows that although there was little party division on this question there was a clear dichotomy between Members with more or less than thirteen years' service. 23 per cent of the Members with less than thirteen years' experience (as against only 7 per cent of longer-serving colleagues) said they found the Library's system for these individual tasks impersonal and 54 per cent of them (as against 74 per cent of their longer-serving colleagues) said that they did not.[1] As well

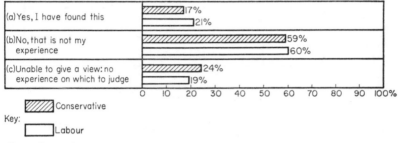

By main parties

(N—106: 54 Conservative and 52 Labour MPs)

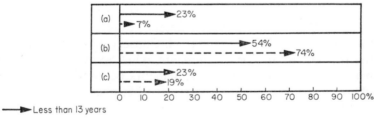

By length of service

(N—109: 54 Conservative, 52 Labour and 3 Liberal MPs)

Figure 33. *Respondents' image of the Library's Research Division—by main parties and length of service.* (See Appendix, Table 30.)

[1] We put this question to all Members, including those who said they never ask for individual jobs: this was to allow us to register the view of any Member who found the Library's service so impersonal (or otherwise unsatisfactory) that he no longer asked them for help. No Member took this position however, and it seemed that all of the 22 per cent who were 'Don't knows' genuinely had no opinion to offer.

as these immediate responses, Members offered comments whose coding into Figure 34 reveals more of the Research Division's image.

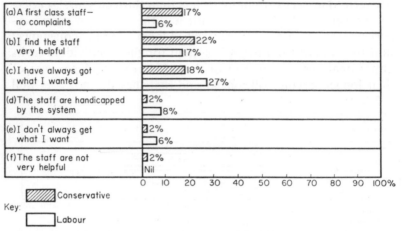

(a) A first class staff— no complaints	▨17% ☐6%
(b) I find the staff very helpful	▨22% ☐17%
(c) I have always got what I wanted	▨18% ☐27%
(d) The staff are handicapped by the system	▨2% ☐8%
(e) I don't always get what I want	▨2% ☐6%
(f) The staff are not very helpful	▨2% Nil

0   10   20   30   40   50   60   70   80   90   100%

Key: ▨ Conservative   ☐ Labour

Figure 34. *Selected reactions on the image of the Library's Research Division.*
(See Appendix, Table 31.)
(N—106: 54 Conservative and 52 Labour MPs)

Looking at Members by their party allegiance and arranging the six statements in a scale from the most to the least favourable, brings out rather more party difference than was apparent from the simpler responses of Figure 34. Conservatives made more of the favourable first two statements, while more Labour Members made the more critical statements below the middle line (if we ignore the single Conservative Member who specifically said that he found the Research Division's staff rather unhelpful). Labour leads, however, on the favourable, although vague, statement, 'I have always got what I wanted'.

The dichotomy of thirteen years' service was also more clearly established by these statements. The Members who said that the staff was 'first-class' and that they had 'no complaints' were mostly those with thirteen or more years in the Commons; the four MPs who replied that they did not always get what they wanted from the Research Division and the one Member who said that he did not find the staff very helpful had all been Members of the House for less than this period (in fact, less than nine years), as were the five MPs who said that the staff

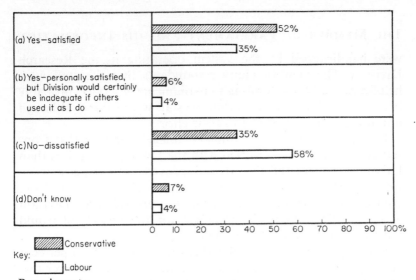

Key:
▨ Conservative

☐ Labour

By main party

(N—106: 54 Conservative and 52 Labour MPs)

Figure 35. Part One

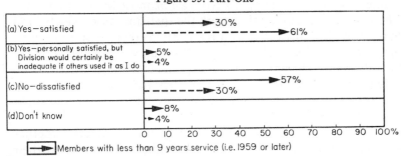

Key:
➤ Members with less than 9 years service (i.e. 1959 or later)

➤ Members with nine years service or more (i.e. pre-1959 entrants)

Figure 35. Part Two

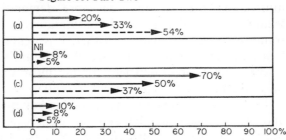

Key:
➤ 1966 entrants
➤ 1964 entrants
➤ Pre-1964 entrants

By length of service

(N—109: 54 Conservative, 52 Labour and 3 Liberal MPs)

Figure 35. Part Three

Figure 35. *Respondents' satisfaction and dissatisfaction with the Library's Research Division—by main party and length of service.* (See Appendix, Table 32.)

315

were handicapped by the system operating in the Research Division. The view of many respondents that the staff were helpful varied little according to parliamentary service, probably because it included the idea that the staff were willing, although not always fully successful in their efforts.

It seemed from this preliminary 'image' question that Conservatives were more satisfied with the Division's services than Labour Members and this, indeed, proved to be the case when we asked the key question on this topic: 'Do you think, from your experience with them, that the Library Research Division is adequately staffed and equipped for the tasks you would most often be likely to give them?'

Looking at all Members together, approximately 40 per cent answered 'Yes' and another 40 per cent 'No', leaving over two small groups. One of these said that, while satisfied personally, they thought the system would certainly collapse under anything like the same demands from all or most Members as they themselves made: they thus took the question more widely, and gave a 'policy' answer, which really aligns them with those who simply replied 'No'. The other small group were unable to make a judgement, through lack of experience: five of these seven Members had already told us that they never ask the Division for jobs and the other two presumably had not done so often enough to feel able to comment.

There was a considerable tendency for Members, whether satisfied or dissatisfied, to say they deliberately restricted their requests for reference jobs below their desired level as they believed that the Library was hard pressed, and as they felt they must already be among the more demanding Members—a feeling composed mainly of considerateness to the staff, plus some sense of 'fair play' to other, less demanding, Members. Some of these Members treated the Library's service as a last resort, after trying elsewhere for the information required, or only when a quick response was essential.

The party difference in reply to this key question was sharp and the symmetry may be seen very clearly in Figure 35·1. Half our Conservative Members replied 'Yes' (satisfied) while almost 60 per cent of Labour Members said 'No'.[1] Their respective

[1] In late 1968, 86 per cent of Labour Members (including Ministers) who responded to a survey question asking whether they found the Library's total reference facilities 'good', 'adequate' or 'bad' replied either 'good' or 'adequate'.

minorities on the matter—dissatisfied Conservatives and satisfied Labour—were exactly equal, at 35 per cent of their respective parties and the two remainder groups were small.

There was a sharp division (producing the equally plain
symmetry of Figure 35·2), according to length of service—nine
years, in this case, being the significant dichotomy. Nearly
three-quarters of the dissatisfied Members had less than nine
years' service. Figure 35·3 brings out the progression of dissatisfied views from the pre-1964 Members to the 1964 entrants
and then to the strongly dissatisfied 1966 intake. Interesting as
that feature is, we feel the real significance lies in the nine-year
dichotomy which incorporates the dissatisfied views of the
significant group of Members (mostly Conservatives) who
entered the House between 1959 and 1964. Their response on
this key question gives weight to the view we shall advance in
Chapter VII that the reformist climate of the present Parliament
is not the creation only of the largely Labour intakes of 1964
and 1966 but also draws strength from the largely Conservative
group of 1959–64 entrants.

We also analysed satisfaction with the Research Division
according to Members' educational background and found, as
with length of service, that the differences ran across party lines.
The most satisfied Members in this context were those who had
only an elementary education while the least satisfied were those
with a secondary, but not a university education. The more
extensive the education received the greater the diversity of
views, so that graduates of all parties tended as a group to be
more or less evenly divided on the matter of satisfaction with
the Research Division. It would seem that the view, which was
expressed to us by several Members (usually Conservatives)
during our interviews, that only the graduate MPs (and particularly the new Labour Members who were lecturers before
entering the House) are critical of the Research Division
facilities is incorrect.

Our fourth analysis of these responses was according to frontbench experience. In general, greater dissatisfaction was displayed by Members without frontbench experience, more than

This question was so much broader than ours in Figure 35 that no comparison
is possible, although it may suggest rather higher Labour satisfaction with the
simpler reference aspects of the Library (which Members operate for themselves)
than they appear in Figure 35 to have felt in 1967 in the Research Division's case.
The 1968 survey was conducted by the PLP's Parliamentary Reform Group.

half of whom replied 'No' (dissatisfied) against less than one third of the ex-Ministers and Opposition shadow Ministers, taken together. When these ex-ministers and shadow Ministers were separated, however, they differed sharply, with the overwhelming majority of the ex-Ministers (70 per cent) expressing satisfaction with the Research Division while only half the shadow Ministers agreed with them, a difference which is probably attributable to the greater use made by the Opposition spokesmen of the Research Division. From the comparative frequency with which shadow Ministers asked for reference jobs, and their comparatively critical views of the current level of provision (bearing in mind the small number we are analysing) it would seem that their relationship with this parliamentary source would be a significant factor in any longer study of the working of modern Opposition in Parliament.

Having established the degree of satisfaction with the Research Division among our 111 respondents we concentrated on the fifty who expressed dissatisfaction and tried to get their specific ideas on how to improve matters by asking them: 'What particularly do they seem to lack in staff and resources?' Beyond these two words, we offered no 'prompts' on this question of possible ways to develop the Research Division nor did we try to correct Members whose idea of what was available in the Division appeared to us wrong or out of date, since we were interested to know how far the critical Members had thought about, or at least heard about, specific proposals and whether their criticism was at all ill-informed. In fact, we found virtually no inaccurate ideas of what services existed and coded the many responses to this open-ended question into five standard statements. In looking at Figure 36, it should be remembered that it shows multiple responses from the fifty Members who found the Research Division inadequate for their needs: nineteen Conservatives, thirty Labour and one Liberal.

As Figure 36 shows, the most common view is that the Research Division is simply underdeveloped: equal proportions of the main parties, felt that general growth was the main need and some of them went on to more specific statements about expert staff and modern equipment. Some Members attributed the inadequacy of the Division more narrowly to either lack of staff or poor facilities; by putting these groups together as we have done in Figure 36, we find 76 per cent of these Members favouring these developments. Two more specific proposals which lie within the demand for 'better staff and facilities', appeared to be fairly popular: the need for more expert, presumably specialised, staff and the need for mechanical and electronic aids, including computers, for the rapid storage and retrieval of information. Although more Labour than Conservative Members (43 per cent against 32 per cent) felt that more expert staff were needed, nearly equal proportions (17 and 16 per cent) from both parties favoured 'more mechanisation.'

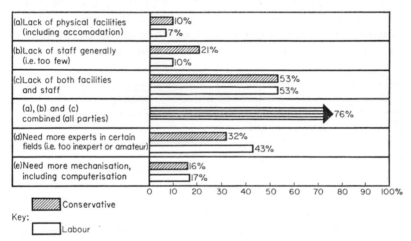

Figure 36. *Weaknesses of the Library's Research Division as seen by those respondents who regarded it as inadequate for their needs.* (See Appendix, Table 33.)

(N—49: 19 Conservative and 30 Labour MPs)

When examining these responses by Members' length of service we should recall that nearly three-quarters of our respondents who were dissatisfied with the Research Division had entered the House in 1959 or since. This group was not of one opinion, however, on exactly what improvements to the Division were needed: the pre-1966 entrants were more general in their view, while 1966 entrants placed more stress on specific matters such as specialist staff and mechanical aids. Over 80 per cent of the 1959–65 entrants mentioned a lack of staff and facilities in general as their criticism of the Division, whereas only half of the 1966 entrants did so.

Having asked Members to describe their Library activity, to assess the adequacy for their needs of the Research Division, and to make suggestions if they were dissatisfied, we hoped to gain further background knowledge from reactions to the next question: 'Taking a general view of the Research Division, what is your conception of their task?' We have coded the responses to display the variety of Members' emphases on this central question. Figure 37 shows these responses broken down by party and also by length of service based on 1966, 1964 and earlier entrants.

The considerable emphasis on the provision of any factual information quickly stands out from Figure 37. Two-thirds of all respondents mentioned this aspect of the service. Many Members pointed out to us that they often needed information at very short notice, not only for forthcoming debates but

	Conservative / Labour
(a) Dig out any facts quickly	74% / 62%
(b) Fill gaps in information not available elsewhere	6% / 6%
(c) Provide non-partisan information	4% / Nil
(d) Provide concise reports on particular issues/policies	13% / 15%
(e) Provide comprehensive information and bibliographies generally	24% / 17%
(f) Act as a clearing house for information	9% / 17%
(g) Provide analytical and expert assistance to Members	13% / 21%
(h) Provide facilities for research in depth	4% / 17%
(i) Provide alternative views on policy	Nil / 6%
(j) Don't know or uncertain	7% / 4%

Key: //////// Conservative   [ ] Labour

By main party

(N—106: 54 Conservative and 52 Labour MPs)

Figure 37. Part One

320

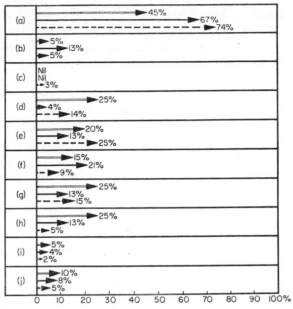

Key:
➤ 1966 entrants
➤ 1964 entrants
-- ➤ Pre–1964 entrants

By length of service
(N—109: 54 Conservative, 52 Labour and 3 Liberal MPs).

Figure 37. Part Two

Figure 37. *Respondents' conceptions of the role of the Library's Research Division—by main party and length of service.* (See Appendix, Table 34.)

sometimes actually during a debate (for which purpose the Library, including a representative of its Research Division, remains available while the House is sitting, even throughout the night).

Conservatives mentioned this need for rapid service noticeably more often than Labour Members, which may be the sign of any party's parliamentary style while in Opposition: a 'cut and thrust' approach based on the need to catch out and generally resist Ministers. While this may be an element in the picture, we suggest that it is more likely to involve the Library in the matter of Members wanting to scan the Press and generally look up material for parliamentary Questions. Preparing Questions, however cutting, is hardly an emergency matter in view of the twenty-one days notice period required for most Questions which are likely to be reached for oral answer.

Evidence lower down the Figure suggests that the even greater Conservative emphasis on speed, compared with Labour views, is linked with a smaller appetite for more elaborate work, as responses (f) to (i) inclusive show. Similarly the Conservative 'lead' on response (e), which refers to 'comprehensive information and bibliographies generally', is part of the more independent and individual approach to research (of which the bibliography is the basic element) which appeared to us to be maintained by many of the Conservatives we interviewed.

For their part, Labour Members as a group put greater emphasis on the provision of 'expert assistance' and facilities for 'research in depth'. These words (which are based on Members' own common phrases) appear in our coded responses in order to convey the idea of a Member receiving a 'report' of already-processed information from a member of the Library staff. Scrutiny by a trained (and preferably specialist) person sifts the significant and telling facts or points and sets them into a background for the Member. This Figure's main burden is to show how this 'secondary' approach to information on the part of some Labour Members contrasts with the 'primary' or 'do-it-yourself' attitude of rather more Conservatives.

Looking at the 1966 and 1964 entrants as separated from all other Members in Figure 37·2 we see this preference for the 'report-writing' or 'processed' information service coming out from the newer Members who are, of course, mainly Labour. The responses referring to 'concise reports'; 'analytical and expert assistance'; 'facilities for research in depth' and 'alternative views'—all have the 1966 entrants 'leading' while they 'lag' behind the other groups in their support for 'quick facts' and 'comprehensive information and bibliographies'. A point of particular interest lies behind response (g) calling for 'analytical and expert assistance'. On this the 1966 group 'leads', as we have noted. The 1964 group lies third in this demand with the pre-1964 group between. The pre-1964 entrants' position is due to the interesting fact that Members who entered the House between 1959 and 1964 mentioned 'analytical and expert assistance' almost as often as the much newer Members who entered the House in 1966. It is true that this 1959–64 group also placed considerable stress on the provision of 'comprehensive information and bibliographies' but the almost equal interest in 'processed' or 'reported' information between these two groups (which are separated by about five to seven years in date of entry into the House and which are predominantly of different parties) reminds us again that the ambitious or reformist attitude to these important matters is not confined to newer and younger Labour Members.

The education distinction between graduates and non-graduates is, to some extent, a reflection of these same 'post-1958' partisan groups. Graduates as a class were rather less interested than non-graduates in the purely reference Library function of getting 'facts quickly' and more interested (20 per cent against 11 per cent) in wishing to see more specialists available in the Library.

Our small group of Conservative shadow Ministers had an interesting position on this question. They did not stress the need for speed in the Library's reference service any more than did Members without any frontbench experience but, of all sub-groups of our respondents, they were the most interested in the more sophisticated functions of the Library. These preferences are obviously connected with their special parliamentary contributions. Shadow Ministers do not have to take their chance of being called to speak in the chamber from the Speaker's list of would-be contributors but must, as it were, recompense the House for their assured place in the debate with particularly well-prepared speeches. As shadow Ministers, like Ministers

Response	Members satisfied with Research Division	Members dissatisfied with Research Division
	per cent	per cent
(a) Dig out facts quickly	81	60
(b) Fill gaps in information not available elsewhere	11	4
(d) Provide concise reports on particular issues or policies	15	14
(e) Provide comprehensive information and bibliographies generally	9	32
(f) Act as a clearing house for information	—	26
(g) Provide analytical and expert assistance for Members	2	32
(h) Provide facilities for research in depth	4	18
(i) Provide alternative views on policy	—	6

Figure 38. *Relationship between satisfaction and dissatisfaction with the Library's Research Division and conceptions of its role.* (See Appendix, Table 35.)

themselves, find themselves moved around among the various different jobs by their Leader, it is likely that they would particularly appreciate a more sophisticated Library service.[1]

Figure 38 cross-tabulates the conceptions of the Research Division's tasks which are maintained by satisfied and dissatisfied Members. The satisfied Member tended to nominate the simple reference tasks as his conception of the Library's role, while his dissatisfied colleague mentioned more demanding and elaborate services which he thought the Library should inaugurate or develop.

Four-fifths of the satisfied MPs nominated 'Dig out facts' as being the Library's role with no more than 15 per cent mentioning any other single task. As the italicised numbers in Figure 38 show, the two purely reference functions (responses (a) and (b) attracted notably more mentions from satisfied Members than from their dissatisfied colleagues. For these dissatisfied Members the speed of getting reference information was comparatively less important, although it still received about twice as many mentions as any other possible Library role. These Members gave more support than did satisfied MPs (as the rest of the italicised numbers show), to the more specific proposals (g), (h) and (i).

These results show a clear demand for growth and improvement among the dissatisfied Members. There is probably no firm line to be drawn between Members who mention the need for general growth in the Research Division and those who made more specific proposals: if pressed, the former group would have made further, more particular, proposals, while the others must logically support general growth as a background to their ideas for specialist staff and computer aids, since these innovations could be economic only within a broader organisation. It is rather a matter of comparative emphasis of Members' comments which we have tried to draw out, based on the standard assumption of this kind of open-ended question that the respondent will mention those matters which are uppermost in his mind and on which he may have the stronger feelings.

[1] As the Conservative Research Department offers its frontbench spokesmen relatively elaborate support, this enthusiasm for more sophisticated services in the Library's Research Division is interesting. It is possible that the Conservatives 'additional spokesmen' (deputy shadow Ministers) feel the need for rather more help than CRD can provide, thus contributing to our results. (We had only a small group of frontbench spokesmen among our respondents.)

Summing up all these responses about the Library, we have seen that just under half our respondents were either personally dissatisfied with the 1967 level of provision by the Research Division or believe that it was inadequate for the House as a whole (although their own demands were well met). Adding to this figure the effect of the widespread caution we detected among both the satisfied and dissatisfied Members when asking the Research Division to do jobs (because of their belief that the staff was overburdened), we may conclude that there is a latent demand among Members for reference services (although it is difficult to establish its exact nature) and that at least half the approximately 530 MPs not serving in the Government want to see more being done.

Most of the fifty dissatisfied MPs whom we asked for particular comments, however, wish to see a generally bigger operation which would bring benefits such as wider reference background, speedier but more comprehensive information retrieval and a swifter and more knowledgeable response to the more demanding jobs based on greater specialisation by the staff. There was also a demand (which was particularly mentioned by some Members and may also appear reasonable and desirable to their colleagues who themselves mentioned only general development of the Division) for deliberate specialisation of function within the Division.

Most Members who mentioned specialist staff envisaged at least one (and preferably a small team) of relevantly trained specialists who would each be extremely well aquainted with the information in their field and masters of its sources, structure, inherent difficulties and reliability. The major policy fields such as social services, economic affairs, foreign affairs, and so on would be covered with increasing penetration as each team was built up.

Some other Members favoured recruiting such information specialists in narrower fields of particular technical difficulty, leaving, by inference, the more 'open' ground around them to continue to be dealt with by 'generalist' researchers or the specialising Member himself. For example, the Division would contain an information specialist with world-wide knowledge of sources and information on medical and hospital costing or on public policies to promote the safety of medicines rather than a specialist on all British 'health' or even 'social services' affairs.

The demand for computers was mentioned by almost equal proportions of Conservative and Labour Members (16 per cent and 17 per cent) and some called for a national data centre on all Government and public affairs of which the Commons Library would be a component part, along with all Government Departments and other agencies producing and demanding social and economic statistics.

3. PERSONAL RESEARCH ASSISTANCE FOR MEMBERS

We wanted to measure the serious, positive demand among our respondents for the services of a personal research assistant, as we knew informally that some such demands existed. To have asked Members whether they would welcome such a service would probably not have helped us. Many Members, who would not refuse the services of an assistant if they were offered (but for whom the matter is not salient), would, no doubt, have answered this question affirmatively.

Instead, we probed respondents informally when they answered our question on the adequacy of the Library's Research Division to discover whether they had a personal research assistant in mind when giving their views on the Division. We did not introduce the phrase 'research assistant', but tried to allow the Member to mention it if he so wished.[1]

Just over one Member in four told us (either directly or in response to the probe we have described) that he would like a research assistant of his own; a further 7 per cent said they would like a share of one. Thus 35 per cent declared this demand. Taking those Members by party (see Appendix, Table 36) the Labour figure for the two views combined was 44 per cent and the Conservatives 25 per cent.[2] Enthusiasm for personal assistants was higher among Members with less than nine years'

[1] The twin dangers of this informal approach are, of course, under-prompting a Member who did have the research assistant scheme in his mind, and over-prompting a Member who did not; an open question would probably have over-prompted many Members. By this stage in the interview we were used to each respondent's style of speech and, in general, feel that almost all Members who had the research assistant matter in mind were drawn out in the way we wanted.

[2] In 1963–4 Malcolm Shaw conducted an enquiry into the support among all MPs and peers for a scheme whereby private funds would provide about twenty parliamentarians per annum with a temporary research assistant. The research assistant would be centrally recruited and also subject to time off for educational activities during his year's 'internship' at Westminster. About two-thirds of the respondents to Mr Shaw's near random sample said they favoured such a scheme

service. Backbenchers who lacked frontbench experience were the most interested group compared with either shadow Ministers (the more senior of whom have very similar assistance offered by the Conservative Research Department) or ex-Ministers who had returned to the backbenches.

There may be a significant link between the secretarial support received by Members and their stated wish for a research assistant. The 1964–6 entrants were rather more inclined to request the research assistant (bearing in mind the rather limited numbers involved) and were also more inclined, in the summer of 1967 at least, to employ a part-time secretary or share the services of a full-time secretary with three or more other MPs. The broad group of longer-serving Members, ex-Ministers now on the backbenches and Conservative shadow Ministers, all had fuller secretarial assistance than backbenchers who had never been on the frontbench, and they may have been influenced in their mentioning the research assistant idea by this fact.

What is the case for backbench MPs being offered the use of a fixed amount of public funds with which to engage a 'research assistant'? Drawing together the remarks of all those Members who expressed this desire we would say their basic point rests on the distinction between 'information work' and 'personal research support'. This is a functional distinction in their minds which is of general application, having nothing to do with their views on the strength and weaknesses of the Library's existing services or any other aspect of parliamentary work at Westminster.

'Information work' is concerned with knowing either certain techniques of mechanising or otherwise arranging information for easy classification and retrieval, or (and perhaps in addition)

(the response rate being about 50 per cent). Although various considerations concerning the particular scheme advanced by this survey (and the inevitably 'leading' nature of the question asked) prevent direct comparison with our study, there are at least two common findings. Firstly, both surveys found many Members praising the Library staff but saying that they held back work for fear of adding to the staff's burdens. Secondly, both found MPs giving quite a wide range of explanations of why they wanted a research assistant and what work they would expect from one. See M. Shaw, 'Assistants for Members of Parliament', *Institute of Social Research*, October 1964. The PLP survey (p. 316 n) found what *The Guardian* described as a 'fairly widespread' demand among Labour Members for personal research assistants, whose salary would be found by the Exchequer and who would enjoy personal use of the Library (which is currently denied to all except Members) (*The Guardian*, November 5, 1968).

mastering the information flows of a chosen special field in a manner designed to help someone else absorb some parts of that material, as their needs require. This, runs the argument, is specialist work, requiring training and judgement and is best done by a collective service which offers its knowledge and skills freely to any Member or other client.

Because it is an impartial and openly available service, however, it cannot go beyond offering the best available materials in the most useful way: even any 'analyses' of materials must be limited to devices for bringing together or highlighting certain of their features. The Library's Research Division and International Affairs Desk staff are very reluctant to 'work up' information into an argumentative brief or case of any kind, partly because they have always been under great pressure of work but also because they wish to avoid any possible charge of partisanship and failure to retain their objective standards. In this sense, the clerks of the House are more flexible, often being prepared to re-draft and discuss a thoroughly partisan Question, amendment, new clause or early day motion (perhaps to make it sharper or subtler) on the purely political terms of the Member's own thinking. But a clerk, who occasionally enjoys a few minutes of partisan skullduggery with a Member who wants to make a point, is hardly a substitute for the continuing working relationship, involving partisan and policy considerations, which a Member could have with a personal assistant—even one whose services were shared with a colleague.

These two characteristics of the MP-assistant relationship— its continuing nature and its policy or partisan commitment— may be taken separately. The Members advancing these views feel that no collective service, however well endowed, could ever be sufficiently close to their own work and interests to follow jobs through in a sequence and thus build up experience of both the Member's affairs and his fields of activity. Thus while the Library's Research Division (particularly an expanded service) may be capable of meeting the Member's specific requests for information, including a series of requests in a particular field, it could never supply the Member with a continuing flow of tailored work in the same way as a personal research assistant. Furthermore, the Research Division will act only on the initiative of the Member, whereas a research assistant may anticipate his Member's needs. As several of these Members said, 'research work', even of the kind which an academic may regard as rather elementary, is often a matter of trial and error, false leads and the realisation afterwards that time was wasted on a point. A Member cannot burden even the most elaborate collective information service with every aspect of a policy interest or project which he may have in train. In order to indulge in such activity, he must either have the service of a personal assistant who can pursue these matters under his supervision or try to find the time to do it himself. The parliamentary life of continual meetings and perambulations simply does not allow the expenditure of his own time on these tasks if he is also to be active among his colleagues on at least some current political issues and interests, while preparing himself to make a worthwhile contribution on others. Even if a shared research assistant's services were available to him on only an intermittent basis (say, two or four weeks at a time) this would still permit a longer-term project to be undertaken which was considerably larger than anything likely to be available from a collective bureau, unless that bureau was of the proportions of the Legislative Reference Service in Washington.

The other characteristic of the MP-assistant relationship—its policy or partisan flavour—is rather less definite because it is so subject to the individual Member's hypothetical preference. We received all three possible answers on the partisanship point from the small number of MPs in whose interviews the point came up: some thought it essential that the assistant should be a committed co-partisan, while others were not very concerned, and one or two thought they would actually shy away from a fellow party member and prefer a young person who was interested in politics but not ideologically committed. In our own view this is not an important matter. The need for balance and possible compromise would be all the greater if assistants were working for small groups of close colleagues who would probably each use the assistant's services in a somewhat different way.

Whether the assistant should be a specialist in any field, or a generalist who must be ready to tackle anything, was also a matter for diverse views and would similarly, in our opinion, be best left for the individual Member to arrange. One Labour Member with a very close knowledge of one area of world affairs said he would ask the assistant, whom he would very much like to have, to be a general aide on home affairs; another

Labour Member wanted, on the contrary, to share his own special interest in overseas and defence affairs with an assistant who would preferably have a reasonably relevant university degree; a Conservative interested in social policy said that the one-third or half of a research assistant's service, which he would like, would be best offered by a 'bright generalist interested in politics, not an expert social scientist'. We did not have the time to pursue these lesser points—although it is interesting to wonder why a Member who is very concerned with topics such as dangerous drugs and social security, as we know this Conservative Member is, should specifically point out that he would prefer someone with no background knowledge of these fields. It is our very informal impression that there is little objective reasoning behind these various preferences and that Members, like any other group, have different approaches to knowledge and work stemming from personality differences.

Naturally, we also acquired some views against the idea of personal or research assistants for Members. Some ex-Ministers now on the backbenches (mostly Conservatives among our interviewed Members) offered generally disparaging remarks on the place of most backbenchers in the political system and, in a few cases, singled out the Labour entrants of 1964–6 who have academic backgrounds for particular displeasure. As we have already noted, these critical Members tended, incorrectly it appears, to equate this group with reformist opinion in the House as a whole.

A Labour Member who entered the House in 1945 felt that an undue stress on research support for politicians carried dangers. It led to a lack of his own outside contacts and a lack of self-reliance and self-confidence—both bad traits in an MP. The research assistant idea would be an interesting (although probably expensive and administratively difficult) development. He thought not more than one hundred assistants would, in fact, be required to satisfy the Members who care about it. 'It's the new, young, educated ones that want it. I'm sure there's a case, but we should be cautious. Hare-chasing is not the MP's job, while responding to public needs is. If the flood of new, young MPs in 1945 and 1964 had been provided with assistants who were under their personal control, they would have pursued their hares instead of learning necessary general political sense.'

In warning against what he saw as the unduly American ways of thought of some of the newer Members, a Conservative, who had been in Parliament since 1950 (and who had served most of the period as a whip) offered a distinction between the two parties in their approach to 'research' and the House of Commons Library: Labour Members were 'more academic' and Conservatives 'more practical'. He is himself a 'gradual, steady expansionist' on the matter of the Library and (unlike some other Conservatives of his age group) has no fears that the demands on it of the newer Labour Members will produce an extended service, which will be seen as a white elephant in a few years' time following those Members' parliamentary demise at the polls or a falling-off of their enthusiasm. We are sure that this Member is correct in his broad 'academic'—'practical' characterisation of Labour and Conservative approaches, at least if those words are used loosely. Our results on Library use and perceptions show that Conservatives tend to have a less demanding approach which is pitched more at the 'reference' rather than the 'research' level.

One Conservative who certainly seemed to adopt a most 'practical' approach (and who was fairly hostile to the 'Labour lecturers' and their alleged ways) spoke against Members being 'spoonfed' with final versions of briefs or reports: personal study and analysis is essential. This applies both to partisan material from the Conservative Research Department and to the first-class information and statistical service which ought to be available from the Library but which (in this Member's experience) unfortunately is not. 'But, better than that, I want a research assistant—for personal, trained, continuing support. However, even a good research assistant is no substitute for one's own expert, up-to-date, practical contacts in the field.' Clearly, the demand for an assistant and the emphasis on being personally involved in the practical affairs of any field of interest can go together in an individual Member.

None of the thirty-nine Members whom we interviewed and who mentioned that they wanted a research assistant dwelt on the administration of an actual scheme. All seemed to share the assumption that public funds, would, in some way, pay people who had been individually recruited by Members, or small groups of Members, and whose responsibility would be solely to the Members. Some respondents stressed the personal and political link necessary to such a working relationship while others (usually Conservatives) stressed only the personal link and discounted the political views of the assistants they would like to have. One Labour Member declared that a 'taxi rank' service in which assistants were detailed off to work for any Member on a *ad hoc* basis of a few days or hours would be hopeless and we suspect almost every other Member we spoke to would agree with that view. Indeed, only one Member spoke of this kind of service, and he also may have preferred personal assistance if we had asked him.

It is interesting that the assumption among Members of a personal-recruitment scheme was so apparent. Members may wish to avoid the distribution of research assistants falling to the party whips or their regulation being part of the House's own administration. It is probable that the essentially personal relationship involved in this work is the decisive factor. Purely personal recruitment has considerable practical advantage for the public, as well as for the Member who wants to get the right person for his needs. To put Members to the trouble and modest expense of advertising for and recruiting their own personal assistant would be a useful barrier against the Member who would otherwise be tempted to 'put his name down' for an assistant to be provided by a central recruiting authority.

4. THE LIBRARY AND SELECT COMMITTEE WORK

Before the establishment in 1966 of the first two specialised select committees the Library dealt with a certain number of requests for information which had been generated by select committee work. A Member who sat on a committee, or a committee clerk, could ask for assistance on sources and their interpretation (the clerk merely operating the long-standing convention of mutual co-operation between the Library and the Clerk's Department). The addition of two new select committees to the established trio (Estimates, Public Accounts and Nationalised Industries), who had regularly studied aspects of Government activity, led to a rather more formal arrangement for Library assistance.

For the two new specialised committees to look to the Library for information support was natural, particularly as the Government had not provided them with more staff of their own than was enjoyed by the established select committees. A precedent for trying to link the select committees to the Library's organisation had occurred in the 1958–9 session: the Nationalised Industries Committee had called for a special section in the Library to study the industries and provide a base for expert assessors (such as seconded university specialists) who would assist the select committee in its work.[1]

There are several ways in which the sources of information available to Members, who either sit on a given select committee or who merely follow its affairs, could be improved as a result of strengthening the committee's own access to information and analysis. Most radically, the committees could (through the House) directly employ senior expert staff to assess their fields of work and advise on the committees' enquiries. Secondly, the committees could engage more junior staff, of a 'research officer' or 'research assistant' type, to work directly under the supervision of the committee's chairman and clerk. As another alternative, senior or junior staff of this type could be employed on salary but attached to the Library, thus placing them closer in organisation terms, to the House's information centre but further away from the committee whose work they would be supporting. A different approach would be to revert to the senior, nationally-recognised experts but have them attend the committees and undertake private study on the committees' behalf, with no question of secondment from normal employment, or of salary arising.

It is this proposal for visiting expert advisers which has now come into effect at the House, the Select Committees on Estimates, Nationalised Industries and Science having begun the process. The advisers come in to the House, or work elsewhere, on a daily basis and receive a fee and expenses; they sit with the committees and answer points during discussions. Their role, according to the additional terms of reference passed by the House for the purpose, is to supply, 'for the purpose of particular enquiries, either . . . information which is not readily available or to elucidate matters of complexity within the committee's order of reference'; the advisers themselves are referred to as 'persons with technical and scientific knowledge'.[2]

---

[1] D. Coombes, *The MP and the Administration*, Allen & Unwin, 1966, pp. 75–9. Mr Coombes considered that an attempt should have been made on this scheme despite the difficulties.   [2] H.C. Debates, April 19, 1967, c. 722.

The role of the Library as a potential information source for select committees who have such experts assisting their work is protected by the finely-wrought caution of this wording (assuming that the select committee concerned always sticks to such instructions). The adviser is not supposed to become the committee's research arm or information source except at the most technical and rarified level. The scheme is, rather, for a partnership between him and the committee's clerk.

The Scientific Section of the Library's Research Division was, as we have said, established in late 1966, at about the same time as the Select Committee on Science and Technology. It was therefore available to help the Committee with its first enquiry (the nuclear reactor programme) and with the second enquiry (coastal pollution following the wreck of the *Torrey Canyon*). Background papers were prepared by the Scientific Section for these enquiries and Press and journal extracts assembled.[1] The mass of papers and memoranda which are submitted to select committees during the course of some enquiries was also subjected to some premastication by the Scientific Section. This service was much appreciated by Members who felt they could not deal with the amount of paper involved.

We were fortunate that the three Members who have, so far at least, probably been the most active members of the Science Committee fell into our sample and granted us interviews. They stressed the importance of good information to such committee work and appeared to share what seems to be the uncontroversial view that select committees are correct in the present course of combining an *ad hoc* expert adviser with a qualified, but less expert, 'information specialist', backed by his reference sources, who is on the Library's staff. The only question on this matter is how quickly a relevantly-trained Library clerk can be recruited for each policy field which may be granted a specialised committee. An agriculture graduate joined the Research Division in 1968 and assisted the Agriculture Committee on a regular basis. (Now that the Committee has disappeared, there is little risk of her feeling under-employed as Members' interests in agriculture share in the general and continuing increase in the Division's workload). The specialised committees on Education and Race Relations also receive help from Library staff. We met no disagreement, among either our interviewed respondents

[1] D. Menhennet and J. Poole in *New Scientist*, op. cit., p. 501.

or the other people with whom we discussed this aspect of our study, with the judgement that servicing select committees is a most valuable new aspect of the Library's work—a view which is, we understand, fully shared by the Librarian and his staff.

The outside expert advisers to select committees (nearly all of whom, so far, have been university staff) are an interesting new development of Members' sources of information. At the time of writing, more than a dozen of them have assisted the Estimates, Nationalised Industries, Science and Agriculture Committees. The advisers' future role will obviously tend to be concentrated on areas of particularly difficult material which needs 'translating' to laymen, science and technology being obvious examples. It is not an easy task for either the committee concerned or their chosen adviser to talk together in a way which preserves at least the outline of the technical point he wants to make and also maintains the committee's full participation in his argument. If this narrow path is not followed, then either the adviser may feel he is excessively and pointlessly popularising his field or the committee may accept the conclusions which their adviser tells them flow from his technical analysis and come to treat him as their guru.

It is, of course, true that the witnesses called by the select committee (most of whom are officials responsible for policy in the matter under review) will not treat the committee's adviser in this way and it may be a good thing for the select committee to observe and record any exchanges which, indirectly, the two individuals may have. If advisers were permitted to question witnesses direct during select committee meetings, this exchange would become much more obvious and, on balance, more fruitful for the process of enquiry and report-writing which is being served—(one adviser did, inadvertently, break the rule against his asking a question of a witness: their exchange was cut from the committee's published evidence).

David Marquand (Labour Member for Ashfield) served on the Estimates sub-committee which retained Professor Graham Pyatt to help assess Government statistical services. He told us that this expert adviser gave invaluable help to the sub-committee, particularly after its original chairman Jeremy Bray (Labour Member for Middlesborough West) had left the committee upon appointment as a junior Minister; (Dr Bray's Ph.D. is in mathematics and he had come into the House from systems analysis work in ICI). 'It did occur to me,' said Mr Marquand in a letter to us

'that there might possibly be a danger in an expert adviser on a very technical matter of this sort conceivably using the committee as a way of furthering his own views. In other words, the committee could be captured by its own technical adviser just as Ministers can be captured by theirs. But, even if this did happen, the clash between the expert adviser and the civil service would probably be a good thing. Also, it is worth remembering that few investigations are conducted into matters as highly technical and abstruse as this one. On balance I should say that the appointment of Professor Pyatt was very well-justified and a proof of the value of expert advisers.'

In practice (and stretching the official formula for his role if need be) the adviser prompts the committee, mainly through its chairman and clerk, with lines of enquiry and argument and generally helps to deepen and enrich the committee's critical approach to their topic: the Nationalised Industries Committee reported that its adviser (Professor Maurice Peston) had been able to devote an average of one-and-a-half days a week to his work for them: 'he read all the evidence, helped in advising the chairman and members of the sub-committee on all important points, particularly on economic matters such as pricing and investment criteria, and, in general, provided much helpful guidance on matters in which he is an expert.[1] One would expect that, just as the Members, who act as chairmen of the House select committees and their various sub-committees, vary in their boldness in the face of the formal terms of reference under which the House has instructed them to operate, so the outside advisers brought in to 'elucidate matters of complexity' will vary in their approach to their task.

This is, of course, very much a matter for the committee concerned—any sub-committee is fully able to control the contribution made by such an adviser and the main committee can equally easily curb its sub-committee if it so chooses. It is possible that there will be rumblings from Whitehall as senior civil servants lobby their Ministers, complaining that select committees

[1] Select Committee on Nationalised Industries, 1967–8, 'Ministerial Control of the Nationalised Industries', H.C. 371—I of 1967–8, p. 7.

are letting their advisers 'go too far', just as some of them have lobbied in recent years against the Estimates Committee's occasionally rather free interpretation of its terms of reference. But even the close supervision over select committees' membership and activities, maintained by the Government through its whips' office and the Leader of the House, is unlikely to present a serious impediment to the growth of these attachments between MPs sitting on select committees and outside experts in various fields of public affairs or interest.

As one observer put it, the process of select committees having advisers and 'information service' from the Library is basically as much educative as political—that is, the internal process by which the House improves its understanding of problems is as important as the external one of 'checking' the Government and making suggestions for improvements in official 'administration' or 'policy'. This internal or educational process recurs each session as each committee begins a new enquiry. In this way a body of Members with background knowledge even in particularly difficult areas, such as science and technology, is built up and the House's general posture in these areas gradually improved.

5. A PARLIAMENTARY INFORMATION SYSTEM

So far in this chapter we have placed the Library in the context of other existing parliamentary sources of information (which are very minor) and described its development and present features. We have presented our survey evidence of Members' attitudes towards existing and potential Library services and discussed the 'research assistant idea', on which we also had some evidence to offer. We briefly described how the Library has begun to provide some direct service to select committees.

Naturally, we now wish to look to the future and ask how the House may be best served by its own information service. A functional or systematic approach to this question provides a useful way of setting the scene for any further advances which the Library may make. We shall, therefore, adopt a theoretical —even utopian—stance in the following two sub-sections of this chapter and sketch an ideal information system for MPs. The final part of the chapter will then assess the priorities for the Library's advance.

(i) *A functional model*

What is a simple view of an information system and how would this view apply to a particular information system required for parliamentary use? With a fairly complicated information service (the Library) already in existence; with a rather diverse set of views among Members and others on how it ought to be equipped and run; and with several schemes for innovation (such as research assistants for Members) current, no apology for undue obviousness need be made if we describe a basic functional model of the situation.

The three elements of an information system are (i) its store of information, (ii) its staff, who constantly feed new information into, and draw information out of the system and who then convey it (possibly in some processed form) to (iii) the system's clients. The items of information which they convey to the clients may be part of a regular prearranged series of messages or may be requested individually on the client's own initiative. The item of information may be sent to all, or some, or just one client: if the item is to be sent only upon a client's request, it is possible that one single client, or some, or perhaps even all of them will happen to ask for it. The regularity of sending out items of information from the information store has no logical connection with the numbers of clients receiving those items.

The information store is a fixed part of the system. It may be big or little, well-tended or neglected and may consist of several electronic computers or a collection of index cards housed in shoe boxes—these particular features do not concern us at the moment. Similarly, the make-up of the clients group (perhaps only MPs, perhaps peers, etc., as well) is not relevant while we are merely noting that the client's position in the system is also fixed: whoever he is, he receives items of information which either come automatically, under some prearrangement, or following his specific request. Figure 39 shows a simple model of the type we are describing.

The staff of such a system are of two kinds: the Information Supply staff (whose skills are in filling and extracting information from the store and presenting its output in a way useful to others) and the Specialist staff (who are mainly concerned to receive that part of the information from the store which comes within their ambit and process it for clients.) So far as 'output' from the store is concerned, the job of the Information Supply staff is to convey the information to the system's clients or to the Specialist staff for their purposes. That received by the Specialists may be a different set of items from those sent direct to clients. It may be more advanced or more difficult information which the Specialists will process before forwarding it to interested clients. The three sets of triple arrows shown in the Figure indicate this flow from the Information Supply staff to the clients—either direct or via the Specialist staff.

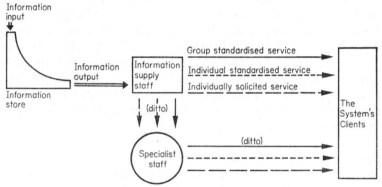

Figure 39.   *A simple information system.*

The arrows run in triplicate in Figure 39 as there are three types of information item which follow these courses. The first of these, the 'group standardised service', represents standard items going by prearrangement to a certain group of clients. They may include a regular item, such as a newsletter or similar list of messages which is standardised in format but not in content—(the Scientific Section's 'Science Digest' is an existing example of this in the House Library); or it may be a fully standardised item in both format and content (such as monthly unemployment or trade returns). The second type of item is the 'individual standardised service' which is exactly similar but goes to only one client. The third type, the 'individually solicited service' is quite different in that the client asks for an item, *ad hoc*, on his own initiative.

The Specialist staff are in exactly the same position in respect of the three-fold flow of information as are the system's clients: some things may be received regularly and automatically from the Information Supply staff by all or some Specialists, some by only one Specialist and some things need to be requested on the Specialist's own initiative. After he has done his work on this information (by mixing it together with his own knowledge) the Specialist passes it as a finished information report to the client along the same trio of arrows—marked 'ditto' in the Figure.

If this simple information system which we have described has the necessary funds, it would naturally expect to consider mechanisation of its routine processes. The input into the information store, and its output to the Information Supply staff are certainly subject to mechanisation. So, too, are many of their 'standard' products which go to their colleagues on the Specialist staff and, also, direct to clients on a regular basis. The 'individually solicited service', in which the client asks for an item on his own initiative is less amenable to mechanisation, either because it is a fairly unusual item he is requesting (which is not to be found in the store) or because the fact that one individual client wants one individual item of information is not worth mechanising.

(ii) *An 'ideal-type' system*
We now add to this functional model a sketch of what would seem to us the 'ideal-type' of parliamentary information system at Westminster. This system (given our present unapologetically utopian context) should be seen as a mere wing of the comprehensive national information system on public policy questions which Britain should develop if attempts to deal with national problems are to have the best basis of factual knowledge.

Looking first at the input of the system, we see that the parliamentary information system would both draw from and contribute to the Public Affairs Information System (PAIS) of which it is part. PAIS would itself draw data from all departments and agencies of the central and local government systems, and from all relevant industries. PAIS would also receive any available data on public policy from a range of other official or private bodies which either have responsibility for or which conduct research into any field of public affairs.

PAIS would consist of several high-capacity memory banks housed within computers, together with whatever number of input and output desks (known as 'remote terminals') the participating organisations wanted to maintain in their various offices around the country, allowing them quick access to the

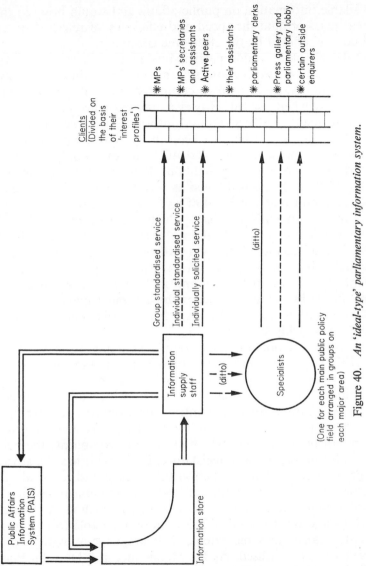

Figure 40. An 'ideal-type' parliamentary information system.

total store of information. A staff of computer workers would prepare data for insertion into the system and would supervise the withdrawal of information by participating organisations and by outside enquirers. The PAIS system would have 'locks' on certain data to prevent its unauthorised withdrawal. On the whole, however, the system is intended to receive only publicly

341

available information on public affairs and would bring to this great mass of data the speed and efficiency of retrieval or 're-discovery' offered by the electronic computer.

Like all other major participants in the PAIS scheme, the parliamentary information system would maintain its own information store in its own computer and call for data from PAIS only when needed. However, the existence of PAIS, with its vast quantity of background information on economic and social affairs would help to keep the parliamentary operation within reasonable bounds and allow its own computer to be filled with the information about Parliament itself which is most likely to be needed.[1] Just as by no means all Parliament's information would come out of PAIS, so not all the data generated by Parliament's business, which the Information Supply staff would prepare to feed into their own computer, would also be fed into PAIS. The PAIS staff would judge which material available from participants was of sufficiently wide interest to justify admittance into PAIS and make informal arrangements on 'thresholds' of admittance with each participant. Any body of information required by PAIS from Parliament's own store could be quickly supplied.

The information on Parliament's activities is very varied. Parliament is so much more than a legislature and receives directly from Ministers such a rich array of information on administrative and international matters which are unconnected with legislation. Also, in contrast to Congress for example, Parliament has a strong tradition of raising grievances and new topics of public concern which enrich and complicate the body of its business. But, as a legislature, Parliament has the advantage of being able to mechanise the storage and retrieval of a certain amount of its output of laws and opinions based on the formal language of legislation. Documents such as Acts, regulations and unsuccessful bills are more amenable to this treatment because, to some extent, their language as well as their format is standardised. As Dr Menhennet and Dr John Poole have pointed out, 'With this, for instance, it would be a relatively simple matter to supply an MP with a print-out giving

---

[1] The existence of a centralised body of data, which obviates the need for broadly interested users (such as Parliament, Government and universities) to hold their own stocks of background information, should offer a considerable economy of scale to the financing of a system such as PAIS.

in chronological order the parliamentary history of a particular bill.'[1]

As for debates, parliamentary Questions, etc., and motions on political matters which are formally set down by Members for debate, their contents may be easily analysed and indexed by an elementary type of content analysis technique. Key words in a field are chosen and the computer stores items of information, such as speeches and Questions, under one or more of these keys. This use of computers as memory systems aids any analysis of the state of the law or what has been said about it. The New York State legislature, which has its legislative record committed to a computer, was able to discover quite easily, once all the laws were fed in, that the dispersion of State banking law needed some attention: 1604 banking provisions were found in laws which were not primarily banking laws.[2]

A basic element of the PAIS system would be its coverage of the laws of the United Kingdom: until the whole field is codified, PAIS would tell any interested participant how all the law on a topic such as property or contract is distributed across the statute book—a service of particular value to the parliamentarians who make laws, as well as to the lawyers who use this service on the level of coping with the statute book as it exists.

It is worth pointing out that, although the PAIS system would use computers merely to store information which was fed in, these machines remain capable of analysing their material in useful ways. Some of the PAIS participants, notably the universities, would see the system through researchers' eyes, while others, such as Government Departments, would use it more as a repository of publicly important facts—Parliament would come somewhere between these two approaches. It would therefore be necessary to design the information-storage and content analysis tasks undertaken by PAIS with some regard to the needs of researchers who wish to analyse the system's data for either policy-making or academic purposes.[3] Parliament's own

[1] D. Menhennet and J. Poole in *New Scientist*, op. cit.

[2] The US Code of Laws is also on a computer tape at a university and will produce all laws requested by a user under a given heading plus other, related items, not listed under that heading in decreasing order of relevance until the user is satisfied. See K. Janda, 'Information Systems for Congress' in de Grazia (ed), *Congress: The First Branch of Government*, Anchor, 1967.

[3] For a general account of the more advanced tasks of content analysis for a more research-oriented application see P. J. Stone, *et al.*, *The General Enquirer: a computer approach to content analysis*, M.I.T. Press, 1966.

343

input to PAIS would therefore be prepared with this consideration in mind.

As Figure 40 shows, the Information Supply staff of the parliamentary information system would be involved in several technical functions, all of a fairly routine and standardised nature. They would receive data from PAIS to hold in their own information store and contribute coded information on Parliament's doings to their own store, some of which would also be taken by PAIS. They would continually pass along information, both to the clients direct and to their own Specialist colleagues, as we saw when outlining the functional model of Figure 39.

The material which we have called 'group (or individual) standardised service' would be based on an expression of interest by the clients. Each client would nominate his fields of interest and would then receive an automatic flow of items which are stored under relevant key words. If his particular 'interest profile' would produce too large a flow for his wishes, the client may receive instead (or in part-exchange for the full flow) a weekly check-list which he returns—exactly similar in intent to the existing check-list of needed parliamentary papers which Members mark and return. As we have noted, there is no essential difference between a standardised item of this kind going to several hundred clients or being directed to just one. We have separated out the 'individual standarised service' in the Figures merely to show that a standard service which is offered repetitively on a given topic on, say, a daily, weekly or monthly basis is not logically connected with a large number of clients— whether the system can afford the cost of 'individual standardised service' would depend solely on its budget and the priorities which flow from it.

The 'individual solicited service' from the Information Supply staff is a simple one: clients would request items of information from the store (or from a manually derived source if this information has not yet been put into the store). Whether clients should themselves have access to the information store in the computer would be, again, a matter of cost and convenience: it may be more appropriate for access to the store to be confined to the staff.

This flow of information from the store would go also to the Specialist staff, as we have seen. It would be 'raw' information—

reprinted Press cuttings and *Hansard* extracts, presented in standardised format.[1] The Specialist staff would receive a good deal more than this standard output (which would be designed rather for clients' direct consumption). They would also, of course, be more likely than the clients to know what data was going into the PAIS system in their specialist fields from its other participants. Thus they would make sure that the parliamentary information system was getting all the PAIS material necessary to give the Specialists proper support for their work.

The task of the Specialists would be to maintain in the information store the best possible level of useful material having regard to the trends of clients' apparent needs and wishes. They would also supervise the dispatch of the standardised material requested by the clients according to their declared 'interest profiles'. In practice they would be likely to deal with self-selected panels of regular clients having special interests in their respective fields. Each Specialist would provide these clients with regular material, while also dealing with their individually solicited jobs in his field. Other clients would come to him for individually solicited service from time to time when their attention is drawn by some event to a problem in his field (such as the question of underground gas storage mentioned in Section 1, above).

The Specialist would not be best described as an 'expert' in his particular field. As an 'information specialist' he would be more of a trained observer of his field than a potential practitioner, although this distinction rests as much on his personal attitude and intellectual style as on any point of formal qualifications. In most cases he would be relevantly qualified for his specialised field in the parliamentary information system, preferably from formal university training in the field, although possibly from in-service specialisation at Westminster which involved him in using the general learning skills of a good honours graduate to master the information flows of the field in question.

Some fields, such as public health and medical statistics, lack a specific undergraduate preparation. A very broad information

---

[1] Standardised format would permit the use by both the staff and their clients of standard filing systems. Once clients, their secretaries and assistants became familiar with such files, a considerable gain in efficiency (and probably a significant advance in the space problems of clients' individual offices) would be made.

system such as Parliament's, could certainly manage with an information Specialist in these matters who is not a doctor and, conceivably, with one who was not a trained statistician either, so long as he or she had the basic taste and feel for such difficult quantitative data as are encountered when attempting, for example, international health comparisons. In other areas, such as the administration of justice, a lawyer's university training would be essential, as would a social scientist's in the various fields of social administration and the personal social services. To these background qualifications (whether they are relevant university degrees or determined personal efforts to master a novel field on an in-service basis) should be added a reasonable familiarity with the workings of the computer, both as an information store and as a research tool. Professional skill in programming could be obtained from outside experts when designing any analysis jobs needed by the parliamentary information system. Routine programming of Parliament's computer would, of course, be the concern of the Information Supply staff, in consultation with the Specialist staff.

The right kind of personality to deal with the often rather elementary needs of clients, while preserving high standards on the more sophisticated jobs would, of course, be an important requirement. The art of absorbing something rather difficult and abstruse and putting it across to both laymen and the semi-expert clients in his field would be central to the success of the Specialist in this parliamentary information system. His talents would be very close to those of another developing group whose impact on politics will be significant: the graduate specialised journalist.

The intellectual pressure towards specialisation (which the graduate Specialist would have seen at first hand in dealing with his teachers during his university years) and the conventional prestige of the 'academic level' of intellectual life are so persistent that the key role in the nation's life of the 'information specialist', who observes and interprets to others a range of work far wider than he could ever hope to 'contribute' to (in the academic sense of the word), needs to be highly regarded, if an advanced country is to understand its own behaviour and problems. Steps need to be taken to establish and preserve the status of people with these valuable skills.

These Specialist staff members in a parliamentary information system would be intellectually akin to specialised journalists, as we have said. This means they would probably not naturally incline toward either professional academic life or to the purely reference and technical functions of librarianship or Information Supply staff work. They would probably like to write and communicate at least some of the interpretations which they form while discharging their duty of providing interested parliamentary clients with a concise, disciplined and completely impartial rendering of what is happening in their special field. This aversion to complete anonymity is natural, given the skills and talents with information for which they are employed. The Information Specialists should, therefore, be free to contribute articles on their fields of an informative kind (raising and discussing issues but avoiding sharply controversial conclusions) to the Press and publications of all relevant kinds, and to domestic and overseas broadcasting networks. The test for approving any such public activity should be whether the points and opinions expressed by the Specialist are at all likely to diminish confidence in him as an impartial Information Specialist in the mind of any of the system's clients: fields vary in their combustibility and it is likely, for example, that the Specialist in technology and automation would have more leeway for any published opinions than his colleagues in housing or social security.

The ambits of these Specialists would be patterned on a mixture of functional and Government departmental breakdowns of the total field of public responsibility. The housing specialist, for instance, would not be tied to the local authority housing sector because of his close observation of the work and problems of the Ministry of Housing and Local Government— the financing of the private housing sector (involving building societies and tax concessions) is, in fact, Treasury business. Similarly, the nationalised industries would be seen as part of the economy's major economic units (except insofar as the Nationalised Industries Committee required assistance from a Specialist in their studies on these industries' special position). Concentration into fields by these information Specialists would not be very highly developed: it does not match that of either the civil servants who are responsible to their superiors for public policies or even of some, at least, of the specialised journalists.

The Specialist in the parliamentary information system would need to adjust the ambit of his tasks to suit his clients' own level of knowledge and try to be rather closer to the material than any client would be (unless the client was professionally engaged in the field). But he should also be prepared to work at different levels of concentration in different parts of his field and to adjust himself to changing levels, perhaps under pressure from topical events or newly perceived 'problems' (such as the 'brain drain' topic of recent years) or merely according to the mood of the times.

This flexibility would be part of the Specialist's general taste for the urgency, the unpredictability and the crucial importance to his client of receiving a sound and accurate information service on which his client will take some political stand. Bearing these points in mind the list of the parliamentary information system's Specialists (gathered into a reasonably convenient, but by no means immutable, grouping of six sections) could be as follows:

I. *External Affairs* (8)

Communist nations; the UN and international bodies and law; Europe; Commonwealth and colonies; other areas . . . (5)

World resources and underdevelopment—UN and international technical agencies (1)

Defence: British forces' administration and equipment; alliances and strategy . . . (2)

II. *Economic affairs* (5)

British financial and fiscal; trade and industry, consumer affairs; labour, employers and productivity; Scottish and regional economies; international financial affairs and overseas economies . . . (5)

III. *Law and Social Services* (7)

Home Office affairs, administration of justice, law reform, legal system, race relations . . . (3)

Health and social security affairs . . . (2)

Education affairs . . . (2)

IV. *Environment* (5)

Transportation and urban planning; housing and rents policy; local government affairs and services (except health and education); building industry and public

works; agriculture, horticulture (grants) and rural
planning . . . (5)

V. *Science and Technology* (5)

Scientific policy and development; technology, automation and aviation affairs . . . (3)

Power . . . (1)

Medical and public health, environmental health
hazards (1)

VI. (3)

Parliamentary affairs; machinery of Government, Civil
Service (1)

Communications: Post Office, broadcasting, Press, etc.,
affairs, official information services (1)

Miscellaneous and other fields; co-ordination and
common service to all six sections; administration and
relief of the Specialist service . . . (1)

Although flexibility in such an organisation of thirty-three
Specialists should be second only to skill and competence as a
priority, there would be obvious limits to a body of individual
'Specialists' doing each others' work, even in an emergency.
More troubling than an emergency (when service from a part
of the Specialists' system would simply have to be suspended
while, for example, particular staff members were indisposed)
would be the short-run increase of the pressure of work on a
section caused by political developments. In cases where clients
are calling for very difficult analyses of information in response,
perhaps, to rapid Government moves to introduce legislation,
it may be necessary to go outside for qualified manpower.
The haste with which legislation was passed during the 1967–8
session on immigration and dangerous drugs serves as a reminder that no advanced parliamentary information system
would be able easily to handle a sudden major increase in demand from its clients on one or more fields.

It is true that the standardised services would be very elastic
in meeting the extra demand: thus, if the Information Supply
staff were already sending a monthly item on some aspect of
dangerous drugs policy to thirty regular clients, it would be
little extra effort to send it to three hundred while the 'heat' was
on the subject, as this task would be mechanised. Less easy
would be the production at short notice of, say, international

data on drugs in response to a range of thirty individual and non-standardised requests. If clients were calling for the assembly of data which had not been assembled before and which was widely scattered, and if that section of the system happens to be already heavily involved in some other topical issue, it would be natural for the system to commission outside specialist manpower to meet clients' needs. This would apply particularly when the information processing required was rather more of an expert matter than the Specialists could handle alone, bearing in mind their other commitments. Thus outsiders (usually in universities and research institutes) could sometimes be retained to help in such circumstances. Similarly outside experts could also be retained to keep a friendly eye on the progress of a section of the information system, particularly when a newly-appointed or newly- 'self-trained' Specialist was settling in. Experts who had served as advisers to select committees of the House could well be retained for this function, as they would have seen the kind of information service required for MPs and other clients of the system at first hand.

But who, in this 'ideal-type' parliamentary information system we are describing, would be the 'clients' to whom we have been referring, following the functional language of our simple model in Figure 39? This would be entirely a matter of opinion and convenience to the principal clients of the system, the MPs. If some Members had research assistants, or employed their secretaries in a similar manner, it would suit them if the information system were to treat these aides as clients. It would suit active peers to be so treated (as it would their assistants and secretaries), and also members of the parliamentary Press gallery and the parliamentary lobby who also appear in Figure 40. Whether the extension to these groups of parliamentary information services inconvenienced MPs would depend entirely on the design of the system. If it was properly set up in adequate accommodation and if access to the computer's information store was made easy and quick, it would not, in practical terms, matter to an MP that the facilities were also enjoyed by, say, another Member's research assistant or secretary, a peer or a political correspondent.[1] Whether it would matter to him in

---

[1] An arrangement for the information system's staff to give Members priority over others in urgent or difficult circumstances would no doubt be made, continuing the established Library practice which admits requests for information

terms of 'principle' (i.e. the MP's exclusive status) is another question: most MPs would probably approach it in a practical spirit.

We have used the term 'client' to establish a functional rather than a hierarchical or institutional view of the job which Parliament's information system would do. Both the Information Supply and Specialist staffs would also take a functional view of their various specialist clienteles whose names emerge from clients submitting their 'interest profiles' to the staff. The various groups of clients would break down and interlock with each other in a fairly complex way (which we express in Figure 40 with a brickwork pattern). If the system is a parliamentary one and if all political actors in that place value access to the system, be they MPs, their assistants, peers or political journalists then, it may be argued, the system would itself prosper from the economies of scale and degree of specialisation possible with a larger clientele (particularly as there is no reason why the British and overseas Press, and the broadcasting authorities should not pay for the convenience of having their people who work on the spot in the Palace accepted as clients of Parliament's information system).[1]

Trying even to conceive of, let alone actually to install, the ancilliary functions of a rationally planned modern legislature within the useful accommodation offered by the Palace of Westminster is a nightmare. Accommodation is a major problem for the development of all aspects of the work of Parliament. It is worth noting that the House's computer, its technical links

---

from peers and others when obligations to Members permit.

[1] There is also no reason why the regular standardised information material produced by the parliamentary information system for its immediate clients should not also be made available to outside users. If copyright law allowed, commercial bodies could subscribe, while a policy decision would be required on whether schools, colleges, public libraries or individuals should pay an economic or subsidised price for the material they receive, or even receive it free.

To make Parliament the source of an information service on British public affairs which penetrated thousands of schools and libraries in both Britain and other countries would do much for Parliament's standing. The large-scale performance by the parliamentary information service of individual tasks solicited by the public is a separate matter. The Legislative Reference Service of the US Congress does a lot of this work, notably for school and college students, as a matter of public policy: much of it is standardised material, however, particularly on constitutional and historical topics of perennial interest. If such a public service developed at Westminster, similar methods would presumably be employed.

with the PAIS and the Information Supply staff handling this machinery would not need to be close to the Palace. Given adequate audio-visual links (and, of course, the data links with the computer) it would not matter even to the Specialist, and certainly not to the client, where the machinery was situated. Both the Specialist and his client would be more interested in how much information had been fed in, how much awaited this process, and how quick and reliable the installation appeared to be.

The long, thin plan of the Palace's useful space would dictate that accommodation for those staff members of such a parliamentary information system who would need to work close to their clients, could be found only in the main suites of the present Commons or Lords Libraries. It would be essential for the system to maintain the Commons Library's established tradition of face to face contact with Members and other clients. The best broad solution would therefore probably be to accommodate the Specialists and other staff members who would be close to clients in the present main suite and other space now used by the Commons Library. The ancilliary staffs, the remainder of the Information Supply staff and perhaps the computer itself, would be housed in the promised Bridge Street extension.

Putting a considerably increased number of Information Specialists, together with their supporting staff and materials, into the present Commons Library would make its atmosphere almost completely that of a reasonably quiet, but busy 'information workshop'. Some of the Library's stock which is currently housed in the main suite would be displaced, as would the amenity functions of the Library for Members who wish to write or read quietly, without reference to the information service, or who wish simply to relax. In a new, overall system, which accepted both MPs and peers as clients of its information services, it would be natural to use the main suite of the present Lords Library for a system which peers and Members would share.

To merge the two separate libraries into a considerably expanded and improved parliamentary information system may be seen in some quarters as raising political, or even 'constitutional' questions. With the question of the reform of the House of Lords in abeyance, at the time of writing, it is difficult to speculate further. Nevertheless, it may be that the active members of a reformed House of Lords would be sufficiently attracted by a greatly improved parliamentary information system, of which they were clients, to agree to the merging of the two separate libraries and the use of the total available space for the benefit of themselves and MPs.

There is, of course, one other aspect to the accommodation problem: useful space in the Palace could be taken over for use by the Commons, Lords or their overall parliamentary information system from the Lord Chancellor's Department and sundry other non-parliamentary users. No Government has ever accepted this policy, preferring instead to build new accommodation for MPs as their demands have risen. Such an attempt to move these users elsewhere could, possibly, succeed if both Houses urged the Government to do so. Commons opinion alone probably would not suffice. The supremacy of the elected chamber, notwithstanding successive constitutional advances, should not be thought boundless.

(iii) *Present provision and priorities for advance*

If the existing House of Commons Library is compared with an 'ideal type' system of the kind described, it may be possible to observe its strengths and weaknesses in the same light. Firstly, there is, of course, no Public Affairs Information System in which the Library participates and there is no likelihood of one being established in the foreseeable future. It is also clear that the Library lacks a computer and has not arranged its stock of material in preparation for obtaining one of its own, or for regularly sharing the time of someone else's.

A start has been made, however, in the handling of information by means of a computer. Collaboration with the Office for Scientific and Technical Information (OSTI) and with the library of Culham Laboratory enabled the Commons Library to run, in the autumn of 1968, a short-term, experimental computerised service. Over 400 Members, and about 100 outside users,[1] received weekly 'Current Literature Bulletins' on the subjects of their choice, from a list of thirty-six subjects (such as Business, Law, Politics, Social Problems, etc.), which between them covered the whole field of British domestic affairs. The Bulletins consisted of edited references to parliamentary and

[1] These users were associates of OSTI.

other material. Generally speaking, this experiment evoked a favourable response among the Members who participated and showed a demand for some sort of permanent, mechanised information service in the social sciences.[1]

The catalogue of 100,000 volumes remains on the London Library system and requires transfer to the Library of Congress system (with conversion to its being machine-readable, in whole or part, as a further possibility). On the staffing side, it would appear at first sight that the staff is not sufficiently differentiated into the Information Supply side and the Information Specialist side; this would be a natural result of the Specialist side (i.e. the Research Division) having grown organically from the existing Information Supply side (i.e. the Library proper, such as it was in 1946) over a period of more than twenty years.

But the two bases for these complementary specialisms (the Library's two divisions) are present and need growth rather than radical alteration to allow their different contributions to emerge more clearly. While one of the four sections of the Library's Research Division carries a 'subject heading' (which was given it as late as 1968) as awesomely broad as 'Home and Parliamentary Affairs', and while the two graduate scientists and one qualified librarian, who currently make up the senior staff of the Scientific Section, are supposed to cover all science, technology and medicine, it is clear that the distinct Information Specialist, each in his particular field, has not yet emerged. When the staffing establishment of the Research Division (including the currently separate International Affairs Desk) is permitted to grow towards the much larger number of graduate information Specialists which is needed to offer an adequate service (a number which we have estimated to be over thirty compared with the actual 1968 figure of about fourteen), it will become more clear that there is a body of graduate staff members both qualified, and perhaps technically trained as information Specialists who are not routinely concerned to 'spot' information on very wide areas, but who manage and refine a steady flow of material in a genuinely specialised field.

Whether computerisation comes about or not, there is still much to be done in expanding the Supply side of the overall information service as the Library is weak on what we have

[1] See an account of this experiment by J. Poole in *Parliamentary Affairs*, XXII, 2 (Spring 1969).

called, in our 'ideal-type' system, the 'standardised services'. There is great scope for gathering Members' 'information profiles' and supplying them with the standard-format and standard-content material we have mentioned above. If the revision of the copyright law, which university and other libraries are currently requesting, liberalises the legal reproduction of materials, the Library would, of course, also benefit by being able to distribute such material as widely as demand required.

If the Library is undeveloped in the establishment of channels to Members along which regular information may flow according to their choice of interests, it is relatively well-developed on what we have called 'individually solicited service' (i.e. the Research Division). This balance between the two kinds of service is hardly surprising in a small and only slowly-developing organisation, as the individually solicited service consists of waiting for the client to make a request rather than going to him with offers of service (which, of course, makes for extra work if he accepts any part of the offer). As it happens, the Library's small staff dealing with these individual requests has been continuously over-burdened, which has prevented the development of the standardised information services beyond the basically bibliographical 'reference sheets' (and their accompanying 'green boxes')[1] and the much more recent and somewhat more sophisticated *Science Digest* with its 'mailing list' of about 90 Members.

The tasks of assessing the present balance between the 'standardised, pre-arranged and regular' information service and the 'individually solicited' information service and of looking to the future are hindered, to some extent, by the rather misleading use by the Library of the word 'research'. The individual information and reference service, which handled 1,937 requests from MPs and others in 1968, is called 'the Research Division' (while a further 450 tasks were performed as 'research jobs' by the International Affairs Desk within the Parliamentary, or main Library, Division). The use of this word goes back to the first appointment of 'research assistants' in 1946 to deal with Members' individual enquiries. Members' enquiries, however,

[1] The Library's reference sheets often report the contents of some of their listed documents. The sheet occasioned in 1967 by the Government's announcement of policy on decimal currency gave the gist of the majority and minority recommendations of the Halsbury Committee, followed by the usual list of the documents available in the green box on the subject.

355

have always been overwhelmingly, and still are, of an information and reference nature, although their sophistication increases steadily as the years pass.

On the infrequent occasions when a Member has asked for a piece of genuine political research (involving the analysis and manipulation of materials according to a certain purpose, or, perhaps, towards a certain conclusion) the Library has been known to decline to go beyond its normal function of offering information and references, either because it is so busy or because it is uncomfortable doing politically-infused work, or both. Material in support of a partisan view may be provided for Members without the inclusion of balancing pros and cons, but this can include only existing published arguments to which the enquirer is merely referred without any discussion of the points concerned.

The Members who have been broadly satisfied with having only an information and reference service naturally do not want a genuine political research service; they prefer, as many told us, to extract their own conclusions and thoughts from the materials to which the Library has drawn their attention. Other Members, who said they were not satisfied with only an information service, and who wanted research support as well, stressed to us the importance of a personal and political link with this support—that is, the personal research assistant idea. There is thus no scope for a collective policy analysis bureau, run by the House along similar lines to the Library's existing services. This was clearly shown by the absence from our survey of any but a tiny demand among Members for such a service (three Members only; see Table 34). Complementing this view among Members themselves is the Library's long-established reluctance to become involved in plainly partisan analysis of affairs.

The Library's handbook for Members makes it clear that requests for assistance can be entertained only if 'a scrupulously factual and impartial form' of reply is accepted by the Member, and, as we have noted, the Library observes this rule by declining or only partly answering the kind of request which calls for a politically shaped treatment. Dr Menhennet discussed this point in his article in *Political Quarterly*:

'. . . what is meant by "research" in the all-important context of Members' actual requirements? Generally speaking, it does not imply original long-term research in the academic sense of the word... Indeed a feature of many research enquiries from Members is that they are unavoidably made at short notice: answers to about two-thirds of the questions asked are sought within forty-eight hours. The main function ... is therefore to provide accurate, precise and scrupulously factual written answers to numerous specific enquiries within the time limit allowed'.[1]

That the work done by the Library for politicians is not of the same scale and character as the research practised by academics is hardly to be doubted. The question is, rather, whether what the Library does, within its official rules requiring a scrupulously factual treatment of enquiries, can be called genuine research by politicians who are trying to analyse and manipulate material appropriate to their role. The distinction to be drawn is not that between the somewhat miscellaneous reference function of the small Library organisation which has so far developed and the highly specialised long-term work of university scholarship, but rather between the reference function for politicians and the analysis, or genuine research, function for politicians.

Dr Menhennet appears to lean more to this interpretation in his article with Dr Poole in which the Research Division's function is described as:

'(to provide) accurate, relevant and politically disinterested facts and figures which will afford Members with the maximum possible assistance in their duties. This last requirement means that, although work has to be free of political bias, it also needs to be geared to the interests and immediate concerns of the individual MP asking for information.'[2]

On the other hand, the authors of this article quote with approval the foreword to an international symposium on legislative library services in various countries which declared: '... more and more Members find the need for a *positive* library service to help them with the immediate provision of information for use in debate. There is a very real need also for

[1] D. Menhennet in *Pol. Quart.*, op. cit.
[2] D. Menhennet and J. Poole in *New Scientist*, op. cit.

library services which provide research in depth on issues of legislative importance.'[1]

This comment, by its use of the word 'also', does indicate its author's appreciation of the difference between a 'positive' information service (of the kind whose ideal-type we have outlined in the previous section) and the entirely separate proposal for an official, collective bureau for policy research on 'issues of legislative importance'. As a matter of fact, this writer's claim that there is a real need among legislators for such a service is not supported by British M Ps, although it may well be true elsewhere. As our survey shows, if M Ps at Westminster want anything provided for them in respect of policy research, they seem to prefer the personal research assistant solution. More than one Member in three among all our interviews (thirty-nine out of 111) registered their view that this solution would be best, although we had carefully avoided asking a direct question on the point. Some of these thirty-nine Members were 'satisfied' with the Library Research Division's provision of service as they found it in 1967 and others were not: where they agreed with each other was on the necessary personal basis for any genuine research support they might enjoy, because of its political nature. Apart from the three Members shown in Table 34, no view favouring a policy research bureau in the House emerged.

The crucial functional distinction between the two concepts of 'information' and 'research' is brought out well in our results by the small group of Conservative shadow Ministers whom we interviewed. They were, of all the sub-groups of respondents, the most interested in getting a sophisticated information service from the Library and were also seen in the data as particularly frequent users of its facilities. This activity of the shadow Ministers to whom we spoke led us to comment in Section 2 of this chapter that the Library of the House should clearly figure in any study of the modern Opposition (assuming that our small group of shadow Ministers was at all typical of the others). Yet these Members, who have a relatively very high demand for an information service, probably have almost no need of policy analysis from any official bureau, whether run by the Library itself or any other parliamentary authority, as their policy views

[1] *Library Services to the Legislature—a Symposium*, op. cit (emphasis in original).

are derived from their party and represent their party's official position. It was almost certainly the clearly partisan nature of their respective speeches and other contributions in the chamber on policy matters which prompted these shadow Ministers to stress particularly strongly to us that 'research' for Members means political research and that they did not expect this from the Library. Some of these shadow Ministers were among those Members who said they want this service from a research assistant: a personal, continuing and often partisan support for the Member's political work.

As a result of our study of existing services and our survey of Members' attitudes towards them, we conclude that the existing House of Commons and House of Lords Libraries should combine resources and be considerably extended to provide a single parliamentary information service along the lines shown in Figure 40 (albeit without the benefits of a public affairs information system).

The new organisation should be divided into an Information Division (including Library functions) and a Specialists' Division, the misleading word 'research' being discarded in favour of the single, and quite sufficiently challenging, concept of providing the best and most sophisticated information service possible within the available resources. This would involve the maximum possible degree of concentration in their respective fields by the Specialists. If this graduate staff of Specialists is allowed to increase from the existing numbers in the Research Division of the Commons Library towards the size required for an adequate coverage of public affairs, and if the Information Division is given adequate resources (preferably including a computer facility) with which to build up the flow of basic raw material to the Specialists and to clients, along the lines of our ideal-type outline, then Parliament will have something approaching a first-class information system.

Ideally, of course, the proposal for Members' individual research assistants should be allowed to develop simultaneously. The parliamentary information system proposals and the research assistants proposal are not in the least competitive with each other as ideas but are, in fact, perfectly complementary. There is, it is true, scope for confusing Members and others on this basic point so long as the Commons Library calls its individual information enquiry service a 'research division' yet remains, at most, highly ambivalent in its attitude towards true parliamentary research, whose nature is political. It is the term rather than this ambivalence which is out of place in an official service such as the Library offers.

The growth of a reasonably adequate information service for MPs and other possible parliamentary clients is, however, obviously in direct competition with the research assistant proposal as a priority for public expenditure. Both advances appear to us to be necessary to meet the legitimate needs of those more active Members who would engage and keep a graduate research assistant,[1] although each development—the good collective service and the research assistants—could quite well exist without the other.

If the information service was radically improved, but no research assistant scheme established, the Member who needs genuine political research done would continue to try to do it himself. He would, of course, be enjoying a better official information service, one of whose Specialists may, if the Member is lucky, be in exactly the same field as the Member's special interest. If the research assistant scheme were brought in and the Library left as it is, the assistants would go to outside sources and, in particular, to other libraries which they would actually be allowed to enter (Members' assistants are, at present, officially prohibited from entering the Commons Library).

It is difficult to say which of these two developments ought to enjoy the higher priority. We would suggest only which of them, looking at our survey, would enjoy the greater support among Members if they were told they could choose only one

[1] An ideal list of the facilities which should be available to a Member on request, in addition to a first-class collective information service and the help of a personal research assistant includes: an office (with a small outer office for his secretary and research assistant) to which the public can gain controlled access at the discretion of the Member or his secretary; a secretarial grant meeting the reasonable current cost of an average salary, similar to the research assistant's salary grant; a telephone, with secretary's extension, which dials out direct to London numbers and via an operator for long distance calls (declared constituency calls being free) and which receives all calls direct, subject to an answering service if his office fails to answer; a television set which not only serves as annunciator of debates, speakers, etc., in the Chamber (which are already being issued to Members' rooms) but also receives radio and television programmes; a type writer and dictation tape recorder; and general filing units together with the special standardised units designed to hold the products of the parliamentary information system as mentioned in our text.

of the two. We feel most Members would probably give the higher priority to a major advance of the House of Commons Library towards a fully developed parliamentary information system, with a Specialists' Division.

Our reasons for this interpretation are as follows. About one respondent in three spontaneously said that they would like a research assistant. About one respondent in five said this and added their view that the Research Division was adequate for their needs. It is, of course, possible that all this latter group would be quite single-minded on this matter and decline to use any collective service, however good it may be—only a research assistant would meet their needs. We do not know how many of this minority group would take this view. Probably not all of them would, but their numbers could not, in any case, exceed one-fifth of the whole. The other Members who mentioned the research assistant proposal also wanted to see a better collective service and so would be pleased to accept half a loaf. In addition, Members who called for a better collective service without mentioning research assistants would be even more pleased, while Members who expressed general satisfaction on these matters would presumably not feel hostile (so long as the existing amenity value currently afforded by the Library suite was not lost or too severely displaced in the process of building a better information service). The extension of collective information services would probably, therefore, give more satisfaction to more Members than would the introduction of the research assistant scheme.

In support of this profile of opinion among Members is the obvious factor that the existing information service (the Library and its supervisory House Services Committee) must, by its very existence, produce pressure in favour of its own extension rather than permitting the birth of a novel scheme such as that for research assistants. It is also possible that even a radical extension of collective information services of the kind we have described would cost less than a research assistant scheme, although it is very difficult to attempt any comparative estimate when the scheme for research assistants is so open-ended a commitment, and when there is the possibility of a parliamentary information service earning outside revenue.

In view of the fact that officials in the Treasury rule over the facilities which the two Houses of Parliament may be permitted to enjoy, virtually as if Parliament were a Government Department, this cost factor is of great importance.[1] One ex-Minister whom we interviewed, and who was in a position to know, remarked that the growth of the House of Commons Library was 'moving ahead against a Treasury brake'. How easily that brake may be released will be a function of how strongly Members are willing to press the Leader of the House and the Government generally to accord a higher priority to parliamentary information services.

[1] See evidence of Treasury control of expenditure by House of Commons departments from the Clerk of the House, Sir Barnet Cocks, to the Science and Technology Committee (sub-committee on Coastal Pollution) May 21 1968. H.C. 167—vi of 1967-8.

CHAPTER VII

CONCLUSION

1. MEMBERS AND MINISTERS

The final questions of our interview were of a very general nature, designed to record each Member's overall attitude to the House's role. We asked, 'Do Ministers (of *any* Government) *wish* to limit M PS' knowledge?'

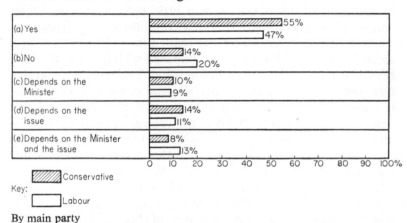

By main party

(N—96: 51 Conservative and 45 Labour M PS)

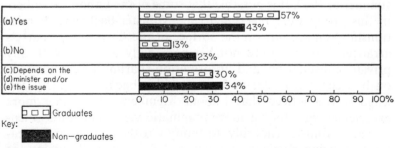

By university education

(N—98: 51 Conservatives, 45 Labour and 2 Liberal M PS)

Figure 41. '*Do Ministers (of any Government) wish to limit MPs' knowledge?'—by main party and university education.* (See Appendix, Table 37.)

363

About half our respondents replied that they believed Ministers did positively 'wish' to limit MPs' knowledge and only one sixth thought not. The rest, just under one third, replied that it depended on the individual Minister, or on the particular issue, or on a mixture of the man and the issue. There were some differences between the parties, rather more Labour Members saying that Ministers as a whole did not entertain this wish—which may well, of course, be a reflection of a less critical view among Labour Members of their own party's Ministers despite our attempt to put the question in a neutral manner.

It is interesting, when looking at these responses in terms of parliamentary service, to see that the 1966 entrants, whose experience was of only Labour Ministers and who were themselves mainly Labour Members, were a little less inclined to acquit Ministers of any positive desire to keep information from MPs. Three-fifths of the 1966 entrants replied that Ministers do wish to limit Members' knowledge, compared with half of all Members who were in the House before 1966. The response that this question turns on the individual Minister or the particular issue is more common with longer parliamentary service and this tendency runs across party lines: the 1966 group was least likely, and the longest-serving group (with thirteen or more years in the House) was most likely to take this pragmatic view, while the Members who had entered the House during the period 1955–65, inclusive, registered a middle position.

As on certain other matters in our survey, we cannot know whether this rather flatly critical view of three-fifths of the 1966 entrants has altered with their greater experience since the summer of 1967. It is possible that some of the Labour Members in this group were reacting to the Minister-backbencher relationship as it appears on the surface of the Government party's arrangements and were not yet personally involved with any private consultation and information-sharing which may go on between a Minister and some of his backbench party colleagues. We noticed that Labour Members with rather more experience, who took a more pragmatic view, sometimes mentioned a Minister (notably Anthony Crosland, then at Education) as being particularly open to advice and discussion, at meetings of the PLP's party groups or elsewhere, which could be described as exchanges of 'information' in the broad, political sense of the word. Some other current Ministers, it was felt by some Labour Members, seemed barely able to blow their noses when in the company of Labour backbenchers without first checking on their Department's official position on the action and perhaps also asking the Prime Minister's permission.

The feeling that Ministers did wish to limit Members' knowledge was more common among graduates, as Figure 41 shows, although this point is subject to the usual pattern of greater diversity of views to be found among the more extensively educated Members. Ex-Ministers generally were a little less likely to answer that Ministers wish to limit knowledge, although all but two of the small group of shadow-Ministers (which, of course, included several ex-Ministers) said that Ministers did have this desire. Ex-Ministers, like longer-serving Members as a whole, tended towards a pragmatic view. Generally, opinion on this broad question was diverse and rather loose—but Members made some interesting comments, some of which we reproduce.

MPs Talking about Ministers

(In response to the question 'Do Ministers (of *any* Government) *wish* to limit MPs' knowledge?')

'No. The Ministers wish to limit our power not our knowledge: there is no lack of knowledge if MPs can absorb it.' (Labour, 1966)

'Yes. Especially the long-term "professional" Minister like Rab (Butler). I was and still am in favour of openness.' (Conservative ex-Minister)

'Some of them are very remote from political reality. Being naturally suspicious, I think we must press on and develop new contacts, e.g. between Parliament and big business; information leads to influence and power.' (Labour, 1964)

'No: they're caught up in an avalanche of information and work. But at the top Wilson epitomises the presidential PM, although he has only put the hallmark on the cup that was shaped by Macmillan. Specialised committees may keep MPs happier in the future but they will not alter the basic facts of power.' (Conservative)

'I'm pretty optimistic: it's a generational feeling. We younger MPs look on the House of Commons as a workshop.' (Conservative, 1966)

'Yes: for example, I pressed for a white paper on a certain topic but the Government knows its publication would focus protest and have therefore refused.' (Conservative)

'Yes, of course they do since it's convenient. Parliament is a nuisance as answers to Questions show: backbenchers drag in party attitudes and frontbenchers have to tag along to keep supporters happy.' (Conservative ex-Minister)

'Yes, of course they do. It's essentially because Ministers act on pretty evenly-balanced advantages. The Civil Service sets a problem up to Ministers like that. If MPs knew how even the balance of advantage often is in Government policy-making they would criticise to try to tilt it the other way.' (Conservative ex-Minister)

'It is unwise to reveal all. The risk of exposure would make the Civil Service too reactionary. The Minister's essential task is to interpret his Department and Parliament to each other: he achieves change by carrying them both along.' (Conservative ex-Minister)

'They can fudge so much. There is a vast difference between what crosses the floor in debate and what Ministers actually know about things.' (Labour, 1964)

'Governments pay lip service to openness but all act the same when they get the chance. Ministers naturally wish to put the best face on things.' (Conservative, 1945)

'Whitehall is indeed very clamped up, but it is understandable and right: they cannot go around telling everyone their thoughts when they are responsible for decisions.' (Conservative ex-Minister)

'Ministers vary very much. I have recently abstained from supporting one Labour Minister's policy and he is very open and amenable.' (Labour, 1966)

'The Civil Service certainly do and only the efficient Minister can stop them.' (Conservative)

'My friends who have become Ministers gradually change their attitudes and resist attempts to secure information.' (Conservative)

'Yes—and private Members act the same when their own motions, bills or party activity puts *them* in the position of knowing something.' (Labour, 1964)

'No: but they get upset with ignorant criticism. Ministers think the onus for getting information is on the MP. I agree.' (Labour, 1966)

'No, but the tendency of paternalism towards Government backbenchers is strong: "If you knew what I know you'd see I'm right. Meanwhile, father knows best." ' (Labour)

'Without "wishing" to, Ministers and civil servants must come to see MPs as a series of barriers and obstacles to be got around: nuisances to be avoided.' (Conservative)

'They don't really—there is no problem of access when your party is in power.' (Conservative)

'It depends on the Minister: some would like to have more confidential discussions but the PLP leaks too much.' (Labour, 1966)

Our final question concerned general 'optimism' or 'pessimism' among our respondents about Parliament's overall 'information position': 'Under our Constitution, must the House of Commons inevitably settle for *about* the level of information it gets at the moment?' At this final stage of each interview our exchanges with Members were fully discussive and Figure 42 therefore consists of coded responses allocated by us from a variety of comments although based on common phrases used by Members.

Between two-fifths and half of our respondents felt that there should be no limit placed on the information made available to them as Members of Parliament. Nearly one-fifth, however, felt that, in various senses of the phrase, 'information' was 'not the real problem'. Of these, four Members thought better physical facilities at the House were important; six considered the supply of information more than adequate and saw its management or digestion by Members as the difficult question;

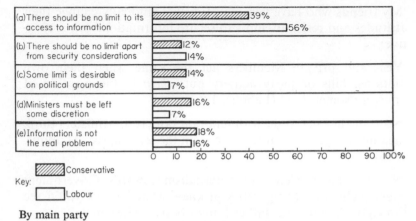

By main party

(N—92: 49 Conservative and 43 Labour MPs)

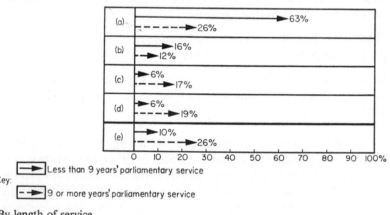

By length of service

(N—93: 49 Conservative, 43 Labour MPs and 1 Liberal MP)

Figure 42. *'Under our Constitution must the House of Commons inevitably settle for about the level of information it gets at the moment ?'—by main parties and length of service.* (See Appendix, Table 38.)

six other Members said that the political problem of making Ministers more accountable to Parliament was the heart of the matter. The remaining Members (rather more than a third) believed that some limit was necessary on grounds such as national security (14 per cent) general political grounds (11 per cent) or the need for ministerial discretion, whether partisan or not (12 per cent).

Far more Labour MPs subscribed to the view that there should be no limit on the information made available to them: this applied to well over half of the Labour Members but to less than two-fifths of the Conservatives. Although similar proportions of Conservative and Labour Members regarded a limit on security grounds as acceptable, twice as many Conservatives subscribed to the view that limits on general political grounds or ministerial discretion were acceptable, or even desirable. The newer MPs were much more strongly opposed to any limit being placed on the information Parliament received than were their longer-serving colleagues: nearly two-thirds of the 1966 entrants and over two-fifths of the 1964 entrants supported this view, compared with fewer than two-fifths of the pre-1964 entrants.

Further analysis brings out another example of the link we have noticed in earlier chapters between Members who entered the House during 1959–63, inclusive, and the 1964–6 newcomers. On this question of the overall flow of official information to Parliament the more established of these two groups was more in sympathy with the recent entrants than with their longer-serving colleagues who were in the House before 1959. The dichotomy around nine years' service shown in Figure 42 is sharp and goes far beyond any party division.

Summing up these responses on these final broad questions, we see that about half the non-ministerial Members in 1967 thought that Ministers deliberately keep back information and that nearly half consider that they should be obliged to reveal virtually all information to the House, newer Members being more often of that opinion than their longer-serving colleagues.

2. INFORMATION AND 'FULL-TIME' MEMBERS

What the House of Commons does depends directly on the contribution which its Members, particularly its non-ministerial Members, are prepared to make to its various processes. This contribution will itself depend very considerably on whether they are also involved in regular, outside employment or other activity and how they see their priorities between the two: a House in which no Member had a regular outside commitment would obviously be a very different assembly from one in which all Members had such jobs and engagements.

The House is, of course, a mixture of these two simple extremes and vigorous arguments have continued, at least since Members were first paid an 'allowance' (as Lloyd George insisted on calling it) of £400 p.a. in 1911, as to whether MPs' involvement in outside jobs is a good or a bad thing for Parliament and the country.

These broad issues are avoided here because our perspective is confined to the flow of information to Members. But these outside links could be a major element in any Member's political conceptions which requires us to consider the matter at least within that context. There is no study available of this matter. Nothing is known, beyond informal impressions, about the effect on a Member's thinking of his having a regular job outside the House which draws him into the particular problems of that type of work and into the company of people who have only modest levels of political interest. Is this Member's attitude to partisan strife (including the alleged 'hothouse' atmosphere of the Palace of Westminster) or to his own or other party's policy proposals different because of his outside occupational links? Do his general ideas on the place of Parliament and politics in the nation's life remain more like the ordinary voter's and less like those of the full-time Member?

We do not know whether this experience makes a Member (of any party, doing any kind of job which may be combined with membership of the House) more 'practical', 'pragmatic', or 'detached' compared with his fellow Member who has no regular tasks to perform outside the House—or whether his political perceptions are, by comparison, merely dulled by the effort and distraction of his non-political work, partly due to his being able to absorb only a reduced amount of information of all kinds about current political and public affairs. A study of these matters, including their psychological aspects, would be a difficult but valuable undertaking.

The basic facts about Members' outside jobs appear in the volumes on the *Business Backgrounds of MPs*, launched in 1957 and published at intervals since by Andrew Roth (fortunately on the basis of a very wide interpretation of the word 'business'), which give details of many different kinds of outside attachments and personal interests.[1] These volumes are compiled from

[1] Andrew Roth, *The Business Backgrounds of MPs*, Parliamentary Profiles Ltd. The latest edition covers the House elected in 1966.

questionnaires filled in by Members themselves (along similar lines to *The Times House of Commons, Who's Who* and other reference books) plus much extra information which Mr Roth has gleaned but which Members themselves did not vouchsafe.

To establish the approximate position regarding outside jobs of our 111 interviewed respondents we analysed their entries in *Business Backgrounds* according to certain 'key words' (i.e., chairman, director, underwriter, farmer, partner, barrister, solicitor and journalist) which, at least, are more likely than some other terms (such as trustee, consultant or author) to indicate a regular job or executive function. Our resulting lists would show any politically informed person the occasional inaccuracies, such as the claim to be a 'journalist and broadcaster' by an MP whose efforts in these fields are rather less than everyday fare for either British or overseas audiences. Similarly, a directorship can mean anything from an almost full-time managerial job to the most marginal of interests—while to be listed as a 'farmer' might indicate a genuine major occupation, a casual inheritance, or a weekend home with fields attached, all of which are let off to the real farmers of the locality. But, with these rather liberal interpretations on words such as 'director', the results are as follows:

(a) All respondents:

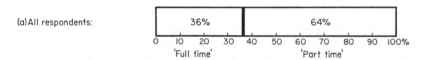

(b) Breakdown by party:

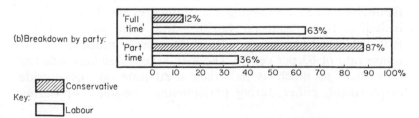

Figure 43. *Part-time and full-time Members among our respondents as analysed from 'The Business Backgrounds of MPs'.* (See Appendix, Table 39.)

(N—111: 56 Conservative, 52 Labour and 3 Liberal MPs)

371

This very striking Figure shows first the overall division of our 111 respondents into 'part-time' and 'full-time' MPs and then gives the party breakdown, showing the far greater preponderance of Conservative 'part-timers'.

As we pointed out in Chapter I, when describing our sample and its respondents, there was a slight under-representation in the sample of the Labour Members who are sponsored by trade unions as opposed to those who are not. This effect was compounded when union-sponsored Labour Members failed to respond proportionately. These Labour Members tend strongly not to have outside jobs, mainly because their previous occupations in factories or mines simply cannot be combined with membership of the House, even if the Member retains the skill and strength to perform it. Thus, apart from this blemish on our sample of 177 and bearing in mind the poorer response from this group of Members, we can say that Figure 43 in analysing our 111 respondents, is slightly under-representing the true presence of 'full-time' Labour Members among our sample of 177—and that this sample slightly tends to do the same thing for the total population of 531 MPs from which it was drawn. These effects will not be major, however.

The Figure shows that only a small proportion of Conservative Members among our respondents—12 per cent—can be regarded, on our definition, as 'full-time' MPs, compared with more than three-fifths of Labour Members. But an important minority of Labour Members—nearly two-fifths—are also 'part-time', and their numbers (and also, in our estimation, their opinions and influence on the matter of the House's organisation), have considerable significance.

Our simple exercise was based on certain descriptions in a reference book: more light was shed on this topic by Members themselves when completing questionnaires on their health—including their 'financial health'—and their work for the British Heart Foundation in 1967 (the survey produced a response rate of 63 per cent).[1] The BHF asked Members whether they spent as much as half their total time on any outside employment, either during parliamentary sessions, or during

[1] *Enquiry into Health and Work in the House of Commons* by H. B. Wright and G. Pincherle, 1967, p. 30, Table 15. We are fortunate that this survey was conducted during our own study period and gratefully acknowledge its value for several aspects of parliamentary studies.

recesses. The percentages of Members who did spend this much time in these pursuits was as follows:

Time spent in outside employment		Labour* per cent	Con- serva- tive per cent	Total per cent
None		73	31	62
Outside Employment	Less than 50 per cent in session	25⎤ ⎬27	57⎤ ⎬69	33⎤ ⎬38
	More than 50 per cent in session	2⎦	12⎦	5⎦
		100	100	100
None		73	31	62
Outside Employment	Less than 50 per cent in recess	12⎤ ⎬27	57⎤ ⎬69	18⎤ ⎬38
	More than 50 per cent in recess	15⎦	12⎦	20⎦
		100	100	100

Figure 44.   *Estimated time spent in outside employment by* MPs.

* The figures for Labour Members do not, of course, include Ministers.

SOURCE: *British Heart Foundation Enquiry into Health and Work in the House of Commons* by H. B. Wright & G. Pincherle, Table 15.

One's first reaction to these figures is that 'half-time' is a heavy commitment: one would certainly classify as 'part-timers' MPs who spent considerably less time than this on an outside job. If only one Conservative in eight, and virtually no Labour backbenchers, say that (while it is sitting) they give the House less than half their time compared to an outside job, we still want to know how many consider themselves 'full-timers'. If Members had been asked about 'one-third' or 'quarter' of their time (based, perhaps, on the idea of the equivalent of one or two days a week spent working outside) we would have a more complete picture of the 'part-timer's' other commitments.

Without detailed and frank answers by Members to questions about their non-parliamentary activities it is very difficult to know the truth about the situation at any given time. The official inquiry into MPs and Ministers' salaries under Sir Geoffrey Lawrence (which reported in 1964)[1] issued a questionnaire to Members in the previous House (dissolved in October

[1] Cmnd. 2516.

373

1964) which asked for views and facts on these matters. Not all this material was published by the Committee, although the general view against the 'full-time' Member of that Conservative-majority House did receive some publicity. It is probable, as D. N. Chester has suggested, that the trend is towards the more nearly full-time Member.[1] As he says, no record is kept of time spent at the House by Members beyond that necessary to record a vote. Some Members virtually confine their attendance to this basic function, as their colleagues no doubt observe. We interviewed one Member soon after his area whip had chided him for some recent absence from the division lobby to which complaint the gist of his reply had been, 'When X is there and I am not: then you can come and complain.' The 'part-timers' may, however, be less vocal than in earlier years: Charles Pannell's man who 'blew in, blew up and blew out' has now almost disappeared from the House.

Although the 'part-timers', especially perhaps the lawyers, are less demonstrative than some years ago, they are, of course, still unwilling to give up their outside work. 'This place is run by two hundred or fewer workhorses', observed a Conservative full-timer in an interview; this Member has risen to be a standing committee chairman and is a typical example of the 'all-day MP' whose committees begin at ten o'clock, but whose whips still occasionally require him to stay on to vote into the small hours of the following day. While the part-timer is also engaged in work from nine or ten o'clock in the morning in his outside job, he is being paid a second salary or other income for his effort.

We should like to have explored further, in the course of our interviews with Members, the differences in the overall patterns of political information and parliamentary activity seen by Members who held regular outside jobs as against those who did not. As we have suggested, the MP with the outside commitment has a different pattern to his life involving a different set of personal contacts. Although he may see the same newspapers and magazines as any other MP and the same television programmes on public affairs and, despite his sharing the rich personal information network of the House's life around Question time and during the evenings, he is rather differently placed in the

[1] D. N. Chester, 'The British Parliament 1939–66', in *Parliamentary Affairs*, XIX. 4 (Autumn 1966), p. 424.

political information network from the MP with no regular out-side connection.

A breakdown of our respondents' answers on a range of inter-view questions according to their full-time or part-time status, as we have defined and presented it above, offers some data on this point. Compared with full-time Members, part-time Mem-bers in our survey claimed to listen to fewer backbench speeches, to consult *Hansard* less frequently and to read fewer books on political and social matters. 'Part-timers' also said that they saw fewer television programmes on public affairs than were claimed by their full-time colleagues, and they reported less frequent constituency surgeries.

The responses of 'part-timers' on the House of Commons Library indicated a more generalised and independent approach. They were less likely either to ask the staff for written informa-tion or to nominate specific improvements which they would like to see in the service. They were rather more likely than full-time MPs to mention their wish for a research assistant and less inclined to favour the rapid extension of specialised committees to many other fields than science and agriculture. These two points may be grounds for tentatively suggesting that, although part-time Members would welcome a reform which would give them help in their present parliamentary work, they maintain a cautious attitude towards new committees (on which their whip may ask them to serve). Such developments would press them towards a professionalisation of their parliamentary role.

Our cross-tabulations of these Members having an outside job with their views on certain key matters in our survey offer only an oblique perspective on their parliamentary and political outlook: further survey work on this central question of the House's approach to its work is needed.

'Part-timers' obviously vary very much in the kind of 'infor-mation' they obtain from their outside jobs which may claim some relevance to public affairs. Three of the younger Con-servatives among our respondents had, respectively, these busi-ness attachments in 1967: a half-time analyst's and adviser's post in the City concerned with the foreign exchange market; a partner in a firm of country-town solicitors; and a part-time executive in a printing firm. Each was getting practical experience —and the information which comes with it—in a particular field and was thus (according to the general Conservative view of the question, at least) contributing towards their party having well-grounded views on various public matters (e.g. exchange control policy, landlord and tenant law and the efficiency of the printing industry).

The essential problem for the House is that while these Members are out gaining practical specialist experience in this and that aspect of the nation's everyday affairs, the House cannot organise itself to become a more authoritative overseer of public affairs as a whole, because these Members will not give up their mornings for parliamentary business. The dilemma is well shown in a pamphlet, *Control by Committee*[1] by Airey Neave (Conservative Member for Abingdon). He calls for more effective Commons control over expenditure and stronger influence over Government decision-making to be achieved by establishing six more of the new type of specialised committees than currently existed. Although he proposes abolishing the existing thirty-three Member Estimates Committee, which would release Members for new committee assignments, this would be done only to permit the establishing in its place of a new senior committee to co-ordinate the others and pursue major inter-departmental topics such as public expenditure and the machinery of Government. Mr Neave is a non-executive director of John Thompson Ltd, a large engineering firm which is associated, among other activities, with the particularly taxing commercial field of nuclear design and engineering. He is a keen advocate of Members having outside attachments and argues that the term 'specialised MP' should be applied to 'part-time' Members with specialised knowledge gained outside, rather than to those 'full-timers' who have no other job and who remain much more inside the Palace of Westminster observing and commenting on public events.

If the chamber of the House is not to be drained nearly dry by many competing activities in committee rooms during the late afternoon and evening, Mr Neave's new committees will have to do at least a significant part of their work in the mornings. But how can a Member with regular responsibilities outside join in, except as a marginal committee man who comes to such meetings only when his outside attachments permit? The availability of MPs to join in the process of information-gathering and to benefit from the fruits of that process is a basic

[1] Conservative Political Centre, 1968.

problem underlying our study and we were thus interested in Mr Neave's more detailed views.

In correspondence with us he reasserted the value to politics of having at least some MPs who are involved (even in a non-executive capacity) in the special problems of 'outside' work, particularly in industry.[1] They can bring practical knowledge to the House's work and are particularly well-placed for valuable service to any select or specialised committee in their professional field which the House may establish. (Mr Neave, with his nuclear and general engineering background, is a prominent member of the Science and Technology Committee.) He continued:

'My experience over the last two years of the Select Committee on Science and Technology, which now has no less than four sub-committees, indicates that it is difficult to give full attendance, especially if business meetings clash. On the other hand, the work of the Science and Technology Committee is of great value to outside industry in probing Government decisions, especially in advanced fields of research and technology.

'I think we should aim at a constant exchange of views between Parliament and industry, and specialist MPs can provide the link. It does, however, mean that they must organise their lives in such a way that they can give their time to both industry and the committees. It also means they can do less active parliamentary work, for example, on the floor of the House. This is not necessarily a bad thing.

'To a certain extent, finding suitable manpower will always be a question of chance after each election. But the system is creating a new type of MP who is commanding some respect in industry and Government establishments.

'The House needs informed debates on the specialised committees' reports. . . . I think the Select Committee on Science and Technology has been a great success and others will follow in due course.'

---

[1] Mr Neave has been an active supporter of the 'Change or Decay' group of Conservative Members who published a CPC pamphlet under that title in 1963. Most of this group are businessmen and their long-standing support for the idea of specialised committees stems, in part, from a belief that industry and politics should be in greater communication with each other. Official Conservative Opposition support for the establishment of a Science and Technology Committee of the House stemmed from the active interest of this group.

377

Given the basic duties which all Members must perform (such as constituency work and waiting around the House when divisions are due), it may seem that organising one's life in order to fulfil obligations to both an outside job and a select committee would be a problem of getting a quart into a pint pot. In response to this view, Mr Neave agrees that a Member who holds an industrial or professional appointment probably could not hope to be one of a specialised committee's most active members, in terms of full attendance at meetings or energetic pursuit of every topic covered.

He sees a partnership between the interested Member who is full-time at the House and the Member who holds an outside post. Each brings rather different strengths to a specialised committee: the 'full-timer' knows the committee's work intimately, while the 'part-timer' brings practical experience to the questioning of expert witnesses and strengthens the committee as an investigating body.

3. REFORMIST OPINION AND 'POLITICAL GENERATIONS' AMONG MPS IN 1967

We noted in Section 1 of this chapter that in 1967, Members who had been in the House for less than four years made up the bulk of those who said that Ministers should be obliged to reveal to the House virtually all information on their Departments' affairs. It may be that after two further parliamentary sessions, some of these Members have moderated their views and it is certain that their 1967 position would, rightly or wrongly, have been thought very naive by some senior Members, particularly those who were, or had been, Ministers.

Some newer Members expressing support for openness by Ministers countered advice to heed the 'facts of political life' with the observation that many aspects of the House's attitude to Governments are, at any given time, matters of convention. Within a framework of its formal supremacy, the House expects certain behaviour from and allows certain discretion and independence to Ministers, the nature of which has changed, albeit gradually, in the past and could continue to do so, if enough Members willed it sufficiently strongly. This consideration led us to analyse the overall situation within our sample of non-ministerial opinion in 1967 on the key topics of our interviews as they affect the House–Government relationship. Such an exercise serves to round off the analysis of our data and to provide an historical base for future research on parliamentary opinion on these very important questions.

It has been common since October 1964 (and, again, since Labour's second electoral victory in March 1966) to label the critical and discontented elements among Members of Parliament with terms such as 'impatient newcomers', 'Labour's young Turks' or even 'the Labour lecturers', whose implication is that such views are not shared by other Members who fall outside these groups. The well publicised activities in 1965 of the new and unofficial Labour Members' Reform Group[1], and the occasional public manifestations of Labour discontent with the House's facilities and arrangements which have occurred since, have quite justifiably thrown the spotlight of Press interest on to the Labour benches.

Labour Members, following the custom and intellectual style of their party, tend to complain when they feel aggrieved and, moreover, tend to make specific proposals to alleviate their situation.[2] Conservatives, behaving equally faithfully to their party's traditions, tend to give support to reformist views on institutional or 'system' matters in a less demonstrative way.

It has become quite plain during the presentation of our survey results that although the 1964–6 group of Labour entrants were the most critical and radical reformist group when we spoke to them in 1967, they were joined in some of the most important matters by other Members to make up a broader range of dissatisfied opinion. Three of these most significant topics are: Members' views on the adequacy of the Library's Research Division; on the desirability of setting up further specialised select committees; and on the personal demand for at least a share of the services of a research assistant. Of course, the strength of feeling on these issues is a highly relevant factor as the strong opinion may motivate an individual or small

[1] See A. Barker, 'Parliament and Patience', *Political Studies*, XV, 1 (February 1967); reprinted in B. Crick, *The Reform of Parliament*, Weidenfeld & Nicolson, 2nd (rev.) ed., 1968).
[2] The PLP survey of Labour Members and Ministers (see Chapter VI, n. 1, p. 316) was a further instance of this approach. It covered secretarial, Library, catering and personal research assistance for Members, besides other topics. See 'MPs want secretaries paid for', *The Guardian*, November 5, 1968.

group of Members to organise and try to persuade their colleagues.

We applied a rank-order index to our respondents' views on these three questions in order to guage both the strength of feeling among particular groups and the numerical size of these groups. A distinction between the strength and the volume of feeling obviously needs to be drawn: a small group of Members, such as the Liberals or the Labour-Co-operative Members hold certain reformist views very strongly—but their numbers are small.

Accordingly, we have produced Figure 45 to show how far innovatory opinions among Members on these three topics come from the same groups. For each of the three topics the various groups were placed in rank order, first on a basis of strength of feeling and then for their numerical size, thus giving three scores in each case. These scores were totalled, giving one rank order for strength of feeling and one for numerical size. The results are summarised in the Figure.

Strength of Feeling		*Numerical Support*	
	Rank Order Score		*Rank Order Score*
Party	(Range 3–9)	*Party*	(Range 3–9)
Labour	4	Labour	3
Liberal	6	Conservative	6
Conservative	8	Liberal	9
Sponsorship	(Range 3–9)	*Sponsorship*	(Range 3–9)
Co-operative	5	CLP	3
Trade union	6	Trade union	6·5
CLP	7	Co-operative	8·5
Age	(Range 3–30)	*Age*	(Range 3–30)
Under 30	5	41–45	3·5
41–45	9	36–40	6
31–35	11	46–50	8·5
36–40	12	51–55	12
Education		*Education*	
(a) *General*	(Range 3–12)	(a) *General*	(Range 3–12)
Elementary/secondary plus	6	University	3
Secondary ⎱ University ⎰	7	Secondary	6
		Elementary/secondary plus	9
Elementary	10	Elementary	12
(b) *Public school*	(Range 3–9)	(b) *Public School*	(Range 3–9)
Non-public school	4	Non-public school	3
Public school only ⎱ Public school & univ. ⎰	7	Public school & univ.	6
		Public school only	9
(c) *University*	(Range 3–9)	(c) *University*	(Range 3–9)
Redbrick	3	Oxford	4
Oxford	6·5	Redbrick	5
Cambridge	8·5	Cambridge	9

Strength of Feeling		Numerical Support	
	Rank Order Score		*Rank Order Score*
Parliamentary Service		*Parliamentary Service*	
(a) Pre-1964 and 1964–66		*(a) Pre-1964 and 1964–66*	
	(Range 3–9)		(Range 3–9)
1966	4	Pre-1964	3
1964	5	1964⎱	7·5
Pre-1964	9	1966⎰	
(b) Years in the House		*(b) Years in the House*	
	(Range 3–18)		(Range 3–18)
3 years or less	4	3 years or less	3
4–8 years	6	4–8 years	6
9–12 years⎫		13–17 years⎱	11·5
13–17 years⎬	12	18–22 years⎰	
18–22 years⎭		9–12 years	13
Over 22 years	17	Over 22 years	18
Frontbench Experience		*Frontbench Experience*	
	(Range 3–9)		(Range 3–9)
Backbenchers	4	Backbenchers	3
Current FB Spokesmen	5	Current FB Spokesmen⎱	7·5
Ex-FB Spokesmen	9	Ex-FB Spokesmen⎰	
Occupation	(Range 3–12)	*Occupation*	(Range 3–12)
Professions	5	Professions	3
Miscellaneous	6	Miscellaneous	6
Workers	9	Business	9
Business	10	Workers	12

Figure 45. *Rank order index of groups of Members by the strength of feeling and numerical support which they gave to innovative views on three key survey topics.*

Note: the three topics were: adequacy of the Research Division of the House of Commons; attitude towards specialised committees; and wish for a research assistant. The rank-order scores were computed as follows: *strength of feeling* was measured by taking the proportion in each group in favour of the relevant response(s) on each topic and placing them in order of *proportionate size; numerical support* was measured by placing the groups in order of *numerical size.* The actual rank-order scores are the sum of the three rankings for each group: for example, in the case of the party breakdown, if the Labour Party were ranked first in each case, the Conservatives second and the Liberals third, then their respective scores would be 3, 6 and 9, with 3 and 9 the minimum and maximum scores or range. Where there were, say, six groups, as in one of the two parliamentary service breakdowns, the range was 3–18. In the case of the age breakdown, where there were originally ten groups, only the first four in each rank-order are shown in the table as these are sufficient to convey to the reader the significance of age on attitudes to these topics. For definitions of these characteristics see the Appendix.

This Figure sums up and confirms the impression gained throughout our previous chapters that a lot of this support for parliamentary reforms comes from the relatively young Labour

381

Members who were elected during or since 1964. To this extent, the popular image of the reformist element in the House is, of course, quite correct. But it has also been apparent in our earlier chapters that a number of divisions of opinion tended to cross party lines and that, in particular, years of parliamentary service, educational background and frontbench experience were also often important as the bases of opinion groupings.

Although the details of strength of feeling in Figure 45 merely confirm the well-known role of the 1964–6 entrants (who were mainly Labour) in giving impetus to demands for reforms, the details of other groups which brought numerical support to these views have not been noticed or publicised by either outside observers or (judging from the remarks made by some Members during our interviews) by some elements in the House itself. There was, in fact, quite widespread agreement with reformist views found among the mainly Conservative group of Members who had, in 1967, between four and eight years' experience in the House and (if our small group is typical) among the Conservative shadow Ministers (both leading and 'additional' spokesmen).

Conservatives bring considerable numerical support to the reformist position on the three topics of the Research Division, the specialised committee and the research assistant scheme: more than half the MPs in the forty-one to fifty age group (in 1967) were Conservatives as were majorities (often substantial) of the groups of Members who had between four and eight years of service; who were Oxford graduates; and who were elected before 1964—each of these groups provides significant numerical strength for the general reformist cause. The Conservative reformers are mainly the younger and the more recently-elected Members; those under forty-six years of age in 1967; and those with eight or fewer years of service. Most of the doubt or opposition concerning reform among Conservatives is found among Members over fifty and among those with thirteen or more years of service.

On the Labour side, although the impetus for reform came mainly from the newer Members, it is by no means without support among their longer serving colleagues. Thus, while three-quarters of the 1966 Labour entrants felt the Research Division was inadequate for their needs. This was also the view of half the 1964 and pre-1964 Labour entrants. On specialised committees and research assistants there was little difference in support among Labour Members as divided by the entry year of 1964.

These findings suggest that the continuation of favourable opinions in the House on parliamentary reform questions does not depend quite so much on the survival at the next General Election of most of the Labour Members who arrived in 1966 and 1964, as has been suggested in some parliamentary quarters.

The nine-year and thirteen-year dichotomies in our survey data, which link Members' opinions on several important matters with their years of parliamentary service, are of considerable interest. In judging their significance we are led to a brief examination of the Conservatives, many of whom have entered the House since 1954 (the thirteen-year point).

The parliamentary Conservative Party did not experience major changes in its members' backgrounds between 1951 and 1966, whether viewed on a basis of occupation, age or education. Taking occupation first, it is true that shifts may have occurred within the rather broad groupings used by the Nuffield College election studies (on which we base these comments) but, if this is so, they were probably minor. The Nuffield studies do show, however, a decline in the proportion of Conservative M Ps who were former members of the armed services, company directors and of those living on private means. These Members were replaced by new MPs drawn from a variety of occupations— including solicitors, chartered secretaries and accountants, ex-civil servants and ex-local government officials—so that no one occupational group could be said to have increased much more than the others. (The rather special and probably least useful classification of 'farmers' is an exception to this, having risen from 5 per cent in 1951 to 11 per cent in 1966.)

Looking at educational backgrounds, there has been no broad shift between the Nuffield studies' categories. The passage of time itself obviously accounts for the decline of the number of Conservative Members who had only an elementary or a secondary education. The proportion of graduates rose during these fifteen years, although by only 6 per cent, and a similar rise in the proportion of those with public school backgrounds was also recorded.

Taken as a whole our respondents (regardless of party affiliation) showed no division of opinion on any of the subjects

383

of our survey on a basis of age; their number of years of service in the House was far more important. We therefore examined the backgrounds of these Conservatives respondents to see whether any link between any one characteristic and the Member's years of service could be suggested. We found no basis for any such links—indeed, such evidence as may be drawn goes rather the other way. Thus the Conservative Members with a public school education—whose proportion in their party rose 6 per cent between 1951and 1966—were, if anything, rather less keen on innovation and reform than their non-public school colleagues (although with only eight non-public school men among our interviewees the distinction cannot be pressed too vigorously).

There has thus been little change in these Conservatives' objective characteristics and no connection can be discerned between these small changes and the 'generational breaks' at nine and thirteen years' service which appear in our findings. We can, therefore, only conclude that these 'breaks' are related to differences in Conservative MPs' parliamentary experiences. The major events and controversies of each of the four Parliaments from 1950 to 1964 were, of course, different and a newcomer in each of them may have encountered different atmospheres. In the particular case of the 1959 newcomers it may have been that the growing prominence of reformist (or, at least, self-conscious) criticism of many national institutions and habits in the post-1959 period gave its flavour to these Members' first few years in the House. The malaise or even unrest on the Conservative Government's backbenches, which political correspondents detected at the time, was usually attributed to the long period of their party's control of the Government, combined with a temptation to provide some 'opposition' of their own while Labour was distracted with internal policy disputes.

We believe that the clear 'generation breaks' among Members according to their length of service are accountable in these terms of personal experience, particularly, perhaps, during a Member's first Parliament. Now this experience has receded, in many cases, well into the past it would be impossible to recreate for purposes of research: the Members concerned are older and more established, with probably only hazy memories of how their views on their new surroundings at Westminster influenced their opinions on matters of parliamentary activity and its possible 'reform'.

The notion of 'political generations' in the House which are, to some extent at least, identifiable by a certain syndrome of opinion on certain parliamentary issues naturally leads to the question of whether long-term and lasting change in the House's aggregate attitude is under way. Is this the case, or are Members more likely to shed their early, more critical, views about the House's affairs as they add to their years of service and maybe also receive promotion to the frontbench? These are very difficult questions as almost nothing can now be recovered from the contemporary experiences of large groups of parliamentary newcomers in such key earlier years as 1950, 1945, 1931 or 1906, when electoral fortune brought in many new Members.

Our survey of 1967 has revealed the outlines of 'political generations' on certain key parliamentary issues but these data offer only a single snapshot of a situation which is obviously changing. There would certainly be considerable value and considerable difficulty in mounting with a fixed group of Members the kind of long-term 'panel' study of their views (on such matters as parliamentary reform) over the years, of the kind now done in studies of voting behaviour. Such a study, if begun now, would certainly illuminate the development of attitudes over the coming years of the post–1954 and post–1958 Conservative intakes, some of whom will undoubtedly become Ministers in a future Conservative Government and thus, possibly, amend some of their views on the House–Government relationship.

On the Labour side, such a study should obviously concentrate on the 1964 and 1966 intakes whose future careers as 'reformers' will obviously hold great interest in view of the attitudes with which many of them began their parliamentary careers.

Long-term data on these and other groups of Members who make up the 'parliamentary generations' in the House would help to answer the key question of whether a permanent change in MPs' attitudes towards their relationship with Governments is now working its way through the House. If so, it seems to have begun slowly in the second half of the Fifties, mainly among the House's new recruits to the successful party of the period, the Conservatives, and then to have received a boost in the mid-Sixties, this time on the Labour side. Or, on the other hand, is the process of absorbing and socialising new entrants a cyclical one in which Members moderate their earlier views as they accumulate years of service and, perhaps also, political seniority and influence? If the truth lies in a mixture of the two, which is the more potent influence: membership of a 'parliamentary generation' or the effects of parliamentary senescence? Whichever is the more potent has, of course, considerable significance for parliamentary reform in general and the improvement of Members' supply of information in particular, since the impact of 'parliamentary generations' is likely to be greater than that of parliamentary senescence.

4. THE MP AND HIS INFORMATION—A FINAL NOTE

At the beginning of this book we established an elementary, three-fold division of the Member of Parliament's role: to support or oppose the Government; to follow certain aspects of Government policy and affairs; and to represent his constituents, either as individuals or as a group. These three very broad descriptions of parliamentary activity have been pursued in various ways in this study, using as a basis for enquiry the flow of 'information on public affairs' to a Member and what he thinks of his access to that part of this vast body of knowledge, which he feels he needs in order to perform his particular political work.

His work requires information of two basic kinds: facts about situations and knowledge of what the people concerned feel or intend to do regarding these situations. The Member of Parliament uses both 'objective' and 'subjective' information and often mixes them together in his mind. He will also, as a rule, want to absorb only that information needed for his current purpose. Normally, therefore, a politician's interest is limited and practical in both the quantity and range of what he is willing to study, although MPs still do have longer-range specialised interests.

As the representative, in some sense, of his constituents the Member receives a wide variety of messages and influences because the British people appear, from comparative studies, to be fairly confident and demanding towards elected representatives. The constituency postbags of most Members thus contain a steady flow of requests for assistance on individual problems, together with rather fewer letters offering constituents' views on public questions of either local or national significance. Members always get some extra experience or information from providing even a routine service to a constituent although there is usually little to learn from this work. The case which really seems likely to provide information which will lead the MP to become involved in a dispute with some public authority (particularly if there is any element in it of alleged 'scandal' or revelation) is not so common.

The custom of the Member being seen as (and seeing himself as) a 'welfare officer' is now solidly established, even to the point of some MPs feeling uncomfortable if their constituents fail to make these demands, as the aggregate of services and actions of an increasingly active Government become more complex. This side of the MP's work is likely to grow, although some observers who are worried about the House's modern role at the level of national and international affairs wish it would decline. Until 'regional' government, or a revivified system of local government is capable of dealing for itself with the problems and complaints of the public arising from local services (thus relieving Members of some of their current welfare load) MPs seem to be firmly hooked on to the welfare officer's role.

In searching for reasons why some MPs' welfare work seems to be more onerous than others we found virtually no objective characteristics of either constituencies or of Members themselves which offered much guidance—although some analyses, such as of rural seats or even of Members' public school backgrounds, did offer some sidelights. The truth seems to be that, within limits set by the nature of his constituency (a factor we assessed in the context of aircraft noise over Chelsea) a Member is himself the main probable determinant of how many constituents approach him for assistance. If he can adjust his own personal and political visibility in the constituency he can probably influence his welfare officer commitments. This realisation is, of course, cold comfort to a Member whose political interests attract him towards a more active role in national affairs but whose conscience requires that he should try to help people so long as no other agency or elected representative appears able to do so with anything like the MP's current status and effectiveness.

The Member's public role in his constituency is often associated with his local party and local authorities. The party is a poor source of local information to many MPs whereas the local authority is, of course, as much a source of decisions on policies and cases as of factual information. Most Members are satisfied with both these local sources, Conservatives in particular stressing that an experienced MP builds up his own contacts on a personal basis which often by-pass the local party and, to some extent, the local authorities: his only source of general continuing information on local events is therefore, the local Press, to which Members seem to pay a good deal of attention. Our respondents' rather resigned criticism of the modest calibre of many local councillors and some council officials was apparent in our interviews, as was the feeling that local government reform would help them considerably by reducing the number of separate authorities and (hopefully) attracting people into elected service who would be willing and able to handle problems and complaints.

The relations of MPs with their constituencies and the informational problems involved stress the need for a study of the public status of the modern MP, both as a national political representative and as a prominent individual in the local community. The public obviously accord him considerable status and appreciate his access to the national and local government systems: indeed, some Members find constituents greatly exaggerating Members' powers in these matters. Of course, many people will vote for or against their incumbent MP at each election on the basis of his party label, almost as if he were a mere cypher. His apparently ambivalent position involves a relationship of some considerable interest.

Members throw away immediately or never manage to examine perhaps 95 per cent of the printed material they are sent, and there has been no noticeable improvement over recent years in its design or suitability which may have helped to improve this situation from the senders' point of view. But those interests who may have thought about this problem (rather than simply following the convention of dispatching stuff to the House of Commons) no doubt consider that such a very limited penetration is worth the total effort and expense. (The exercise also serves to show their membership or clients that they are doing something to advance their interests, even though it is not a very productive use of the available funds.)

CONCLUSION

There is a variety of types of written material sent to Members, ranging from the well-argued individual letter to the most impersonal of printed brochures: we noted that Members welcome 'quality' letters (and may weigh the views they contain rather heavily) particularly when they are seeking knowledge in a novel and difficult field such as abortion law reform. Together with William Plowden, we have offered findings and comments on the 'information' offered to Members by some thirteen organisations and specialised bodies, ranging from the British Road Federation to the Kuwaiti Embassy. These thirteen are a few cases from the enormous variety of sources which go to make up a national information network in which the MP is one of the main concentrations of activity and interest.

MPs therefore receive a great range of facts, arguments, exhortations and pleas and are granted little respite from the demand to diversify and spread their mental energies over a broad field —unless, of course, they either never look at this material or (as one Member told us he occasionally feels he has to do) throw the lot away and read a book over the weekend instead.

Many Members therefore try to discipline this miscellaneous flow of facts and opinions which comes to them daily (not merely in their post but also in the Press, the business of the House and their other activities about the House) by concentrating their own attention in certain fields. For this purpose each main party maintains a range of specialised groups, with the national party headquarters offering some additional services. Twenty years ago on the Labour side, some of these specialised groups of Members tended, in the opinion of the leaders of the Attlee Government and the PLP, to get a little out of hand—less politically demanding regionally based groups were therefore introduced into the PLP to offset the influence of the specialised ones. It is possible that, having consented to introduce the specialised group idea into the select committee system of the House itself, the Wilson Government and the current PLP officers are considering the same tactic by bowing to pressure for a Scottish select committee (possibly to be followed by one or more regional English groups) while settling most of the other specialised committees on to a temporary base.

The major device for organising and holding the great mass of information on public affairs ready for Members' use is, of course, the House's Library. It has been permitted by successive Governments to grow at only a slow pace and faced an apparently continuous rise in Members' demand for its services. Using limited resources it is slowly evolving into a sophisticated information service designed for the special needs of the House. We have put special stress on the Library to show how far it has come since development began in 1946, what Members thought about it in 1967 and how far it has yet to go towards an adequate provision. We have noted that its general reference and information service has been relatively well developed and now needs to grow further, while being matched by striking advances in the regular dissemination of carefully organised information to various elements among Members, arranged according to these Members' interests.

In this concluding chapter we have tried to register three basic points. Firstly, Members overwhelmingly believe that their colleagues feel inadequately informed on Government affairs—and few thought themselves any better off. Thus, in 1967, Members were giving very strong support to both the principle and the vigorous practical extension of the new specialised select committees of the House. This impetus may have weakened since then, possibly under Government pressure, but it is unlikely to have disappeared.

Secondly, we raise the basic question of full-time service by MPS, although we have not pursued and presented the forceful, and often bitter, arguments to be found among Members on the matter. Most MPS combine their duties with an outside job of some kind, which may offer advantages to the House but which does constrict the development of a more elaborate committee system or other devices for encouraging Members to adopt a more active role. Whether developing the committee system and so forth is the best way for the House to attempt to gain more influence (and whether the House should try to gain more influence) is, of course, part of the arguments about full time membership. What is certain is that full or part time service in a legislature is very much a function of the culture of that assembly's political system. Parliamentarians' behaviour will, in general, follow the practices and standards expected by people outside. In view of this, we would hazard a guess that, fifteen years from now, part-time MPS will be clearly on the defensive, and possibly in a minority, and that by the turn of the century the issue will be concluded. By then, Members may be stressing their attachment to undivided public service as strongly as they now emphasise their belief in rendering services to their constituents in tones which would have surprised Members sitting in 1939.

Thirdly, we would suggest, on the basis of patterns to be found in our survey results, that any major change in the customs and values of the House (such as the possible growth of full-time service) is likely to come about in successive 'waves' of opinion established over the years by groups of Members who enter the House at the same time. Whether or not Members always retain the opinions about the House's ways which they brought in with them or developed during their first few years, the evidence of our survey suggests the presence of 'parliamentary generations' among Members. The profiles of these 'generations' may be objectively identified in terms of their years of service. Subjectively it is difficult to explain them except on the grounds of Members' common experiences during their first few years in the House.

In each of these three basic matters—Members' feelings of inadequate knowledge; their behaviour on the matter of full-time service; and their opinion profiles based on the apparent existence of 'parliamentary generations'—we conclude our study on an interrogative note. This book has been presented as a survey report, although with commentary and background material designed to interest the less specialised reader. It is offered as an illumination of a very wide and varied field using the concept of 'information' as a key to discovering how both Members and some of the people who send them information try to meet their political needs and responsibilities. We have been willing to speculate and interpret our survey results where it seemed justified and interesting to do so and hope that others may pursue some of the many possible lines of further research.

The present climate of the Commons is most interesting, with backbench Members being more active than ever before. This is bound to produce occasional friction between private Members and Ministers and, possibly, between the parties as well. The party composition and personal motivations of the Members of the next Parliament will be most important in maintaining, weakening or reversing the trend towards activism (notably in select committees and in matters of party discipline) which has characterised the 1964 and 1966 Parliaments. Whichever way the internal distribution of power between frontbenchers and backbenchers may shift and however the norms of the parliamentary culture may adjust to the public's demands, there will be a clear need for further parliamentary research, much of it based on survey interviews and other quantitative studies of Members' behaviour and stated opinions. It is hoped that this broad study of the field may assist such efforts of future parliamentary scholarship.

APPENDIX 1

A further note on our sample of Members

1. *The Constituencies*
(a) *Electoral Status*. All constituencies were classified as follows: the majority of the incumbent party at the General Election of 1966 was expressed as a percentage of the total votes cast, thus enabling all constituencies to be compared on a common basis, regardless of the size of the electorate or the percentage poll in any one constituency. Constituencies were divided into five categories:

(i) Marginal: majority less than 5 per cent of the total votes cast.
(ii) Semi-marginal: majority 5 to 10·9 per cent of the total votes cast.
(iii) Comfortable: majority 11 to 16·9 per cent of the total votes cast.
(iv) Safe: majority 17 to 30·0 per cent of the total votes cast.
(v) Impregnable: majority over 31·0 per cent of the total votes cast.

This classification was first used by Finer, Berrington and Bartholomew in *Backbench Opinion in The House of Commons, 1955–59* (Oxford, Pergamon, 1961), and was more recently adopted by Mitchell and Boehm in *British Parliamentary Election Results, 1950–64* (London, 1966) and *The Gallup Analysis of the Election '66* (London, 1966).

(b) *Urban and Rural Character*. Following Mitchell and Boehm constituencies were divided into four categories according to the relative concentration of urban or rural population:

(i) Primarily urban: those with an urban proportion of the population of 75 per cent or over.
(ii) Mixed with urban areas predominating: 50 to 74·9 per cent urban population.

393

(iii) Mixed with rural areas predominating: 25 to 49·9 per cent urban population.
(iv) Primarily rural: less than 25 per cent urban population.
Urban population was defined as those people living in (i) Boroughs or Urban Districts with a population of 5,000 or more; or (ii) in smaller Boroughs or Urban Districts which are contiguous with others with a total population of 5,000 or more; or (iii) Civil Parishes (Registration Districts in Scotland) of an urban or suburban character which are contiguous with Boroughs or Urban Districts with a population of 5,000 or more.

2. *The Members*

(a) *Age.* The Members were divided into ten age groups, ranging from under thirty to over seventy and broken down into five year intervals between these two categories.

(b) *Education.* Members were divided into six categories:

(i) Elementary: Members whose full-time education terminated at elementary school and including candidates who had further education at night school, adult education courses, etc.
(ii) Elementary/secondary plus: Members who, after attending elementary or secondary schools, had some form of technical or teacher training.
(iii) Secondary: Members whose full-time education terminated at secondary level.
(iv) University: all graduates, including attendance at the Inns of Court and various military colleges.
(v) Not known.
(vi) Self-educated.

The public school background of Members was also examined, following basically the categories used by Finer *et al.* Public schools in general comprised members of the Headmasters' Conference and the Association of Governing Bodies of Public Schools, together with the list of overseas public schools and the list of principal girls' schools annually published in *Whitaker's Almanack.*

The university background of Members was analysed according to whether they had attended Oxford or Cambridge on the one hand, or other universities or degree-awarding institutions on the other.

(c) *Occupation.* Members were divided into five categories:

(i) Workers: self-explanatory, but including all full-time trade union officials.

(ii) Professional: lawyers, doctors, dentists, school, university and adult education teachers, retired officers of the regular forces, and all recognised professions.

(iii) Business: all employers, directors of public and private companies, business executives, stock-brokers, farmers and landowners, and small businessmen.

(iv) Miscellaneous: housewives, professional politicians, welfare workers, local government officers, insurance agents and estate valuers, journalists, party publicists, professional party organisers, miscellaneous administrators.

These are the categories used by D. E. Butler in the Nuffield Election Studies and by Finer *et al.,* but following Finer's practice of classifying by the subject's current or most recent occupation, rather than Butler's practice of using the earliest or formative occupation.

(d) *Parliamentary Service.* Members were divided into groups according to the length of their parliamentary service, ranging from those with three or fewer years' service to those with over twenty-two years' service and broken down into four year intervals between these two categories.

(e) *Frontbench Experience.* Members were divided into groups according to whether they had had ministerial experience, were current Opposition frontbench spokesmen, had served as whips or had no frontbench experience at all.

Table. *An analysis of the characteristics of the original population, the sample and the respondents, together with the response rates of each group*

	Original population	Sample	Respondents	Response rate
	Percentages			
PARTY				
Conservative and U.U.	46·9 (249)	47·4 (84)	50·5 (56)	66·6
Labour	50·5 (268)	50·3 (89)	46·8 (52)	58·4
Liberal	2·2 (12)	2·3 (4)	2·7 (3)	75·0
Welsh Nat.	0·2 (1)	—	—	—
N.I. Repub. Lab.	0·2 (1)	—	—	—

Table—*continued*

	Original population	Sample	Respondents	Response rate
	Percentages			
AGE				
Under 41	23·2 (123)	23·2 (41)	26·1 (29)	70·7
41 to 60	58·4 (310)	58·7 (104)	60·4 (67)	64·4
Over 60	18·4 (98)	18·1 (32)	13·5 (15)	46·9
EDUCATION				
Elementary only	11·3 (60)	10·2 (18)	5·4 (6)	33·3
El./Second. plus	7·9 (42)	7·9 (14)	5·4 (6)	42·9
Secondary	21·8 (116)	23·2 (41)	24·3 (27)	65·8
University	58·6 (311)	58·7 (104)	64·9 (72)	69·2
Not known	0·2 (1)	—	—	—
Self-educated	0·2 (1)	—	—	—
UNIVERSITY EDUCATION				
'Oxbridge'	37·7 (200)	37·8 (67)	44·2 (49)	73·1
Other univs.	19·2 (102)	18·7 (33)	18·9 (21)	63·6
Service colls.	1·7 (9)	2·3 (4)	2·7 (3)	75·0
Non-univ.	41·4 (220)	41·2 (73)	34·2 (38)	52·0
OCCUPATION				
Workers	17·7 (94)	15·2 (27)	9·0 (10)	37·0
Professions	31·6 (168)	32·2 (57)	34·2 (38)	66·6
Business	29·4 (156)	28·8 (51)	29·8 (33)	64·7
Miscellaneous	21·3 (113)	23·8 (42)	27·0 (30)	71·4
PARLIAMENTARY SERVICE				
'New' Members	36·9 (196)	36·2 (64)	39·6 (44)	68·7
'Old' Members	63·1 (335)	63·8 (113)	60·4 (67)	59·3
FRONTBENCH EXPERIENCE				
Ministerial	16·6 (88)	17·5 (31)	18·9 (21)	67·7
Opp. spokesmen	6·8 (36)	6·8 (12)	7·2 (8)	66·6
Whip	5·1 (27)	5·1 (9)	5·4 (6)	66·6
None	71·5 (380)	70·6 (125)	68·5 (76)	60·8
Totals	100·0 (531)	100·0 (177)	100·0 (111)	62·7
SPONSORSHIP OF LABOUR MEMBERS				
Trade union	37·3 (100)	30·3 (27)	21·2 (11)	40·7
Co-op Party	4·9 (13)	5·6 (5)	9·6 (5)	100·0
CLP	57·8 (155)	64·1 (57)	69·2 (36)	63·2
Totals	100·0 (268)	100·0 (89)	46·8 (52)	58·4

APPENDIX 2
Text of the Interview Guide

Member's name:
Party:
Constituency:

Sample serial no.:
Personal details: (e.g. electoral and ministerial history; business links, etc.)

I want to ask you some fairly factual questions about how information comes to you—and then perhaps we can discuss some of your special interests . . .

I Postbag
First, on the post you receive as an MP:

1. How many letters do you receive from constituency sources (i.e. individual constituents, firms and organisations in the constituency)?
2. Apart from these constituency letters, how much other stuff of all kinds do you get?
3. Within this total, how many individual letters from outside your constituency are there?
4. How much of your parliamentary time is spent dealing with all this incoming post? (hours per day/week).
5. What do you think about spending this amount of your parliamentary time in this way?
6. What is your general opinion of the printed and published material sent to you by organisations, firms, embassies, etc.? Supplementary: Is it generally worth their sending it?
7. What's your opinion of the value of any of this material which falls within your special interests?
8. Do you file away any of this printed material?

II Local Party
I'm interested in your local constituency party (association) as a source of information to you on local affairs . . .

397

1. How do you receive information from them?

> *Prompts:* Agent, by letter or contact; Party's magazine; Executive Committee, by resolution or informal approach; party officers or activists, by letter or contact; other.

III Local Authorities

Could you also tell me about your constituency's local authorities as a source of information on local affairs?

1. Firstly (excluding those respondents representing county borough constituencies), what types of local authority (excluding parishes) do you have in your constituency?
2. May we take just one, preferably the most significant, and ask about your contacts with them as our example?

> *Prompts:* receive council minutes; receive committee minutes; contact with the Clerk; contact with other officials; information in any form from councillors—if so, your own party's group or other councillors?

> *Supplementary:* Generally, do you have to ask for things or do they offer information?

3. What do you think of this local authority as a source of information on local affairs?

> *Supplementary:* How could they improve?

4. To sum up on information about your constituency, can we put these three items, plus your local Press, in order of importance to you for local information?

> Your postbag from your constituency;
> Your local party;
> Your local authorities;
> Your reading of your local Press.

IV Party Headquarters

May we turn to national affairs? About your party's headquarters in Smith Square . . .

1. Would you say that your party headquarters offers backbenchers a major source of briefing and information?
2. Can backbenchers in your party personally obtain an individually written brief or research report from your party headquarters?

3. Are you satisfied with the research and information provided to backbenchers by your party headquarters?
4. (If No): What advantage would their work have that other sources lack?

V **Information from Sponsoring Organisations** (Sponsored Labour Members only)

1. How do you receive information your union/the Co-operative Party as a *sponsored* Member? (i.e. not merely as a union/party member).
   Prompts: receive Executive's agenda, documents or minutes; letters from officers or officials; regular or occasional briefings; continual informal contact; union/party publications, statements etc.; other.
2. Does your union/the Co-operative Party usually offer information or do you usually have to ask for it?

VI **House of Commons Debates**
On the House itself as a source of information . . .

1. Leaving aside frontbench speeches (opening and winding up debates) do you often listen to many backbench speeches in a debate?
2. When you're not able to listen to much of a debate in the House for yourself, about how often do you read or look at the *Hansard* report of it?
3. Do you normally read or look at the Press coverage of Commons debates?
4. Your attending debates in the chamber or reading *Hansard* is obviously linked with your own special interests. How would you assess the chamber as a source of information in one of your own special fields of interest?
   Supplementary: Which field of interest have you in mind here?
5. What about oral and written Questions in this field?

VII **The House of Lords**
About the House of Lords . . .

1. About how often do you go up and listen to a Lords debate?
2. About how often do you read or look at the Lords *Hansard*?

3. Do you normally read or look at the Press coverage of the Lords?

VIII The House of Commons Library

I'd like to ask you about the House of Commons Library services . . .

1. Have you read the Library Handbook?
2. How often, when the House is sitting, do you visit or contact any part of the House of Commons Library?
3. Do you more often go there, or ring up or write?
4. What do you most often go there for?
    Prompts: consult newspapers etc.; consult Press cuttings; look at indexes of parliamentary Questions, debates, etc.; take out or return a book; consult the staff with a query or request for a task; other.
5. Do you ever ask the Library's Research Division to do an individual research or fact-finding job for you (i.e. something you ask for and they send in written form after an interval)?
6. How often do you request these individually-prepared jobs?
7. Can you recall any examples?
8. Some MPs who generally admire the Library's Research Division say they find the system makes the staff seem rather detached and impersonal to the Member: what's your experience of this?
9. Do you think, from your experience, that the Library's Research Division is adequately equipped for the tasks you would most often be likely to ask for?
10. (If 'Yes, service is adequate for me) Taking a general view of the Research Division, what is your conception of its task?
11. (If 'No, service is inadequate') What particularly do they seem to lack in staff and resources?
12. (If 'No') How exactly would this extra provision help you?
13. (If 'No'—supplementary) Taking a general view of the Research Division, what is your conception of its task?

IX Special Interest

Finally about your special interests . . . would you suggest one, as an example for our discussion?

1. Broadly, how do you keep informed on this?
   Prompts: printed material received in the post; Press and specialist publications; having an outside job in the field; personal contacts; Questions and enquiries to Ministers and Government Departments; others.
2. Speaking generally, do you think MPs feel they're adequately informed about the many administrative acts of the Government and civil service?
3. And again, speaking generally, do you think more parliamentary select committees like Estimates, or these two new ones on Science and Agriculture, are going along on the right lines to help with the problem?
4. Do Ministers (of *any* Government) *wish* to limit MPs' knowledge?
5. Under our Constitution must the House of Commons inevitably settle for about the level of information it gets at the moment?

Supplementary Questions (Respondents often filled in the form containing these questions and returned it by post, but some Members answered orally after the Interview Guide was completed).

1. What secretarial assistance do you have?
2. Which of the weekly periodicals do you give most time to reading? Which other periodicals do you regularly see and read, at least in part?
3. When the House is sitting are you usually in the course of reading all or most of a book which is about political, international or social affairs? Do you read more periodicals and books on these matters during recesses?
4. When the House is sitting do you see current affairs programmes on TV—either individual features or regular magazines like 'Panorama', '24 Hours' or 'This Week'? Do you usually watch more current affairs TV during recesses?
5. Do you run a constituency surgery?
   (If 'Yes'): How often? Do you think your surgery work helps you to get the 'feel' of the electorate?

APPENDIX 3
Tables of Survey data

Table 1—*Respondents' reading on public affairs*

a. *Respondents usually reading a book on public affairs during parliamentary sessions*

Response	Conservative MPS	%	Labour MPS	%	Liberal MPS	Total MPS	%
Yes	36	69·2	40	80·0	3	79	75·2
No	16	30·8	10	20·0	—	26	24·8
Respondents	52	100·0	50	100·0	3	105	100·0
No answer	4	—	2	—	—	6	—
Total	56	—	52	—	3	111	—

b. *Respondents reading more such books and periodicals during recesses*

Response	Conservative MPS	%	Labour MPS	%	Liberal MPS	Total MPS	%
Yes	42	80·8	33	66·0	1	76	72·4
No	10	19·2	17	34·0	2	29	27·6
Respondents	52	100·0	50	100·0	3	105	100·0
No answer	4	—	2	—	—	6	—
Total	56	—	52	—	3	111	—

402

Table 2—*Frequency of watching public affairs TV programmes*

a. *During sessions*

Response	Conservative MPS	%	Labour MPS	%	Liberal MPS	Total MPS	%
Sees at least one every week	13	25·0	21	42·0	—	34	32·4
Sees average of about one per month	20	38·5	12	24·0	1	33	31·4
Sees more rarely than one per month	17	32·7	14	28·0	2	33	31·4
Never see them *	2	3·8	3	6·0	—	5	4·8
Respondents	52	100·0	50	100·0	3	105	100·0
No answer	4	—	2	—		6	—
Total	56	—	52	—	3	111	—

b. *During recesses*

	Conservative MPS	%	Labour MPS	%	Liberal MPS	Total MPS	%
Yes	37	72·6	33	66·0	3	73	70·2
No—same amount or less during sessions	12	23·5	15	30·0	—	27	26·0
No—none at all during recess	2	3·9	2	4·0	—	4	3·8
Respondents	51	100·0	50	100·0	3	104	100·0
No answer	5	—	2	—	—	7	—
Total	56	—	52	—	3	111	—

* This response was a 'write in' and it is possible that other respondents who 'never' see such programmes reported that they see them more rarely than once a month.

Table 3—*Respondents' estimates of the average weekly number of individual letters received from outside their constituencies.* (See Figure 5)

Average weekly number of letters	Conservative		Labour		Liberal	Total	
	MPS	%	MPS	%	MPS	MPS	%
Less than 25	23	50·0	17	38·6	1	41	44·1
25–49	4	8·7	6	13·6	—	10	10·7
50–74	3	6·5	2	4·5	—	5	5·4
75–100	—	—	—	—	—	—	—
Over 100	—	—	—	—	—	—	—
Varies too much to estimate	16	34·8	19	43·2	1	36	39·8
Respondents	46	100·0	44	99·9	2	92	100·0
Don't know	9	—	5	—	—	14	—
Question omitted	1	—	3	—	1	5	—
Total	56	—	52	—	3	111	—

Table 4—*Respondents' estimates of the average weekly number of postbag items received from outside their constituencies.* (See Figure 6)

Average weekly number of items	Conservative		Labour		Liberal	Total	
	MPS	%	MPS	%	MPS	MPS	%
Less than 25	3	8·1	3	7·3	—	6	7·6
25–49	13	35·1	13	31·7	1	27	34·2
50–74	7	18·9	13	31·7	—	20	25·3
75–100	8	21·6	5	12·2	—	13	16·4
Over 100	6	16·2	7	17·1	—	13	16·4
Respondents	37	99·9	41	100·0	1	79	99·9
Don't know	17	—	8	—	1	26	—
Question omitted	2	—	3	—	1	6	—
Total	56	—	52	—	3	111	—

Table 5—*Respondents' general opinions of printed circulars etc.*
(See Figure 7)

Response	Conservative MPS	%	Labour MPS	%	Liberal MPS	Total MPS	%
A complete waste of time and money	13	23·2	9	18·0	1	23	21·1
Largely a waste of time and money but some useful	26	46·4	34	68·0	1	61	56·0
Without circulars I miss important and useful information	3	5·4	2	4·0	—	5	4·5
Many organisations have no other effective means of contacting MPS	2	3·6	3	6·0	—	5	4·6
Probably worthwhile if an organisation contacts 5 per cent of the MPS it sends to	1	1·8	1	2·0	—	2	1·8
I welcome circulars generally	11	19·6	3	6·0	—	14	12·8
I find them useful in my special field	15	26·8	19	38·0	1	35	32·1
No opinion: I don't see them—secretary discards or files them	2	3·6	—	—	—	2	1·8
Respondents	56	—	50	—	3	109	—
Question omitted for lack of time	—	—	2	—	—	2	—
Total	56	—	52	—	3	111	—

Note: Percentages total more than 100 per cent because of multiple responses to this question.

Table 6—*Respondents' opinions of printed circulars etc. relevant to their special interests*

Response	Conservative MPS	%	Labour MPS	%	Liberal MPS	Total MPS	%
Often excellent/well presented	22	40·7	21	43·7	2	45	42·9
Vary considerably	23	42·6	23	48·0	—	46	43·8
Generally poorly presented	7	13·0	4	8·3	1	12	11·4
Don't know—I never see them	2	3·7	—	—	—	2	1·9
Respondents	54	100·0	48	100·0	3	105	100·0
Question omitted for lack of time	2	—	4	—	—	6	—
Total	56	—	52	—	3	111	—

Table 7—'*Do you listen to many backbench speeches?*' (See Figure 9)

Response	Conservative MPS	%	Labour MPS	%	Liberal MPS	Total MPS	%
Yes, it keeps me in touch	8	14·5	9	18·0	1	18	16·7
No, I attend when I'm interested or to hear a particular speaker	22	40·0	20	40·0	2	44	40·7
No, only when I want to speak	7	12·7	6	12·0	—	13	12·0
No, not very often	18	32·8	15	30·0	—	33	30·6
Respondents	55	100·0	50	100·0	3	108	100·0
Question omitted for lack of time	1	—	2	—	—	3	—
Total	56	—	52	—	3	111	—

Table 8—*Respondents' use of House of Commons 'Hansard'.*
(See Figure 10)

Response	Conservative MPS	%	Labour MPS	%	Liberal MPS	Total MPS	%
Read regularly	5	9·1	4	8·1	—	9	8·4
Skim regularly	13	23·6	9	18·4	1	23	21·5
Only read particular debates	19	34·5	22	44·9	1	42	39·2
Only skim particular debates	4	7·3	7	14·3	—	11	10·3
Seldom or never look at it	14	25·5	7	14·3	1	22	20·6
Respondents	55	100·0	49	100·0	3	107	100·0
Question omitted for lack of time	1	—	3	—	—	4	—
Total	56	—	52	—	3	111	—

Table 9—*Respondents' use of Press reports of Commons debates.*
(See Figure 11)

Response	Conservative MPS	%	Labour MPS	%	Liberal MPS	Total MPS	%
Yes, read regularly	40	72·7	40	81·6	2	82	76·6
Yes, use as a prompt for *Hansard*	7	12·7	2	4·1	1	10	9·3
No	8	14·6	7	14·3	—	15	14·0
Respondents	55	100·0	49	100·0	3	107	99·9
Question omitted for lack of time	1	—	3	—	—	4	—
Total	56	—	52	—	3	111	—

Table 10—*Respondents' view of the chamber as a source of information in a field of special interest—by party and length of service. (See Figure 12)*

Response	Conservative MPS	%	Labour MPS	%	Liberal MPS	Length of service Less than 9 years MPS	%	9 or more years MPS	%	Total MPS	%
A valuable source of information generally	19	34·6	18	36·8	—	18	30·0	19	40·4	37	34·6
Varies considerably as a source of information but sometimes valuable	12	21·8	6	12·2	1	8	13·3	11	23·4	19	17·8
The information is only political, i.e. people declaring themselves	12	21·8	9	18·4	—	11	18·3	10	21·3	21	19·6
Neither the information nor declarations of opinion are usually worth having	12	21·8	16	32·6	2	23	38·4	7	14·9	30	28·0
Respondents	55	100·0	49	100·0	3	60	100·0	47	100·0	107	100·0
Question omitted for lack of time	1	—	3	—	—	3	—	1	—	4	—
Total	56	—	52	—	3	63	—	48	—	111	—

Table 11—*Respondents' use of parliamentary Questions.*
(See Figure 13)

Response	Conservative MPS	%	Labour MPS	%	Liberal MPS	Total MPS	%
Does not use PQS	3	6·0	14	30·4	—	17	17·3
Uses PQS only to obtain information: uses only written PQS	19	38·0	13	28·3	1	33	33·7
Uses PQS only to obtain information: uses both oral and written PQS	22	44·0	16	34·8	1	39	39·8
PQS are mainly a political weapon, rather than an information source	9	18·0	5	10·9	—	14	14·3
Reads through PQS of particular departments for information	4	8·0	3	6·5	—	7	7·1
Reads through PQS generally for information	2	4·0	6	13·0	—	8	8·2
Respondents	50		46		2	98	—
Question omitted for lack of time	6	—	6	—	1	13	—
Total	56	—	52	—	3	111	—

Note: Percentages total more than 100 per cent because of multiple responses to this question.

Table 12—*Respondents' attendance of Lords debates.*
(See Figure 14)

Response	Conservative MPS	%	Labour MPS	%	Liberal MPS	Total MPS	%
Never	5	10·2	9	23·7	—	14	15·6
Once or twice a year	7	14·3	12	31·6	2	21	23·4
More than twice a year	24	49·0	6	15·8	1	31	34·4
Don't know: too irregular or infrequent to estimate	13	26·5	11	28·9	—	24	26·6
Respondents	49	100·0	38	100·0	3	90	100·0
Question omitted for lack of time	7	—	14	—	—	21	—
Total	56	—	52	—	3	111	—

Table 13—*Respondents' perception of whether MPs as a whole feel adequately informed on government administration.*
(See Figure 15)

Response	Conservative MPS	%	Labour MPS	%	Liberal MPS	Total MPS	%
(a) No	42	82·4	36	81·8	3	81	82·6
(b) No, but I feel I am personally	4	7·8	4	9·1	—	8	8·2
(a) plus (b)	46	90·2	40	90·9	3	89	90·8
(c) Yes	5	9·8	3	6·8	—	8	8·2
(d) Don't know	—	—	1	2·3	—	1	1·0
Respondents	51	100·0	44	100·0	3	98	100·0
Question omitted for lack of time	5	—	8	—	—	13	—
Total	56	—	52	—	3	111	—

410

Table 14—Respondents' attitudes to extending the system of select committees on government activity—by party; by local council experience; University education; and length of service. (See Figure 16)

Response	Conservative MPs	%	Labour MPs	%	Liberal MPs	Council experience MPs	%	None MPs	%	Graduates MPs	%	Non Graduates MPs	%	Less than 13 years service MPs	%	13 or more years' service MPs	%
(a) Yes, extend to all Government Departments or fields	12	21·8	27	57·4	2	21	53·8	20	30·3	23	34·3	18	47·4	32	42·7	9	30·0
(b) Yes, but only a limited extension	19	34·5	11	23·4	—	11	28·2	19	28·8	20	29·9	10	26·3	24	32·0	6	20·0
(c) Yes, in favour of principle of specialised committees, but critical of type adopted	4	7·3	2	4·3	—	1	2·6	5	7·6	4	6·0	2	5·3	3	4·0	3	10·0
(a), (b) and (c) together	35	63·6	40	85·1	2	33	84·6	44	66·7	47	70·2	30	79·0	59	78·7	18	60·0
(d) No, opposed to the idea	8	14·6	2	4·3	—	1	2·6	9	13·6	7	10·4	3	7·9	3	4·0	7	23·3
(e) Undecided/open mind/wait and see	12	21·8	5	10·6	1	5	12·8	13	19·7	13	19·4	5	13·1	13	17·3	5	16·7
Respondents	55	100·0	47	100·0	3	39	100·0	66	100·0	67	100·0	38	100·0	75	100·0	30	100·0
Question omitted for lack of time	1	—	5	—	—	3	—	3	—	5	—	1	—	3	—	3	—
Total	56	—	52	—	3	42	—	69	—	72	—	39	—	78	—	33	—

	Pre-1964 entrants MPs	%	1964 entrants MPs	%	1966 entrants MPs	%	Total MPs	%
(a)	22	34·9	8	36·4	11	55·0	41	39·0
(b)	18	28·6	6	27·3	6	30·0	30	28·6
(c)	3	4·8	3	13·6			6	5·7
(a), (b) and (c)	43	68·3	17	77·3	17	85·0	77	73·3
(d)	8	12·7	1	4·5	1	5·0	10	9·5
(e)	12	19·0	4	18·1	2	10·0	18	17·2
Respondents	63	100·0	22	99·9	20	100·0	105	100·0
Omitted	4	—	2	—	—	—	6	—
Total	67	—	24	—	20	—	111	—

411

Table 15—*Respondents' estimates of the average weekly number of letters received from constituencies.* (See Figure 17)

Average weekly number	Conservative MPS	%	Labour MPS	%	Liberal MPS	Total MPS	%
Less than 25	7	13·5	6	12·8	—	13	12·9
25–49	21	40·4	20	42·5	1	42	41·6
50–74	11	21·1	15	31·9	—	26	25·7
75–100	7	13·5	3	6·4	1	11	10·9
100+	6	11·5	3	6·4	—	9	8·9
Total	52	100·0	47	100·0	2	101	100·0
Respondents unable to estimate	3	—	2	—	—	5	—
Question omitted	1	—	3	—	1	5	—
Total	56	—	52	—	3	111	—

Table 16—*Comparison of estimated weekly number of constituency letters and the size of respondents' electorates.* (See Figure 18)

Average weekly number of letters	Under 40,000 MPS	%	40,000–49,000 MPS	%	50,000–59,000 MPS	%	60,000–69,000 MPS	%	70,000–79,000 MPS	%	80,000+ MPS	%
Less than 25	—	—	5	20·8	6	14·6	2	11·8	—	—	—	—
25–49	4	100·0	10	41·7	19	46·4	7	41·2	—	—	2	50·0
50–74	—	—	7	29·2	11	26·8	5	29·4	2	18·2	1	25·0
75–100	—	—	2	8·3	3	7·3	1	5·9	5	45·4	—	—
100+	—	—	—	—	2	4·9	2	11·8	4	36·4	1	25·0
Total		100·0	24	100·0	41	100·0	17	101·0	11	100·0	4	100·0

Table 17—*Urban and rural constituency postbags*

Average weekly number of letters	Urban MPS	%	Rural MPS	%
49 or less	34	58·6	21	48·8
50 or more	24	41·4	22	51·2
Total	58	100·0	43	100·0

Table 18—*Proportion of respondents holding constituency surgeries.* (See Figure 19)

	Conservative MPS	%	Labour MPS	%	Liberal MPS	Total MPS	%
Yes	47	88·7	49	94·2	2	98	90·7
No	1	1·9	1	1·9	—	2	1·9
No, only by appointment	5	9·4	2	3·9	1	8	7·4
Respondents	53	100·0	52	100·0	3	108	100·0
No answer	3	—	—	—	—	3	—
Total	56	—	52	—	3	111	—

Table 19—*Frequency of respondents' surgeries—by party (see Figure 20); by length of service; and by local council experience*

Frequency	Conservative		Labour		Liberal	Less than 9 years service		9 or more years service		Experience as councillor		No experience		Total	
	MPS	%	MPS	%	MPS	MPS	%	MPS	%	MPS	%	MPS	%	MPS	%
Once a week	7	14·9	8	16·3	1	11	18·6	5	12·8	9	23·7	7	11·7	16	16·3
Once a fortnight	11	23·4	17	34·7	1	24	40·7	5	12·8	11	28·9	18	30·0	29	29·6
Once every three weeks	6	12·8	8	16·3	—	10	16·9	4	10·3	4	10·5	10	16·7	14	14·3
Once a month	16	34·0	13	26·6	—	12	20·4	17	43·6	12	31·6	17	28·3	29	29·6
Less often	7	14·9	3	6·1	—	2	3·4	8	20·5	2	5·3	8	13·3	10	10·2
Respondents	47	100·0	49	100·0	2	59	100·0	39	100·0	38	100·0	60	100·0	98	100·0
No answer	3	—	—			—		3	—	—		3	—	3	—
Respondents not holding surgeries	6	—	3	—	1	4	—	6	—	4	—	6	—	10	—
Total	56		52		3	63		48		42		69		111	

Table 20—*Respondents' views on whether surgeries give them the 'feel' of the electorate*

Response	Conservative MPS	%	Labour MPS	%	Liberal MPS	Total MPS	%
Yes	31	68·9	39	79·6	1	71	74·7
No	8	17·8	8	16·3	—	16	16·8
Don't know/doubtful	6	13·3	2	4·1	—	8	8·4
Respondents	45	100·0	49	100·0	1	95	99·9
No answer	5	—	—		1	6	—
Respondents not holding surgeries	6	—	3		1	10	—
Total	56	—	52		3	111	—

Table 21—*Respondents' estimates of the average time they spend in dealing with their postbags.* (See Figure 21)

Hours per day	Conservative MPS	%	Labour MPS	%	Liberal MPS	Total MPS	%
Less than 1 hour	9	18·8	6	12·5	—	15	15·1
1 hour	15	31·2	6	12·5	—	21	21·2
1½ hours	10	20·8	7	14·6	—	17	17·2
2 hours	6	12·5	12	25·0	2	20	20·2
More than 2 hours	8	16·7	17	35·4	1	26	26·3
Respondents	48	100·0	48	100·0	3	99	100·0
Unable to estimate	6		1		—	7	—
Question omitted for lack of time	2		3		—	5	
Total	56		52		3	111	—

Table 22—*Respondents' attitudes to the time spent on their postbags (i.e. the 'welfare officer' role)—by party; length of service; university education; and local council experience. (See Figure 23)*

	Conservative MPs %	Labour MPs %	Liberal MPs	Pre-1964 entrants MPs %	1964 entrants MPs %	1966 entrants MPs %	Graduates MPs %	Non-Graduates MPs %	Council experience MPs %	None MPs %	Total MPs %
'A great personal satisfaction'/'The most valuable part of my work'	19 33·9	22 44·0	1	20 30·3	8 34·8	14 70·0	25 35·7	17 43·6	18 45·0	24 34·8	42 38·5
'I welcome (expect/accept) the "welfare officer" role'	32 57·1	32 64·0	2	43 65·1	13 56·5	10 50·0	43 61·4	23 59·0	27 67·5	39 56·5	66 60·5
'Many of these cases are not properly for me as an MP at all'	14 25·0	7 14·0	1	14 21·2	5 21·7	3 15·0	18 25·7	4 10·3	7 17·5	15 21·7	22 20·2
'The "welfare officer" role has been taken too far'	6 10·7	7 14·0	—	8 12·1	4 17·4	1 5·0	8 11·4	5 12·8	3 7·5	10 14·5	13 11·9
Respondents	56	50	3	66	23	20	70	39	40	69	109
Question omitted for lack of time	—	2	—	1	1		2	—	2	—	2
Total	56	52	3	67	24	20	72	39	42	69	111

Note: Percentages total more than 100 per cent because of multiple responses to this question.

Table 23—*Respondents' views of their local constituency parties as sources of information.* (See Figure 24)

Response	Conservative MPS	%	Labour MPS	%	Liberal MPS	Total MPS	%
Personal contacts with the local party agent	43	78·2	34	66·7	2	79	72·5
Personal contacts with party officers and activists	38	69·1	34	66·7	2	74	67·9
Attending formal meetings of the local party committee	3	5·5	20	39·2	—	23	21·1
Receiving resolutions from the local party	2	3·6	18	35·3	—	20	11·3
Receiving local party publications	2	3·6	3	5·9	—	5	4·6
Attending local trade union meetings	—	—	2	3·9	—	2	1·8
Local party is NOT really a source of information on local affairs at all	10	18·2	9	17·6	1	20	18·3
Respondents	55		51		3	109	
Question omitted for lack of time							
Question omitted for lack of time	1		1		—	2	
Total	56		52		3	111	

Note: Percentages total more than 100 per cent because of multiple responses to this question.

Table 24—*Respondents' views of their local authorities as sources of information.* (See Figure 25)

Response	Conservative MPS	%	Labour MPS	%	Liberal MPS	Total MPS	%
Receives council minutes regularly	19	35·2	27	52·9	1	47	43·5
Receives minutes only on occasional request	3	5·6	2	3·9	2	7	6·5
Deals direct with several chief officers	28	51·8	35	68·6	1	64	59·3
Deals with the Clerk on nearly all matters	22	40·7	16	31·4	1	39	36·1
Has regular discussions with councillors of own party	3	5·6	9	17·6	1	13	12·0
Has only ad-hoc discussions with councillors	40	74·1	34	66·7	1	75	69·4
Stresses personal contacts with officials and councillors rather than formal links	41	75·9	39	76·5	3	83	76·8
Is a current member of a local authority in own constituency	—	—	3	5·9	—	3	2·8
Respondents	54	—	51	—	3	108	—
Question omitted for lack of time	2	—	1	—	—	3	—
Total	56	—	52	—	3	111	—

Note: Percentages total more than 100 per cent because of multiple responses to this question.

Table 25—*Respondents' satisfaction or dissatisfaction with their local authorities as sources of information by party and by experience as a local councillor*

	Conservative MPS	%	Labour MPS	%	Liberal MPS	Council experience MPS	%	No experience MPS	%	Total MPS	%
Satisfied: information and contact about right	48	88·9	43	87·8	2	37	97·4	56	82·4	93	87·7
Dissatisfied: local authority could do more	6	11·1	6	12·2	1	1	2·6	12	17·6	13	12·3
Respondents	54	100·0	49	100·0	3	38	100·0	68	100·0	106	100·0
Question omitted for lack of time	2	—	3	—	—	4	—	1	—	5	—
Total	56	—	52	—	3	42	—	69	—	111	—

Table 26—*Respondents' views of their party headquarters as sources of information.* (See Figure 26)

(a) *Is your party headquarters a major source of information?*

Response	Conservative MPS	%	Labour MPS	%	Liberal MPS	Total MPS	%
Yes	44	80·0	9	18·0	2	55	50·9
Yes, with qualification	3	5·5	4	8·0	—	7	6·5
No	6	10·9	37	74·0	1	44	40·7
Don't know (insufficient experience)	2	3·6	—	—	—	2	1·9
Respondents	55	100·0	50	100·0	3	108	100·0
Question omitted for lack of time	1	—	2	—	—	3	
Total	56	—	52	—	3	111	

(b) *Can you obtain an individual brief from party headquarters?*

Response	Conservative MPS	%	Labour MPS	%	Liberal MPS	Total MPS	%
Yes	46	83·6	21	42·0	3	70	64·8
No	6	10·9	12	24·0	—	18	16·7
Don't know: no experience	3	5·5	17	34·0	—	20	18·5
Respondents	55	100·0	50	100·0	3	108	100·0
Question omitted for lack of time	1	—	2	—	—	3	—
Total	56	—	52	—	3	111	—

(c) *Are you satisfied with your party headquarters as a source of information?*

Response	Conservative MPS	%	Labour MPS	%	Liberal MPS	Total MPS	%
Yes	26	48·1	14	28·0	1	41	38·3
Yes, within its resources	23	42·6	6	12·0	1	30	28·0
No	5	9·3	25	50·0	1	31	29·0
Don't know: no personal experience	—	—	5	10·0	—	5	4·6
Respondents	54	100·0	50	100·0	3	107	99·9
Question omitted for lack of time	2	—	2	—	—	4	—
Total	56	—	52	—	3	111	—

Table 27—*Respondents' estimated average frequency of visits to the House of Commons Library.* (See Figure 29)

Frequency of visits	Conservative MPS	%	Labour MPS	%	Liberal MPS	Total MPS	%
At least once a day	37	67·3	37	75·5	3	77	72·0
Three times per week	6	10·9	9	18·4	—	15	14·0
Twice a week	4	7·3	2	4·1	—	6	5·6
Once a week	5	9·1	—	—	—	5	4·7
Less than once a week	1	1·8	—	—	—	1	0·9
Seldom or rarely	2	3·6	1	2·0	—	3	2·8
Respondents	55	100·0	49	100·0	3	107	100·0
Unable to estimate	1	—	1	—	—	2	—
Question omitted	—	—	2	—	—	2	—
Total	56	—	52	—	3	111	—

Table 28—Respondents' estimates of the principal purposes of their visits to the House of Commons Library—by party and length of service. (See Figures 30 and 31)

Purpose of visit	Conservative		Labour		Liberal	Pre-1964 entrants		1964 entrants		1966 entrants		Total	
	MPS	%	MPS	%	MPS	MPS	%	MPS	%	MPS	%	MPS	%
Read newspapers, journals, etc.	31	56·4	36	70·6	1	36	55·4	18	75·0	14	70·0	68	62·4
Use *The Times* press-cuttings service	27	49·1	30	58·8	2	30	46·1	15	62·5	14	70·0	59	54·1
Use visible strip index of PQS, etc.	31	56·4	29	56·9	2	37	56·9	13	54·2	12	60·0	62	56·9
Borrow or return a book	32	58·2	37	72·5	1	40	61·5	16	66·7	14	70·0	70	64·2
Ask the staff a reference question	38	69·1	42	82·3	2	44	67·7	22	91·7	16	80·0	82	75·2
For personal reference generally	3	5·4	2	3·9	—	5	7·7	—	—	—	—	5	4·6
Respondents	55		51		3	65		24		20		109	
Question omitted	1		1		—	2		—		—		2	
Total	56		52		3	67		24		20		111	

Note: Percentages total more than 100 per cent because of multiple responses to this question.

Table 29—*Respondents' estimated average frequency of requesting an individual reference or fact-finding job from the Library's Research Division.* (See Figure 32)

Frequency of requests	Conservative MPS	%	Labour MPS	%	Liberal MPS	Total MPS	%
At least once a fortnight	10	28·6	13	40·6	2	25	36·2
At least once a month	12	34·3	7	21·9	—	19	27·6
At least three times a year	6	17·1	5	15·6	—	11	16·0
Less than three times a year	4	11·4	1	3·1	—	5	7·2
Only once or twice ever	3	8·6	6	18·8	—	9	13·0
Respondents	35	100·0	32	100·0	2	69	100·0
Unable to estimate	10		10		—	20	
Respondents making no requests	11		9		1	21	
Question omitted for lack of time	—		1		—	1	
Total	56		52		3	111	

Table 30—*Respondents' image of the Library's Research Division—by party and length of service.*
(See Figure 33)

'Staff remote and inaccessible?'	Party					Length of Service				Total	
	Conservative		Labour		Liberal	Less than 13 years		13 or more years			
	MPs	%	MPs	%	MPs	MPs	%	MPs	%	MPs	%
Yes, I have found this	9	16·7	11	21·2	—	18	23·1	2	6·5	20	18·4
No, that is not my experience	32	59·2	31	59·6	2	42	53·8	23	74·1	65	59·6
Unable to give view: no experience	13	24·1	10	19·2	1	18	23·1	6	19·4	24	22·0
Respondents	54	100·0	52	100·0	3	78	100·0	31	100·0	109	100·0
Question omitted for lack of time	2		—		—	—		2		2	
Total	56		52		3	78		33		111	

Table 31—*Selected reactions on the image of the Library's Research Division.* (See Figure 34)

Response	Conservative		Labour		Liberal	Total	
	MPS	%	MPS	%	MPS	MPS	%
A first-class staff: no complaints about the system	9	16·7	3	5·8	1	13	11·9
I find the staff very helpful	12	22·2	9	17·3	2	23	21·1
I have always got what I wanted	10	18·5	14	26·9	—	24	22·0
I don't always get what I want	1	1·8	3	5·8	—	4	3·7
The staff are not very helpful	1	1·8	—	—	—	1	0·9
The staff are handicapped by the system	1	1·8	4	7·7	—	5	4·6
Respondents	54		52		3	109	
Question omitted for lack of time	2		—		—	2	
Total	56		52		3	111	

Note: These are *selected* reactions and percentages do not therefore total 100 per cent.

Table 32—Respondents' satisfaction and dissatisfaction with the Library's Research Division—by party and by length of service. (See Figure 35)

Response	Party					Length of service										
	Conservative		Labour		Liberal	Less than 9 years		9 or more years		Pre-1964 entrants		1964 entrants		1966 entrants		Total	
	MPS	%	MPS	%	MPS	MPS	%	MPS	%	MPS	%	MPS	%	MPS	%	MPS	%
Yes, satisfied	28	51·8	18	34·6	1	19	30·2	28	60·9	35	53·8	8	33·3	4	20·0	47	43·1
Yes, personally satisfied, but Division would collapse if more MPS used it	3	5·6	2	3·8	—	3	4·8	2	4·3	3	4·6	2	8·3	—	—	5	4·6
No, dissatisfied	19	35·2	30	57·7	1	36	57·1	14	30·4	24	36·9	12	50·0	14	70·0	50	45·9
Don't know	4	7·4	2	3·8	1	5	7·9	2	4·3	3	4·6	2	8·3	2	10·0	7	6·4
Respondents	54	100·0	52	99·9	3	63	100·0	46	99·9	65	99·9	24	99·9	20	100·0	109	100·0
Question omitted for lack of time	2		—		—	—		2		2		—		—		2	
Total	56		52		3	63		48		67		24		20		111	

Table 33—*Weaknesses of the Library's Research Division as seen by those respondents who regarded it as inadequate for their needs.* (See Figure 36)

	Conservative		Labour		Liberal	Total	
	MPS	%	MPS	%	MPS	MPS	%
Lack of physical facilities (including accommodation)	2	10·5	2	6·7	—	4	8·0
Lack of staff generally	4	21·0	3	10·0	—	7	14·0
Lack of both facilities and staff	10	52·6	16	53·3	1	27	54·0
Sub-total	16	84·1	21	70·0	1	38	76·0
Particular reactions							
Need more experts in particular fields	6	31·6	13	43·3	—	19	38·0
Need more mechanisation including computers and data-processing facilities	3	15·8	5	16·7	1	9	18·0
Research Division should be separated from the library	—		1	3·3	—	1	2·0
Don't know: not familiar with the system	1	5·3	—	—	—	1	2·0
Respondents	19		30		1	50	
Not applicable because satisfied with library or don't know	35		22		2	59	
Question omitted for lack of time	2		—		—	2	
Total	56		52		3	111	

Note: Percentages total more than 100 per cent because of multiple responses to this question.

427

Table 34—*Respondents' Conceptions of the role of the Library's Research Division—by party and length of service.* (See Figure 37)

Role of Research Division	Party					Length of service						
	Conservative		Labour		Liberal	Pre-1964 entrants		1964 entrants		1966 entrants		Total	
	MPS	%	MPS	%	MPS	MPS	%	MPS	%	MPS	%	MPS	%
Dig out any facts quickly	40	74·1	32	61·5	1	48	73·8	16	66·7	9	45·0	73	67·0
Fill gaps in information not available elsewhere	3	5·6	3	5·8	1	3	4·6	3	12·5	1	5·0	7	6·4
Provide non-partisan information	2	3·7	—	—	—	2	3·1	—	—	—	—	2	1·8
Provide concise reports on particular issues/policies	7	13·0	8	15·4	—	9	13·8	1	4·2	5	25·0	15	13·8
Provide comprehensive information and bibliographies generally	13	24·1	9	17·3	1	16	24·6	3	12·5	4	20·0	23	21·1
Act as a clearing house for information	5	9·3	9	17·3	—	6	9·2	5	20·8	3	15·0	14	12·8
Provide analytical and expert assistance to Members	7	13·0	11	21·1	—	10	15·4	3	12·5	5	25·0	18	16·5
Provide facilities for research in depth	2	3·7	9	17·3	—	3	4·6	3	12·5	5	25·0	11	10·1
Provide alternative views on policy	—	—	3	5·8	—	1	1·5	1	4·2	1	5·0	3	2·7
Don't know or uncertain	4	7·4	2	3·8	1	3	4·6	2	8·3	2	10·0	7	6·4
Respondents	54		52		3	65		24		20		109	
Question omitted for lack of time	2		—		—	2		—		—		2	
Total	56		52		3	67		24		20		111	

Note: Percentages total more than 100 per cent because of multiple responses to this question.

428

Table 35—*Relationship between satisfaction and dissatisfaction with the library's Research Division and conceptions of its role.* (See Figure 38)

'Is the Research Division adequately equipped . . . ?'

Role of Research Division	Yes MPS	Yes %	Yes, but . . . MPS	No MPS	No %	Don't know MPS
Dig out any facts quickly	38	80·8	3	30	60·0	2
Fill gaps in information not available elsewhere	5	10·6	—	2	4·0	—
Provide non-partisan information	1	2·1	1	—	—	—
Provide concise reports on particular issues (policies)	7	14·9	1	7	14·0	—
Provide comprehensive information and bibliographies generally	4	8·5	2	16	32·0	1
Act as a clearing house for information	—	—	1	13	26·0	—
Provide analytical and expert assistance to Members	1	2·1	1	16	32·0	—
Provide facilities for research in depth	2	4·3	—	9	18·0	—
Provide alternative views on policy	—	—	—	3	6·0	—
Don't know or uncertain	2	4·3	—	—	—	5
Respondents	47		5	50		7
Question omitted for lack of time	2	—	—	—	—	—
Total	49		5	50		7

Note: Percentages total more than 100 per cent because of multiple responses to this question.

429

Table 36—*Proportion of respondents mentioning their wish for a research assistant*

Mentioned wish for research assistant	Conservative		Labour		Liberal	Total	
	MPS	%	MPS	%	MPS	MPS	%
Would like an individual research assistant	10	17·9	19	36·5	2	31	27·9
Would like to share a research assistant	4	7·1	4	7·7	—	8	7·2
Sub-total	14	25·0	23	44·2	2	39	35·1
Other respondents	42	75·0	29	55·8	1	72	64·9
Total	56	100·0	52	100·0	3	111	100·0

Table 37—'Do ministers (of any Government) wish to limit MPs' knowledge?'—by party and by university education. (See Figure 41)

Response	Conservative MPS	%	Labour MPS	%	Liberal MPS	Graduates MPS	%	Non-graduates MPS	%	Total MPS	%
Yes	28	54·9	21	46·7	2	36	57·1	15	42·9	51	52·1
No	7	13·7	9	20·0	—	8	12·7	8	22·8	16	16·3
Depends on the Minister	5	9·8	4	8·9	—					9	9·2
Depends on the issue	7	13·7	5	11·1	—	19	30·2	12	34·3	12	12·2
Depends on both the Minister and the issue	4	7·8	6	13·3	—					10	10·2
Respondents	51	99·9	45	100·0	2	63	100·0	35	100·0	98	100·0
Question omitted for lack of time	5		7		1	9		4		13	
Total	56		52		3	72		39		111	

Table 38—'Under our Constitution must the House of Commons inevitably settle for about the level of information it gets at the moment?'—by parties and length of service. (See Figure 42)

Response	Conservative MPS	%	Labour MPS	%	Liberal MPS	Less than 9 years service MPS	%	9 or more years service MPS	%	Total MPS	%
No limit on information	19	38·8	24	55·8	—	32	62·7	11	26·2	43	46·2
No limit apart from security	6	12·2	6	13·9	1	8	15·7	5	11·9	13	14·0
Some limit is desirable on political grounds	7	14·3	3	7·0	—	3	5·9	7	16·7	10	10·7
Ministers must be left some discretion	8	16·3	3	7·0	—	3	5·9	8	19·0	11	11·8
Information is not the real problem	9	18·4	7	16·3	—	5	9·8	11	26·2	16	17·3
Respondents	49	100·0	43	100·0	1	51	100·0	42	100·0	93	100·0
Question omitted for lack of time	7		9		2	12		6		18	
Total	56		52		3	63		48		111	

Table 39—*Part-time and Full-time Members among our respondents as analysed from 'The Business Backgrounds of MPs'.* (See Figure 43)

Part-time or Full-time	Conservative		Labour		Liberal	Total	
	MPS	%	MPS	%	MPS	MPS	%
Full-time	7	12·5	33	63·5	—	40	36·0
Part-time	49	87·5	19	36·5	3	71	64·0
Total	56	100·0	52	100·0	3	111	100·0

GENERAL INDEX

Abortion, Abortion Act 1967, 51, 229; social clause, 67; Abortion Law Reform Association, 54, 56, 97; Society for the Protection of Unborn Children, 54, 56, 97; Roman Catholic Church policy, 54–6; NHS (Family Planning) Bill, 55

Agents, MPS', 205–6, 231–2

Aims of Industry, 87

Aircraft noise, 221–30

Amalgamated Engineers and Foundryworkers (AEF), 266–70, 277

Anglo-French parliamentary group, 115, 117

Anglo-Kuwait parliamentary group 110–17 *passim*

'Animal lobby', 57, 97, 100, 111, 177

Animal Welfare Group (of MPS), *see* 'Animal lobby'

ASLEF, 271

Automobile Association (AA), 70–95 *passim*, 96, 97

Bank of England, 164

Bank reviews, MPS' material from, 35, 37, 66

Board of Trade, 222–7 *passim*

Books, on public affairs, MPS' readership, 37–9

Booms, supersonic, 53

Bow Group, 260

Breathalyser, 59

British Airline Pilots' Association (BALPA), 223, 226–7

British Airports Authority, 223–9 *passim*, 281

British Association for Control of Aircraft Noise (BACAN), 223, 228

BBC, 132, 171, reports of debates, 52; Audience Research, 43n.; MPS' material from, 66; also *see* Broadcasting

British Field Sports Society, 97

British Heart Foundation, 69, 93, 372

BISAKTA, 267

British Iron & Steel Federation, MPS' material from, 66; links with Conservative h.q., 252–3

British Road Federation (BRF), 70–94 *passim*, 96, 119, 389

Broadcasting, on political affairs, interest in parliamentary reform c. 1963–7, 24; TV programmes viewed by MPS, 33, 39–46; social class viewing surveys, 42–4; growth of election coverage, 45; broadcasting Commons debates, 45; status with overseas govts, 116; 'Reithian' restraints, 122; as platform for Ministers, 127; — for MPS, 51–2, 178–9 *passim*; public appetite, 42–4, 169; broadcasters as specialists, 16; — as lobby members, 341, 350–1

Cabinet decision-making, 16–17, 26, 167

Carlton Club, 121–2

Chatham House, *see* Royal Institute of International Affairs

Chelsea & Kensington Action Committee, *see* Aircraft noise

Civil Liberties Group (of MPS) *see* National Council for Civil Liberties

Civil servants, contacts with interest groups, 69–95, *passim*; use of clubs, 119–22 *passim*; contacts with MPS, 142, 143–4, 187, 223–4; drafting official letters and speeches, 204, 224, 250; public attitude towards, 169–71; MPS' attitudes, 187, 366–7; before select cttees, 159, 163–4, 335–6

Clerks, parliamentary, 287–9 *passim*, 329, 332–7 *passim*, 341

Clubs, Pall Mall, 119–22

437

GEORGE ALLEN & UNWIN LTD

Head office:
40 Museum Street, London, W.C.1
Telephone: 01–405 8577

Sales, Distribution and Accounts Departments
Park Lane, Hemel Hempstead, Herts.
Telephone: 0442 3244

Athens: 7 Stadiou Street
Auckland: P.O. Box 36013, Northcote Central, N.4
Barbados: P.O. Box 222, Bridgetown
Beirut: Deeb Building, Jeanne d'Arc Street
Bombay: 103/5 Fort Street, Bombay 1
Calcutta: 285J Bepin Behari Ganguli Street, Calcutta 12
Cape Town: 68 Shortmarket Street
Delhi: 1/18D Asaf Ali Road, New Delhi 1
Hong Kong: 105 Wing on Mansion, 26 Hankow Road, Kowloon
Ibadan: P.O. Box 62
Karachi: Karachi Chambers, McLeod Road
Madras: 2/18 Mount Road, Madras 6
Mexico: Villalongin 32, Mexico 5, D.F.
Nairobi: P.O. Box 30583
Pakistan: Alico Building, 18 Motijheel, Dacca 2
Philippines: P.O. Box 157, Quezon City, D–502
Rio de Janeiro: Caixa Postal 2537–Zc–00
Singapore: 36c Prinsep Street, Singapore 7
Sydney, N.S.W.: Bradbury House, 55 York Street
Tokyo: C.P.O. Box 1728, Tokyo 100–91
Toronto: 81 Curlew Drive, Don Mills

Further titles in the P.E.P. Series

EUROPEAN UNITY

'Having so much information in one volume is not only useful, but serves as reminder of the vast complex of levels in which European Governments are in touch with each other. It deserves to be widely read and consulted.' *Public Administration*

'A valuable reference work for students of international affairs.'
Contemporary Review

ECONOMIC PLANNING AND POLICIES IN BRITAIN, FRANCE AND GERMANY

D. DENTON   M. FORSYTH   M. MACLENNAN

'The most valuable feature is the way in which the authors have combined their contributions according to topics, and have avoided dividing the book into three separate sections on Britain, France and Germany.' *The Financial Times*

THE COMPANY

Edited by CHARLES DE HOGHTON

In the spring of 1967 PEP organised a seminar on 'The Future of the Enterprise and the Reform of Company Law'. This seminar was attended by academics and businessmen from eleven countries and their contributions, later fully revised, form the basis of this book.

The Company is divided into four parts, together with a number of appendices. Part I deals with the distinctions between different legal forms of company and between public and private enterprise. Part II discusses the objectives of the company. Part III is concerned with company organisation and control. Here, among other topics, are considered the powers and accountability of chief executives, the purposes and extent of disclosure, the role and rights of shareholders, employees and consumers and the degree to which private firms are subject to public control. These three parts are based on contributions from eight countries: Belgium, Britain, France, Germany (Federal Republic), Italy, The Netherlands, Sweden and the USA. Part IV contains three separate chapters on Japan, India and Yugoslavia which have been set apart from the others because of their special circumstances.

EUROPEAN POLITICAL PARTIES

It is more than ten years since the publication of the last major comparative study of political parties in Western Europe. Yet the party remains a crucial unit for political organisation and the wielding of political power in practically every Western European country; and in view of recent changes in the system and structure of many of these parties there is a pressing need for this new book on the subject. At the same time, the development of ever closer links between the major countries in Western Europe must focus particular attention on political parties. In any integration process they obviously have a major role to fulfil, and a good deal of discussion already centres on the question of the formation of trans-national parties.

POLITICS AND BUREAUCRACY IN THE EUROPEAN COMMUNITY

DAVID COOMBES

The key institution in the European Common Market is its Commission, and a critical assessment of its role raises new and crucial issues about the basic principles on which the Common Market is based. This book, which is a definitive study of the Commission, is therefore most opportune, especially now that the question of Britain's entry into the European Communities is becoming so vital.

EUROPEAN ADVANCED TECHNOLOGY

CHRISTOPHER LAYTON

The challenge posed to Europe by American technology has been well publicised in terms of generalities. This book expounds a programme of action for Europe's response.

'Mr Layton's detailed and thoughtful book. Certainly it should be compulsory reading for governments, for civil servants, for industrialists, and for lectures on European affairs.' *Times Educational Supplement*

'... the most comprehensive and pungent commentary that has yet appeared on Europe's struggle for technological survival ... The more it is read, the better will be the prospects for a more productive dialogue between science and politics ...' NEVILLE BROWN in *New Scientist*

INTERNATIONAL POLICY FOR THE WORLD ECONOMY

J. O. N. PERKINS

The recent crises in international monetary arrangements have drawn attention to the urgent need for reforms. This book emphasises the importance of proceeding with such reforms in the context of the other main areas of international economic co-operation. These include the various policies adopted by different countries to achieve full employment and a strong balance of payments; the promotion of world trade by reductions in tariffs and other obstacles to trade, both generally and among groups of countries; and policy towards capital flows and economic aid.

Dr Perkins emphasises the various ways in which policy in each of these areas interacts with the others and the effects on the less developed countries. His viewpoint is that of the world economy as a whole and will appeal equally to readers in differently situated countries. His book is intended for courses in international economics, but will present no difficulties to the businessman on whom these problems now daily impinge. Detailed treatments already exist of some of the topics dealt with by Dr. Perkins, but there appears to be no similar work considering together all the urgent, inter-related aspects of policy for world trade and emphasising their effects on each other.

INTERNATIONAL TRADE AND ECONOMIC GROWTH

HARRY G. JOHNSON

'... by any standards, an important book. In a period when this part of economic theory made some very notable advances in the hands of others also, Professor Johnson was able to push analysis beyond the existing frontiers at a surprising number of points. He has, moreover, in an unusual degree the gift of relating, compressing and frequently simplifying the works of other theorists ... the high eloquence of his work ... will probably continue for a long time to impress itself on everyone who wants to be considered a serious student of international theoretical economics.' *Economic Journal*

LONDON : GEORGE ALLEN AND UNWIN LTD